T0317391

HIS MAJESTY'S OPPONENT

HIS MAJESTY'S OPPONENT

SUBHAS CHANDRA BOSE AND INDIA'S STRUGGLE AGAINST EMPIRE

Sugata Bose

THE BELKNAP PRESS OF HARVARD UNIVERSITY PRESS

Cambridge, Massachusetts, and London, England

First Harvard University Press paperback edition, 2012

Library of Congress Cataloging-in-Publication Data
Bose, Sugata.
    His majesty's opponent : Subhas Chandra Bose and India's struggle against empire /
Sugata Bose.
        p.   cm.
    Includes bibliographical references and index.
    ISBN 978-0-674-04754-9 (cloth: alk. paper)
    ISBN 978-0-674-06596-3 (pbk.)
    1. Bose, Subhas Chandra, 1897–1945.   2. Nationalists—India—
Biography.   3. Statesmen—India—Biography.   4. India—Politics and
government—1919–1947.   I. Title.
DS481.B6B68 2011
954.03′5092—dc22
    [B]   2010038250

In honor of
Sisir Kumar Bose
(1920–2000)

Contents

Preface

Subhas Chandra Bose was an uncle of my father, Sisir Kumar Bose, and a younger brother of my paternal grandfather, Sarat Chandra Bose. I never met Subhas Chandra Bose, since he passed from the scene in 1945, a good eleven years before I was born. I never met Sarat Chandra Bose either; he died in 1950. Growing up during the early decades of independent India, I knew them not as relatives but as historical public figures. Like millions of other South Asians, I thought of Subhas Chandra Bose as Netaji—"Revered Leader"—one of those who spearheaded India's freedom struggle. I was also aware of how controversial he was in the West, because of his wartime alliances. According to my father, Netaji believed that his family was coterminous with his country. I was taught, from childhood, never to claim a special relationship with him based on an accident of birth.

Though I belong to a generation that never knew Netaji in person, I had the opportunity to meet the men and women who had worked closely with him. They were frequent visitors and guests at my family's home in Calcutta, first at 1 Woodburn Park, and after 1974 at 90 Sarat Bose Road (the house we called "Basundhara"). Sitting on the verandah of Woodburn Park, I heard Abid Hasan recount the thrilling story of the hazardous submarine voyage he took with Netaji in 1943. S. A. Ayer told many vivid anecdotes about Netaji's time in Singapore and Rangoon, including the process of writing the proclamation of the provisional government of free India. Another visitor, Lakshmi Sahgal, described the formation of the women's regiment of the Indian National Army in 1943. Janaki Thevar Athinahappan spoke of the regiment's retreat with Netaji from Burma to Thailand in 1945. The battles fought in Imphal, Kohima, and Burma came alive in the words of Prem Kumar Sahgal, Gurbaksh Singh Dhillon, Abid Hasan, Mehboob Ahmed, and many others. Their voices became thick with emotion whenever they spoke about Netaji, and they wept for their lost leader decades after he was gone.

One afternoon in early December 1940, Netaji called my father to his side and inquired, "Amaar ekta kaj korte parbe?" The *kaj* ("work") that my father was being asked to do was to help his uncle escape from British-ruled India. From that day on, my father never stopped doing Netaji's work. Despite his busy professional life as one of India's leading pediatricians, he was deeply committed to upholding the best traditions of India's freedom struggle. In 1957, he established the Netaji Research Bureau (NRB)—an institute devoted to history, politics, and international relations—in Netaji's ancestral house at 38/2 Elgin Road. I grew up in tandem with that institution, to which he devoted far more time and attention than to his children.

I did not fully appreciate the scale of my father's achievement until I turned to writing this book. Through half a century of dedicated effort, he had managed to collect a trove of documents, letters, manuscripts, relics, memoirs, photographs, voice recordings, and film footage connected to Netaji and the Indian independence movement—materials gathered from all corners of Asia and Europe and beyond. Though I have made extensive use of archives in London, Delhi, and elsewhere, no truly substantive biography of Netaji would have been possible without the priceless resources available at the Netaji Research Bureau. I remember with much fondness its first archivist, Naga Sundaram, who as a young civilian recruit in the Indian National Army had fought at the Battle of Imphal, and Benode Chandra Chaudhuri, who in the NRB's early decades ran its publications division with unflagging zeal.

During my research and writing of this book Kartik Chakrabarti, Sukhamoy Chowdhury, and Manohar Mondal cheerfully responded to my endless demands for source materials of every kind from the NRB archives. This is the first book I have written in Calcutta. I wrote during the day at 38/2 Elgin Road and during the night at 90 Sarat Bose Road.

Though I participated in the NRB's academic programs and activities beginning in my student days, my role as joint editor of Netaji's *Collected Works* was a matter of necessity rather than choice. Sisir Kumar Bose had already published the first five volumes by 1992, when his health suddenly declined. I therefore joined him as editor of the next seven volumes of the twelve-volume set. This task gave me a close familiarity not just with Netaji's own writings, but with the whole range of documentary material associated with him. Of special significance was the work I did during 1993–1994 in connection with the seventh volume, entitled *Letters to Emilie Schenkl, 1934–1942*. I had often visited my great-aunt Emilie in Vienna and Augsburg when I was a student and then a Fellow at Cambridge. She was a relative, and not a historical public figure like her husband, Netaji. I admired her independence of spirit and her refusal to take any help from the Indian state during the difficult days when she was bringing up their daughter Anita by herself. She had a dignified bearing and was a storehouse of knowledge about India, a country she never saw. She was loving, affectionate, and kind to me, and we shared a fondness for good wine. In 1993–1994, once she had given the NRB permission to publish the Subhas-Emilie correspondence, I had to put on my historian's hat and ask her some searching questions. She answered with her characteristic grace and candor. The most enjoyable of my field trips to places associated with Netaji was the one I took in the company of my aunt Anita, my uncle Martin, my mother Krishna, and my brother Sumantra to Badgastein, Subhas and Emilie's favorite hill resort in Austria. Had I not visited Badgastein, I would never have understood why my subject was so enchanted by that place.

For a very long time, I was hesitant about writing this book. But I knew that I would have to write it one day. A few years ago, Nandini Mehta, then commissioning editor at Penguin India, persuaded me that I must really overcome my inhibitions and write what she thought should be the definitive biography of Subhas Chandra Bose. Joyce Seltzer, editor extraordinaire at Harvard University Press, with whom I had worked on *A Hundred Horizons,* liked my book proposal concerning the man I described as "His Majesty's Opponent." And so, to borrow a phrase used by Netaji in July 1943, I "began work." Ranjana Sengupta, editor at Penguin India, was as keen about the book as Nandini had been and entered into an agreement with Harvard University Press to publish the book in South Asia. Writing for a diverse worldwide readership was a daunting task, but seemed like a challenge worth taking.

The timing of my decision to take the plunge had something to do with my sense that I had achieved enough critical distance from the subject to offer my interpretation of a historical figure who was attracting interest among the younger generation in South Asia and beyond. More salient, however, was my own deepening interest in connective interregional and global history. The life of Subhas Chandra Bose seemed to me a prism through which all the contradictory forces of world history during the first half of the twentieth century had been refracted. Only after I had acquired a grasp of key elements of European, East and Southeast Asian, and Indian Ocean history did I feel capable of doing justice to the global odyssey of Subhas Chandra Bose. I have subtly tried to expand the boundaries of historiography in the mode of biography—an endeavor that I hope will not be lost on students of history who read this book.

Though I composed the text in Calcutta, I was deeply influenced by the interdisciplinary scholarly milieu in the Boston area. I benefited much from the stimulating company and friendship of Homi Bhabha, Leila Fawaz, Emma Rothschild, and Amartya Sen. My former and current graduate students at Harvard—Kris Manjapra, Manjari Miller, Faisal Chaudhry, Sana Aiyar, Antara Datta, Sandy Polu, Nico Slate, Aliya Iqbal, Tariq Ali, Johan Mathew, Gitanjali Surendran, Julia Stephens, Dinyar Patel, and Benjamin Siegel—kept me intellectually alert. Across the Atlantic, Chris Bayly's support was invaluable. In Vienna, Ranajit Guha was a source of inspiration. Seema Alavi, Jayati Ghosh, and Kris Man-japra each read a couple of chapters and offered helpful comments.

Only five persons—Krishna Bose, Joyce Seltzer, Ayesha Jalal, and two readers for Harvard University Press—read the manuscript in its entirety. Krishna Bose is a walking reference library on Subhas Chandra Bose, especially on his overseas activities in Europe and Southeast Asia. Her own books in Bengali—*Itihaser Sandhane* and *Charanarekha Taba*—are literary classics in their own right. By casting her eyes over the text, she helped to ensure both factual accuracy and a sensitive understanding of the more contentious issues surrounding the life and times of Subhas Chandra Bose. Joyce Seltzer's close reading and critical marginal comments in pencil did much to improve the book in both style and substance. She encouraged me to write for a wide audience of non-specialists and at the same time to retain the depth of scholarly research. She also showed me ways of balancing a portrait of the man's greatness with a perception of his human flaws and failures. Both the praise and the constructive suggestions contained in the two readers' reports were an enormous help in the final revision and refinement of the manuscript.

Ayesha Jalal's marginal comments were as incisive as her oral criticisms. She provided encouragement and support in good measure. Her own exemplary work on the relationship of the individual to larger historical processes served as an inspiration. I hope she will see this book as a worthy product of our three decades of emotional companionship and intellectual comradeship.

HIS MAJESTY'S OPPONENT

1

A Flaming Sword Forever Unsheathed

The enemy has already drawn the sword. He must, therefore, be fought with the sword.

—SUBHAS CHANDRA BOSE, 1943

"Indian nationalists are working day and night to build up Bose as the 'George Washington' of India," the *New York Times* reported on February 8, 1946. "This is particularly true of the revolutionary element in the Congress party, which spares no efforts to eulogize Bose, create a 'Bose legend' and wrap his sayings and beliefs in sanctity."[1]

The admiration for Netaji Subhas Chandra Bose, who had crossed swords with the forces of British imperialism during the Second World War, was rampant in India. Reverence for Bose was not limited to the radical elements of the Indian National Congress, who were clamoring for independence from British rule. Mahatma Gandhi best captured the significance of the armed struggle for freedom that unfolded from 1943 to 1945. The court-martial of some leading officers at Delhi's Red Fort had just transmitted the story of the Indian National Army and its Netaji ("revered leader," as Bose had come to be called) to every Indian home. "The whole country has been roused," Gandhi observed, "and even the regular forces have been stirred into a new political consciousness and have begun to think in terms of independence."[2] The man whom Bose had been the first to hail as the "Father of Our Nation" now regarded his rebellious "son" as a prince among patriots. "Netaji's name," Gandhi said, "is one to conjure with. His patriotism is second to none." "The lesson that Netaji and his army brings to us," the Mahatma wrote in *Harijan* on February 12, 1946, "is one of self-sacrifice, unity—irrespective of class and community—and discipline."[3]

With World War II raging across Europe and Asia, an American journalist named Louis Fischer had come to see Mahatma Gandhi in early June 1942. The young American was puzzled by the Indian reluctance to line up unambiguously on the side of the Allies against the Axis powers. Hosted for a week in Gandhi's guest house—"a one-room mud hut with earthen floor and bamboo roof"—in the village of Sevagram in western India, Fischer had a series of candid conversations with the Mahatma. There were "powerful elements of Fascism in British rule," Gandhi told his interlocutor, and these were the elements Indians encountered on a daily basis. "Your President," Gandhi continued, "talks about the Four Freedoms. Do they include the freedom to be free? We are asked to fight for democracy in Germany, Italy, and Japan. How can we when we haven't got it ourselves?" If these were points Gandhi gently raised in a low voice during conversation, he struck a harsher tone in written replies to Fischer's questions. "I see no difference between the Fascist or Nazi powers and the Allies," he declared. "All are exploiters, all resort to ruthlessness to the extent required to compass their end. America and Britain are very great nations but their greatness will count as dust before the bar of dumb humanity, whether African or Asiatic." Although the United States and Britain may have been focused on the war against Germany and Japan, Gandhi made it clear that his priority was the battle to free the colonized.[4]

Two months later, on August 8, 1942, the Indian National Congress under Gandhi's leadership formally passed a resolution calling upon the British to "quit India." The Mahatma asked his followers to "do or die" in their quest for independence. The British arrested all the top-ranking Congress leaders and cracked down hard on the movement in urban and rural areas alike. Wartime imperatives ensured that British policies were hardly benign. To severe political repression was added intensified economic exploitation of India's resources. By the spring of

1943, the back of the nationalist resistance within India was broken and the eastern province of Bengal on the front line of the war against Japan was engulfed in a gigantic man-made famine in which some three million people were to perish.[5]

One leader, however, had escaped the clutches of the British in 1941 and was now ready to raise the Indian flag of independence abroad. Louis Fischer, in the course of his conversations with Gandhi, asked about this man: Subhas Chandra Bose. In his response, Gandhi described Bose as "a patriot of patriots," albeit "misguided." What Fischer learned about Bose from Kurshed Ben ("Sister Kurshed"), who was deputed by Gandhi to take care of his guest, was even more revealing. Kurshed Naoroji was the granddaughter of Dadabhai Naoroji, a founding father of the Indian nationalist movement and the first Indian member of the British House of Commons, in the late nineteenth century. For the previous fifteen years, she had been a constant disciple of Gandhi, the apostle of nonviolence. "If Bose entered India at the head of an Indian army," Kurshed Ben told Louis Fischer, "he could rally the whole country." Bose, according to this feisty forty-year-old woman, was "more popular than Nehru, and in certain circumstances had a stronger appeal than Gandhi."[6]

On July 4, 1943, India's would-be George Washington rose to accept the leadership of the Indian freedom movement in Southeast Asia. Wearing a light suit and tie and a white Gandhi cap, Subhas Chandra Bose looked more like a philosopher than a military commander as he faced some two thousand representatives of the Indian Independence League in the packed Cathay Theater of Japanese-occupied Singapore. The words he spoke, however, were reminiscent of Giuseppe Garibaldi, the hero of Italian unification. In ringing tones and elegant Hindustani, he told those who were prepared to follow him that he could offer "nothing but hunger, thirst, privation, forced marches and death." The passion of the delivery was often drowned by the enthusiasm of the audience's response. "When we reach Delhi's Red Fort and hold our victory parade there . . . ," Subhas Chandra Bose began before thunderous cheers interrupted him. Once the applause died down, he continued his sentence: ". . . no one can say who among us will be there, who among us will live to see India free." "Whether we live or die," the leader asserted, "that is of no consequence. The only thing that matters, the only truth, is that India shall be free."[7]

When the sun rose next morning over Singapore harbor, it was the "proudest day" in Bose's life. On July 5, 1943, he appeared looking resplendent in a simple khaki military uniform on the balcony of Singapore's green-domed municipal building, flanked by its majestic Corinthian columns. The soldiers of the Indian National Army stood in serried ranks in front of him on the *padang*, the expanse of green, that stretched from the steps of the city hall toward the sea. It had pleased Providence, their supreme commander told them, for him to be able to announce to the whole world that India's army of liberation had come into being. "George Washington of America could fight and win freedom," he told the vanguard of India's struggle, "because he had his army. Garibaldi could liberate Italy, because he had his armed volunteers behind him." History had taught him the lesson of the inexorable decline and fall of empires. He and the pioneers of the Indian National Army (INA) were standing on what had been once a bulwark, now reduced to a graveyard, of the mighty British Empire. "How many of us will individually survive this war of freedom," he said in a somber warning, "I do not know. But I do know this: that we shall ultimately win, and our task will not end until our surviving heroes hold the victory parade on another graveyard of the British Empire—the Lal Qila, or "Red Fortress," of ancient Delhi."[8]

Bose gave his soldiers the slogan "Chalo Delhi" ("On to Delhi"), reminiscent of the 1857 rebellion in India, when Indian soldiers had revolted against the British under the banner of the last Mughal emperor. He introduced the inspiring national greeting "Jai Hind" ("Victory to India"). From the millions of Indian civilians in Southeast Asia, he called for "total mobilization for a total war"—not to aid the Axis powers against the Allies, but to wage the struggle against the British raj. In return for such mobilization of men and women, money and resources, he promised "a real second front for the Indian struggle."[9] On September 26, 1943, a ceremonial parade and prayers were held in Rangoon, at the tomb of the last Mughal emperor, Bahadur Shah Zafar, to signal the INA's determination to march to the Red Fort of Delhi. He was fond of quoting the emperor's Urdu couplet: "So long as *ghazis* [heroic warriors] are imbued with the spirit of faith / The sword of Hindustan will reach London's throne."[10]

On October 21, 1943, Bose proclaimed the formation of the Provisional Government of Azad Hind ("Free India") in Singapore. He wrote the proclamation himself, well past midnight on October 19–20, 1943, drawing on Indian history and on elements of the Irish and American declarations of independence.[11] In early January 1944, the headquarters of the provisional government were moved forward from Singapore to Rangoon. Having first seen action on the Arakan Front in February 1944, the INA moved into northeastern India toward Imphal and Kohima on March 18, 1944. With "Chalo Delhi" on their lips, the INA soldiers crossed the Indo-Burma frontier and carried the armed struggle to Indian soil.

The promised march to Delhi was, however, halted in Imphal. The British and Britain's Indian Army, with American air support, were able to break the siege of Imphal after three and a half tense months, and to beat back the Japanese forces and the INA from the outskirts of Kohima as well. The military debacle in Imphal by August 1944 gave way to a harrowing retreat speckled with a few determined rearguard actions by the INA in Burma during late 1944 and early 1945. Bose retreated on foot from Burma to Thailand with the soldiers of the INA, including the women he had recruited into a women's regiment named after the Rani of Jhansi, a heroine of the 1857 uprising. A dangerous trek under constant enemy fire in late April and early May 1945, the retreat helped to fortify his reputation as a selfless and fearless leader. The atom bombs dropped on Hiroshima and Nagasaki in early August 1945 brought the war in East Asia to an abrupt end. On the day of Japan's defeat on August 15, 1945—exactly two years before India's independence—Netaji issued his last order of the day and a special message to Indians in East Asia. "The roads to Delhi are many," he told his soldiers, "and Delhi still remains our goal." Urging his civilian followers never to falter in their faith in India's destiny, Bose expressed confidence that "India shall be free and before long."[12]

The victory parade at the Red Fort came to be enacted in a most unusual way. When the Second World War ended, the Indian independence movement seemed in disarray. The Quit India movement launched by Mahatma Gandhi in August 1942 had been crushed. Bose's armed thrust from outside India's borders had been repulsed. At such a moment of despondency in the nationalist ranks, thousands of Netaji's soldiers arrived at the Red Fort of Delhi as prisoners. The triumphant British decided to teach a demoralized nation a lesson by putting on public trial three officers of the Indian National Army. Bose himself could not have made a better choice of the Red Fort three. The British charged a Hindu, a Muslim, and a Sikh—Prem Kumar Sahgal, Shah Nawaz Khan, and Gurbaksh Singh Dhillon—with high treason for waging war against the king-emperor. "The trial," Nehru wrote, "dramatized and gave visible form to the old contest: England versus India. It became in reality not merely a question of law or of forensic eloquence, and ability—though there was plenty of ability and eloquence—but rather a trial of strength between the will of the Indian people and the will of those who hold power in India."[13]

As the drama unfolded in the winter of 1945 and the spring of 1946, Netaji Subhas Chandra Bose commanded in absentia the dénouement of the plot. The conquering hero, whose name was on everyone's lips, did not make an appearance on the stage at its climax. Bose had been reported killed in the crash of a Japanese bomber in Taipei on August 18, 1945. "You will understand our pressing anxiety," a British intelligence officer wrote on February 19, 1946, "to get to the truth of whether Bose is actually and permanently dead."[14] British imperialists may have wanted him "permanently dead," but most people in India wished exactly the opposite and longed for him to be permanently alive! No one man could have elicited such conflicting emotions as Bose did upon the approach of Indian independence. Britain's imperial hands could not forgive him for subverting the loyalty of the prized instrument of colonial control: Britain's Indian Army. He had escaped to Germany and Italy via the Soviet Union in 1941, looking to recruit soldiers being held as prisoners-of-war by the enemies of Britain. A ninety-day voyage on German and Japanese submarines in early 1943 had brought him to Southeast Asia. The taint of Axis collaboration and negative wartime propaganda had definitively sullied his image in the West. In the South Asian subcontinent, by contrast, Bose was a great popular hero—the object of almost blind and uncritical adulation, on a par with Mahatma Gandhi.

Indians never had any difficulty in combining reverence for saints with admiration for warrior-heroes. The great Indian epics, especially the *Mahabharata*, had placed warriors engaged in a just cause, such as Arjuna, on the highest pedestal. "The sword of the warrior," an early twentieth-century nationalist had asserted, "is as necessary to the fulfilment of justice and righteousness as the holiness of the saint."[15] A people forcibly disarmed since the defeat of the 1857 rebellion had deployed Gandhi's weapon of nonviolent noncooperation since 1919, but were equally enthused by Bose's decision during the international war crisis of the 1940s to meet force with force. During the war, the British had tried to impose tight censorship on news in India about Bose and the Indian National Army. The public trial at the Red Fort provided an occasion for nationalist newspapers and magazines to widely disseminate the story of the INA saga. By February 1946, the British had to release nearly eleven thousand INA prisoners, who returned to their home villages to tell of their wartime experiences. Putting on trial a few INA men to set an example to Britain's Indian subjects proved to be a catastrophic error on the part of the colonial masters.

Subhas Chandra Bose had been twice elected president of the Indian National Congress, in 1938 and 1939—with Gandhi's blessings on the first occasion and against Gandhi's wishes on the second. Even though he had parted ways with the Gandhian leadership in 1939, he had wholeheartedly supported Gandhi ever since the Mahatma had called upon the British to quit India in 1942. The Indian National Congress now decided to defend the Indian National Army at the Red Fort trial of November 1945. In the process, it managed to regain some of the political momentum it had lost. A highly skilled and experienced lawyer with liberal political views, Bhulabhai Desai, led the legal defense team established by the Congress. Nehru donned his barrister's robes for the first time in a quarter-century, in solidarity with the army led by his erstwhile comrade and rival (though he had been skeptical of Bose's wartime exploits). The arguments of the defense failed to sway the military judges, but found wide acceptance in the court of public opinion.

Sahgal, Shah Nawaz, and Dhillon were found guilty of the weighty charge of having forsaken their oath of loyalty to the British king-emperor and taken up arms against him. "When you are nominally fighting against the King but really fighting to liberate your country," the defense counsel had argued, "then the point is whether the question of allegiance can arise at all. Unless you sell your soul, how can you ever say that when you are fighting to liberate your country, there is some other allegiance, which prevents you from so doing. If that happens, there is nothing but permanent slavery." The INA, Desai claimed, had fought under Bose's duly constituted government, which had declared war and waged it in observance of international law.[16]

The Cambridge-educated Subhas Chandra Bose had plunged into Gandhi's Indian freedom movement after resigning from the Indian Civil Service in 1921. In the subsequent two decades of mass agitation against colonial rule, the soldiers in Britain's Indian Army had re-mained insulated from the swirling currents of civilian political dis-content. They were the ones who were deployed, wherever and when-ever necessary, to defend Britain's imperial interests worldwide. Bose had made up his mind that at the climactic moment of India's anti-imperialist struggle, the loyalty of Indian men in arms to the British king-emperor had to be replaced by a new allegiance to the cause of Indian independence. A world at war afforded him the opportunity to gain access to these soldiers taken as prisoners-of-war by Britain's ene-mies. An armed thrust from outside India coinciding with an uprising within, Bose believed, could bring about the final dissolution of the British raj.

"When Netaji arrived in Singapore," Shah Nawaz Khan testified at the Red Fort trial, "I watched him very keenly. I heard a number of his public speeches, which had a profound effect on me. It will not be wrong to say that I was hypnotized by his personality and his speeches. He placed the true picture of India before us, and for the first time in my life I saw India through the eyes of an Indian." Shah Nawaz came from a Punjabi Muslim family of Janjua Rajputs (a royal warrior clan) in Rawalpindi; they had a tradition of serving in the British Indian Army. His father had served the British for three decades, and more than eighty members of his clan were enlisted as officers during the

Second World War. Until he met Bose, in July 1943, he was by his own admission "politically almost uneducated," interested only in soldiering and sport. The question that Bose posed for him was: Did he owe allegiance to "the King or the country"? "I decided to be loyal to my country," he told the court, "and I gave my word of honor to my Netaji that I would sacrifice myself for her sake."[17] If Bose had hypnotized the INA in 1943, "the hypnotism of the INA," Gandhi recorded in 1946, "has cast its spell upon us."[18]

The trial of Sahgal, Shah Nawaz, and Dhillon began on November 5, 1945, and was adjourned for two weeks the following day. In the interim, the nationalist press published Bose's speeches and orders of the day, as well as stirring accounts of the heroism of the men and women of the INA. When the trial reconvened on November 21, violent protests erupted in Calcutta, Bombay, Karachi, Rawalpindi, Allahabad, Banaras, Patna, and numerous other cities and towns. Between November 21 and 24, British and American military and police personnel came under attack in Calcutta, Bose's home city. One British soldier was killed, and 188 were reported wounded; 49 British and American vehicles were destroyed, and 97 damaged. At least 32 Indian protesters were killed when the police opened fire, and 150 to 200 were injured. Political leaders were stressing Hindu-Muslim unity, and trucks packed with political activists were flying the Congress tricolor and the Muslim League's green flag side by side.[19]

Of even greater concern to the British authorities than widespread civilian anger was the overwhelming opinion among their own Indian officers against the trial of the INA officers. The Royal Indian Air Force based in Calcutta condemned "the autocratic action" of the government and lauded the men on trial as the "brightest jewels of India," whose "noble ideal" and course of action were "commendable and inspiring." The Royal Indian Navy in Bombay and Karachi would rise up in a major mutiny in late February 1946. During the winter of 1945–1946, senior Indian officers attended Gandhi's prayer meetings and called on Sarat Chandra Bose, Subhas's elder brother, at his home.

The trial concluded on the last day of 1945. The court sentenced the three INA officers to deportation for life, exactly the same verdict as the one imposed on the last Mughal emperor in 1858. Its implementation on this occasion, however, proved untenable. On January 3, 1946, Claude Auchinleck, the commander-in-chief of the British Indian Army, issued an order commuting the sentences and setting the three Red Fort prisoners free, to a tumultuous reception by the Indian public. He explained to his senior officers in February that "any attempt to force the sentence would have led to chaos in the country at large and probably to mutiny and dissension in the army, culminating in its dissolution."[20]

The view of Subhas Chandra Bose as a warrior-hero who snatched political victory for his country out of the jaws of his own military defeat is no more than a partial glimpse of a multifaceted personality. The warrior paused between battles, often involuntarily in British prisons, to give expression to his dreams for India and the global role that he saw for his country free of bondage. His spirit of service to suffering humanity had been inculcated early in life, under the influence of the teachings of the Hindu sage Swami Vivekananda. In public life he transcended the boundaries of religious community in the manner of his political mentor Deshbandhu Chittaranjan Das, making the cause of Hindu-Muslim unity his top political priority. It was his mastery on this score that most impressed Mahatma Gandhi and that accounts for his salience today on a subcontinent which continues to face the specter of religious conflict. "Though the INA failed in their immediate objective," Gandhi noted, "they have a lot to their credit of which they might well be proud. The greatest among these was to gather together, under one banner, men from all religions and races of India, and infuse into them the spirit of solidarity and oneness to the utter exclusion of all communal and parochial sentiment." The modern proponent of nonviolence wanted this example to be emulated. If unity were achieved only "under the glamour and romance of fighting," he would be disappointed. He wanted the feeling of oneness to "persist in peace."[21]

Bose was acutely aware that Indian society was extensively fissured along lines not just of religious community, but also of caste, class, and gender. He chose to side with the underdogs, having identified the subordinated castes, the laboring masses, and women as the three oppressed collectivities who had to be empowered. He worked to bring the peasants and workers into the anticolonial movement, willing to accept a measure (though not a surfeit) of class conflict—in contrast with Gandhi's absolute commitment to class conciliation. He described himself as a *samyavadi,* a believer in equality, preferring the ancient Indian term for an egalitarian aspiration not inconsistent with balance and harmony. His ideological predilection was toward a form of socialism imbued with an Indian spirit and suited to Indian conditions, rather than the doctrinaire varieties imported without appropriate modifications. Yet his political career, traversing complex international itineraries, required a constant negotiation of the global forces of imperialism and nationalism, fascism and communism. His life, in that sense, encapsulated all of the dramatic contradictions of world history in the first half of the twentieth century.

Bose was an uncompromising anti-imperialist, but by no means an uncritical nationalist. He recognized the Janus-faced character of nationalism, favoring its benign aspect that inspired creativity and instilled an ethic of service, and condemning the malignant obverse that transmuted into imperialistic arrogance, aggression, and hubris. He denounced the racism of Nazi Germany and the militarism of 1930s Japan, but allied with them in the 1940s in his single-minded pursuit of Indian freedom from British colonial rule. Always keen to articulate an ethical conception of human affairs, he could put on blinkers to ignore horrific outrages committed by the enemies of Britain if these did not directly affect his own people. His pragmatic analyses of international relations sat uneasily with the fiery idealism that inspired the mission of his life. He believed in his ability to lead India to freedom, and therefore set in motion the processes of planning for its social and economic reconstruction. He envisioned free India as a modern industrial power breaking the shackles of poverty and illiteracy to be able to make creative contributions, material and spiritual, to the world.

A brave man, he was prone to taking enormous risks, such as his daring escape from India in 1941, his submarine voyage from Europe and Asia in 1943, and his final decision to board a Japanese bomber to try to reach a new battlefield in 1945. His complete disregard for his safety meant that he was lost to India when his country perhaps needed him most. He was sorely missed when the calamity of partition overtook the subcontinent at the moment of decolonization. He was not present at the famous midnight hour of Indian freedom. "Only now, fifty years on," historians Christopher Bayly and Tim Harper wrote in 2004, "has Subhas Chandra Bose begun to claim his still deeply controversial legacy as the greatest military hero of India's modern history."[22] On August 15, 1997, the fiftieth anniversary of India's independence, three voices were played at a special midnight session of India's Parliament—those of Gandhi, Nehru, and Bose—and it was Bose who drew the loudest and longest applause. Untarnished by the disappointments and disenchantments of the postcolonial era, Bose lives in popular memory as an alternative beacon of hope.

What perpetuates the Bose legend is that his appeal cuts across religious, linguistic, and national boundaries. All those who see themselves as fighting for freedom—political, social, and economic—claim his mantle, including those who battle against the Indian state. Many Kashmiri and Naga militants seeking independence from India, for instance, believe Bose would have understood the justness of their cause.[23] Sheikh Mujibur Rahman, the founding father of Bangladesh, spoke eloquently of Bose's "ideal of sacrifice and suffering," which would serve as an undying inspiration to aspirants for liberty in all places and times.[24] Nelson Mandela, on his first visit to India after his release from prison in 1990, paid tribute to the iconic leaders of India's struggle against empire. "Your heroes of those days," he told his Indian audience, "became our heroes. Netaji Subhas Chandra Bose was amongst the great persons of the world whom we black students regarded as being as much our leader as yours. Indeed, Netaji united all militant youth of all the colonially oppressed world. We followed with pride his great contributions, as we did that of the Mahatma and Pandit Nehru."[25]

Soon after he proclaimed the Provisional Government of Free India in October 1943, Bose was presented with a ceremonial Japanese sword bearing the inscription, "Destroy evil, establish justice." Twenty years after independence, that sword was brought to India by General Fujiwara Iwaichi, who as a major during the Second World War had worked closely with the Indian National Army. As the sword was welcomed in Calcutta, an astute observer noted a not uncommon paradox in South Asian history: that "men of spiritual yearnings with the strain of mysticism" were often associated with "the cult of the sword."[26] Netaji's sword then made a journey from Calcutta to Delhi. At the crowded Howrah railway station, heart-rending cries asking the leader to return reverberated as the train moved off. Huge numbers of people gathered at Mughalsarai, Allahabad, Kanpur, Ghaziabad, and smaller wayside stations as the relic traveled across the Gangetic Plain. From Delhi station the sword was taken in a gigantic procession to the Red Fort, with thousands of people lining the streets and showering flowers from balconies and treetops along the way. "So many of us who knew Netaji have assembled here today," Prime Minister Indira Gandhi said at the Red Fort, "with hearts laden with emotion. His slogan was 'Onward to Delhi.' He himself could not reach Delhi. But his sword has come here today and we welcome it warmly. Netaji was an example of India's courage. I can still remember when we were young and we looked into his inspired eyes, our hearts also filled up with fervor. We can therefore well understand how and with what fervor he organized the Azad Hind Fauj (Indian National Army)."[27]

The symbolism of the sword has sometimes led people to make easy assumptions about the muscular quality of Bose's nationalism, and to ignore the tender aspects of his personality. In a chapter titled "My Faith—Philosophical" in his unfinished autobiography, he identified love as "the essential principle in human life."[28] A model of leadership, he inspired awe among his followers, but did not instill fear. It was through expressions of unbounded love that he elicited devotion and a fierce loyalty that remained with those whose lives he touched decades after he had passed from the scene. Mehboob Ahmed, Bose's young military secretary in 1945, had the good fortune of working with Gandhi and Nehru later in his career. He acknowledged the greatness of the Mahatma and the Pandit, but there was only one man at whose call he was prepared to lay down his life, and that was Netaji.[29] Bose wept when he sent his soldiers into battle and did not restrain his tears when he witnessed and shared their suffering. One could speak of Bose in the words that Carl Sandburg used to describe the heartbroken Abraham Lincoln: "on occasions he was seen to weep in a way that made weeping appropriate, decent, majestic."[30]

Many in India coped with the tragedy of Subhas Chandra Bose by denying his death. As he became shrouded in myth and mystery, a great deal was lost—namely, a genuine understanding of who he was as a human being and of his place in history. Yet the life was, in important ways, greater than the legend and certainly as fascinating. The more rationally minded accepted the reality of his mortal end, but they understandably chose to concentrate on celebrating the birth of this deathless hero. During his lifetime, Bose himself was apt to forget his own birthday. He was not permitted to do so on January 23, 1945, his forty-eighth, when much to his embarrassment he had to acquiesce in using the occasion to raise funds for the Indian National Army. He had told the organizers that he was "frankly against the celebration of his own birthday" and urged them to "concentrate on and popularize ideas and ideals and not personalities."[31] Yet he was not present after the war to prevent his own deification by devotees who cast his image according to their own fancies. His human qualities and the forces that impelled his mission became immersed in the mystical haze created around him. The tradition of observing his birth anniversary in India as a popular festival began in his absence in 1946 and continues to this day, with the blowing of conch shells and the bursting of firecrackers minutes after midday to mark the moment of his arrival. Seven days before being assassinated on January 30, 1948, Gandhi had been "very glad" to take note of Subhas's birthday, even though he "generally did not remember such dates" and "the deceased patriot believed in violence," while Gandhi himself was wedded to nonviolence. Subhas, according to the Mahatma, "knew no provincialism nor communal differences" and "had in his brave army men and women drawn from all over India without distinction and evoked affection and loyalty, which very few have been able to evoke."[32] Bose was born on January 23, in the year 1897—the high noon of the Raj. He would devote his life to ensuring that the sun finally did set on the British Empire.

2

God's Beloved Land

India is God's beloved land. He has come into being in many countries in human form but not so many times in any other country—that is why I say, India, our motherland, is God's beloved land.

—SUBHAS CHANDRA BOSE to his mother, Prabhabati, 1912

"I rose early," Janakinath Bose, a lawyer in Cuttack, Orissa, wrote in his diary on January 23, 1897, "but found Prabha was still suffering. A son was born at midday. Prabha felt very ill—but thank God she somehow got through."[1] The sixth son and ninth child of Janakinath and Prabhabati was named Subhas, "One of Good Speech"—a name that would prove prophetic when his stirring words inspired India's army of liberation during the Second World War. The boy was born into a well-to-do family, though not into opulence. The country of his birth was, by contrast, mired in poverty.

"Many babies have already been born at the works," the *Times* of London reported that January morning in a news item titled "The Famine in India." The "works" referred to were the relief operations the British had initiated in the Punjab on the new Jhelum irrigation canal, where forty thousand "coolies" labored. "The mothers are then maintained gratuitously for a time," the report continued, "and receive two pice extra for each baby. Young infants who have been deserted or whose mothers are unable to nurse them are fed with prepared Swiss milk by means of feeding bottles." This story of human interest from Jhelum was supplemented by a factual report provided by Reuters from

Calcutta. The number of people employed in the relief works all over India now exceeded 1.75 million, of whom 175,000 were receiving "gratuitous relief." The main increase in numbers had come from the eastern province of Bengal and the North-West Provinces. The daily cost of providing relief was nearly 200,000 rupees, or 20,000 pounds. The *Times*'s own correspondent added from Ottawa that the Bank of Montreal had contributed $5,000 (Canadian) to the Indian Famine Relief Fund.[2]

The year 1897 was no ordinary one in the history of the British empire. Britain was celebrating the diamond jubilee of Queen Victoria's reign with much pomp and ceremony. It was also the twentieth anniversary of Victoria's assumption of the title "Empress of India," which had been translated for the benefit of her colonial subjects as "Kaiser-e-Hind." Romesh Chunder Dutt opened his 1903 book, *The Economic History of India in the Victorian Age,* with a reference to the celebration in London that had taken place six years earlier. He noted "one painful thought" that "disturbed the minds of the people": "Amidst signs of progress and prosperity from all parts of the Empire, India alone presented a scene of poverty and distress. A famine, the most intense and the most widely extended yet known, desolated the country in 1897."[3] Dutt may have been off the mark in his claim about Indian exceptionalism, since "late Victorian holocausts" had a global spread.[4] But he was right about the scale of the calamity that had tarnished the jewel in the Victorian crown.

"The shadows darkened and deepened in their horrors as the year advanced," Mahadev Govind Ranade, an intellectual from western India, grimly recorded in 1897, "and it almost seemed as if the seven plagues which afflicted the land of the Pharaohs in old time were let loose upon us, for there is not a single province which had not its ghastly record of death and ruin to mark this period as the most calamitous year of the century within the memory of many generations past."[5] The premier British medical journal, *The Lancet,* estimated famine mortality in India during the 1890s at 19 million, which was about half the population of Britain.[6] The death toll for the 1897 famine ranged from the official figure of 4.5 million to unofficial claims of up to 16 million.[7] After a brief interregnum in 1899, another huge famine gripped India in 1900. It lasted nearly three years, and claimed a toll ranging from 1.25 million lives (according to official figures) to nearly 5 million (in the estimates of Indian nationalists). When the viceroy of India, George Nathaniel Curzon, organized his glittering Delhi *Durbar*—a courtly gathering of Indian princes and notables—in January 1903, there were still tens of thousands of famine victims eking out a wretched existence in relief camps.

Newspaper readers in London and Manchester were aware of the tragedies unfolding in India during the 1897 famine. The best that concerned citizens in the imperial metropolis could do for the less fortunate subjects of Queen Victoria was to contribute to charity in aid of the relief works in India. For Indian critics, charity was not the answer to the problem of poverty and famines. These had been caused by colonial policies that had drained India's wealth and could be remedied only by changing them. There was nothing ancient about India's poverty, Indian nationalists told their colonial masters, and famines were not natural disasters but products of a deeply flawed colonial political economy. It was at this moment, when economic debates between imperialists and nationalists were taking on a sharper political edge amid the specter of famine, that Subhas Chandra Bose was born in a remote corner of Britain's Indian empire.

Cuttack

In the 1890s, Cuttack, located by the great river Mahanadi about 300 miles southwest of Calcutta, was a town of some 45,000 inhabitants. Unlike the temple towns of Puri, Bhubaneswar, and Konarak in its environs, Cuttack was an administrative center both for the British and for the numerous princely chiefs of Orissa, who had by then accepted British "paramountcy"—a form of indirect imperial rule in return for a measure of internal autonomy. The sprawling province of Bengal, where the British had first obtained a political foothold in 1757, included Bihar, Assam, and Orissa. A rail link had yet to be established between Calcutta, the capital of British India and second city (after London) of the British Empire, and Cuttack, the premier town of Orissa. Travel by cart exposed one to the risk of encountering "thieves and robbers," while on the journey by sea one had to contend with "the winds and the waves." Boat was the preferred mode of travel, since it was deemed "safer to trust in God than in brother man."[8] Passengers would travel on seagoing ships to Chandbali, and from there on smaller steamers to Cuttack, through an intricate network of rivers and canals.

In 1885, the twenty-five-year-old Janakinath had moved from Calcutta to Cuttack in search of a career in the British law courts. The genealogy of the Boses could be traced back twenty-seven generations to one Dasarath Bose, the progenitor of their southern Bengal clan. They belonged to the Kayastha caste, one of the three upper castes among the Hindus of Bengal. If the Brahmans were the sacerdotal elite and the Vaidyas made their mark in the field of medicine, the Kayasthas formed a literati that generally did well in government service. The glory days of the Boses, based in a village called Mahinagar, fourteen miles south of Calcutta, lay in the era of the pre-Mughal Muslim sultans of Bengal. Mahipati, eleventh in descent from the founder, Dasarath, rose high as minister of finance and war and was honored with the title Subuddhi Khan, no doubt in recognition of the *subuddhi* ("good counsel") he had offered the king. One of Mahipati's grandsons, Gopinath Bose, became a *vazir,* or minister, in charge of finance and the navy in the court of the great Sultan Husain Shah (1493–1519) and acquired the proud title of Purandar Khan. He combined an aptitude for war with considerable literary talents and was a noted composer of devotional poems. It was a "misnomer," Subhas Chandra Bose later wrote in his unfinished autobiography, "to talk of Muslim rule when describing the political order in India prior to the advent of the British," as "the administration was run by Hindus and Muslims together."[9]

By the 1800s, after experiencing many turns of fortune through the centuries, the Boses were still ensconced in their cluster of villages in the Twenty-Four Parganas, a district to Calcutta's south. Men belonging to the family were finding opportunities in the services and the professions under the new British dispensation. Janakinath, born in 1860, was well versed in English, having studied at Albert School, St. Xavier's College, and Scottish Church College in Calcutta before graduating from Ravenshaw College in Cuttack and taking his law degree

from Calcutta University. The Boses tended toward the Shakta strand
of Bengali Hinduism, which worshiped the Supreme Being as an em-
bodiment of strength in the form of the mother goddess Durga, or
Kali. But some family members were also attracted to the Vaishnava
current, which sought union with the godhead through devotion or
the way of love. Janakinath himself was deeply influenced by the reformist Brahmo Samaj, a religious society founded by Rammohun Roy
in 1828 that emphasized the monotheism of the Upanishads and took
a stand against the more egregious forms of caste and gender discrimination in contemporary Hindu society. He was a great admirer of the
Brahmo leader Keshub Chunder Sen, whose powerful oratory on social
issues inspired many young Bengalis in the 1880s. Subhas later passed
the rather harsh judgment that despite "a profound moral awakening
among the people during the formative period of my father's life," "politically the country was still dead."[10]

Subhas's mother, Prabhabati, born in 1869, was an offspring of the
Dutts of Hatkhola, in northern Calcutta, a prominent family who had
acquired education and wealth under British rule. Prabhabati was of
a more orthodox religious bent than her husband, with whom she settled in Cuttack after their marriage. From 1887 onward, her life was
dominated by a series of pregnancies and childbirths. But she possessed a strong personality and "ruled the roost" on the domestic front;
in family matters, "hers was usually the last word." A grandson remembered her as "Queen Victoria of the Bose Empire and a hard taskmas-
ter."[11] As a child, Subhas felt lost among a large brood of siblings and
cousins. He held his father in awe, and relations with both parents were
marked by a distant reserve.

It was no wonder, then, that Subhas looked forward to going to
school just before his fifth birthday, in January 1902. His parents had
chosen to send him to the Protestant European ("P.E.") School, run by
the Baptist Mission. The P.E. School was primarily designed for European and Anglo-Indian boys and girls, but the Bose children formed
part of the 15 percent minority of Indians who enrolled in it. Subhas
and his classmates "loved" their teacher Miss Sarah Lawrence, while lik-
ing, tolerating, or hating a range of other teachers. The Latin declen-
sions—*bonus, bona, bonum*—were taught early, and daily Bible lessons

involved the boring routine of memorizing passages from the sacred text. The children gained a solid grounding in the English language, but no Indian language was taught. British history and geography became part of the mental world of the young Subhas. The curriculum aimed, as he remembered later, "to make us as English in our mental make-up as possible."[12]

Subhas was not unhappy in his primary school. He was good at his studies and usually at the top of his class. He was too young and too far away in Cuttack to be influenced by the anticolonial Swadeshi ("Own Country") movement that swept Calcutta and Bengal proper from 1905 onward. That year, Curzon had partitioned Bengal into a Muslim-majority province, comprising eastern Bengal and Assam, and a Hindu-majority province that included western Bengal, Bihar, and Orissa. Bengali nationalists were determined to undermine what Curzon regarded as the "settled fact" of partition through a campaign of passive resistance and boycotts of British goods and institutions. The antipartition political agitation had coincided with a new flowering of Bengali literature, art, music, and culture, along with an effort to revive indigenous industries and promote national education. The P.E. School remained a European island in the political backwater of Orissa, its children protected from the powerful currents of change unleashed by the forces of Bengali patriotism, Indian nationalism, and Asian universalism. The school atmosphere presented a contrast to the broader cultural environment. It was only toward the end of his seven years at the P.E. School that Subhas realized that he had been inhabiting "two distinct worlds" which "did not always match." He felt a vague sense of "maladaptation" and "a strong desire to join an Indian school." When he finally bid goodbye to the Protestant European school, in January 1909, he did so "without a momentary pang."[13]

With the move from the P.E. School to the Ravenshaw Collegiate School, a sense of alienation yielded to a feeling of promise and possibility, tinged with anxiety.[14] Ravenshaw, consisting mainly of Bengali and Oriya teachers and students, proved far more congenial for making lasting friendships. Initially, Subhas's lack of training in reading and writing Bengali was a challenge, and the grammatical mistakes in his first Bengali essay elicited much laughter from his fellow students when the teacher read it out in class. Displaying a kind of dogged determination, Subhas made sure that on the annual examinations he obtained the highest marks in the subject. His family background and mastery of English in any case won him respect and gave him a sense of self-confidence. An inspiring headmaster of the school, Beni Madhav Das, instilled in him a sense of moral values and a love for nature that had both aesthetic and ethical dimensions. Subhas took to "a species of nature-worship," choosing beautiful spots by a river or on a hill or in a meadow to "practise contemplation."[15]

On reaching his teens, Subhas entered "one of the stormiest periods" in his "psychical life." Part of the tumult could be explained by the usual changes of adolescence and the challenge of coming to terms with his sexuality, which he struggled to "suppress or transcend." But his precocity and introverted nature made Subhas's torment more intense than that of other teenagers. "I had in some respects," he would later recall, "a touch of the abnormal in my mental make-up." His higher self impelled him to rise above the attractions of worldly pursuits. He embarked on an incessant search for "a central principle," "a peg to hang my whole life on." It was not just the choice of his life's goal, but directing his "entire will to that single goal" that presented the major challenge. As he negotiated the existential crisis and "trials of becoming" of his adolescent years, books containing the works of one man, Swami Vivekananda, appeared to him as God-sent.[16]

"I was barely fifteen," Subhas Chandra Bose wrote, "when Vivekananda entered my life." The message of this great Hindu sage, who had preached a life of service to suffering humanity and died at the early age of thirty-nine in 1902, gave him "an ideal" to which he could devote his "whole being." Vivekananda inspired an entire generation, but none so profoundly as the young Subhas. From a comprehensive reading of Swami Vivekananda's letters and speeches, Subhas "emerged with a vivid idea of the essence of his teachings" captured in the Sanskrit maxim, "Atmano Mokshartham Jagaddhitaya[ca]." That aspiration—"For your own salvation and for the service of humanity"—was to be his "life's goal." The *hita* ("good") of humanity was rendered here as achievable through *seva* ("service"). To this formulation Subhas added another element: the service of humanity included the service of one's country. The spirit of self-fulfilling yet selfless service was distinct in Subhas's mind from "the selfish monasticism of the Middle Ages," as well as "the modern utilitarianism of Bentham and Mill." It was Vivekananda's radically modern interpretation of the ancient scriptures that appealed to Subhas. His religion was based on "a rational philosophy" of the Vedanta, and he dedicated his life to bringing about "a reconciliation between science and religion." His stirring call for equality was a harbinger of modern democracy in a hierarchical society. He had envisaged India's future as belonging to the Sudras, "the downtrodden masses." His passionate cry, "Say brothers at the top of your voice, 'The naked Indian, the illiterate Indian, the Brahman Indian, the pariah Indian is my brother!'" was not just a plea for equality, but an invocation of the value of *shraddha*, "faith"—faith in oneself built on profound respect. If Swamiji taught the virtues of *seva* and *shraddha*, the teachings of Vivekananda's spiritual preceptor Ramakrishna Parahamsa, who had been the high priest at the Kali temple in Dakshineshwar on the outskirts of Calcutta, brought home to Subhas the indispensability of *tyag* ("sacrifice") through his oft-repeated dictum that "only through renunciation was realization possible."[17]

The path prescribed by Vivekananda led Subhas toward a combination of individualistic *yoga* and social service in the form of voluntary work in the villages. The practice of *yoga*, representing the individual's pursuit of union with the godhead, was supplemented with an effort to relieve human suffering. The master's teaching that "revolt is necessary for self-fulfillment" inspired a rejection of anachronistic familial and social conventions that restricted the sphere of community service. Sanskrit verses enjoining obedience to one's parents were now discarded in favor of those that extolled defiance. Friends who were prepared to follow Vivekananda's ideals seemed closer than family members who showed little empathy or understanding. Subhas remembered later that he felt "more at home when away from home." Yet the dramatic transformation that Subhas underwent in 1912 was best captured in a series of intense letters that the fifteen-year-old boy wrote to his mother.[18]

Until December 1911, the year the partition of Bengal was rescinded, Subhas was "politically so undeveloped" (as he recorded in his autobiography) that he took part in an essay competition on King George V's coronation. His father had been government attorney and public prosecutor in Cuttack since 1905, and would be rewarded with the official title of Rai Bahadur in 1912. Politics was a taboo in his house, and he had removed the pictures of Bengali revolutionaries his sons had put up in their study.[19] The appearance of Vivekananda's works in Subhas's life in 1912 caused "a revolution within and everything was turned upside down."[20] It was with his own country and his own people that Subhas could be "in touch with humanity in all its concreteness."[21] Vivekananda had famously described his motherland as the queen of his adoration. Once under the spell of the sage's magical words, Subhas's love for the country was tinged with a religious sensibility and expressed as devotion to the Mother. Yet he was dismayed at the current state of both the country and of religion: "Now, wherever religion is practised there is so much bigotry and sin." He asked his own mother, "Will the condition of our country continue to go from bad to worse— will not any son of Mother India in distress, in total disregard of his selfish interests, dedicate his whole life to the cause of the Mother?"[22]

The stream of consciousness that flowed in the nine letters he wrote in Bengali to his mother in 1912–1913 was the product of a precocious and ultrasensitive mind. "Ideas come surging within me from time to time," he wrote, "as when flowers come to bloom in a garden and I offer them at your feet as outpourings of my heart." He wanted to see less pomp and more sincerity in the worship of the Mother Goddess, and questioned the purpose of education of the kind on which his parents were spending so much if it did not produce real men prepared to do God's work. He derided his own class of Babus, who were not prepared to use their legs to walk or let their precious hands engage in manual labor. He castigated Bengali gentlemen who had become "ease-loving, narrow-minded, characterless, and given to jealousy." He disliked reading and writing letters on "the worldly things of life" and wanted letters "full of ideas." The purpose of human existence was to find God. Like rivers flowing inexorably toward the sea, human lives could attain finality only in the Supreme Being. Despite the plethora of sin and corruption that vitiated the contemporary world, he still had faith that India was "God's beloved land" which had been blessed with Saviors more often than any other country "for the enlightenment of the people, to rid this earth of sin and to establish righteousness and truth in every Indian heart."[23]

If Subhas's missives to his mother in Bengali were mostly concerned with nation and religion, his letters to his elder brother Sarat in English, during the same period, reveal his curiosity about the wider world. It was with this particular brother, the second son of Janakinath and Prabhabati, that Subhas developed a special bond. As Sarat prepared to leave for England in 1912 to study law, Subhas asked him to describe what he saw on his journey and how he felt among "strange and foreign associations." He wondered, when the ship left port, which of the American author Washington Irving's lines would ring true to his brother: Would he find "time for meditation" upon closing one book and before opening another, or would he feel "sent adrift upon a doubtful world"? He pleaded for a description of a sunset at sea and provided one of his own imagining. He wrote to his brother about Rabindranath Tagore, a year before the poet's Nobel Prize, and lamented "how indifferent Bengal had been in showering laurels upon him" while foreigners "extolled him as the greatest poet the world has produced." Subhas was overjoyed to receive his brother's vivid descriptions of the voyage and of England, and peppered him with more probing questions about life in England. "Another year has rolled by," he wrote on January 8, 1913, "and we find ourselves responsible to God for the progress or otherwise that we have made during the last twelve months." Subhas, not yet sixteen, saw darkness, despair, and decline engulfing India, but "the angel of hope" had appeared in the form of "the saintly Vivekananda." That seemed to provide some solid ground for Tennyson-like optimism. "A brighter future is India's destiny," Subhas told his brother. "The day may be far off—but it must come."[24]

The Cuttack phase of Subhas's life was drawing to a close. In his autobiography, he noted some of the advantages of having grown up in Orissa. He had the opportunity to forge interprovincial contacts, and his Bengali immigrant family enjoyed cordial relations with their Oriya-speaking hosts. The Bose family lived in a predominantly Muslim quarter of Cuttack, with Muslim neighbors, teachers, and classmates, and took part in Muslim festivals. Subhas believed his "mental attitude" toward Muslims was influenced by his early contacts, and reported that "friction or conflict between Hindus and Muslims was unknown" in his formative years. The diverse and liberal social setting was a boon, but did not preclude the tortuous individual trials of coming of age in an era of incipient nationalism. Reflecting back, he had little doubt that he "must have appeared to others as wayward, eccentric, and obstinate."[25] His parents were worried that he was neglecting his studies. In March 1913, Subhas took his school-leaving matriculation examinations and was ranked second in the entire university. A very wide range of institutions throughout the province was affiliated with Calcutta University, and so this was an outstanding result. Subhas's parents were relieved, and decided to send him to college in Calcutta.

Calcutta

"This great city had intrigued me, bewildered me beyond measure," Subhas Chandra Bose wrote of the city of Calcutta.[26] He had visited this great metropolis before, but it was in the spring of 1913 that he came to live there. Calcutta had been the capital of British India since the late eighteenth century, but in 1911 the colonial masters had decided to move their headquarters from troublesome Bengal to the old Mughal center of Delhi. Subhas came to stay in the three-story house at 38/2 Elgin Road that his father had built in 1909–1910. In a letter to his mother in March 1913, he wrote that he did not want to study at Presidency College.[27] But it was at this premier educational institution of Western learning that he did enroll, to read for honors in philosophy. He had already made up his mind that he was "not going to follow the beaten track" but instead "lead a life conducive to [my] spiritual welfare and the uplift of humanity." Convinced that "life had a meaning and a purpose" that had to be fulfilled by resolute training of the body and the mind, he wished to make "a profound study of philosophy" and "emulate Ramakrishna and Vivekananda."[28]

The Indian students of Presidency College were divided into various groups. There were the earnest studious types and the rich dilettantes, those attracted to secret revolutionary activities and those steering clear of radicalism to engage in spiritual pursuits. Subhas found the heirs of Ramakrishna and Vivekananda's mantle the most congenial to associate with. This group was led by Suresh Banerjee, a medical student, and had as one of its key members Hemanta Kumar Sarkar, who became Subhas's close friend during his early years in college. The religious calling was to Subhas "a pragmatic necessity" which he felt able to reconcile with a "rational philosophy."[29] The battle with sexual desires persisted, since he believed at this stage of his life that the overcoming of sexual urges was a *sine qua non* for achieving spiritual progress. But from individualistic *yoga*, he turned increasingly toward social service.

Subhas traveled with his friends to Murshidabad in search of Bengal's history, met Rabindranath Tagore in 1914 to learn about village reconstruction, discussed plans with the poet to set up an excellent educational institution, and spent some time in a camp on the River Hooghly wearing ocher robes in the manner of Hindu ascetics. He began reading Aurobindo Ghose's essays in the journal *Arya* from 1914 onward. Aurobindo had inspired Bengal's young revolutionaries of the Swadeshi era, before retiring into a life of religious contemplation in 1910. Shankara's doctrine of *maya*, or the illusoriness of human life, had been troubling Subhas. Aurobindo's metaphysics was based on "a reconciliation between Spirit and Matter, between God and Creation," and a synthesis of *yoga*—the union of the human with the divine—as a means to attaining the truth, and for Subhas it supplied a way out of "the cobwebs of *maya*." Subhas was impressed by Surendranath Banerjee, the moderate leader of the Indian National Congress, but he was inspired by Aurobindo's stirring call: "I should like to see some of you becoming great; great not for your own sake, but to make India great, so that she may stand up with head erect amongst the free nations of the world."[30]

During vacations Subhas returned to Cuttack, where he joined a group to nurse cholera patients in the surrounding villages during an epidemic. This experience unfolded before him "a picture of real India, the India of the villages—where poverty stalks over the land, men die like flies, and illiteracy is the prevailing order."[31] Subhas's discovery of India, unlike that of his great contemporary Jawaharlal Nehru, occurred very early in his life, while he was still in his teens. It happened before rather than after (as in Nehru's case) a direct encounter with Europe, and was intimately connected with a spiritual quest. In the summer vacation of 1914 Subhas quietly left home with a friend, without telling his parents, in search of a guru or a spiritual preceptor. He visited all of the major pilgrimage sites of northern India, including Lachhman-Jhola, Hrishikesh, Hardwar, Mathura, Brindaban, Benares, and Gaya. At Hardwar, a third friend joined the search party for a guru. The two-month expedition made possible a few meetings with some truly holy men, but overall it ended in disillusionment and disenchantment. Subhas witnessed first-hand the deeply ingrained caste prejudices in northern India and the petty sectarian rivalries of the men of religion. Brought face to face with "the patent shortcomings of Hindu society," he returned to Calcutta "a wiser man, having lost much of [my] admiration for ascetics and anchorites." Within a few days of his return, he came down with typhoid—"the price of pilgrimage and guru-hunting."[32] As he lay ill in bed, he received news of the outbreak of the First World War.

It was at this time that Subhas's political consciousness was aroused. The racism that Indians suffered at the hands of the British in the city of Calcutta was constant and ubiquitous. Subhas encountered this haughty superiority on his daily tram-car journeys from home to his college. He often had to engage in verbal duels with arrogant Englishmen. At the same time, the shock of the eruption of global war affected him greatly. Lying in bed and reading the newspapers, he began to question whether it was possible "to divide a nation's life into two compartments and hand over one of them to the foreigner, reserving the other to ourselves."[33] He doubted the efficacy of separating the home from the world, the inner spiritual life from the outer material domain. Yet the year 1915 passed without any major crisis. Subhas immersed himself in the study of the philosophy of Kant, Hegel, and Bergson. His extracurricular activities were numerous: he was the elected class representative on the students' consultative committee, the secretary of the debating society and of a famine relief committee for east Bengal, and a member of the board of the newly launched college magazine. While recruiting debaters, he got to know a fellow student named Dilip Kumar Roy, son of the famous poet and songwriter Dwijendralal Roy, and forged what was to be a life-long friendship. Dilip later reminisced that from their earliest meetings he noticed that Subhas "had a native power to lead, and he knew it."[34]

A dramatic incident in early 1916 shattered the normal routine at Presidency College. On January 10, Subhas was studying in the college library when he was told that Edward Farley Oaten, a history professor, had "manhandled" some students who were in Subhas's year. As class representative, he took up the matter with the principal, Henry R. James, and demanded that Oaten should apologize to the students. The professor claimed that having been disturbed by the chatter of these students outside his classroom, he had merely "taken them by the arm," a gesture that could not be interpreted as an insult. He was a member of the government's educational service, and the principal did not have the power to extract an apology from him. The disaffected students then called a general strike for the next day. The news of the successful strike in a college that was meant to be a bastion of loyalism caused much excitement in the city and encouraged young students at other institutions to follow the rebellious example. Toward the end of the second day of the strike, Oaten met the student representatives and settled the dispute. The principal, however, refused to withdraw the fine of five rupees that he had imposed on the striking students. The next day Oaten ordered ten students out of the twelve in his history course—those who had taken part in the strike—to leave the class.[35]

On February 15, the students learned that Oaten had "manhandled" another student belonging to the first-year chemistry class for being noisy in the corridor. On this occasion, a group of students decided to "take the law into their own hands." At the bottom of Presidency College's imposing main staircase, Oaten was given a solid thrashing. The incident lasted forty seconds, according to the official inquiry. Oaten later recalled that he suffered "no injury except for a few bruises." "Subhas Chandra Bose was supposed to be connected with the affair," he wrote, "although I never had any proof of this."[36] He had seen ten or fifteen students milling around as he came down the stairs and could not be sure who had hit him, as he was putting up a notice about a cricket match. An orderly identified Subhas and another student, Ananga Dam, as being among those he had seen leaving the scene.

The news of the shocking assault spread like wildfire and dominated the media for weeks to come. The government immediately issued a communiqué closing down the college indefinitely. This order was issued without consulting the principal, who went to the Writers' Building to remonstrate with the member in charge of education on the governor's council. Another communiqué was issued suspending the principal for showing "gross personal insult" to the honorable member. Before his own suspension could take effect, James summoned the suspected students to his office. Turning toward Subhas, he snarled, "Bose, you are the most troublesome man in the College. I suspend you." The governing body confirmed the principal's order and expelled Subhas from Presidency College. His appeal to the university for permission to study in another college was turned down. For all practical purposes, he was "rusticated" from Calcutta University.[37]

Had Subhas actually taken part in the physical assault on a professor? In his deposition before the Enquiry Committee, Subhas did not admit his own guilt, but steadfastly refused to name any others or criticize the action of the students. His mother maintained that striking a blow at a teacher was completely out of character for Subhas and that he could never have done such a thing. In his autobiography, written in 1937, Subhas described himself as "an eyewitness" to the incident, even though in a letter written to Sarat in 1921 he had stated that he should have taken responsibility for the assault in a more forthright manner instead of simply remaining silent and refusing to implicate others. When prodded later in life on this question, especially by his young nephews, he simply smiled and did not give a direct answer.[38] If he did lay hands on Oaten, it can only be explained in terms of the peer-group psychology inciting the behavior of a number of agitated students.

The Oaten incident took place at a time when relations across the racial and generational divides were fraught with tension. The aftermath of the antipartition Swadeshi movement of 1905–1908 had polarized the views of the colonizers and the colonized on what constituted proper demeanor on the part of Indian youth. Professors like Oaten often harbored beliefs about Britain's racial superiority and civilizing mission in India that were anathema to the proud post-1905 generation in Bengal. Even the official Enquiry Committee mentioned "the harm done by the occasional use of tactless expressions by certain European professors in addressing students." It cited the example of professors' employing the phrase "barbarian peoples" ("those who need to be civilized") without explaining "the literal Greek sense" of "non-Hellenic," in which the term might have been used.[39] During 1916, there was much commentary in the Indian press on the breakdown of the old paternalistic social norms. Perhaps the most astute intervention came from Rabindranath Tagore, in essays he wrote in English and Bengali. To his mind, the incident was a symptom of the rebellious spirit of Bengali students engendered by the arrogance of British professors and perceptions of unfair treatment meted out to Indian professors. The British demanded a relationship based on fear and hatred, rather than aspiring to a rule of love, and for Indian students this meant that "the least insult pierce[d] to the quick."[40] The government, for its part, disbanded the recently instituted system of having elected class representatives to articulate students' grievances and interests. Those elected had been, in the government's view, "the demagogue type who are not necessarily the most desirable members from an intellectual and moral standpoint."[41] The authorities may have been justified in punishing students suspected in a case of physical assault. Yet by deeming democracy to be antithetical to the colonial imperative of maintaining order even in the field of education, they did away with a possible channel of communication with a new generation of students unlikely to be as deferential as their predecessors.

Subhas was clearly dismayed at the time to see his studies cut short, and hoped for a reprieve. His father and elder brother Sarat tried their best to use their family connections in high places and their access to the dictatorial vice-chancellor, Ashutosh Mookerjee, to get Subhas admitted elsewhere, but their efforts were not immediately successful. For the moment, they thought it prudent to put the expelled student on a train back to Cuttack. In retrospect, the Oaten affair looked like a defining moment in Subhas's life. "Lying on the bunk in the train at night," Subhas would write in his autobiography three decades later, "I reviewed the events of the last few months." The "inner significance" of "the tragic events of 1916" would emerge only later, when he realized that his expulsion from college had given him "a foretaste of leadership though in a very restricted sphere—and of the martyrdom that it involves."[42]

The "tragic events" had more to do with social tensions than with individual animosities. Oaten was by no means the only British professor to be assaulted by his Indian students in Calcutta in the early twentieth century. The episode surrounding him was best remembered because of its association with the early life of Subhas Chandra Bose, a future iconic figure of India's independence movement. Professors who later suffered a similar fate at the hands of their students were said to have been "oatenized." The professor whose name became a verb was for decades portrayed as a villain in popular accounts of the incident in India. But his reputation was redeemed more than two decades after independence when a poem composed by him on the Indian leader came to light:

Did I once suffer, Subhas, at your hands?
Your patriot heart is stilled, I would forget!
Let me recall but this, that while as yet
The Raj that you once challenged in your land
Was mighty; Icarus-like your courage planned
    To mount the skies, and storm in battle set
The ramparts of High Heaven, to claim the debt
Of freedom owed, on plain and rude demand.
High Heaven yielded, but in dignity
Like Icarus, you sped towards the sea.[43]

Such a grand historical reconciliation lay in the distant future. In March 1916, a promising young student's future looked bleak as he returned to Cuttack. Yet Indian society accorded him sympathy and respect, while his immediate family showed him understanding in his predicament. If anything, a distance developed between him and his spiritual circle of friends, whom he had not cared to consult during the tribulations of January and February. Subhas was setting his own course now by cutting loose from the group given to esoteric exercises. Instead, he threw himself more resolutely into social service. He spent his enforced year away from college in the environs of Cuttack, nursing patients suffering from cholera and smallpox. He also devoted some time to organizing youth for community work. At one of the students' hostels, he found a Santhal student named Arjun Majhi facing the all-too-familiar discrimination from the upper castes that was the lot of this tribal community. When this student fell ill with typhoid, Subhas took a stand against such prejudice and made sure he was nursed with extra care. To his "surprise and joy," his mother joined him in nursing this Santhal student back to health, allying herself with her son's chosen path.[44]

After a year's absence, Subhas journeyed to Calcutta to try his luck with the university authorities once more. Bengalis were deemed by the British to be a "nonmartial race," based on a spurious anthropological theory about martial races and castes formulated in the late nineteenth century. The bulk of the British Indian Army was drawn from the so-called "martial races," which included Punjabis, Pathans, and Gurkhas. The exigencies of war, however, had led the British to start recruiting for the "49th Bengalee Regiment" in 1917. Kazi Nazrul Islam, who was to become Bengal's greatest revolutionary poet, enlisted in this regiment ostensibly because he wished to forsake the university for the universe. Subhas too quietly applied for recruitment at the army's office on Beadon Street in Calcutta. He was disqualified because of his poor eyesight, even though he passed all the other medical tests. So he headed back to the university and showed up at the office of Dr. Urquhart, the principal of Scottish Church College. He explained his situation and expressed his desire to enroll in the honors course in philosophy. Urquhart wanted a note from the new principal of Presidency College that he had no objection. Subhas was able to obtain this with the help of his brother Sarat. In July 1917, Subhas returned to his studies in philosophy "with zeal and devotion."[45]

At Scottish Church College, he began to enjoy the philosophy lectures and Bible lessons given by Urquhart, and found him a "tactful and considerate" principal. Subhas became an active participant in the seminars of the college philosophical society. On February 1, 1918, he presented a paper entitled "A Defence of Materialism," which was sharply criticized by members of the society. On September 6, when he gave a talk entitled "A Defence of Idealism," the audience extended

warm approbation. On this occasion he was speaking more from conviction than from a desire to simply sharpen his forensic skills. The
minutes of the society recorded that the speaker "supported Idealistic
Monism of the Hegelian type but differed from Hegel and Schopenhauer in conceiving the absolute not as Pure Reason or Pure Will but as
Spirit in all his fullness, striving through all the processes of the world
to rise into the bliss of Self-consciousness in the life of man."[46]

Subhas chose to match his mental exercises with some solid military
training. In the final year of the war, the British set up a university unit
of the India Defence Force, and Subhas joined it with great enthusiasm.
"What a change it was," he wrote. "From sitting at the feet of anchorites
to obtain knowledge about God, to standing with a rifle on my shoulders taking orders from a British army officer!" He liked Captain Gray,
a Scotsman, who despite his gruff voice and brusque manners had "a
heart of gold." The young men under his command were prepared
to "do anything" for him. Subhas took "positive pleasure" in the pa-
rades and musketry training. He recalled that the first day the trainees
marched into the otherwise out-of-bounds Fort William to fetch their
rifles, they felt "a queer feeling of satisfaction" of "taking possession of
something" to which they had "an inherent right" but of which they
had been "unjustly deprived."[47] Civilian Indians, as colonial subjects,
had been deprived of the right to bear arms ever since the failure of the
great rebellion of 1857. The forcible disarming of the populace still
rankled.

As the B.A. examinations drew closer, Subhas turned his attention
from soldiering to study. He received first-class honors in philosophy
and placed second in the university's order of merit. He was awarded
various medals and prizes for his accomplishments, though he felt his
performance was not up to his own high standards. For his master's
degree, Subhas decided to switch from philosophy to experimental psychology. He had barely started his researches in psychology when, one
evening, his father sent for him. Subhas found Janakinath closeted with
Sarat. The father asked whether Subhas would like to go to England to
study for the Indian Civil Service and requested a reply within twenty-
four hours. The ICS formed the steel frame of Britain's bureaucratic
administration of India. It was mostly British in composition. Indian

nationalists had been clamoring since the late nineteenth century for greater Indianization of this service, but progress toward that goal had been painfully slow. In 1893, the House of Commons had passed a resolution favoring simultaneous examinations in London and India for entry into the service, but this administrative reform had not been implemented. For those Indians willing to serve the British raj, the ICS was regarded as the "heaven-born service" in which a handful of them could serve alongside British civil servants in the upper echelons of the bureaucracy.

Subhas took counsel with himself and, having persuaded himself that he could not possibly pass the difficult ICS examination with only eight months left to prepare for it, decided to accept his father's offer anyway. He was more interested in using this opportunity of going abroad to get a university degree in England. Subhas had to leave in a week's time. His decision to travel to England elicited disapproval from two entirely different quarters. With the members of the group who had joined him in spiritual pursuits, there was an unstated "parting of the ways": "they threw cold water on the project." He then went to see the provincial adviser for studies in England, a Cambridge alumnus and professor at Presidency College, who advised him that he had no chance whatsoever in the ICS examination "against the 'tip-toppers' from Oxford and Cambridge" and asked why he was going to throw away ten thousand rupees. Subhas was by now determined to follow his own path and was not easily dissuaded. Seeing there was no hope of persuading this man to help him gain admission to Cambridge, he simply replied, "My father wants me to throw away the ten thousand rupees." And then he left.

Cambridge

On September 15, 1919, Subhas Chandra Bose set sail for England from Bombay on the S.S. *City of Calcutta*. It was a slow and tedious journey. The ship was delayed by a week at Suez because of a coal strike. At long last, on October 25, a typically gray London day, the *City of Calcutta* steamed into Tilbury. The academic year had already commenced in England. Subhas hastened to see the adviser to Indian students at his office on Cromwell Road. The adviser was not of much help, and so, at the urging of friends, Subhas boarded a train for Cambridge. He called on Mr. Reddaway, the censor (head) of Fitzwilliam Hall, who granted him permission to enroll for the Moral and Mental Sciences Tripos—the degree course at Cambridge in philosophy— even though the deadline had passed. "Without Mr. Reddaway," Subhas wrote later, "I do not know what I would have done in England."[48]

The general elections of December 1918 in Britain had led to the installation of a coalition government of the Liberals, led by David Lloyd George, with the Conservatives, under Andrew Bonar Law. From 1919 to 1921, the country witnessed the rise of the Labour party and a spate of strikes by miners and other workers, even as the British Empire contended with anticolonial challenges in Ireland, Egypt, and India. Cambridge was politically conservative at war's end, more so than Oxford, which was beginning to take a liberal turn. But after enduring the stifling atmosphere of wartime Calcutta, Subhas enjoyed breathing the air of freedom in Cambridge and was deeply impressed by the esteem that was shown to young students. He attended the debates at the Union Society, where he found the atmosphere enabling the freedom of expression "so exhilarating." Coming from a British colony where dissent amounted to sedition in the eyes of the government, he could appreciate the biting humor of a pro-Irish speaker who drew a contrast between "the forces of law and order on the one side and of Bonar Law and disorder on the other" (Andrew Bonar Law was then home secretary in the U.K. government). In addition to taking part in extracurricular activities, Subhas regularly went to lectures on ethics, psychology, and metaphysics for his Philosophy tripos. But the bulk of his time had to be devoted to diligent preparation for the ICS examination. He studied nine diverse subjects: English composition, Sanskrit, philosophy, English law, political science, modern European history, English history, economics, and geography. Of these, he found delving into political science, economics, English history, and modern European history to be "beneficial" in the long run. A reading of Bismarck's autobiography, Metternich's memoirs, and Cavour's letters gave him a sense of the distinctiveness of continental Europe in relation to Britain and aided his understanding of "the inner currents of international politics." He was also curious about the historical struggle for liberty in England, which he felt had some relevance for contemporary India. His copies of the books he read, such as A. F. Pollard's *Factors in Modern History,* Arthur D. Innes's *A History of England and the British Empire,* and John Maynard Keynes's *Indian Currency and Finance,* were heavily marked and filled with extensive marginal notes.[49]

In Subhas's experience, relations between British and Indian students at Cambridge tended to be cordial, but not intimate. More generally, the Indians were saddened to see the support among the British middle classes for General Reginald Dyer, who had given the order to shoot that resulted in the Amritsar massacre of April 1919. Nearly four hundred innocent men, women, and children had been killed and three times that number wounded in an enclosed park. Yet Dyer had received a hero's reception for teaching recalcitrant colonial subjects a stern lesson and was given a sizable financial reward on his return to Britain. There were smaller instances of racial discrimination that rankled. The Indian tennis champion was not allowed to captain Cambridge University's team in the interuniversity tournament. Indian students were not permitted to enlist in the university unit of the Officers' Training Corps. Subhas and a fellow student, K. L. Gauba, were sent as representatives of the Indian Majlis, a students' organization in Cambridge, to present their case before Secretary of State E. S. Montagu, and the Earl of Lytton, Under-Secretary of State for India. Lytton claimed that the India Office had no objection to admitting Indians to a course on officers' training, but the War Office was worried that Indians who received training would seek commissions in the British army. Indian officers commanding white soldiers was not yet something that Britain's military brass was prepared to countenance. The Indian students reassured the authorities that they were interested only in the training and promised not to seek military commissions, but to no avail. As the India Office and War Office passed the buck between them, the Indian students felt the cold winds of exclusion.[50]

During his Cambridge years, Subhas forged and deepened a number of friendships with fellow students from India, including Dilip Kumar Roy, Kshitish Prasad Chattopadhyay, and C. C. Desai. The Bengali trio of Subhas, Dilip, and Kshitish found a home away from home at the

Lancashire residence of the Dharmavir family—a Punjabi doctor, his European wife, and their two little daughters, Sita and Leila. Subhas developed an affectionate relationship with Mrs. Dharmavir, whom he called "Didi" ("Elder Sister"). He later confessed to her that he was never really happy in England, except during his brief stay with the Dharmavirs at Burnley, Lancashire. He could not quite say what gave him such joy, but he knew "both you and Doctor were responsible for it." He wished Mrs. Dharmavir would come to India, where "civilization consists in the elevation of the human spirit and in the increasing approximation of the human spirit to the Divine." He was grateful to her for showing an interest in his lonely thoughts. When she gave packets of nuts and fruits to him and his friends as their train departed, he was "reminded of what an Indian mother would do under similar circumstances."[51]

The Dharmavirs' living room was the venue for lively conversations about politics. Sitting in front of a crackling fire, the Cambridge friends, as Dilip remembered, "often talked far into the night with a glow of heart that only youth can command." They discussed the rising Labour party in England and the communist revolution in Russia. Drawing an analogy between India and Ireland, Subhas told his friends that the Bengali revolutionaries of the Swadeshi era had not failed: "You might just as well say that the Sinn Féin movement is a failure also, since it hasn't delivered the goods yet. When de Valera was sentenced the other day to death, whoever thought he would be released and then reimprisoned again in 1918 only to escape from Lincoln Jail and visit America where he would raise six million dollars for the Irish Republican movement?" The Bengali revolutionary movement was "the first real movement" that instilled strength in a supine people and "created the nucleus of national consciousness."[52]

Writing to another friend, Charu Chandra Ganguly, in India, Subhas observed that in England he had come to fully grasp the need for mass education and labor organization in India. He recalled Vivekananda's view that India's progress would be achieved "only by the peasant, the washerman, the cobbler, and the sweeper." The West had already shown what "the power of the people" could accomplish—and "the brightest example" of this was Russia, the world's first socialist republic. "The

Sudras or the untouchable caste of India," he wrote, "constitute the Labour Party. So long these people have only suffered. Their strength and their sacrifice will bring about India's progress."[53]

These ruminations about India's future were written while Subhas was studying hard to qualify for the ICS—what many called the "heaven-born service." The examinations began in mid-July 1920 and the "agony" dragged on for a month. Subhas was convinced that he had not done well. He had thrown away "150 sure marks" by neglecting to transcribe his rough translation of a Sanskrit text into the proper answer book. So he was surprised, one night in mid-September, to receive a cable from a friend that read: "Congratulations See Morning Post." The *Morning Post* revealed that Subhas had qualified for the ICS, ranking fourth in the order of merit.[54] He had got the highest marks for English Composition, along with another Indian student. While the three ranked above him had done well in Latin, Greek, and mathematics, Subhas had excelled in history, moral and metaphysical philosophy, political economy and economic history, and psychology and logic.[55] He had achieved a stunning success by the standards set by the colonial masters, and was now faced with "a serious crisis of conscience."[56] Were his ideals of service to humanity compatible with entering the Indian Civil Service and serving the British raj?

For the next seven months, Subhas struggled to resolve this crisis, seeking counsel and support in long letters he wrote to Sarat, his elder brother and confidant. He was careful to distinguish between the British people and British rule in India. In September 1920, Subhas was staying as a paying guest of one Mr. Bates at Leigh-on-Sea in Essex. Even as he debated with himself whether or not to serve the British raj, he wrote to his brother with great warmth about his British host. Mr. Bates "represents English character at its very best," he told Sarat, as he was "cultured and liberal in his views and cosmopolitan in his sentiments." He admired Mr. Bates for having friends drawn from many different nationalities and for his familiarity with Russian, Irish, and Indian literature. He asked his brother if he could arrange to send a miniature model of the Taj Mahal from Calcutta, as a present for this broad-minded Englishman. Respect for the best in English character, however, did not translate into a positive assessment of the British raj.

Subhas was not delighted at the prospect of joining the ICS. "Given talents, with a servile spirit," he wrote with some sarcasm, "one may even aspire to be the Chief Secretary of a provincial Government." His temperament, which fed on "eccentric" ideas, was not well suited to easily accepting a life of "worldly comfort." "Life loses half its interest if there is no struggle—if there are no risks to be taken," he told his elder brother. He was emphatic that "national and spiritual aspirations" were "not compatible with obedience to Civil Service conditions." His father was "sure to be hostile" to his idea of declining to enter the service, and he had not yet decided on the path of disobedience. If he were "given the option," Subhas would be "the last man to join the Indian Civil Service." An ICS man was naturally the recipient of many marriage proposals, and many poured in for Subhas. "If the *ghataks* [matchmakers] come to trouble you again," he instructed his elder brother, "you can ask them straight away to take a right about turn and march off."[57]

Subhas had to contend with the argument that some Indians, such as Romesh Chunder Dutt, the economic historian and critic of colonial policies, had done a lot of good work despite being a member of the civil service. He felt, however, that a question of principle was involved, and he just could not countenance being a part of the machinery that had "outlived the days of its usefulness" and was now associated with "conservatism, selfish power, heartlessness, and red-tapism." The choice before him seemed clear. He must either "chuck this rotten service" or "bid adieu to all [my] ideals and aspirations." He did not care that many of his relatives would "howl" when they heard his rash proposal not to join the service. "But I have faith in your idealism," he wrote to Sarat, "and that is why I am appealing to you." He alluded to the Oaten incident and recalled the moral support his brother had given him on that occasion. He was now going to write to his father seeking his consent, and wanted his barrister brother to plead his case.[58]

Subhas faced a profound psychological dilemma in deciding whether to defy his father on the ICS question. He informed Sarat that he had sought the permission of their father and mother to take "the vow of poverty and service." He found the "very principle" of working for an alien bureaucracy "intensely repugnant." The path blazed by Aurobindo Ghose, the revolutionary of the Swadeshi era, appeared to him to be "more noble, more inspiring, more lofty, more unselfish, though more thorny" than that of the moderate Romesh Dutt. If the elderly Chittaranjan Das—popularly known in India as "Deshbandhu" ("Friend of the Country")—could "give up everything and face the uncertainties of life," so could young Subhas.[59] C. R. Das, who would become Subhas's father figure in politics, had been Aurobindo Ghose's defense lawyer in the Alipore bomb trial of 1909. By now he had emerged as the preeminent leader of the Indian National Congress in Bengal. Addressing C. R. Das as "the high priest of the festival of national service in Bengal," Subhas wanted to know what work the leader might assign him once he resigned from the service. He believed that he had the skills to teach in the National College and write for the Deshbandhu's nationalist newspaper. While seeking advice from C. R. Das, the young Subhas did not hesitate to forcefully communicate his own ideas about the Congress. The premier nationalist party had "no definite policy" regarding Indian currency and exchange, relations with the princely states, or the franchise for men and women. Because of the party's "lack of effort" in relation to the "Depressed Classes," India's hapless untouchable castes, the non-Brahmins of Madras had "become pro-Government and anti-nationalist." The Congress needed permanent quarters and a permanent staff of researchers to work on national problems and devise policies.[60]

Subhas displayed amazing self-confidence in pointing out the shortcomings of the Congress to C. R. Das, a redoubtable leader of the party. He lamented the Congress's lack of a clear-cut policy on labor and factory legislation, as well as on vagrancy and on relief for the poor. Worst of all, the Congress had "no determined policy as to the type of the Constitution" that should be adopted. The scheme worked out by the Congress and the Muslim League in 1916 seemed to him to be out of date. "We must now frame the Constitution of India," he urged C. R. Das, "on the basis of *swaraj* [self-rule]." The work of creation had to begin, even as the Congress went about dismantling the established order.[61]

By late February of 1921, Subhas had made up his mind to turn his back on the ICS. He had written to Sarat on February 23 that the "illustrious example" of Aurobindo Ghose loomed before him and "he was ready to make the sacrifice which that example" demanded of him. He was sure that Sarat would "respond favourably," but that "hardly anyone else" among his relatives would approve of his "eccentric plans." "My decision is final and unchangeable," he wrote to his brother, "but my destiny is at present in your hands. Can I not expect your blessings in return and will you not wish me Godspeed in my new and adventurous career?"[62]

The doting elder brother was prepared to be indulgent, but in early March their father, Janakinath, communicated his firm disapproval. Subhas's decision about the colonial bureaucracy would now have to be taken in defiance of his father's express wishes. On April 6, 1921, Subhas sat down in Oxford to compose a detailed rebuttal of their father's arguments to Sarat. He began by recounting his painful mental struggle as he tried to reconcile his duty to his parents and his duty to himself. He was aware that he had caused his parents grievous hurt, especially in view of the loss of some close relatives, and was the primary source of discord in the family. His father believed that since the constitutional reforms of 1919 had made some concessions at the provincial level, the position of an Indian civil servant would not be incompatible with a sense of self-respect. "Should we under the present circumstances own allegiance to a foreign bureaucracy," Subhas retorted, "and sell ourselves for a mess of pottage?" In their father's opinion, Home Rule would come to India in ten years. Such an outcome was possible, according to the skeptical son, only if Indians were prepared to pay the price. "Only on the soil of sacrifice and suffering," Subhas declared, "can we raise our national edifice." He was dismayed that in the entire history of British rule in India, not a single Indian had renounced the civil service motivated by patriotism. "If the members of the services withdraw their allegiance or even show a desire to do so," he reckoned, "then and then only will the bureaucratic machine collapse."[63]

While Subhas grappled with his own future, the nonviolent noncooperation movement led by Mahatma Gandhi raged in India. After two decades as an expatriate in South Africa, where he earned a reputation as a practitioner of passive resistance, Mohandas Karamchand Gandhi had returned to India in 1915. During 1917 and 1918, he had led two local campaigns of nonviolent protest in his home province of Gujarat and another against European indigo planters in the Champaran district of Bihar. At war's end, he launched his first all-India *satyagraha* —"quest for truth," through mass political activity—against what he described as the "satanic" British government which had turned a wartime ordinance into peacetime legislation enabling the imprisonment of Indians without trial. With the support of Indian Muslims worried about the fate of the Khilafat (Caliphate) in Turkey, Gandhi had risen to the leadership of the Indian National Congress by 1920. The party had launched a mass campaign for boycotting British textiles, schools, courts, and representative institutions.

Subhas's father thought that the so-called leaders of this movement were not genuinely unselfish. But did that give him any right, Subhas countered, to prevent him from taking the unselfish path of a conscious and deliberate sacrifice? He could not see how he might persuade his father that the day he resigned would be one of "the proudest and happiest moments" in his life. Sarat had gently suggested that perhaps he could resign after returning to India. Subhas was not persuaded. For him, it would be "a galling thing" to "sign the covenant which is an emblem of servitude." In Sarat's assessment, the movement his younger brother wanted to join was in a "nebulous and chaotic condition." Subhas turned that argument around: it was the "apprehension of failure or slackening" that impelled him to take the plunge before it was "too late to mend matters." In case he changed his mind about his decision to resign, he would cable his father to "relieve his anxiety."[64]

On April 20, 1921, Subhas informed Sarat that he was going to send in his resignation "day after tomorrow." He had been touched profoundly by his elder brother's "magnanimous spirit" and could not have expected "a more cordial and sympathetic response." "I know how many hearts I have grieved," he concluded, "how many superiors of mine I have disobeyed. But on the eve of this hazardous undertaking my only prayer is—may it be for the good of our dear country."[65] Subhas had decided to give up all that he had been groomed for and strike out on an uncertain path. It was a decision that placed him outside the framework of the British raj and shaped the rest of his life. On April 22,

1921, from his lodgings at 16 Herbert Street, Cambridge, Subhas Chandra Bose dispatched his letter of resignation from the Indian Civil Service to E. S. Montagu, Secretary of State for India.[66]

"The die is cast," Subhas wrote to Sarat the day after, "and I earnestly hope that nothing but good will come out of it." Even though Sarat had sent "warmest felicitations on whatever course" he chose, Subhas knew he had disobeyed his father and acted against his brother's advice. He felt that he needed to justify his stand once more. He had come to believe that "compromise is a bad thing—it degrades the man and injures his cause." He was not enamored of the course followed by the moderate Congress leader Surendranath Banerjee, whose philosophy of expediency, learned from Edmund Burke, was bringing him a knighthood at the end of his career. "We have got to make a nation," he insisted, "and a nation can be made only by the uncompromising idealism of Hampden and Cromwell." The time had come to "wash our hands clean of any connection with the British Government." The best way to undermine that regime was to withdraw from it. This was not merely Tolstoy's doctrine as preached by Gandhi, but a matter of his own inner conviction. He had been happy to receive a recent letter from his mother saying whatever might be the views of his father and others, she preferred "the ideal for which Mahatma Gandhi stands." C. R. Das had replied to him pointing out the shortage of sincere workers at home. Mr. Reddaway, the head of Fitzwilliam Hall who had granted Subhas admission into Cambridge, had "heartily approved" of his future course of action.[67]

Subhas's resignation caused consternation in the corridors of power. During the next month or so, various attempts were made to persuade him to reconsider his decision. Sir William Duke, Permanent Under-Secretary of State for India, tried to intervene using old family connections from his days spent in Orissa, and wrote to Subhas's eldest brother Satish. Subhas was also approached by lecturers in Cambridge to change his mind. The most intriguing overture came from Mr. Roberts, Secretary of the Civil Service Board in Cambridge, with whom Subhas had clashed not so long before over some instructions for ICS probationers on the "Care of Horses in India." These instructions contained gratuitous statements about Indian grooms eating the same food as their horses and the habitual dishonesty of Indian traders. When Subhas asked to have these remarks removed, Mr. Roberts had said that he would have to "clear out" if he did not accept the official point of view. Subhas should not "look out for offenses," Mr. Roberts had advised, to which Subhas replied that he had not "looked out" but the instructions were there right in front of him. After his resignation, Subhas met a very different Mr. Roberts: the man was "so sweet," pleading long and hard to persuade him to try the service for two years. Subhas thanked him for his concern, and let him know that his mind was made up, since he "could not serve two masters."[68]

On May 18, 1921, Subhas told Sarat he had sent word to Sir William Duke that he had acted after "mature deliberation." His tripos examination would end on June 1, and he planned to sail home from Marseilles in late June or early July. He would book his passage on one of the Nippon Yasen Kaisha boats as soon as his resignation was accepted.[69] Subhas's letter of resignation on April 22, 1921, had been a rather prosaic one. He had expressed his desire to have his "name removed from the list of probationers in the Indian Civil Service." He had received an allowance of £100, and he would remit the amount "as soon as my resignation is accepted."[70] On the day he sent in his resignation, he wrote another letter to an old college friend, Charu Chandra Ganguly, which captured the poetry of the moment:

> You are aware that once before I sailed forth on the sea of life at the call of duty. The ship has now reached a port offering great allurement— where power, property and wealth are at my command. But the response from the innermost corner of my heart is—"You will not find happiness in this. The way to your happiness lies in your dancing around with the surging waves of the ocean."
>
> Today in response to that call, I am sailing forth again with the helm in His hands. Only He knows where the ship will land.[71]

3

Dreams of Youth

Ideas will work out their own destiny, and we who are but clods of clay encasing sparks of the Divine Fire have only got to consecrate ourselves to these ideas.

—SUBHAS CHANDRA BOSE to Sarat Chandra Bose, from Insein Jail, May 6, 1927

Having completed his Cambridge degree in philosophy, Subhas Chandra Bose set sail for India with an unwavering sense of mission to serve his country's cause. He landed in Bombay on July 16, 1921, and that very afternoon he rushed to see Gandhi at Mani Bhavan, the Mahatma's usual residence in the city.

Gandhi sat in the middle of a large room decorated with Indian carpets. He was surrounded by some of his closest followers, who all wore Indian garments made of *khadi*, handspun and handwoven cotton. Gandhi had adopted the *charkha*, the spinning wheel, as one of the key symbols of Indian mass nationalism. Feeling somewhat out of place, Subhas opened the conversation by apologizing for his European attire. He was soon put at ease by the Mahatma's "characteristic hearty smile" and warm indulgence. The eager and impatient young recruit bombarded the leader, who was more than double his age, with a series of insistent questions. How would the movement of nonviolent noncooperation that Gandhi had been spearheading since 1920 accelerate in stages toward its climax in the nonpayment of taxes to the government? How could that and civil disobedience compel the foreign rulers to concede Indian freedom? How would Gandhi fulfill his promise to the people of delivering *swaraj* ("self-rule") within one year?

Bose was satisfied with Gandhi's answer to the first question on how he planned to ratchet up the agitation as it gathered momentum. He was not persuaded, however, by Gandhi's vague responses to the other questions. Perhaps the commander of the nonviolent campaign to boycott British goods and institutions did not wish to divulge all the secrets in his armory, the new lieutenant tried to persuade himself. Giving the leader the benefit of the doubt, Bose tried to believe that there must be a lack of comprehension on his own part. His reason, however, told him that there was "a deplorable lack of clarity" in Gandhi's political strategy.[1] One thing was clear after the very first meeting between Gandhi and Bose. The Mahatma had failed to cast his hypnotic spell on Subhas, as he had done with so many of his followers—those who chanted in unison, "Gandhi Maharaj ki Jai!" ("Victory to the Great King Gandhi!").

Another admiring skeptic, Rabindranath Tagore, had traveled on the same ship with Subhas on the return voyage from Europe to India. During the journey, the poet and the patriot had discussed the Congress policy of noncooperation. Tagore had not been actively involved in anticolonial politics since the Swadeshi ("Own Country") movement of 1905–1908. He had seen how the boycott of educational institutions in those days had—in the absence of a successful alternative—blighted the future of an entire young generation. He did not want another generation to suffer the same fate. Besides, the mechanical pursuit of spinning and weaving at Gandhi's urging would, he feared, dull the critical faculties of the people. Subhas found in his conversations that Tagore was not opposed to the idea of noncooperation as such, and was "only anxious that there should be more of constructive activity." This line of thinking Bose saw as "analogous to the constructive side of the Irish Sinn Féin movement" and "completely in accord" with his own views.[2] After their arrival in India, Tagore was persuaded that Gandhi's personal antagonism to modern science and medicine was influencing the tenor of the political movement. This, according to Bose, led Tagore to deliver his powerful speech in Calcutta on the

"Unity of Culture," lamenting the boycott of educational institutions and what he saw as an attempt to isolate India from the global circulation of ideas.

On Mahatma Gandhi's advice, Subhas hastened by train to Calcutta in order to report for duty to Deshbandhu Chittaranjan Das, the towering Congress leader from Bengal, with whom he had corresponded from Cambridge. C. R. Das had harbored initial doubts about Gandhi's strategy, but accepted the path of noncooperation once he saw that a majority in the Congress party favored it. The Deshbandhu ("Friend of the Country") was away on tour in the rural interior of the province, and so Subhas had to wait. He settled down to live with his elder brother Sarat, sister-in-law Bivabati, and their children in a rented house at 38/1 Elgin Road, adjacent to his father's house at 38/2. Having renounced the civil service, Subhas relied on the unstinting financial and emotional support provided by Sarat. As soon as C. R. Das returned to Calcutta, Subhas called on him. Unlike Bose, Das had failed the ICS examination but had been later successfully called to the bar at the Inner Temple in London. If there was one quality that distinguished Das, it was his magnanimity. He had given up his princely income as a leading barrister in the Calcutta High Court to devote himself full-time to the noncooperation movement. A peer of Gandhi, he connected well with young people and with youthful aspirations. Speaking with Das, Subhas felt that "here was a man who knew what he was about." By the end of the conversation, Subhas "had found a leader" and "meant to follow him."[3]

In Quest of *Swaraj*

At its annual session in December 1920, the Indian National Congress had declared its goal: *swaraj* ("self-rule"), to be achieved by "all peaceful and legitimate means." In Gandhi's definition, *swaraj* meant "Self-Government within the empire, if possible—and outside, if necessary." He combined the negative value of *ahimsa* ("nonviolence") with the positive value of *satyagraha*—a righteous mass political campaign—to offer a novel method of resistance against British rule. The program of nonviolent noncooperation advocated by the Gandhian Congress included the triple boycott of legislatures, law courts, and educational institutions.

The Montagu-Chelmsford constitutional reforms of 1919—so named after the secretary of state and the viceroy of India—aimed at pacifying Indian protest and at diverting Indian political attention to local and provincial arenas, while keeping real power firmly in British hands at the center. Even at the provincial level, there was to be a system known as "diarchy" in which the more important departments of government would be reserved for the British governor and his civil servants. Indian ministers drawn from the elected members of the provincial legislative council could be put in charge of less sensitive departments. The Congress party had chosen to shun the elections to these councils, and was determined to subvert the colonial attempt to provincialize Indian politics. It wanted to instigate an all-India movement that would broaden the political arena far beyond the limited sphere of British-sponsored institutions.

The spirit of the reforms had been swiftly contravened in March 1919 by the passage of the Rowlatt Act, which transformed wartime ordinance into peacetime legislation enabling the British to hold Indians in detention without trial. Protests against this lawless law had been answered on April 13, 1919, with the Amritsar Massacre in Punjab, which left at least 379 innocent men, women, and children dead and some 1,200 wounded. To add insult to injury, the official Committee of Enquiry had not indicted the perpetrators of the crime, and the House of Lords had even congratulated Reginald Dyer, the military officer who ordered the shooting. The flouting of the pledge made by Lloyd George, the British prime minister, not to dismember Turkey and not to take over the holy lands in the Hejaz had angered many Indian Muslims. The resolve to right the Punjab wrong and the Khilafat wrong had galvanized Hindus and Muslims to come together under Gandhi's leadership to challenge the might of the British raj.

Amid the political ferment and the socioeconomic discontent of the postwar years, C. R. Das was quick to harness the talents of young Subhas in the service of the noncooperation movement in Bengal. Subhas was put in charge of publicity for the Bengal provincial congress committee and appointed principal of a newly established national college. He made his mark as an able writer and editor for the vibrant anticolonial press, but efforts to lure students away from the government curriculum toward national education were largely unsuccessful. Bonfires of British textiles burned much brighter in the late summer and autumn of 1921 than the lamps of Indian learning that some nationalists, including Subhas, tried to light. As winter approached, the government supplied fresh fuel to the conflagration by announcing a visit to India by the Prince of Wales. The Congress called for a *hartal*, or general strike, on November 17, 1921, the day the heir to the British throne arrived in Bombay. While the streets of Bombay witnessed a pitched battle between those who wished to welcome the prince and those determined to boycott him, Congress volunteers directed by Subhas Chandra Bose ensured a complete shutdown in the city of Calcutta. The government was provoked, and in retaliation declared all national volunteer organizations illegal.

The noncooperators now decided to put the British ban to the test by organizing small groups of five volunteers each to go out into the streets of Calcutta to hawk *khadi,* the cloth that served as the emblem of Gandhi's movement. To give a spur to the campaign, Das decided to send his wife at the head of one group aimed at provoking arrest. Subhas, the chief organizer, objected, but was overruled. The sight of Basanti Devi, the revered wife of the Deshbandhu, being hauled to prison caused a furor across the city and upset even loyalist politicians and police constables. Basanti Devi was set free by midnight, much to the relief of an emotional Subhas, who had come to look upon her as a second mother.[4] The colonial government's miscalculation in arresting her meant there was no dearth of volunteers on the following day. The two large prisons in the city were filled to overflowing, as were the makeshift detention camps. On December 10, 1921, in sheer exasperation, the government arrested Chittaranjan Das and Subhas Chandra Bose. This was the first of Subhas's eleven journeys to British jails.

"We are proud of Subhas and proud of you all," Janakinath Bose wrote to Sarat on December 12, 1921. The father who had strenuously opposed his son's resignation from the ICS now professed his belief in "the doctrine of sacrifice."[5] During the eight months of that first stint in jail, Subhas took care of the father-like figure of Chittaranjan Das with utmost devotion. Jailmates joked that C. R. Das had even acquired the services of an "ICS cook" in his prison cell. The intimacy of prison life together gave Subhas an opportunity to observe the Deshbandhu at close quarters: he found a model of generous and inspiring leadership. On the eve of the Prince of Wales's scheduled visit to Calcutta on December 24, 1921, the viceroy of India, Lord Reading, made an overture to C. R. Das through an emissary. In return for a lifting of the boycott, he offered the release of political prisoners and an invitation to a round-table conference to discuss the future constitution of India. The young firebrands, including Subhas, initially opposed a truce on these terms. C. R. Das explained, however, that the *swaraj* Gandhi had promised by the end of the year was nowhere on the horizon. A readiness to negotiate at this stage could be interpreted by the Congress as tangible progress toward the goal of self-rule. Das, from his prison cell, sent a message to Gandhi urging him to accept the viceroy's proposal, but the Mahatma demurred.[6] The year drew to a close with spectacular success in bringing the masses into politics, but freedom was still a distant dream.

Early in 1922, Gandhi announced that in late February he would begin the climactic phase of the protest: nonpayment of taxes to the government in the Bardoli district of his home province, Gujarat. But on February 5, 1922, news came from Chauri Chaura, a remote village in the United Provinces of north India, that insurgent peasants had set fire to a police station and twenty-one policemen had died. Citing this act of violence, Gandhi unilaterally called off the noncooperation movement. The other leaders, who were in prison, were dismayed. Das was furious and believed Gandhi had bungled badly in pulling the plug on the campaign without getting anything in return. So far, the British had not dared to arrest the Mahatma. Now, on March 10, 1922, they took him into custody in Ahmedabad and charged him with sedition for essays he had published in his journal *Young India*—"the finest he has ever written and which will rank for all time among his inspired writings," in Subhas's opinion.[7]

In the articles that so impressed Subhas and so offended the colonial masters, Gandhi had defended his compatriots Mohamed Ali and

Shaukat Ali for calling on Indian soldiers not to serve the British. "I have no hesitation in saying," Gandhi had proclaimed in September 1921, "that it is sinful for anyone, either soldiers or civilians, to serve this Government which has proved treacherous to the Mussalmans of India, and which has been guilty of the inhumanities of the Punjab." When the time was ripe, he would not hesitate, "at the peril of being shot, to ask the Indian sepoy individually to leave his service and become a weaver." He spelled out his reasons in unambiguous terms:

> For, has not the sepoy been used to hold India under subjection, has he not been used to murder innocent people at Jalianwala Bagh, has he not been used to drive away innocent men, women, and children during that dreadful night at Chandpur, has he not been used to subjugate the proud Arab of Mesopotamia, has he not been utilized to crush the Egyptian? How can any Indian having a spark of humanity in him, and any Mussalman having any pride in his religion, feel otherwise than as the Ali Brothers have done? The sepoy has been used more often as a hired assassin than as a soldier defending the liberty or the honor of the weak and the helpless.[8]

For nearly six months, the British had been forced to tolerate such stinging indictments of their rule. "We are challenging the might of this Government because we consider its activity to be wholly evil," Gandhi had written in another article. "We want to overthrow the Government." In yet another essay, Gandhi had described the British Empire as one "based upon organized exploitation of physically weaker races of the earth, and upon a continuous exhibition of brute force." Such an entity could not last if there was "a just God ruling the universe."[9] The Mahatma paid the price for his outspoken criticism. He was sentenced by a British judge and sent to Poona to be imprisoned in Yeravda Jail.

Subhas, confined in the Alipur Central Jail of Calcutta, was taking part in confabulations that C. R. Das had initiated on the nationalists' future course of action. Das contended that the boycott of the legislatures did not make any further sense, now that Gandhi had scuppered the mass movement. It simply allowed loyalists of the British raj to hold positions of advantage within the political system. He favored a tactical shift and suggested entering the legislatures to wreck the inadequate and hypocritical constitutional reforms from within. Yet before Bose could embark on this mission, another crisis took priority; politics could not be his first call of duty. Once their prison sentences came to an end, Subhas and the band of young workers he had gathered around him headed for the districts of northern Bengal, which had suffered devastating floods in late September. Social service had always been Subhas's forte. He organized a thousand Congress volunteers and spent six weeks directing relief operations in the affected districts. Their outstanding work in providing succor to the distressed villagers earned the appreciation of Lord Lytton, the governor of Bengal.[10]

In December 1922, C. R. Das, head of the Indian National Congress, presented his ideas about a change in political strategy at its annual session held at Gaya. His proposal to work from within the legislatures was rejected by a majority of "no changers," who followed Gandhi in wanting a continued boycott of these bodies. Das resigned as Congress president; and soon after, he and Motilal Nehru, leader of the Congress in northern India, announced the formation of the Swaraj party in pursuit of their activist strategy. During the course of 1923, Das gradually regained support within the Congress, and by September 1923 an accommodation was reached between the "pro-changers" and the "no changers." Congress members were permitted to compete in elections to the legislatures under the banner of the Swaraj party led by C. R. Das and Motilal Nehru, while Gandhi's followers spent their time at the spinning wheel and doing constructive work in the villages.

The Swarajists, supported by Hindus and Muslims, did remarkably well in the elections of 1923 to the Bengal legislative council. Under the leadership of C. R. Das, they kept up a barrage of criticism and defeated the government in key votes. When it came to measures that had no legislative sanction, the British governor had to approve these by executive fiat, revealing the 1919 reforms to be a sham. Subhas worked energetically as a Swarajist and a Congressman. In addition to editing the Bengali paper *Banglar Katha,* he managed a new English newspaper, *Forward,* which made a mark in the field of journalism as soon as it was launched in the autumn of 1923. Around the same time, Subhas took charge as general secretary of the Bengal provincial Congress committee, a post in which he showed great organizational skill.

An amended Calcutta municipal act of 1923 laid the basis for elections to the Calcutta Corporation, the city government: as of March 1924, it broadened the electorate and strengthened the mandate for elected representatives. The Swarajists decided to field candidates in the elections, in an attempt to take over India's largest municipality, and they succeeded in winning a comfortable majority. Deshbandhu Chittaranjan Das was elected mayor of Calcutta, while Husain Shaheed Suhrawardy, a promising young Muslim politician, became the deputy mayor. Sarat Chandra Bose was elected an alderman, and Das appointed the twenty-seven-year-old Subhas as the chief executive officer of the municipal administration. Initially hesitant to accept this role, Subhas obeyed his leader's instructions after deciding to donate half his salary to charity.

He took to his work with the earnestness which was by now his hallmark. He paid particular attention to education and health, setting up free primary schools across the city and health associations in every ward. He made careful plans for an informative weekly paper called the *Calcutta Municipal Gazette,* which made its first appearance later in the year. He took an active interest in developing infrastructure—water supply, lighting, roads—and in administering municipal affairs. Subhas was intent on proving that Indians were more than capable of running their own government. He was not satisfied with the mere symbolism of his office: hosting civic receptions for visiting nationalist leaders, instead of British viceroys and governors.

More significant than the nationalist victory in Calcutta was the Hindu-Muslim unity that underpinned the triumph. Though Muslims formed slightly more than 50 percent of the population of Bengal, they lagged behind Hindus in access and opportunity in education, the professions, and government services. C. R. Das was determined to rectify this imbalance: he proposed a pact between Hindus and Muslims for an equitable sharing of power and positions acquired by nationalists from the British. He failed to get his pact accepted by the Indian National Congress at its annual session at Cocanada in December 1923, but the proposal was adopted at the Bengal provincial conference at

Sirajganj in May 1924. Subhas Chandra Bose implemented his leader's policy, and came in for withering criticism from conservative Hindus for appointing a disproportionate number of Muslims to posts in the Calcutta Corporation. He retorted that in the past Hindus had enjoyed "a sort of monopoly" when it came to appointments, and he would support the "just claims" of Muslims, Christians, and members of the depressed classes even if that caused "heart burning" among Hindus.[11] Both C. R. Das and Mahatma Gandhi sprang to his defense—the latter in the pages of the journal *Young India*. "I note," Gandhi observed, "that the chief executive officer of the Calcutta Corporation has come in for a good deal of hostile criticism because of his having given twenty-five out of thirty-three appointments to Mussalmans. I have read the statement made by the chief executive officer. It is a creditable performance. If Hindus wish to set India free, they must be willing to sacrifice in favor of their Mussalman and other brethren."[12] Subhas was already displaying the sense of fairness toward all religious communities that would win him the trust of minorities later in his political life.

Throughout the summer and early autumn of 1924, Subhas was immersed in his administrative and political work. His parents had come around to supporting his choices. He felt happy living with his elder brother Sarat's family, with the rest of the extended family nearby. He had found another home at C. R. Das's residence and had adopted Das's wife, Basanti Devi, as a second mother. After an arduous day's work, he would drop in on her late at night and ask to be served *bhate-bhat*, a simple vegetarian rice dish of Bengal.[13] Such a happy state of affairs was too good to last, especially for someone who had opted for the uncertainties of a life of adventure.

Mandalay

As dawn broke on October 25, 1924, Subhas was awakened and told that some police officers wanted to see him. "Mr. Bose, I have a very unpleasant duty to perform," the deputy commissioner of the Calcutta police said to him. "I have a warrant for your arrest under Regulation III of 1818."[14] Under this statute, which was more than a hundred years old, the colonial masters could detain their subjects indefinitely without trial, and without even making the charges against them public. The house was searched for arms, ammunition, and explosives. Nothing of the sort was found, and the police had to be satisfied with seizing some papers and letters. Seventeen others were arrested in the police swoop on that day, including two Swarajist members of the Bengal legislative council. Secret intelligence reports claimed that Subhas was "the leading organizer of the revolutionary movement in Bengal" and had been in touch "with Bolshevik propagandists."[15] The suggestion of a communist connection was totally unfounded; C. R. Das had in fact rejected an overture from the Communist International. The internal files of the Home Department (the Ministry of the Interior) asserted that Das was "supported by the terrorists" and that terrorist members of the Swaraj party had backed Bose's candidacy for chief executive officer of the Calcutta Corporation.[16] Three British and Anglo-Indian newspapers alleged that he was the "brain" behind a revolutionary conspiracy. An indignant Subhas asked Sarat to sue them for libel on his behalf, and after lengthy legal proceedings he eventually won damages and costs against two of them. The government confessed in a communication to these newspapers that there was not a shred of documentary evidence against Subhas, only the word of anonymous "credible witnesses."[17] C. R. Das was outraged by the government's resort to "brute force." "If love of country is a crime," he thundered, "I am a criminal. If Mr. Subhas Chandra Bose is a criminal, I am a criminal."[18] Das was convinced that the British were simply unwilling to countenance the fact that nationalists were running the second-largest city of the British Empire.

Das and Bose did not support acts of individual terrorism and did not believe *swaraj* could be won by terrorist methods. Bred in the Bengali political tradition, however, they did not subscribe unquestioningly to Gandhian nonviolence either. Bose may not have been averse in principle to an organized armed struggle, but he realized it was not an option for a subject population lacking any weaponry. As early as 1907, Aurobindo Ghose had written that a subject nation had to make its choice of strategy by taking account of "the circumstances of its servitude," and that Indian circumstances indicated passive resistance to be the correct path. While anticipating many elements of Mahatma Gandhi's methods, Aurobindo argued from a different ethical standpoint. He was certainly not prepared to regard other methods as "in all circumstances criminal and unjustified." "It is the common habit of established Governments and especially those which are themselves oppressors," he wrote, "to brand all violent methods in subject peoples and communities as criminal and wicked." The refusal to listen to "the cant of the oppressor," who was attempting to lay "a moral as well as a legal ban on any attempt to answer violence by violence," had the approval of "the general conscience of humanity." Passive resistance could well be transformed into a battle in which the morality of war ruled supreme. In those situations, to "shrink from bloodshed and violence" deserved "as severe a rebuke as Sri Krishna addressed to Arjuna" on the battlefield of Kurukshetra in the great ancient Indian epic *Mahabharata*.[19] This interpretation of Krishna's message of strength and disinterested action, as embodied in the holy book *Bhagavad Gita*, appealed to the votaries of anticolonialism in Bengal.

In late 1920, Das had arranged a meeting of some of Bengal's revolutionaries with Gandhi, who had persuaded them to renounce violence temporarily and give his method of nonviolent noncooperation a try. Once Gandhi suspended the mass movement in 1922, the revolutionaries felt they were no longer bound by that tacit agreement. The difference in the perspectives of Das and Gandhi on terrorism was evident in the controversy over Gopinath Saha, a young man who had attempted to assassinate Charles Tegart, the police commissioner of Calcutta, but had instead killed a certain Mr. Day in a case of mistaken identity. During his trial, Saha stated in court that he had intended to kill Tegart, was full of remorse that he had fired at the wrong man, and was prepared to pay for his deed with his life. He was duly found guilty and executed. In May 1924, the Bengal provincial conference in Sirajganj, presided over by C. R. Das, passed a resolution that read as follows: "This conference, whilst denouncing (or dissociating itself from) violence and adhering to the principle of non-violence, appreciates Gopinath Saha's ideal of self-sacrifice, misguided though that is in respect of the country's best interest, and expresses its respect for his great self-sacrifice."[20] Gandhi's supporters narrowly defeated the same

resolution when it was brought before an All-India Congress Committee meeting in Ahmedabad. Subhas Chandra Bose was not present
either at Sirajganj or at Ahmedabad, being occupied with municipal
work in Calcutta. But he had met Gopinath Saha's brother and offered
condolences at the jail gate when the brother emerged with the clothes
of the prisoner, who had been hanged and cremated inside the prison
compound.[21]

Despite the lack of evidence and trial, Subhas was incarcerated. For
the first six weeks of his imprisonment, the chief executive officer of
the Calcutta Corporation found himself lodged in the Alipur Central
Jail of Calcutta. After he managed to turn his prison cell into a political
and administrative office, the government decided, in early December
1924, to move him to Behrampur Jail in northern Bengal. "I am quite
well here," Subhas wrote reassuringly to Sarat. "Stone walls do not a
prison make, nor iron bars a cage—the poet's words are true indeed."[22]
On January 25, 1925, Subhas was suddenly served an order to be transferred to Calcutta; no reason was given. By midnight he was in a lockup
at Lalbazaar, Calcutta's police headquarters, which he described as "a
hell on earth." After spending the night in "a dirty hole" swarming with
mosquitoes and bugs, he and seven others were bundled into a police
van before morning light and driven to the riverbank. They were made
to wait in a small motorboat for several hours, then transported to a
larger ship and put aboard on the side facing away from shore. It was
now obvious that Subhas was being sent somewhere far from Bengal.
In fact, they were taken to Rangoon—a voyage that lasted four days,
which Subhas spent chatting with Mr. Lowman, the assistant inspector-
general of police, on various subjects, including police torture. Even
though he began with a strong prejudice against this police officer, he
came to hold "a favorable opinion of him" as a result of their conversations.[23] It took another twenty hours by train to go from Rangoon to
Mandalay.

Mandalay, the capital of the last independent kingdom of Burma,
had fallen to the British in 1885. Rampaging foreign troops had dese-
crated the palace marching through in their heavy boots and looting its
treasures. The prison to which Subhas and his companions were taken
formed part of the fort, which had been attached to the palace. Manda-

lay in the 1920s was an unhealthy place with high mortality from plague and smallpox epidemics. In a letter to his brother written soon after his arrival, Subhas described the town as "a kingdom of dust": "In Mandalay the dust is in the air—therefore you must inhale it. It is in your food, therefore you must eat it. It is on your table—your chair and your bed—therefore you must feel its soft touch. It raises storms, obscuring distant trees and hills—therefore you needs must see it in all its beauty. Verily, dust in Mandalay is all-pervading—it is everywhere." The cellblocks in Mandalay Jail were made not of brick but of wooden bars or palisades. "I am sure that when we are locked in at night," he wrote to Sarat, "we look like so many human beasts prowling about in a lighted cage. It gives one an uncanny feeling—at the same time, no one who possesses any sense of humor can fail to enjoy the experience."[24]

Subhas bore the rigors of prison life with a combination of stoicism and humor. He was inspired by the fact that Balwantrao Gangadhar Tilak, the veteran nationalist leader from Maharashtra in western India, had written his "monumental and epoch-making" commentary on the *Gita* as a prisoner in Mandalay from 1908 to 1914. This jail was, to Subhas, "a place of pilgrimage sanctified by one of India's greatest men by continuous residence for a period of six years."[25] He felt that he would be "spiritually a gainer" through his imprisonment. "When I pause to reflect calmly," he wrote to his friend Dilip, "I feel the stirring of a certitude within that some Vast Purpose is at work in the core of our fevers and frustrations." But he gently rejected his friend's description of his detention as martyrdom. Since he had "some sense of humor and proportion," he could "hardly arrogate" to himself "the martyr's high title."[26]

In those years in Burmese prisons, from 1924 to 1927, Subhas Chandra Bose grew from a lieutenant into a leader. During the noncooperation movement and its aftermath, he had wholeheartedly accepted Deshbandhu Chittaranjan Das as his political mentor. He displayed total devotion to that magnanimous and far-sighted statesman, who was prepared to make great personal sacrifices for the cause of India's independence and Hindu-Muslim unity. But the apprenticeship was cut short by the Deshbandhu's untimely death, on June 16, 1925. When

Subhas received this terrible news as a prisoner in Mandalay, he felt "desolate with a sense of bereavement."[27] Dazed and stunned though he was by the demise of his leader, he wanted all important papers and documents to be carefully preserved. "A biography will be written in due time"—and in anticipation of that task, he wanted the materials for it to be gathered now. When they had been in jail together in 1921–1922, Das had been preparing a book on the philosophy of Indian nationalism. If his leader's notes were available, Subhas thought he might be able to construct something definitive out of those.[28]

Subhas's lengthy prison essay on the Deshbandhu, written in February 1926, contains insights into the fundamentals of his own political beliefs. "I do not think that among the Hindu leaders of India," he wrote, "Islam had a greater friend than in the Deshbandhu. Hinduism was extremely dear to his heart; he could even lay down his life for his religion, but at the same time he was absolutely free from dogmatism of any kind. That explains how it was possible for him to love Islam." It was this spirit of broad-minded generosity in the matter of India's religious diversity that Subhas sought to emulate in his own politics, and it was a quality he found to be sorely lacking in most of the other nationalist leaders. This was not secularism in the sense of a separation between religion and politics, but a politics based on respect for and reconciliation of religious differences. "That Swaraj in India meant primarily the uplift of the masses, and not necessarily the protection of the interest of the upper classes," he emphasized, "was a matter of conviction with the Deshbandhu." This, too, was an ideal not shared by many of the other front-rank leaders, but to which Subhas Chandra Bose was deeply committed.

To the large question of whether "culture" was unitary or diverse, his answer was that it was "both one and many." The Deshbandhu, he pointed out, was first and foremost a friend of Bengal. He "loved Bengal with all his life," but that did not make him forget India as a whole. The pursuit of *Nyaya*, a philosophical system developed in the district of Nadia in Bengal during the early modern period, had shaped the "logical and argumentative" strand within Bengal's intellectual tradition. It was a talent that made Das a great barrister in the modern era, but he would have been a famous logician of the Nabadwip school had he been born a few centuries earlier. Nadia was not just the home of rational logic, but a locus of effervescent devotion. Das thought it was "a matter of pride" rather than embarrassment that Bengalis were "susceptible to emotions." "The fulfillment of the Deshbandhu's nationalism," Subhas wrote with obvious admiration, "was in international amity; but he did not try to develop a love of the world by doing away with love for his own land. Yet his nationalism did not lead him to exclusive ego-centricity." C. R. Das's unfulfilled dreams and hopes were, in Subhas's view, his "best legacy."[29]

In Mandalay Jail, Subhas studied much harder than he had for the ICS examination. He read voraciously and filled his prison notebooks with copious notes and analyses of the books that he requested endlessly from family and friends. His markings in multiple volumes of Friedrich Nietzsche's collected works showed that his interest in philosophy was still alive. He read Bertrand Russell's works on industrial civilization and free thought. The great Russian novelists, Turgenev and Dostoyevsky, figured on his reading list of European literature. The broad range of subjects he studied included European history, histories of empires and revolutions, social anthropology, political memoirs, comparative religion, psychology, criminology, exercise and dietetics, and the color line in human relations.

He became something of a specialist in Irish history and literature. He recorded in a marginal note that more human beings perished in Ireland during the 1840s famine than had fallen by the sword in any war England had ever waged. He transcribed Irish poems that touched him, such as P. H. Pearse's "Renunciation," "The Rebel," and "The Wayfarer," and Dora Siegerson's "The Dead Soldier." Pearse had been a leader of the Easter Rising in 1916, and was executed by the British on May 3 of that year. Pearse's lines about the rebel who came of "the seed of the people that sorrow" must have seemed especially poignant to Subhas:

I say to my people that they are holy,
That they are august despite their chains,
That they are greater than those that
Hold them, and stronger and purer,

That they have but need of courage, and
To call on the name of their God,
God the unforgetting, the dear God that
Loves the peoples
For whom he died naked, suffering shame.[30]

Closer to home, Subhas undertook a careful study of Burmese culture, ancient Indian history, and Bengali literature through the medieval, early modern, and modern periods. He even believed he could supply Rakhaldas Banerjee, a famous ancient Indian historian, with missing links in the history of early and medieval Bengal from his study of Burmese records. He found Burma to be "a wonderful country" that had developed "a perfect social democracy." He noted admiringly that women were more powerful in Burma than in any European country. The indigenous and inexpensive system of primary education had resulted in much higher rates of male and female literacy in Burma than in India. Subhas pursued and urged the acquisition of a deeper knowledge of history, literature, and art. A revival of ancient and medieval Bengali culture, he believed, could serve as the foundation of national reconstruction, much the way "a revival of classicism laid the foundation of modern Europe."[31]

"Writing letters has become a problem," Subhas had lamented to Sarat soon after his arrival in Mandalay: the sword of Damocles was hanging over his head, in the form of the police censor. "But write I must," he had concluded, even if his letters hardly ever reached his recipients intact.[32] Correspondence with family and friends sustained him during his two-and-a-half-year ordeal in Burmese prisons. Despite being subjected to the scrutiny of the government censor, Subhas's prison letters supply some of the deepest insights into the workings of his mind. The letters covered a wide array of topics—art, music, literature, nature, education, folk culture, spirituality, and of course politics.

The correspondence between Subhas and Dilip exemplified the meaning of friendship. They dwelled on debates about the variable capacity to bear suffering and the question of individual aptitude and sense of fulfillment. Dilip had suggested that it must be Subhas's philosophical bent of mind that gave him fortitude in adversity. Subhas countered that "even the unphilosophic" may possess "an idealism of their own." Among his compatriots in jail, Subhas found some who were "neither thoughtful, nor philosophic," yet they dealt with pain calmly, "even like heroes." He conceded that the philosophically inclined can channel suffering to a higher purpose, but then asked: "Is it not true that we are all philosophers in embryo and it only requires a touch of suffering to awaken the philosophical impulse?"[33]

Dilip looked forward to Subhas taking on the mantle of "our future beloved political leader," and asserted that the younger generation had pinned their faith on him as "the one man who can lead us." He was sure that Subhas's *adhara* ("innate nature") and humility would not permit him to become "a narrow patriot or a common demagogue for the so-called good of our country." Even though Subhas believed in the principle of the greatest good for the greatest number, he did not equate that good with the purely material. Unlike economists, he did not look upon art as unproductive. "The time is out of joint," Subhas wrote on October 9, 1925. He urged Dilip to flood the country with songs and "recapture for life the spontaneous joy we have forfeited." "He who has no music in his composition," he wrote, "whose heart is dead to music, is unlikely to achieve anything great in life." He had been captivated by the *gambhira* music and dance of the Maldah district of northern Bengal. Subhas asked Dilip to visit this place to give a boost to the simple and spontaneous folk music of Bengal. Only after realizing one's *swadharma* ("inner calling") could one claim one's *adhikar* ("inalienable right") to real service. "To put it in the language of Emerson," he told Dilip, "we must be molded from within."

Forced inactivity through incarceration strengthened Subhas's belief that for most people "action in a spirit of service" ought to be "the main plank of their *sadhana* [quest]." He had reverence for Sri Aurobindo, who had become a *dhyani,* immersed in meditation, but he warned of the danger that the active side of man might become atrophied through prolonged seclusion. "For a variety of reasons," Subhas observed, "our nation has been sliding pauselessly down to the zero line in the sphere of action; so what we badly need today is a double dose of the activist serum, *rajas*." Dilip sent this letter from Subhas to Rabindranath Tagore. "Subhas has written a very fine letter," the poet said in reply. "I was gratified to know about the qualities of his head and heart through the letter. What Subhas has said about art is unexceptionable."[34]

On an impulse, Subhas wrote a letter to another popular literary figure of early twentieth-century Bengal, Sarat Chandra Chattopadhyay. He felt that this novelist had penned the only truly insightful tribute to the Deshbandhu, which had touched him deeply. Chattopadhyay wrote and published his novel *Pather Dabi* (The Demand of the Road), about a Bengali freedom fighter in Burma, during Subhas Chandra Bose's Mandalay years. "If I had not come here," Subhas wrote to this master of fiction, "I would never realize the depth of my love for golden Bengal. I sometimes feel as if Tagore expressed the emotions of a prisoner when he wrote: 'Sonar Bangla, ami tomae bhalobashi [Golden Bengal, I love you]!'"[35]

This song, along with others by Tagore, Dwijendralal Roy, and various devotional and folk poets, figured prominently in a notebook in which he had transcribed his favorite songs. He believed that the songs of Kazi Nazrul Islam, the revolutionary poet laureate of Bengal, had been enriched by the composer's lived experience in colonial prisons. Distance strengthened his yearning for his regional homeland. "When I see patches of white clouds floating across the sky in the morning or the afternoon," he wrote, referring to Kalidasa's ancient epic poem, "I momentarily feel—as the exiled Yaksha of Meghdut did—like sending through them some of my innermost feelings to Mother Bengal. I could at least tell her in the Vaishnavic strain: 'To face calumny for your sake, / Is to me a blessing.'"[36]

The quotidian aspects of prison life were best captured in delightful anecdotes that Subhas related in his letters to his sister-in-law Bivabati. He felt happy that Bivabati found his stories to be highly entertaining. Citing a Sanskrit saying that "God is but all-pervading delight," he expressed relief that he had not lost all sense of humor in jail, for that would have meant being bereft of the cream of life—*ananda* ("bliss"). He narrated with sympathy the predicament of common convicts: Maloy, an erstwhile village raja of Burma; Shyamlal, the foolish burglar who had been awarded the title of "pundit"; and Yankaya, the illiterate jailbird from Madras who communicated with the Bengali political prisoners in an Indo-Burmese pidgin language. Vivid reports were sent home on the well-being or otherwise of the pigeons, chickens, a parrot and other cellmates from the bird and animal kingdoms, including the tomcats who created a nuisance and occasionally ate the pigeons.

The inadequacies of the basic amenities of life were the subject of wry comments. "You have asked about my clothing," Subhas wrote in reply to a query from Bivabati. "Do you not know that we are guests of the Emperor? How can we be in want of anything?" As for food, "anything" was "available in our hotel":

> The other day the Manager fed us with hot *jilebis* [a sweet delicacy]— and we blessed him whole-heartedly, praying he may ever remain in prison. Some time ago he entertained us with *rosogollas* [soft, round milk-based sweets]; although the balls were floating in the syrup all right, they had no syrup inside and if you threw them at anybody, there was the risk of his head getting fractured. Nevertheless, we swallowed the hard-as-iron *rosogollas* without a tear and in gratitude prayed for the Manager's long life.

"From time to time," he conceded, "I miss scent and music. But what can one do?" When the government informed the political prisoners, two years after their arrival in Mandalay, that their detention without trial would continue, Subhas wrote to Bivabati: "We had a feast on a small scale to celebrate our continuance in our jobs."[37]

The everyday issues of bad food and poor clothing, not to mention the absence of music, about which Subhas wrote to his sister-in-law with wit and sarcasm, were precisely the matters of serious contestation between the prisoners and the prison authorities. "If man is regarded as a being possessing a soul, music is as much a necessity as food and drink," Subhas had claimed while demanding permission from the governor of Burma to play musical instruments in prison. As early as May 1925, Subhas and his compatriots had threatened a hunger strike to protest against "highly insulting and humiliating behavior" by the jail authorities and a miserly diet, clothing, and bedding allowance.

On February 18, 1926, they actually began a fifteen-day hunger

strike. The ostensible reason was the refusal of the government to sanction funds for the observance of Durga *puja,* the annual worship of the
mother goddess, in October of the previous year. A sympathetic jail
superintendent, Major Findlay, had granted permission for this religious festival in anticipation of approval by higher authorities, since
Christian prisoners in India were typically allotted modest resources
for their religious observances. But the government refused and up-
braided Findlay for showing such indulgence. The political prisoners
denounced this refusal as "an unwarranted interference" with their
right to religious freedom that militated against the spirit of Queen
Victoria's proclamation of 1858 and was "a violation of God's law."[38]
They did not relent until the government conceded their point in principle and allotted an annual sum of thirty rupees per prisoner for the
exercise of their religious rights. Subhas later confided to Sarat that the
whole story of their decision to go on a hunger strike could not be told
until their release, but that it had been taken after "mature deliberation."[39] It is hard not to surmise that the specific issue at hand was less
important than the determination to bring pressure to bear on those
who held them in detention. Even though the authorities tried to stop
all communication by the prisoners with the wider world, the news of
their fast was reported in the *Forward* within three days of their having
started it and caused an uproar in India.

The end of the hunger strike, on March 4, 1926, returned life to
"normal" for the prisoners, but with some guarantee of better treatment. On the Ides of March, a storm—this time an act of nature—
broke over Mandalay Jail. As Subhas described it, "the dust like a moving canopy completely shrouded us."

Papers began to fly, lanterns were smitten down and sundry articles
began to take wings. But the wrath of Heaven did not last long and the
"twice-blest" drops of mercy soon began to fall from above. Philosophers say that God's mercy shines even in darkness. . . . So, to complete
the harmony of the situation the electric current conveniently failed
and we were enveloped in what Milton would describe as "Cimmerian
darkness." The lurid flashes of lightning served only to make the "darkness visible" (I am again using a Miltonic expression, for is not saintly

Milton as effective in his descriptions of darkness as Shakespeare is sweet in his descriptions of fairy moonlight?) and to reveal to the more devoted the terrible beauty of the smile of Kali—the Queen of the Dark (Chinmoy mukhamandale shobhe attahashi).[40]

Dry sheets and blankets were obtained from the chief jailer, out of his own surplus store, before the prisoners yielded to the lockup man for the night.

By now, Sarat was less impressed by his younger brother's poetry and philosophy and more concerned about Subhas's rapidly deteriorating health. He noted with alarm that Subhas had lost about forty pounds while in jail.[41] His moral courage could not endlessly compensate for his physical infirmities, which had been aggravated by the resort to the hunger strike. Seeing no legal option for securing the release of his brother, Sarat now began to explore a political solution. New elections to the Bengal legislative council were due late in 1926. Sarat began to consider deploying the Sinn Féin tactic of nominating political prisoners for election based on the principle, "Vote him in, to get him out."

At first, Subhas rejected the suggestion that he should stand for election. He was getting disgusted with council members who were not doing any good work for the country, and he thought the time had come for the pendulum to swing back in the old Gandhian anticouncil direction. Sarat got him to realize, however, that there was "good reason" behind his advice. Subhas agreed to be nominated in the north Calcutta constituency against Jatindra Nath Basu, a stalwart of the Liberal party who had beaten the Swarajist candidate in 1923. "God willing, we shall give him a damned hollow defeat," wrote Sarat, who was confident of his younger brother's prospects. Subhas could not even release his manifesto: political prisoners were not permitted to issue appeals to the public.[42] Throughout the autumn of 1926, Sarat managed Subhas's election campaign, as well as his own from the university constituency, with consummate skill. Both were rewarded in the winter with thumping victories. The supporters of the Bose brothers celebrated with fireworks, and "Victory to Subhas Chandra" in glittering Bengali letters illuminated the Calcutta sky.[43] The colonial authorities in India, however, proved more obdurate than their counterparts in Ireland. Winning the vote was not sufficient to get Subhas out of jail.

Subhas chose to be philosophical about his continued imprisonment. "The purpose for which Providence sent me here still remains unfulfilled," he wrote to Basanti Devi, "and my apprenticeship in prison is yet incomplete." Since he did not accept *sannyasa,* the asceticism of a world renouncer, memories of the outside world did cause him sorrow. But he was prepared to spend his entire life in prison if that was necessary for the good of his motherland.[44] To a political comrade, he reiterated that his ideal of service was to give away what he could and ask for nothing in return. "You have asked about myself—what can I say?" he wrote. "One of Rabindranath's poems I like very much. Will it sound impertinent if I replied to you in the poet's words?

> Who knows when I shall be able
> To declare with all my heart:
> I have reached my Realization,
> Come all, follow me,
> The Master is calling you all,
> May my life bring forth new life in you all
> And thus may my country awake."[45]

He could only pray, once again in Tagore's words, for strength: "Give unto your chosen one / The strength to carry your banner."[46]

Subhas's physical strength, however, was steadily dissipating during the course of 1926. Low-grade fever was a routine occurrence; and with the onset of winter, matters came to a head with a serious attack of broncho-pneumonia. On February 9, 1927, he was sent to Rangoon Central Jail to be examined by a medical board. His doctor brother, Sunil Chandra Bose, who was allowed to see him, was shocked to find that for eighteen months he had been kept in close proximity to someone suffering from tuberculosis; Sunil feared that Subhas may have contracted the disease. Kaviraj Shyamadas Vachaspati, a famous Ayurvedic doctor, tried treating him long-distance from Calcutta using reports he received of the patient's symptoms. The doctors, including those approved by the government, recommended against holding the sick prisoner any longer in Burmese jails, but the powers-that-be refused to relent. Meanwhile, Subhas's patience snapped and he lost his temper with Major Flowerdew, the superintendent of the Rangoon Jail. Accusing him of highly discourteous behavior, Subhas demanded to be transferred to another prison.[47]

On March 25 he was dispatched to Insein Jail, where the friendly jailer, Major Findlay, who had known Subhas in Mandalay, was appalled to see him in his emaciated state. After receiving Findlay's report on the poor state of his prisoner's health, the government made an offer through a statement in the Bengal legislative council: they would release Subhas if he went straight from Rangoon to Switzerland, at his own expense, to regain his health. He also would not be permitted to return to India, Burma, or Ceylon until the expiration in 1930 of the Bengal criminal law amendment act—a different law from the 1818 regulation used for his arrest, under which he was now being held.

Subhas was contemptuous of this offer of indefinite European exile. It did not even give him an opportunity to visit his elderly parents, whom he had not seen for two and a half years. He had come to regard *tyaga* ("renunciation") and *amrita* ("realization") as "two faces of the same medal"; "to attain hundred per cent and to sacrifice hundred per cent" had become a passion with him.[48] In a long letter to Sarat on April 4, 1927, he explained why he was going to reject the government's offer. If he had "the remotest intention of becoming a Bolshevik agent," he would have jumped at it and "joined the gay band who trot from Paris to Leningrad talking of world revolution and emitting blood and thunder in their utterances." He was not inclined in that direction. The government seemed to have forgotten that they had inflicted suffering on him for two and a half years with no justification, and that he was "the aggrieved party," not they. He could not persuade himself that permanent exile from his homeland "would be better than life in a Jail leading to the sepulcher." "I do not quail before this cheerless prospect," he wrote, "for I believe as the poet does, that 'the paths of glory lead but to the grave.'" He asked Sarat to console their dear parents, but warned that more suffering was in store before "the priceless treasure of freedom" could be secured.[49]

Sarat replied that the sentiments Subhas had expressed were worthy of him, but did not stop negotiating with the government for his brother's transfer from Burma. He wanted the government to move him in detention to the north Indian hill resort of Almora, where he could meet his relatives and recover his strength.[50] On April 11, 1927, Subhas went ahead and formally snubbed the authorities. "Much as I value my life—I love honor more," he wrote to the superintendent of Insein Jail, "and I cannot for the life of me barter away those sacred and inviolable rights which will form the future body politic of India."[51] On May 6 he reaffirmed this attitude, which (he explained to Sarat) flowed from his general outlook on life. "Ideas are the stuff of which human movements are made," he passionately proclaimed to Sarat, "and they are not static but dynamic and militant. They are as dynamic as the Absolute Idea of Hegel, the Blind Will of Hartmann and Schopenhauer, the *élan vital* of Henri Bergson." A life consecrated to ideas was "bound to fulfill itself." He then invoked Saint Paul's famous words: "We wrestle not against flesh and blood but against principalities, against powers, against the rulers of the darkness of this world, against spiritual wickedness in high places."[52] Subhas had unflinching faith in the ultimate triumph of the ideas for which he stood.

The offer of European exile having been rejected, the government ordered that Subhas be transferred to Almora Jail. On May 11, 1927, he was taken from Insein Jail to a boat departing from Rangoon. A four-day voyage across the Bay of Bengal brought him to Diamond Harbor, where he was met by the same police officer, Mr. Lowman, who had escorted him to Mandalay in 1924. Subhas was suspicious when he was asked to disembark, thinking this was a ploy to smuggle him away without taking him to Calcutta. He was assured, however, that the new governor of Bengal, Sir Stanley Jackson, had put the gubernatorial boat at his disposal and that he was to be examined by a high-powered panel of doctors, including the governor's own physician. The next morning, Mr. Lowman arrived with a telegram in hand and informed Subhas that the governor had ordered his release. Bose concluded that Stanley Jackson had arrived with "an open mind," and with "the unerring instinct of a trained politician he had sensed the grievance of the people."[53] Jackson wanted to end police tyranny; and so after two and a half years of detention without trial in Burmese prisons, Subhas Chandra Bose was suddenly a free man.

Leader of Youth

Despite his rigorous apprenticeship in prison, Subhas was initially reluctant to assume the mantle of leadership upon his return from Burma. He pleaded with Basanti Devi to lead Bengal in place of her late husband, C. R. Das. "The spiritual quest of Bengal," he wrote to her, "has always been voiced through the cult of the Mother." The "pack of vagabonds" he represented was pleading with her not because they lacked self-confidence but because "no worship is complete if we leave the mother out." He held up the examples of Madame Zaghlul Pasha and Madame Sun Yat-sen, who had responded to the call of the Egyptian and Chinese nations after the death of their illustrious husbands. Basanti Devi, however, wanted to avoid the public limelight. She was prepared to stay in the background and offer her adopted son emotional support. "May my life not wither away in the desolation of *sannyasa* [renunciation]," Subhas wrote to her. "May my life blossom forth in beneficent fulfillment with the touch of the inspiration that is behind this desolation—I crave for this blessing."[54]

Subhas had to recover his health before he could play an active role in politics. From the governor's launch, he had been transported to Sarat's home in Calcutta. The hill resort of Shillong, in India's northeast, was chosen as the most suitable place for the ailing Subhas during the months of summer and monsoon rains. Several family members accompanied him to the hills. Subhas spent the days playing with the children on the mountainside and the nights reading, writing letters, and preparing questions to be posed in the legislature. The eminent doctor Bidhan Chandra Roy came to treat him, along with his seven-year-old nephew Sisir, who was suffering from fever.[55] Eventually, his sister-in-law Bivabati and her children had to return to Calcutta. Sarat, a leading light of the Calcutta bar, was then building a palatial home at 1 Woodburn Park, around the corner from his father's house at 38/2 Elgin Road. Bivabati had to be in charge of the Calcutta domestic scene and prepare to move house. "I felt rather uncomfortable after you all left suddenly," Subhas wrote to Bivabati. "The empty house gave a forlorn feeling—the mind became restive—I seemed to have lost for a while the moorings of my daily life—it will be no exaggeration to say that I felt a pang in my heart." He had imagined that he had transcended worldly attachments, but now had been given a stern reminder that he was not wholly unattached. Basanti Devi and Bivabati were the two significant women in his life at this stage, both of whom he had elevated to a motherly status. He blamed the long lectures he had inflicted on them through his letters on the colonial masters. Arguing with the English, "even a shy and diffident person" like him had "become garrulous." It took some time to readjust to his quiet surroundings. "The azure sky, green fields, the mountain ranges all around, the play of light and shade in the forests, the continuous roar of the waterfall," he wrote to his sister-in-law reassuringly, "all this keeps me contented." When the rains cleared he would go out to commune with nature, as he had done as a child in Cuttack, and be reminded of Shakespeare's lines in *As You Like It*:

And this our life, exempt from public haunt
Finds tongues in trees, books in running brooks
Sermons in stones, and good in everything.[56]

The exemption from public haunt did not last long. No sooner had he descended from the hills to the plains than Subhas was elected president of the Bengal provincial Congress committee. In December 1927, at the annual session of the Indian National Congress held at Madras, he—along with Jawaharlal Nehru and Shuaib Qureshi—was appointed a general secretary of the All-India Congress Committee. After several years of slumber, Indian anticolonial politics had been galvanized by the announcement of an all-white seven-member commission, chaired by Sir John Simon, to look into the constitutional future of India. The 1919 reforms had provided for a review in ten years. The Conservative government of Stanley Baldwin in Britain brought it forward, fearing a loss of power to the Labor party at the next elections.

The Simon Commission seemed to deny the very basis of Indian nationhood, seeing the country as a collection of squabbling communities and interests over which British parliamentarians alone could arbitrate. Its composition and mandate were seen as an affront not only by the Congress, but also by the Liberals, under the leadership of Tej Bahadur Sapru, and the All-India Muslim League, represented by Mohammed Ali Jinnah. All parties decided to boycott the Simon Commission, which arrived in February 1928. The Simon seven were met with shouts of "Go back!" and black-flag demonstrations wherever they went. An all-parties conference tried to draw up a constitutional framework that Indians could agree on, and in May 1928 the Congress formed a small committee for that purpose. It was chaired by Motilal Nehru, and Subhas Chandra Bose was invited to be a member.

In addition to taking part in deliberations among the inner circle of the Congress leadership, Bose vigorously pursued his active interest in student and youth organizations, labor unions, and the incipient women's movement. He emerged along with Jawaharlal Nehru, eight years his elder, as the leader of the radical, left-leaning younger generation of anticolonial nationalists. His spell in Burmese prisons had created an aura around him, and he was already being seen as the rising star in all-India anticolonial politics. In May 1928, he called on Mahatma Gandhi at his *ashram* in Sabarmati and asked him to lead a new mass movement. He then undertook an extensive tour of the country, addressing countless student and youth organizations and labor conferences. "Democracy," he told the Maharashtra provincial conference over which he presided, "is by no means a Western institution; it is a human institution." He also put forward a reasoned defense of nationalism against its critics. Refusing to believe that nationalism necessarily hindered cosmopolitanism in the domain of culture, he espoused a variant of Indian nationalism that was not narrow, selfish, or aggressive, but instilled "the spirit of service" and aroused "creative faculties" in its people. He argued the case for "a coalition between labor and nationalism," using the term "labor" "in a wider sense to include the peasants as well." India, he believed, should become "an independent Federal Republic." He warned Indian nationalists not to become "a queer mixture of political democrats and social conservatives." He declared in unequivocal terms:

> If we want to make India really great, we must build up a political democracy on the pedestal of a democratic society. Privileges based on birth, caste or creed should go, and equal opportunities should be thrown open to all irrespective of caste, creed or religion. The status of women should also be raised, and women should be trained to take a larger and a more intelligent interest in public affairs.

While not opposed to "any patch-up work" needed for "healing communal sores," he sought a "deeper remedy" through "cultural rapprochement." He regretted that the various communities inhabiting India were "too exclusive." "Fanaticism is the greatest thorn in the path of cultural intimacy," he told his audience, "and there is no better remedy for fanaticism than secular and scientific education." This was the first occasion on which Bose used the term "secular." For him, secularism was not hostile to religiously informed cultural identities, but could help to foster "cultural intimacy" among India's diverse religious communities. He was staking out a middle ground between Nehru's secularism, with its distaste for expressions of religious difference, and Gandhi's harnessing of various religious faiths in energizing mass politics. He underscored three cardinal principles for the framers of India's constitution: popular sovereignty, equal citizenship rights, and a system of joint electorates rather than separate ones for different religious communities.[57]

In July 1928, Subhas had warmly endorsed the candidacy of Motilal Nehru for the presidency of the Indian National Congress.[58] He could not, however, bring himself to support the majority view on the Motilal Nehru Committee: that dominion status within the empire should be India's political objective. He joined Motilal's son Jawaharlal and other young radicals at an August meeting in Lucknow and decided to form an "Independence for India League" to advocate the goal of complete independence. In November the league was inaugurated in Delhi, and branches were set up in many parts of the country to pressure the

Congress toward a bolder articulation of its aims. The Indian National Congress met in Calcutta for its annual session in December 1928. It was by far the largest gathering in the history of the organization, and all the arrangements were made on a massive scale.

Subhas had by now moved into Sarat's new home at 1 Woodburn Park, which became the headquarters for his organizational work. He formed a Congress volunteer corps to run the Congress session smoothly. It was an unarmed and peaceful body with cavalry and motorcycle units and a women's wing; its members were trained in military discipline and put in uniform. When Bose appeared as general commanding officer of his corps, in a resplendent military uniform, it was not so much a spectacle as an evocation of his vision for the future. The young Subhas elicited reverence from his admirers. A mother told her young son, later one of India's most renowned historians, as they watched that impressive figure standing on the running board of a car moving in a procession along Calcutta's College Street: "There goes Subhas Bose—fold your palm and salute him, my child."[59] Mahatma Gandhi was unimpressed by the display, likening the volunteers to performers in the Bertram Mills Circus. Undeterred, Bose proposed a more radical alternative to Gandhi's political program.

At the open session of the Calcutta Congress, Subhas sponsored an amendment demanding "complete independence" instead of "dominion status," in opposition to Mahatma Gandhi. He simply did not believe that there was any "reasonable chance" that the British would grant "dominion status" within twelve months, as demanded in the main resolution. The resolution on "complete independence" would help to foster a "new mentality," overcoming the "slave mentality" that was at the root of India's political degradation. While meaning no disrespect to the elders, including Mahatma Gandhi and Motilal Nehru, Bose opted to give priority to "respect for principle."[60] His amendment was defeated by 1,350 votes to 973. Gandhi promised that if the year 1929 did not bring dominion home rule, he would himself become an "independence-wallah."

During 1929, Subhas Chandra Bose preached the ideal of universal freedom for the individual and the nation. His audiences of students and other young people responded enthusiastically. Speaking to the

Hooghly district students' conference in July 1929, he argued that both individual and national fulfillment should be achieved through the innate diversity of human life and by striking a balance between "the one" and "the many." He reminded the students that Deshbandhu C. R. Das had been a staunch believer in a "federation of cultures," and "in the realm of politics, he liked a federal state for India better than a centralized state." He exhorted the young to call the disadvantaged and downtrodden social groups to their side: "In our country, three large communities are lying absolutely dormant; these are the women, the so-called depressed classes and the laboring masses. Let us go to them and say: 'You also are human beings and shall obtain the fullest rights of men. So arise, awake, shed your attitude of inactivity and seize your legitimate rights.'"[61]

These social groups, especially the working class, had indeed arisen in 1929 to demand their rights through a wave of strikes. Seething labor unrest in Bombay and elsewhere was one of the reasons that Gandhi wished to postpone a confrontation with the colonial government. A staunch believer in class conciliation, he was not inclined to launch an anticolonial mass movement while class-based radicalism was at its peak. Subhas Chandra Bose, by contrast, provided leadership to the workers in an industrial action against the owners of the Tata iron and steel company in Jamshedpur, and aided the legal defense of Bombay-based labor activists charged in the Meerut conspiracy case.

Gandhi's decision to mark time during 1929 in the face of British repression had another consequence: it created political space for the recrudescence of revolutionary terrorism, especially in the province of Punjab. On October 30, 1928, Lala Lajpat Rai had been severely beaten by the police during a peaceful protest against the arrival of the Simon Commission in Lahore. On November 17, this veteran nationalist leader of Punjab died. To avenge his death a twenty-year-old Sikh named Bhagat Singh shot dead a British police officer in the streets of Lahore exactly a month later, on December 17. On April 8, 1929, Bhagat Singh and Batukeshwar Dutt hurled a couple of small bombs and flung a few leaflets inside the central legislature in Delhi, claiming that it took "a loud voice to make the deaf hear." The government responded by arresting a large number of young men in different parts of the country and initiating the Lahore conspiracy case against them in mid-1929. Several of the accused began a hunger strike in Lahore Jail against abysmal prison conditions. The government retaliated by trying to amend the criminal law in the central legislature, so that the fasting prisoners could be tried and sentenced in absentia.

Several Indian members of the central legislative assembly, including M. A. Jinnah, Motilal Nehru, and M. R. Jayakar, staunchly opposed the government's attempt to subvert the elementary principles of criminal jurisprudence. Jinnah, in particular, spoke eloquently of the "universal resentment" against "this damnable system of Government," and demanded humane treatment of prisoners whose cases were being tried. "The man who goes on hunger-strike has a soul," he urged. "He is moved by that soul and he believes in the justice of his cause; he is not an ordinary criminal who is guilty of cold-blooded, sordid, wicked crime."[62] The government did not budge. While most of the hunger-strikers gave up their fast after days or weeks, one twenty-five-year-old man from Bengal—Jatindranath Das—continued resolutely until, on the sixty-third day, life finally ebbed away from him. When Rabindranath Tagore received the grim news in Bengal, he composed one of his finest Bengali songs:

> All meanness is devoured by the fire of your anger—
> O God, give us strength, have mercy on your devotees.
> Sweep away, Almighty, what is false and petty—
> May death be dwarfed by the ecstasy of life.
> By churning the depths of suffering, one will find immortality,
> Those who fear death will be freed of their terror.
> Your resplendent scorching power will melt and let flow,
> Freed of the chain of stones, a stream of sacrifice.[63]

The family of Terence MacSwiney, the mayor of Cork who had died in Brixton Prison under similar circumstances in 1920, sent a telegram saying they had learned with "grief and pride" of the death of Jatin Das and that "freedom will come." Huge crowds came to pay their last respects at railway stations as his body was taken from Lahore to Calcutta. Jatin Das had served in the Congress volunteer corps in 1928 under Subhas Chandra Bose, who now took charge of the funeral rites. After the rites were completed, Subhas returned home with a small packet and stood somber-faced like a marble statue on the marble stairs of 1 Woodburn Park. "I have brought a little bit of the remains of Jatindranath Das," he said to Bivabati. "Please preserve them with care."[64]

In October 1929, Subhas made the journey from Calcutta to Lahore and delivered his message of complete emancipation to the Punjabi students' conference. He lauded the sacrifice of Jatin Das in the cause of freedom. "Jatin today is not dead," he insisted. "He lives up in the heavens as a star 'of purest ray serene' to serve as a beacon light to posterity." Bose saw the students' movement as a school for "the training of the future citizen." He felt that the Congress "should depend, for its strength, influence and power on such movements as the labor movement, youth movement, peasant movement, women's movement, students' movement." "To be free or at least to die in the pursuit of freedom" was the motto he gave to the students.[65] The people of Punjab, he reported in a letter, had given him "love, kindness and honor in an abundant measure." But there was also a hint of loneliness in the midst of the crowds. "I have been shy by nature since my boyhood," he confessed, "and I continue to be so until today—in spite of the fact that I go about making speeches at public meetings."[66]

On October 31, 1929, the viceroy, Lord Irwin, announced that he had been authorized by the Labour government in London to state that dominion status was the logical culmination of India's constitutional progress and that a round-table conference would be convened after the Simon Commission's report was published. A majority of the Congress leaders signed a manifesto in response to this overture, looking forward to the framing of a dominion constitution for India. Jawaharlal Nehru was initially hesitant, but eventually fell into line, as he had been selected by Gandhi to preside over the Lahore session of the Indian National Congress in December. "Jawaharlal has now given up Independence at the instance [sic] of the Mahatma," Subhas informed Basanti Devi.[67] Subhas Chandra Bose and two others, Saifuddin Kitchlew of Lahore and Abdul Bari of Patna, issued a separate manifesto calling for complete independence and rejecting the round-table conference. They saw it as a ploy similar to Lloyd George's constitutional convention for Ireland, which Sinn Féin had rightly spurned. It turned out, after further talks between Gandhi and Irwin, that the viceroy was in no position to give any assurance regarding dominion status. The stage was thus set for history to be made on the banks of the River Ravi in Lahore before the year was out.

When the Congress met for its annual session at Lahore, Mahatma Gandhi redeemed his promise made a year earlier to become an "independence-wallah." He proposed the momentous resolution declaring that *purna swaraj* ("complete independence"), based on a severance of the British connection, was the political goal of the Indian National Congress. The Congress constitution was amended to reflect this change. Subhas Chandra Bose put forth a resolution stating that the Congress's aim should be the establishment of a parallel government in the country, with the help of workers, peasants, and youth organizations. His resolution did not pass, but it was a sign that he was, as always, a step ahead of his contemporaries. He was satisfied that the Congress had accurately described India as a country that was under an alien army of occupation.

The Congress announced that January 26, 1930, would be observed as Independence Day. Unfortunately, Subhas Chandra Bose was not free to celebrate that occasion. On his return to Calcutta from Lahore, he had been arrested once again: his birthday present on January 23, 1930, the day he turned thirty-three, was a one-year prison sentence on charges of sedition and taking part in an unlawful procession. "We are all well," he wrote to Basanti Devi. "We shall joyfully begin our victory march to the Royal temple."[68] From behind prison bars, Bose watched with admiration as Gandhi made his next moves toward civil disobedience. They were "some of the most brilliant achievements of his leadership" and revealed "the height to which his statesmanship" could rise in a crisis.[69] Goading his followers to forsake mute passive nonviolence for "non-violence of the most active type," Gandhi launched the civil disobedience movement in March 1930 with the violation of the government's salt monopoly. His march to the sea with a small band of seventy-eight *satyagrahis* electrified the whole country. Gandhi had chosen a powerful symbolic issue to start another mass movement against the British raj. Defiance of the salt laws was followed by a boycott of British goods, the picketing of liquor shops to deny the government excise duties, and nonpayment of taxes in some parts of the country. The British responded with police actions and mass arrests.

Subhas Chandra Bose spent the first couple of months of his imprisonment in quiet reading and meditation. In April 1930, he and several other Congress leaders lodged in Alipur Central Jail were severely beaten with *lathis* (wooden sticks) when they protested against an assault on other prisoners by the guards. Subhas suffered head injuries and was left unconscious for an hour.[70] In Bengal, the civil disobedience movement escalated greatly and became intertwined with revolutionary terrorism. On Easter weekend in 1930, revolutionaries led by Surya Kumar Sen raided the armory in Chittagong in commemoration of the 1916 uprising in Ireland, and fought a running battle with British forces in the district for several weeks. Sarat Chandra Bose led the legal defense of several revolutionaries accused in the Chittagong armory raid case. In December 1930, three young men—Benoy Bose, Badal Gupta, and Dinesh Gupta—stormed the Writers' Building, the seat of the British government in Calcutta, and shot dead the inspector general of prisons. They then engaged Calcutta's police force in combat along the verandahs of the building until their ammunition ran out. Benoy Bose and Badal Gupta succumbed to their injuries, while Dinesh Gupta was tried and executed. In Midnapur district, the British district magistrate, James Peddie, who had ordered the police to shoot down peasants refusing to pay taxes, was himself assassinated by revolutionaries. Two of his successors suffered the same fate. A new, more radical phase of the independence movement had begun.

As emotions ran high, Subhas Chandra Bose was elected mayor of Calcutta while in prison, defeating the incumbent, Jatindra Mohan Sengupta. Both belonged to the Congress party, so the election was something of an internecine conflict. More than just a factional fight within the Bengal Congress, the tension between Bose and Sengupta reflected the complex relationship between the province and the central leadership of the Congress. Sengupta had been appointed to his posts by Gandhi after C. R. Das's death, and was generally inclined to obey the dictates of the Congress high command. Bose represented the rebellious tendency in Bengal, not just against the British but against the all-India leadership of the Congress as well. During the brief period that he was able to serve as mayor upon his release from prison, Subhas tried to keep alive his mentor's legacy in municipal affairs. On January 26, 1931, as he was leading a peaceful independence day procession, he was brutally attacked by mounted police and hauled away to Calcutta's police headquarters at Lalbazaar. The next day, Calcutta's mayor was presented in his blood-soaked clothes at a local court. He was charged with rioting and sent once more to prison. The colonial government recognized the threat to their rule that Bose represented, and was determined to stifle him.

All significant Indian political parties had rejected the Simon Commission's report, published in July 1930, and the first round-table conference in London boycotted by the Congress had made no headway. In early 1931, therefore, the viceroy, Lord Irwin, invited Mahatma Gandhi for talks. Winston Churchill may have found it "nauseating" to see "the half-naked fakir" striding up the steps of the viceregal palace to parley on equal terms with the representative of the king-emperor. But Gandhi was the king-emperor for India's peasant masses, and the identity of appearance and aspiration between the leader and his followers seemed absolute. In return for the release of political prisoners, the restoration of some of the confiscated land, and the freedom of coastal people to make salt free of duty, Gandhi agreed to suspend the civil disobedience movement and take part in the second round-table conference, to be held in London.

It appeared once more to those who were in jail that their leader had conceded too much for too little, through the Gandhi-Irwin pact of March 1931. Subhas was disappointed by the terms of the truce, but decided to hold his fire until he had a chance to meet the Mahatma and hear his point of view. Upon his release, he rushed to Bombay to meet Gandhi and was satisfied that the leader had not diluted his stand on independence. Subhas continued his talks as he traveled by train with the Mahatma from Bombay to Delhi, and saw for himself from the ovation at wayside stations that Gandhi was at the zenith of his popularity. Upon their arrival in Delhi, Subhas was shocked to hear that the government had decided to execute the Punjabi revolutionary Bhagat

Singh and his comrades. There had been widespread expectation that their death sentence would be commuted. Once it became clear to the viceroy that Gandhi would not break the pact on this question, Bhagat Singh, Rajguru, and Sukhdev were sent to the gallows.

The annual session of the Congress met at Karachi under the dark shadow of this tragedy. In 1931, as Jawaharlal Nehru noted, Bhagat Singh's amazing popularity rivaled that of Gandhi. He was seen to have defended Lala Lajpat Rai's honor, and songs written about his exploits soon turned him into a folk legend.[71] Subhas Chandra Bose found that the twenty-three-year-old revolutionary had, upon his death, become the symbol of the new awakening among India's youth. The people were not prepared to consider whether he was really guilty of the murder charge brought against him; it was his fearless demeanor as a prisoner and his ability to rise above Punjab's religious conflicts that impressed them. The Karachi Congress passed a resolution praising the courage and sacrifice of Bhagat Singh and his comrades, while decrying all acts of violence. It was similar to the Gopinath Saha resolution of 1924, which Gandhi had disapproved of; but in the atmosphere prevailing in the country in 1931, it had to be swallowed by the votaries of nonviolence.[72] The left wing within the party did not oppose the ratification of the Gandhi-Irwin pact, though they were not happy with it and won a commitment from the Congress to strive for the fundamental rights of the Indian people.

While in Karachi for the Congress meeting, Subhas Chandra Bose was invited to preside over the second annual session of the All-India Naujawan Bharat Sabha, a militant youth organization inspired by Bhagat Singh. Bose clearly felt more at home in this radical company than among the Congress stalwarts, and enunciated his political philosophy in a forthright manner. He articulated the meanings of five principles—justice, equality, freedom, discipline, and love—which ought to "form the basis of our collective life." Bolshevism he felt had "many useful lessons for humanity," but he did "not believe that abstract principles could be applied in the same manner, form or degree to different nations and countries." He wanted the Indian variant to be "a new form or type of socialism." "While seeking light and inspiration from abroad," he told the radical youth, "we cannot afford to forget that we should not blindly imitate any other people and that we should assimilate what we learn elsewhere with a view to finding out what will suit our national requirements as well as our national genius."[73]

In addition to students and youth, Bose sought to build a constituency for the anticolonial movement among laboring people, who were suffering the consequences of a dramatic economic downturn. In late 1929, Bose had been elected president of the All-India Trade Union Congress. In his presidential speech, delivered to this labor congress in July 1931, he addressed the specific problems of unemployment, retrenchment, and wages in the context of the Great Depression. He also tried to carve out a middle ground between a "reformist program" of the "Right Wing" of the trade union congress and "Communist friends" who were "adherents and followers of Moscow." He reiterated his belief in "full-blooded socialism," but wanted India to "evolve her own form of socialism as well as her own methods."[74]

Subhas Chandra Bose believed that the Indian National Congress had made a grave tactical error by deciding to send Mahatma Gandhi as its sole representative to the second round-table conference in London. As one among a hundred invitees—mostly "non-descripts, flunkeys and self-appointed leaders," in Bose's view—Gandhi would find it difficult to keep the focus on national issues, with the British keen to highlight myriad sectional interests. Nevertheless, Bose wished Gandhi well and sent him a warm message on his departure for London, expressing confidence that India's honor would be safe in the Mahatma's hands.[75] Gandhi's charm and wit made a mark on common people in England outside the conference chamber, but inside he could make no headway in winning the substance of independence. From September 12 to December 1, 1931, Gandhi spoke a dozen times at the round-table conference, but had to struggle throughout to differentiate the status of the Indian National Congress, as the premier nationalist organization, from various other groups that had been given a place at the table by the British hosts. The Muslim minority and the subordinate castes had certain legitimate demands, but Gandhi was wary of a government keen to use these to split national unity. Gandhi returned from London empty-handed via Paris, Geneva, and Rome. In Geneva he met the French savant and friend of India, Romain Rolland, and Benito Mussolini gave him a warm reception in Rome. On December

28, 1931, Mahatma Gandhi arrived in Bombay as a deck-passenger on the S.S. *Pilsna*.

With the new viceroy, Lord Willingdon, in a bellicose mood and utterly unwilling to make concessions to the nationalists, Gandhi and the Congress leadership had little option but to announce the resumption of civil disobedience in January 1932. British goods and institutions were boycotted once more, and nonviolent protesters courted arrest by violating what they deemed to be unjust laws. In the interim, the British government had perfected their plans to crush a renewed rebellious movement. The Congress organization was declared unlawful and its leaders were put under arrest. Even though larger numbers of civil resisters—more than a hundred thousand—were imprisoned in 1932 than in 1930, this was more an indication of the effectiveness of British repression than the vitality of the Indian resistance. The surprise element in Gandhi's 1930 strategy, which had centered around the novel undermining of the salt laws, was missing on this occasion, making it easier for the government to deal with the movement. Subhas was naturally among the Congress leaders who were arrested; he was sent to a rather remote jail in a place called Seoni in the Central Provinces. The only saving grace on this occasion was that he soon had his brother Sarat as his companion in prison. Sarat had suspended his legal practice to join the civil disobedience movement, and now paid the price by being put away for four long years in British jails.

In prison, Subhas kept himself busy reading Henri Bergson's *Creative Evolution* and other philosophical works. He asked a friend to send him recent biographies of Lenin and Trotsky, the four-volume memoirs of Alexander Herzen, and literature on Thoreau. From late February 1932 he began to experience severe abdominal pain, and by mid-May had lost twenty-eight pounds. The civil surgeon of Chindwara thought there was something wrong with his gallbladder, but the doctors could offer no definite diagnosis.[76] As the health of both brothers deteriorated—Sarat had early diabetes—they were transferred to Jubbulpore Central Jail. Subhas was subsequently shifted to the Madras Penitentiary, the Bhowali Sanatorium, and Lucknow Jail in quick succession, and thus was kept far from Bengal. Stringent bureaucratic instructions were issued by the government to the superintendents of the Bhowali Sanatorium, the Balaram Hospital in Lucknow, and the Madras Penitentiary regarding the treatment of "state prisoner" Subhas Chandra Bose. These included minute details about the furniture, clothing, and quantity of food that he would be permitted, as well as the conditions under which family members could visit him, the scrutiny of letters that he could receive and write, and the newspapers and books he might be allowed to read.[77] With Sarat languishing in jail as well, it fell upon Bivabati to express concerns to the authorities about her brother-in-law's illness in detention. Eventually, the government agreed to allow him to travel at his own expense to Europe for treatment. Subhas usually depended on Sarat for financial support. Now family friends came forward with loans to Sarat, to meet both his family's needs in Calcutta and Subhas's expenses in Europe. These benefactors included luminaries within Calcutta's legal fraternity, including Nripendra Nath Sircar, Provas Chandra Basu, and Nripendra Chandra Mitra, as well as Debendra Lal Khan, a nationalist leader from Midnapur district. Sarat would repay these loans once he returned to his practice in 1936.[78]

It was out of the question that the British would set Subhas free on Indian soil, or allow him to go to Bengal to see his parents before his departure for Europe. He would not see his father again. The government permitted him to spend some time with Sarat in Jubbulpore Central Jail, where the brothers had a visit from Basanti Devi, Bivabati, and her children.[79] On February 13, 1933, Subhas was carried in an ambulance to the port in Bombay and released from detention only after he was put on board the Italian ship S.S. *Gange,* sailing for Europe.

As the ship left the shores of India, Subhas wrote a parting message for Bengalis. After more than a year of exile from Bengal, he was embarking on what would turn out to be more than three years of exile from India. "One of the dreams that have inspired me and given a purpose to my life," he wrote, "is that of a great and undivided Bengal devoted to the service of India and of humanity—a Bengal that is above all sects and groups and is the home alike of the Muslim, the Hindu, the Christian and the Buddhist. It is this Bengal—the Bengal of my dreams—the Bengal of the future still in embryo—that I worship and strive to serve in my daily life."[80]

"Proudest Day of My Life": Subhas Chandra Bose taking the salute at the parade of the Indian National Army in Singapore, July 5, 1943, with Mohammad Zaman Kiani to his left. Courtesy: Netaji Research Bureau.

A Flaming Sword: Holding aloft a ceremonial Japanese sword, Tokyo, November 1943. Courtesy: Netaji Research Bureau.

The Bose Family: Subhas standing on extreme right, Cuttack, ca. 1905. Courtesy: Netaji Research Bureau.

India's Progress: A page from a letter to Sarat Chandra Bose, January 8, 1913. Courtesy: Netaji Research Bureau.

Friends in Cambridge: K. P. Chattopadhyay, Subhas C. Bose (standing right), Dilip K. Roy, and C. C. Desai, Cambridge, England, 1920. Courtesy: Netaji Research Bureau.

5

If anybody else has come forward, I might have had cause to withdraw or wait. Unfortunately nobody is coming yet and the precious moments are flying away. Inspite of all the agitation going on there, it still remains true that not a single civil servant has had the courage to throw away his job and join the people's movement. This challenge has been thrown at India and has not been answered yet. I may go further and say that in the whole history of British India, not one Indian has voluntarily given up the Civil Service with a patriotic motive. It is time that members of the highest service in India should set an example to members of the other services. If the members of the service ~~strike together~~ ~~will~~ withdraw their allegiance or even show a desire to do so — then and then only will the bureaucratic machine collapse.

I therefore do not see how I can save myself from this sacrifice. I know what this sacrifice means. It means poverty, suffering, hard work and possibly other hardships to which

Withdrawing Allegiance: A page from a letter to Sarat, April 6, 1921. Courtesy: Netaji Research Bureau.

c/o D.I.G., I.B. C.I.D., Bengal
13, Elysium Row
Calcutta.

Mandalay Jail
11.9.25.

My dear Dilip,

My last letter to you was unfinished and I intended to follow it up with another one the next week. But a terrible calamity intervened – which swept us off our feet. Even today, I do not know where I stand and I am sure the feelings of all are much the same – though in my case there is an irrecoverable personal loss to deepen my misery, as well as a doubled dose of bondage to heighten my suffering. The sense of personal loss may wane with the passage of time, but I am sure that the magnitude of the loss to the public will become more & more manifest as the days roll by. So versatile was his talent and so many-sided his activities – that people in different and widely separate spheres – will be hard hit by the loss. I used to criticise him by saying that he had too many irons in the fire – but creative spirits do not submit to pragmatic or logical limitations and I have no doubt that it was only the fullness of life and realization that impelled him to attempt reconstruction in so many different spheres of our national life.

You all had at least the opportunity of paying your last homage and even now you can find some solace in trying to perpetuate his memory. But it has pleased God to drive home into our minds a feeling of utter destitution as a result of confinement in remote Manda-

---

A Terrible Calamity: A page from a letter to Dilip K. Roy, September 11, 1925, lamenting the death of Deshbandhu Chittaranjan Das. Courtesy: Netaji Research Bureau.

Prisoner in Mandalay, 1926. Courtesy: Netaji Research Bureau.

2

Ideas are the stuff of which human movements are made and they are not static but dynamic and militant. They are as dynamic as the Absolute Idea of Hegel, the Blind Will of Hartmann and Schopenhauer, the "elan vital" of Henri Bergson. Ideas will work out their own destiny and we who are but clods of clay encasing sparks of the Divine Fire have only got to consecrate ourselves to these ideas. A life so consecrated is bound to fulfil itself regardless of the vicissitudes of our material and bodily existence. My faith in the ultimate triumph of the idea for which I stand is unflinching and I am not therefore troubled in thoughts about my health and future prospect.

I have stated my point of view clearly and unambiguously in my letter to Govt: and no sophistry is possible thereafter. I am sorry that some critics should be so unkind as to say that I am bargaining for better terms. I am not a shopkeeper and I do not bargain. The slippery paths of diplomacy I abhor as unsuited to my constitution. I have taken my stand on a principle and there the matter rests. I do not attach so much importance to my bodily life that I should strive to save it by a process of higgling. My conception of values is somewhat different from that of the marketplace and I do not think that success or failure in life should be determined by physical or material criteria. Our fight is not a

Ideas and Destiny: A page from a letter to Sarat, Insein Jail, Burma, May 6, 1927. Courtesy: Netaji Research Bureau.

Commanding Congress Volunteers: Subhas in military uniform with Motilal Nehru, taking the salute at the Calcutta session of the Indian National Congress, December 1928. Courtesy: Netaji Research Bureau.

Leader of Youth: Subhas with Congress volunteers, 1929. Courtesy: Netaji Research Bureau.

Exiled to Europe: Subhas being carried out of an ambulance to the ship at the pier in Bombay, February 13, 1933. Courtesy: Netaji Research Bureau.

India's Spokesman Abroad: A portrait of Subhas Chandra Bose, Prague, 1933. Courtesy: Netaji Research Bureau.

Author of *The Indian Struggle:* A portrait of Subhas Chandra Bose, Vienna, 1934. Courtesy: Netaji Research Bureau.

Recuperating in Karlsbad: Bose sitting on a bench in Karlsbad, Czechoslovakia, 1934. Courtesy: Netaji Research Bureau.

In Mourning: Subhas soon after his father's death, December 1934; photo by Sisir Kumar Bose. Courtesy: Netaji Research Bureau.

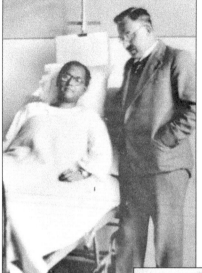

Recovery: Subhas with his surgeon, Rudolf Demel, after his gallbladder operation in Vienna, April 1935. Courtesy: Netaji Research Bureau.

The Magic Mountains: Subhas Chandra Bose and Emilie Schenkl at Badgastein, March 1936. Courtesy: Netaji Research Bureau.

My darling! Even the iceberg sometimes melts and so it is with me now. I can no longer restrain myself from penning these few lines to convey my deep love for you — my darling — or as we would say in our own way — the queen of my heart. But do you love me — do you care for me — do you long for me? You called me "pranadhik" — but did you mean it? Do you love me more than your own life? Is that possible? With us it may be possible — for a Hindu woman has, for centuries, given up her life for the sake of her love. But you Europeans have a different tradition. Moreover, why should you love me more than your own life? I am like a wandering bird that comes from afar, remains for a while, and then flies away to its distant home. For such a person why should you cherish so much love —

My dearest! In a few weeks I must fly to my distant home. My country calls me — my duty calls me — I must leave you and go back to my first love — my country. So often have I told you that I have already sold myself to my first love. I have very little left to give to any one. What little I have — I have given you. It may not be worthy of you and of your great love for me — but that is all that I have to give — and you cannot expect anything more from me.

I do not know what the future has in store for me. May be, I shall spend my life in prison. May be, I shall be

"My First Love": A page from a letter to Emilie, March 1936. Courtesy: Netaji Research Bureau.

Nephews in Arms: Subhas with Amiya and Sisir in Kurseong, June 1936. Courtesy: Netaji Research Bureau.

The Bose Brothers: Subhas and Sarat at 38/2 Elgin Road, Calcutta, 1937. Courtesy: Netaji Research Bureau.

Playing Host to the Mahatma: Bose receiving Gandhi at a suburban station near Calcutta, October 1937. Courtesy: Netaji Research Bureau.

Leaders of the Left: Bose and Nehru at 1 Woodburn Park, Calcutta, October 1937. Courtesy: Netaji Research Bureau.

Confabulations: Gandhi and Bose in a train compartment, November 1937. Courtesy: Netaji Research Bureau.

Winter in Badgastein: A. C. N. Nambiar, Hedy Fülöp-Miller, Subhas Chandra Bose, A. N. Bose, and Emilie Schenkl, December 1937; photo by A. K. Chettiar. Courtesy: Netaji Research Bureau.

President-Elect: A portrait of Subhas Chandra Bose, Prague, January 1938. Courtesy: Netaji Research Bureau.

The Nationalist Leadership: Gandhi, Bose, Patel, and Nehru at Haripura, February 1938. Courtesy: Netaji Research Bureau.

The Saint and the Warrior: Gandhi and Bose at Haripura, February 1938. Courtesy: Netaji Research Bureau.

The Smiling President: Subhas Chandra Bose at Haripura, February 1938. Courtesy: Netaji Research Bureau.

The Socialists: Bose with Jawaharlal and Indira Nehru, 1938. Courtesy: Netaji Research Bureau.

The Hindu-Muslim Question: Negotiating with M. A. Jinnah in Bombay, 1938. Courtesy: Netaji Research Bureau.

Deshnayak ("Leader of the Country"): A portrait of Subhas Chandra Bose, 1938. Courtesy: Netaji Research Bureau.

The Poet and the Patriot: Rabindranath Tagore, Sarat Chandra Bose, and Subhas Chandra Bose in Calcutta, August 19, 1939. Courtesy: Netaji Research Bureau.

4

Exile in Europe

My country calls me—my duty calls me—I must leave you and go back to my first love—my country.

—SUBHAS CHANDRA BOSE to Emilie Schenkl from Badgastein, Austria, March 1936

Vienna, once the dazzling center of the sprawling, multiethnic Austro-Hungarian Empire, was greatly diminished at the end of World War I: it had become the capital of a small, landlocked, agrarian nation-state. In the afterglow of fin-de-siècle Vienna, the finest expressions of sober bourgeois high culture met and struggled with the youthful avant-garde. The death of the city's two most brilliant painters, Gustav Klimt and Egon Schiele, in 1918 symbolized the passing of an era. Vienna remained the home of the father of psychoanalysis, Sigmund Freud, and it was gripped by a neurosis attending the transition from empire to nation—a trauma masterfully depicted by the novelist Robert Musil.[1] It was to this beautiful and angst-ridden city on the Danube that Subhas Chandra Bose came in March 1933, as a political exile seeking a cure from the illness that had beset him in colonial prisons and hoping to promote his country's freedom struggle in Europe.

On March 11, Bose was admitted to Fürth Sanatorium and underwent thorough X-ray and clinical examinations.[2] He had suffered a serious attack of bronchial pneumonia in Mandalay Jail and doctors suspected that he might even have contracted tuberculosis from a fellow prisoner. More recently, severe abdominal pains had indicated the possibility of stones in the gallbladder. The medical facilities in Vienna were outstanding. Even though his chest and stomach ailments were not immediately remedied, Bose soon felt rejuvenated after the stresses and strains of being shunted from one jail to another during the previous year. His passport had been endorsed for Austria, Italy, Switzerland, and France, but it was marked invalid for Britain and Germany. The British claimed that it was "not uncommon to indicate on the passport countries for which it is not valid." Bose had been allowed to visit Europe solely on health grounds, and the reason he had been confined still held good—namely, "his connection with the movement of revolutionary violence."[3] An exaggerated view of the sympathy Bose felt for the revolutionaries led the British to be quite paranoid about his intentions.

Despite the restrictions imposed on him, Bose soon found ways to travel around the European continent as the spokesman for India's freedom. He had long felt that Indian nationalists underutilized international diplomacy in furthering their cause, and now he wanted to rectify that shortcoming. Despite his recurring health problems, Bose traveled tirelessly for the next three years, inspiring Indian students studying abroad, establishing associations to promote friendship between India and various European countries, and meeting opinion-makers and leaders of governments wherever possible, to win their support for Indian independence. He wanted Indians overseas to serve as unofficial ambassadors of their enslaved country, and he set a personal example by becoming the doyen among them. During those years, he grew from a radical leader into an international statesman.

In 1930s Europe, the forces of imperialism and nationalism, fascism and communism, were arrayed against one another. Navigating that political minefield was no easy task. It involved carefully balancing ethical principles and the inexorable realities of power. The worldwide economic crisis of the Great Depression had unleashed xenophobic tendencies across European societies and polities. It was a terrible time for vulnerable minorities, who quickly became the convenient scapegoats for all ills and deprivations. A monstrous dictatorship had just come to power in Germany through formally democratic means. The echoes of a recent catastrophic war did not deter a new race for armaments, as Europe rushed headlong toward an even more devastating conflagration. Subject peoples in Europe's colonies knew that their destinies would unravel in conjunction with the global conflicts. Their dreams of liberty became mired in the battles between totalitarianisms of different ideological hues. Europe was a more challenging terrain than ever for an individual from Asia fired with a missionary zeal to free his country from bondage.

Delivering India's Message

"One chapter of my life has ended," Subhas wrote to a friend in April 1933. "I am trying to start a new one." Even though he was living far away in the city of Vienna, he had only one *sadhana* ("quest")— and that was to enable India, "this half-awake nation," to attain self-fulfillment and independence. He had to give up everything and be alone, in order to achieve a rich and fully realized life. He felt like a "lonely traveler" in an "endless desert of solitude," singing "If nobody hearkens to your call, march ahead alone."[4] In a Viennese sanatorium, Subhas was fortunate to find a kindred spirit and fellow convalescent who was impressed by his single-minded dedication to his homeland. This was Vithalbhai Patel, a leader of the Swaraj party founded by Motilal Nehru and Bose's late mentor, C. R. Das. A former president of the central legislative assembly in Delhi, Patel had just returned from a three-month tour of the United States. Subhas reported with concern on this elder statesman's health in his correspondence with an American author, Reverend J. T. Sunderland, whose sympathetic book *India in Bondage* had been banned by the British in India.[5] Vithalbhai's younger brother, Vallabhbhai Patel, was a loyal lieutenant of Gandhi in Gujarat, but it was the rebellious spirit of the young man from Bengal that captured Vithalbhai's imagination. When Gandhi suspended the civil disobedience movement in May 1933, the two were dismayed and jointly issued a toughly worded statement, the Patel-Bose Manifesto, calling for a new radical leadership of the independence movement.[6]

Subhas Chandra Bose received an invitation to preside over the third Indian political conference in London, to be held on June 10, 1933. The British government was very keen to keep Bose away from London and its large congregation of Indian students. Subhas believed that he needed special permission to visit Britain, but this was not true: his passport was that of a British subject, and thus he could not be legally prevented from entering the country. The British authorities sent instructions to their embassies and consulates not to tell Bose he was mistaken.[7] Since he thought he was denied permission to visit the imperial metropolis, his presidential address, entitled "The Anti-Imperialist Struggle and *Samyavada*," was read in absentia to the London gathering. It contained both an appreciation and a critique of Gandhian *satyagraha* from 1920 to 1933.

Bose accepted that Gandhi had opted for the correct method of struggle in 1920 and had roused the entire country. In his view, however, the movement had been neither sufficiently militant nor sufficiently diplomatic. Gandhi had surrendered at the wrong moments, in 1922 and 1931, and on poor terms. Bose went on to enunciate his own ideal: that of *samyavada*. Attracted by European political experiments in socialism, he nevertheless preferred to use the ancient Buddhist Indian term to articulate his ideology of socialism suited to Indian conditions, one that invoked equality in an atmosphere of balance and harmony. "*Samya* means 'equality,'" he explained to a young European interlocutor. "*Samyavadi* means 'one who believes in equality.' The idea of *samya* is a very old Indian conception—first popularized by the Buddhists five hundred years before Christ. I therefore prefer this name to the modern names now popular in Europe." Bose closed his London address by expressing his messianic faith in the mission that India would fulfill in world history. He gave credit to England for contributing ideas of constitutional and democratic government in the seventeenth century, to France for the transformative ideas of liberty, equality, and fraternity in the eighteenth century, to Germany for the gift of Marxian philosophy in the nineteenth century, and to Russia for achievements in proletarian revolution and culture in the twentieth century. "The next remarkable contribution to the culture and civilization of the world," he asserted, "India will be called upon to make."[8]

The address had been printed at the appropriately named Utopia Press, London, in the form of a twelve-page pamphlet. Printed copies of Bose's speech were prevented from entering India, through a ban imposed under the Sea Customs Act. In the British view, Bose was seeking "to advertise himself as the Lenin of the coming Indian revolution." He had made reference to an organization called the Samyavadi Sangh that might be formed to spread his message of *samyavada*. Several colonial officials wanted to outlaw this "new political society" and its "militant policy." One sensible official pointed out that the government had "no information to prove that the Sangh really exists except on paper and in the brain of Subhas Chandra Bose," and so the plan of banning the utopian organization was abandoned.[9]

Wishing to blend the old and the new, Bose was keen to learn from social and technological innovations in Europe. He was impressed by the practice of municipal socialism, which had been working effectively in Vienna for more than a dozen years. He met the socialist mayor of Vienna, and urged the mayor of Calcutta to emulate the Viennese example. He noted the progress Vienna had made in housing, education, medical relief, and social welfare. He was especially admiring of the socialist municipality's ability to provide housing to nearly 200,000 people by taxing luxuries and amusements, and without falling into debt. He visited the *Kindergarten* houses, where children from poor families were well looked after and given a decent education while their parents were at work. In Vienna, Subhas became friends with Naomi Vetter, who translated his speeches into German, and with her husband, a state official and the director of two theaters. Through an introduction supplied by his friend Dilip, he also formed close ties with Hedy Fülöp-Miller, a Hungarian singer and wife of the writer René Fülöp-Miller. These friends, along with Betty Hargrove, an American, and Helen Ashkanazy, the head of several women's associations in Vienna, were of great help to him in building bridges with Austrian society, media, and political circles. In 1933, Austria stood on the cusp of its socialist past and its fascist future. What Bose most admired about Vienna was soon to be swept away by the Nazi tide, unleashed by an Austrian in neighboring Germany.[10]

Czechoslovakia and Poland were two central and east European countries of special interest to Bose. He carefully studied the way a Czechoslovak legion had been formed during World War I, with British and Russian help, to win Czechoslovakia's freedom from Austrian domination; and the way a Polish legion had benefited from Japanese help to enable its homeland to throw off the Russian yoke. Years later, he would cite these examples—of weaker nations needing help from stronger ones to win independence—when he formed the Indian National Army during World War II. On June 29, 1933, Bose arrived in Prague by plane from Vienna. "Prague," he wrote, "has a peculiar charm about it—especially in the old buildings and medieval relics— but of course Vienna is unsurpassed." Czechoslovakia, however, was more relevant as an example for achieving national self-determination.

Bose had an interesting talk with Edouard Benes, Czechoslovakia's foreign minister, who along with Thomas Masaryk had led the Czechoslovak independence movement. The mayor of Prague received him and arranged for him to survey the city's urban and industrial infrastructure. The Masaryk Home for Children and Invalids was of special interest to Bose, as was the Oriental Institute in Prague, where he met with Professor V. Lesny, a scholar who had spent time at Tagore's university in Santiniketan. He and Lesny discussed the establishment of a Czechoslovak-Indian Association to promote commercial and cultural ties. The following year, Bose returned to Prague, where this bilateral friendship association was inaugurated at the Lobkowitz Palace on May 4, 1934. A good friend and colleague of both Nehru and Bose, A. C. N. Nambiar of Kerala, was based in Prague at that time, having been expelled from Nazi Germany in March 1933. His presence enabled Bose to carry forward his work of organizing Indian students and building ties with politicians and intellectuals in Czechoslovakia.[11]

The Polish consul in Prague gave Bose a visa for his country, and the British consul there innocently endorsed his passport for Poland and other countries on the Continent. The Briton's diplomatic superiors in London were furious when they heard of it, and called him "stupid" for following normal rules of diplomatic procedure in the case of a known revolutionary.[12] As Subhas walked through the streets of Warsaw, he could feel "the throb of a new life." He was warmly received by the municipal authorities and given a tour of a municipal bakery that made bread for one third of the city's population. He was impressed greatly by Warsaw's Physical Culture Institute, the largest of its kind in Europe and organized according to the latest medico-scientific principles. He was given a reception by the Oriental Institute of Warsaw and introduced to prominent citizens, including Professor Michalski, a venerable scholar of Sanskrit. Bose found his visit to Poland inspiring: it showed how a people "held down for centuries could rise to the occasion."[13]

The Czechoslovak and Polish nationalist movements fascinated Bose. He felt a deep sense of empathy with the trials and tribulations of these aspiring nations living under the shadow of great powers. For him, they presented both negative and positive examples of various strategies for coping and staying independent in the face of tremendous pressures from larger neighbors. He studied how they took advantage of the international war crisis of 1914–1918 to wage an armed struggle for freedom, and he analyzed the prospects of applying some of their tactics to the Indian situation as it evolved.

Bose's first visit to Germany was as disappointing as the ones to Czechoslovakia and Poland had been encouraging. On July 17, 1933, he traveled by train from Warsaw to Berlin. Lothar Frank, a young liaison officer deputed by the Indo-German Society, received him on his arrival at the Friedrichstrasse train station. The German government offered him accommodation at the place where Rabindranath Tagore had been put up in 1926. Bose declined; he preferred to stay at the Grand Hotel am Knie in the Charlottenburg neighborhood of Berlin at his own expense.[14] Berlin was a key diasporic space where Indian revolutionaries had gathered since World War I to strengthen the international dimension of the anticolonial movement, and Bose was following the trail of his predecessors in deciding to travel to this German metropolis. Now it had become the capital of the Third Reich, led by Adolf Hitler, who would "rather see India under English rule than under any other."[15]

It was unrealistic to expect any sympathy for India's cause among officials in Nazi Germany, its rivalry with Britain notwithstanding. Hitler viewed the British as a superior race, but it was not just his deep-seated racial prejudices that influenced his dim view of Indians. A streak of brutal rationality in the German Führer led him to believe in the possibility of an imperialist collaboration between Germany and Britain for mastery over the world.[16] In such circumstances, Bose's unhappiness in

Germany was understandable. He had an interview with the mayor of Berlin and meetings with a few officials in the German Foreign Office; none of these exchanges amounted to much. He established contact with Franz Thierfelder, director of the Deutsche Akademie in Munich, with whom he explored prospects for improving Indo-German relations. Even though he remained in Germany for over a month on this first visit, he was laid up for nearly three weeks with severe abdominal pain, probably caused by his gallbladder ailment, and was forced to restrict his activities.[17]

It was here in Berlin that Bose was befriended by Kitty Kurti, a young Czech Jewish woman. As she walked along the Kurfürstendamm, her gaze was caught by a strange figure approaching from the opposite direction: "It was a tall, slender man, obviously Indian. He was clad in a dark suit, not unlike a priest's. He wore a small cream-colored Gandhi cap that made him stand out. His face, a dark olive, was round and childlike, yet strikingly intelligent. His slow, erect gait gave the impression of singular dignity and control." Kitty next encountered this man at the American Cultural Club, where he was the featured speaker. His talk was political in nature, and not, as she had expected, philosophical. "Still," she remembered, "as I carefully watched his countenance, I realized that he was by no means merely a politician; he was, above all, a true philosopher. A man who, though fighting valiantly for the liberation of his country, was equally interested in man's fate and destiny, in all humanity." After the lecture, two British agents berated the American host for inviting this anti-British Indian. Kitty, however, was enthralled by Subhas Chandra Bose and had her husband, Alex, invite him to their house. In the intimate setting of this young couple's home, Bose answered their eager questions about India and wanted to learn from Kitty, a keen student of psychoanalysis, more about Freud and Jung.[18] This was an aspect of his German experience that Bose enjoyed, and he would call on the Kurtis during his future visits. His sensibilities had led him to those who would be marginalized and eventually victimized by the new regime.

After leaving Germany, Subhas spent much of the early autumn of 1933 taking care of the ailing Vithalbhai Patel, his close friend and political ally, in Franzensbad, Vienna, and Geneva. On September 21,

Bose addressed a public meeting on India—the largest of its type ever held in Geneva—under the auspices of the International Committee on India, which published bulletins in French, German, and English. He was, however, bitterly disappointed by the apathy of the League of Nations toward the aspirations of colonized countries. On October 4, he became a patient at Clinique La Lignière in Gland, where Vithalbhai Patel was being treated after a serious heart attack. Bose's abdominal pain was back in acute form, and he could not decide whether to undergo surgery.[19] For the moment, he was less concerned about himself than about Vithalbhai Patel. And with reason: Patel declined further, and died on October 22, 1933. The old man had willed a portion of his fortune to Bose, to be spent "for the political uplift of India and preferably for publicity work on behalf of India's cause in other countries." But a legal challenge by the Patel family, including his younger brother Vallabhbhai, ensured that Subhas did not receive a single penny designated for propagating India's message abroad.[20] For financial support, Subhas continued to rely mostly on Sarat's friends, whose generous loans would be repaid by the elder brother in 1936, after his release from prison.

Bose did, however, inherit a more intangible legacy left by Vithalbhai Patel, who had helped set up the Indian-Irish Independence League. Subhas had always been a keen student of the Irish freedom struggle. He began correspondence with the league's president, the legendary Maud Gonne McBride (whom Sarat had met in 1914), and with the organization's key functionary, Mrs. E. Woods. "In my part of the country (Bengal)," he wrote, "recent Irish history is studied closely by freedom-loving men and women and several Irish characters are literally worshipped in many a home." Even though a visit to Ireland had to wait until February 1936, contact had been established, and information was being exchanged from 1933 onward.[21]

Bose's contact with Italy happened rather unexpectedly. In December 1933, Subhas went to Nice "in search of clear sky and sunshine." There, he suddenly received an official invitation to the opening ceremony of the Italian Oriental Institute in Rome, scheduled for December 21. An admirer of Mazzini and Garibaldi, Bose accepted the invitation with alacrity. An Asian Students' Congress followed the in-

auguration of the Institute, from December 22 to 28. Some six hundred
Asian students converged on Rome from different universities and colleges in Europe. The Italian railways offered free travel, and the students were given accommodation in Rome for a week. The fascist dictator Benito Mussolini addressed the congress on the opening day. In
his opinion, the salvation of the world depended on a rapprochement
between East and West. Il Duce pointed out that while Rome had colonized Europe in the past, its relations with Asia had always been one of
friendly cooperation. "The speech was a fine one," Bose commented,
"whatever we might think of the speaker."[22] His ambivalence toward
Mussolini was obvious.

Bose was not the first prominent Indian visitor to encounter Mussolini. On a visit in 1926, Rabindranath Tagore had met the Italian leader,
who seemed to him "modeled body and soul by the chisel of Michelan-
gelo, whose every action showed intelligence and force." The poet was
subsequently annoyed when the official Italian news media attempted
to use and exaggerate his remarks to legitimize Italian fascism, and
he tried to retract his praise. Yet Tagore drafted a warm letter to Mussolini in 1930 while forging scholarly ties between India and Italy at
Santiniketan, and expressed the hope that the misunderstandings of
1926 would be forgotten.[23] In 1931, Gandhi met Mussolini and found
him a "riddle." While lamenting the leader's "iron hand," the Mahatma
confessed that "many of his reforms attract me." "What strikes me is
that behind Mussolini's implacability," he wrote to Romain Rolland, "is
a desire to serve his people. Even behind his emphatic speeches there
is a nucleus of sincerity and of passionate love for his people. It seems
to me that the majority of the Italian people love the iron government of Mussolini."[24] Bose's phrase—"whatever we might think of the
speaker"—suggested at the very least a degree of skepticism about the
Italian dictator. His decision to engage with Mussolini was motivated
not by romanticism or ideology, but rather by the pragmatic consideration that Mussolini was the leader of an important country with certain conflicts of interest with Britain in the Mediterranean. The Indian
students' convention that met in Rome simultaneously with the Asian
congress decided, with Bose's support, to shift the central office of the
Federation of Indian Students in Europe from London to Vienna. After

completing his engagements in Rome, Bose traveled to Milan, where he addressed the renowned Circolo Filologico Milanese (Philological Society of Milan) on the subject of "Italy and India." He dwelt on the way in which Italy's nineteenth-century movement toward national unification was relevant to the challenges facing India.[25]

From his base in Vienna, Bose embarked on another major tour: Germany, Italy, Czechoslovakia, Hungary, Romania, Turkey, Bulgaria, and Yugoslavia—a trip lasting from late March to early June of 1934. He had two clear aims. First, he sought to mobilize Indian students and young professionals residing in each of those countries to become part of the Indian freedom movement. Second, he wanted to lay the foundation of bilateral friendship associations between India and those European countries, in an effort to counteract what he saw as pernicious anti-Indian British propaganda.

As before, there was much unpleasantness during the trip to Germany. On April 5, 1934, Bose submitted a memorandum to the German Foreign Office listing his grievances regarding Indo-German relations. He complained about the negative attitude of the German press toward India; unfriendly statements by German leaders, including Hermann Göring's bizarre depiction of Gandhi as a "Bolshevik agent"; and the pernicious racial propaganda. He had been called *Neger* in the streets of Munich, and Indian students had suffered similar abuse while being pelted with stones. Indians resented the draft legislation against Jews and people of color. Bose called for a halt to the anti-Indian propaganda and asked that the proposed racial legislation be dropped.[26] Later in the year, he started exploring opportunities to shift talented Indians—eager to receive practical training after their formal studies—from Germany to Czechoslovakia.[27]

Beyond his dedication to promoting the cause of Indian independence, Subhas took pure joy in traveling and in discovering new places and peoples. He found Budapest "picturesque and the natural scenery to be very attractive." He had been a great admirer of Turkish nationalist resistance in the aftermath of World War I and held Kemal Atatürk in high regard. He was inspired by Atatürk to press for the adoption of the Roman script in India, to further the process of modernization and unification. Istanbul, however, fell short of his expectations and gave the impression of a collapsing state. It possessed neither "the romance of the East" nor "the material prosperity of the West." The Balkan countries were "very interesting." The movements of national self-determination in this region fascinated him. He thoroughly enjoyed his visits to Sofia, Belgrade, and Zagreb, despite British success in stopping the leading paper in Yugoslavia from publishing an interview with him.[28]

From the second week of June 1934, Bose settled down in Vienna, since he had a contract from the publishing company Wishart to write a book on the Indian struggle since 1920. In the course of looking for clerical help with preparing the manuscript, Subhas met a woman who would bring about a dramatic change in his personal life. Until then, he had been immersed in the freedom struggle and had taken little interest in relationships with women. "So many did love me before," he would write later, "but I never looked at them."[29] Family elders, his political mentor C. R. Das, and Das's wife, Basanti Devi, had been inundated with marriage proposals for Subhas, all of which he had spurned. He was particularly indignant on one occasion when Das was offered a large political donation by a wealthy benefactor, if only the Deshbandhu would persuade Bose to marry his daughter. Another aspiring father-in-law went further. On being told by Basanti Devi that Subhas would probably be sent to the gallows one day, he responded that his daughter would be proud to be Bose's widow. Basanti Devi, who discussed the subject of women with Subhas, always maintained that her adopted son never said he would not marry—he simply gave precedence to the fight for his country's freedom.[30] His more ardent followers thought he had taken a vow of celibacy and was determined to lead an ascetic life until Indian independence had been won. In Europe, Subhas managed to break free of the tyranny of these expectations.

It was June 24, 1934. A petite and pretty young woman named Emilie Schenkl arrived to be interviewed for the clerical job. Born on December 26, 1910, to an Austrian Catholic family, she knew English, could take dictation in shorthand, and had competent typing skills. Jobs were scarce during the Depression. Her father, a veterinarian, was initially somewhat reluctant to let his daughter work for a strange Indian man, but in time her whole family—father, mother, and sister

—developed a warm relationship with Subhas. Emilie had a gentle, cheerful, straightforward, and unselfish nature, which Subhas found appealing. He came to respect her strength of will and affectionately called her "Baghini," meaning "Tigress" in Bengali. "He started it," Emilie stated categorically about the romantic turn in their relationship. Their intimacy grew as they spent time together in Austria and Czechoslovakia from mid-1934 to March 1936.[31]

During the summer of 1934, Bose worked hard at his manuscript in his Vienna apartment. He did not have easy access to relevant books and papers, and consequently had to rely greatly on his memory of events. He either dictated or wrote in longhand, and Emilie typed up the pages. "I am getting on with my work," he wrote to Naomi Vetter in mid-August, "but do not feel satisfied with the quality of the stuff I am producing."[32] He was still unwell, and had to choose between going to Karlsbad in Czechoslovakia for a cure or trying a gallbladder operation in Vienna. He went with his unfinished manuscript to Karlsbad in early September, accompanied by Emilie, and stayed at the Kurhaus Königin Alexandra. He was worried about the looming deadline of September 30 given by his publisher, but managed to meet it with the help of Emilie and the thermal waters in the spa town. Emperor Charles IV had founded Karlsbad in 1349, and the resort became famous for the healing properties of its sixteen hot mineral springs. What made the place especially attractive to Subhas were "the lovely walks leading up to all the surrounding hill-tops."[33]

Bose's manuscript was shaping up to be a major study of the movement for independence in which he himself was a leading participant. It provided a lucid, analytical narrative of the freedom struggle, from the gathering clouds of the noncooperation and Khilafat movements of 1920 to the stormy civil disobedience and revolutionary campaigns of the early 1930s. The dramatic story of the political upheavals during the interwar period was enriched by Bose's own reflections on key themes in Indian history and a finely etched assessment of Mahatma Gandhi's role in it. In assessing the phenomenon that was Gandhi, he had fulsome praise for the Mahatma's "single-hearted devotion, his relentless will and his indefatigable labor." He was critical, however, of Gandhi's inability to comprehend the character of his opponents or to make use of international diplomacy in his efforts to win *swaraj*. Gandhi's efforts in reconciling capital and labor, landlord and peasant, had their limits. In the ultimate analysis, Mahatma Gandhi had failed, in Bose's view, because "the false unity of interests that are inherently opposed is not a source of strength but a source of weakness in political warfare."[34]

In a penultimate chapter titled "A Glimpse of the Future," Bose made certain comments about communism and fascism that would be seized upon years later to make him the target of hostile criticism from various quarters. The context in which he made those remarks was an attempted answer to the question that was on everyone's lips in Europe: "What is the future of Communism in India?" Bose wanted to differentiate his own response from the emphatic one that Jawaharlal Nehru had given in December 1933. Nehru saw a stark choice before the world between "some form of Communism and some form of Fascism" and declared himself to be "all for" communism. "There is no middle road between Fascism and Communism," he asserted. "One has to choose between the two and I choose the Communist ideal." Bose believed Nehru's view to be "fundamentally wrong" and saw no reason to hold that the choice was "restricted to two alternatives." Whether one adhered to a Hegelian or Bergsonian theory of evolution, the end of history and creativity had not been reached. And then, in a rather mechanistic application of Hegelian dialectics, Bose announced that he was "inclined to hold that the next phase in world-history will produce a synthesis between Communism and Fascism. And will it be a surprise if that synthesis is produced in India?" He went on to list a series of quite convincing reasons why "Communism will not be adopted in India." Its lack of sympathy with nationalism, the inward-looking nature of contemporary Russia, and the antireligious and atheistic element in the ideology would combine to make communism unappealing to Indians. It would therefore be "safe to predict that India will not become a new edition of Soviet Russia." With "equal strength" it could be said that "all the modern socio-political movements and experiments in Europe and in America will have considerable influence on India's development." In the future, India would take "more and more interest in what goes on in the outside world."[35]

Bose had barely finished correcting the proofs for his book in late November when he received an urgent telegram from his mother: his father was critically ill. He set off from Vienna at once by air. "I may not be able to write to you till I reach India," he wrote to Emilie from Rome on November 30, 1934. "Do not worry. I am always a bad correspondent—but not a bad man I hope." He did manage to write to Emilie from all the places where the plane stopped—Venice, Athens, Cairo, and Baghdad. He had just enough time to see the Acropolis and a few other ancient sites in Greece. In Cairo, he enjoyed visiting the pyramids, mosques, tombs, and especially the wonderful Tutankhamen Museum. "I am back again in the bosom of the East," he happily informed Emilie from Egypt. "While coming from Athens, we flew above the clouds in the early morning and saw a gorgeous sunrise, which we can sec only in the East." In Baghdad he was thrilled to see "a mosque with golden domes" built nearly half a millennium ago.[36] After further halts in Karachi and Jodhpur, the KLM flight landed in Calcutta at about four in the afternoon on December 4. Subhas's father had passed away on December 2. The airport was surrounded by police, and as soon as Subhas stepped off the plane he was placed under house arrest, like his brother Sarat. On the portico of their father's house at 38/2 Elgin Road, Sarat and Subhas had an emotional reunion after nearly two years.[37]

A month of mourning was observed for the departed patriarch. During this period, Subhas lived like a prisoner in his own house. Looking like a Buddha, with his head shaven, he joined his six surviving brothers in performing an elaborate and traditional *shraddha* ceremony for the peace of their father's soul.[38] On December 31, 1934, he informed Emilie that he saw no alternative but to undergo an operation on his return to Europe. On January 8, 1935, he left Calcutta for Europe, and on January 10 he boarded the M.V. *Victoria* sailing from Bombay. He had severe pains on the boat, but felt better on land. He arrived in Naples on January 20 and decided to spend a week in Italy, so he could meet with Mussolini before returning to Vienna. While in Naples, he saw Pompeii and the active volcano Solfalara. In Rome, he had a long meeting with Amanullah, the former king of Afghanistan, and called on Maxim Litvinov, foreign minister of the Soviet Union, at the Russian Embassy.[39] He wrote to Emilie from Rome on January 25, thanking her for remembering his birthday two days before, which he himself had forgotten. He also informed her that he would have an interview with Mussolini that evening and was going to present Il Duce with a copy of his book, adding that she should "treat this matter as strictly private."[40] In the book's preface, dated November 29, 1934 (their daughter would be born on that date in 1942), Emilie was the only person he mentioned by name. "In conclusion," he wrote, "I have to express my thanks to Fraulein E. Schenkl, who assisted me in writing this book, and to all those friends who have been of help to me in many ways."[41]

The Indian Struggle, Bose's interpretation of the freedom movement from 1920 to 1934, was published by Lawrence and Wishart in London on January 17, 1935. The colonial government in Delhi, with the approval of London, lost no time in proscribing the book and banning its entry into India. Samuel Hoare, the secretary of state for India, alleged in the House of Commons in reply to a question from the Labour MP Colonel J. Wedgwood that the action had been taken because the book "tended generally to encourage methods of terrorism and direct action." This was rather a strange charge to make, since the book, if anything, made some constructive suggestions on how to deter revolutionaries from the path of terrorism and turn them toward peaceful methods of struggle.

Despite the hostility of the British government, *The Indian Struggle* was particularly well reviewed in the British press and warmly welcomed in European literary and political circles. Reviewing the book in the *Manchester Guardian,* J. T. Gwynne, a British officer of the elite Indian Civil Service, gave the following assessment:

> This is perhaps the most interesting book which has yet been written by an Indian politician on Indian politics. His history of the last fourteen years, though written avowedly from the standpoint of the Left-Wing, is as nearly fair to all parties and everyone as can be reasonably expected of an active politician. He is interested in trade union movements, the peasants' revolt, and the growth of Socialism. Alto-

gether the book leaves us with a wish to see Mr. Bose take a lead in Indian politics.

The *Sunday Times* review by Sir Alfred Watson was more critical, but still found *The Indian Struggle* "a valuable book for the enlightenment of opinion. It has a point of view difficult for the British mind to comprehend, but it accurately describes a side of the Indian movement that cannot be ignored." The renowned diplomatic correspondent W. Norman Ewer, of the *Daily Herald,* described it as "calm, sane, dispassionate" and "the ablest work I have read on current Indian politics. This is the book of no fanatic, but of a singularly able mind, the book of an acute, thoughtful, constructive mind, of a man who, while still under forty, would be an asset and an ornament to the political life of any country." Sir Frederick Whyte, writing in the *Spectator,* found the book "valuable as a document of contemporary history." The reviewer in the *News Chronicle,* J. Stuart Hodgson, described Bose as "unusually clear-headed for a revolutionary" and added: "His picture of Gandhi is very interesting as an Indian view. It is firmly and convincingly drawn. He does full justice to the marvelous qualities of the saint without condoning in the least the 'Himalayan blunders' of the politician." The banning of the book in India created a stir among left-leaning British politicians and intellectuals. George Lansbury thanked Bose for the book, from which he was "learning a great deal."[42] The proscription in India of a book that was circulating freely in Europe was a blatant application of the rule of colonial difference. "Is English law to have one interpretation in Great Britain and another in India?" Bose asked indignantly in a letter to the editor of the *New Statesman and Nation.*[43]

From continental Europe, the most insightful commentary on the book came from Romain Rolland, who found it so interesting that he ordered a second copy so that his wife and sister would each have one. "In it, you show the best qualities of the historian," he wrote to the author, "lucidity and high equity of mind. Rarely it happens that a man of action as you are is apt to judge without party spirit." He was full of admiration for Bose's "firm political sense" and thought it "a pity that all the ablest leaders of the Indian Social Movement," including Bose

and Nehru, were either in prison or in exile. Eamon de Valera of Ireland likewise read the book with great interest, and expressed the hope
that "freedom and happiness" would come to the Indian people in the
near future.[44]

First Love

Subhas Chandra Bose, according to his close friend and political associate A. C. N. Nambiar, was a "one-idea man: singly for the independence of India." "I think the only departure," he added, "if one might
use the word 'departure,' was his love for Miss Schenkl; otherwise he
was completely absorbed. He was deeply in love with her, you see. In
fact, it was an enormous, intense love."[45] This love blossomed during
1935, in Vienna and in the mountain retreats of Austria and Czechoslovakia. The hills and valleys of Karlsbad, Hofgastein, and Badgastein
were the only witnesses to this romantic side of Subhas's life—a side
that remained hidden from public view. Yet no understanding of his
personality and psychology can be complete without taking account of
the way in which he dealt with the tension between private joy and
public duty. The stifling social conventions of Indian society had given
him little opportunity to forge genuine friendships with women. His
shy and reticent manner with them had not helped. In the cultural
world of the anticolonial revolutionaries of Bengal, women were ideal-
ized into mother figures. Any romantic attachment with a woman
tended to be viewed as an unworthy distraction from ascetic devotion to the motherland. In the freer atmosphere of Europe, Subhas developed real friendships with women. Most of them happened to be
married European or American women, with a broad international
outlook and an interest in India. Young and single, Emilie was different, and what started as a working relationship soon developed into a
close personal bond.

The year 1935 was dominated by Subhas's own illness, including major surgery and a long drawn-out convalescence. This was aggravated
by grief at the illness and death of loved ones. Before he could address
his own health problems, he felt compelled to travel to Gland, in Switzerland, to participate in a memorial ceremony for Vithalbhai Patel.[46]

He took this opportunity to call on Romain Rolland at his Villa Olga in Villeneuve, a site that afforded sweeping views of Lake Geneva. He had long admired the French savant, and wrote a detailed account of their two-and-a-half-hour conversation for the *Modern Review*. Bose asked Rolland some leading questions about the potential conflict between Gandhi's priorities and the rights of labor, and was "delighted and amazed" by Rolland's unambiguous support for the workers' cause. Rolland declared himself to be in favor of internationalism, justice for workers, freedom for suppressed nationalities, and equal rights for women. Toward the end of the conversation, Bose ventured to say: "For suppressed peoples and nationalities, war is not an unmixed evil." "But for Europe," Rolland replied, "war will be the greatest disaster. It may even mean the end of civilization."[47]

On April 24, 1935, after delaying the decision as much as possible, Bose finally agreed to have a gallbladder operation. Professor Rudolf Demel carried out the surgery at the Rudolfinerhaus, a sanatorium in Vienna. Before being put under anesthesia, Subhas asked for a piece of paper. "My love to my countrymen, my debts to my elder brother Sarat," he wrote.[48] Professor Demel removed the gallbladder, which contained a large stone. A team of nurses led by Sister Elvira cared for Subhas, and Emilie was a regular visitor. After three weeks, once he was able to walk about a little, he moved from the Rudolfinerhaus to the Westend Sanatorium in Purkersdorf, on the outskirts of Vienna. He was rather impatient with his slow recovery, and as late as September reported having to wear an abdominal belt and avoid strenuous exercise.

Bose left Vienna in mid-June for Karlsbad, where he remained for nearly three months. From Vienna to Prague, he accompanied Kamala Nehru, Jawaharlal's wife, who was in Europe to be treated for pulmonary tuberculosis while her husband was imprisoned in India. Bose spent the period of enforced rest and recuperation reading a variety of books, including H. G. Wells's *The New America: The New World*. In September, at the suggestion of his doctor, he decided to try the "cure" in Hofgastein. On his way from Karlsbad to Hofgastein, he made a detour to Badenweiler to see Kamala Nehru. As her condition deteriorated, the British relented and released Jawaharlal from jail so that he

could be with his wife. Bose met Nehru upon his arrival in the Black
Forest resort, and the two stayed in the same boardinghouse.[49] Once
Kamala Nehru's condition improved a little, Subhas went on to Austria.
"If I can be of any service in your present trouble," Subhas wrote to
Jawahar from Hofgastein on October 4, 1935, "I hope you will not
hesitate to send for me."[50] He himself found solace in the company of
Emilie in both Karlsbad and Hofgastein.[51]

Bose felt well enough to leave Hofgastein on October 23, 1935, and
traveled to Vienna after seeing the Nehrus once more in Badenweiler.
During November and December of 1935, he readied himself for another major European tour in early 1936, to advocate freedom for India. He was denied a visa to go to the Soviet Union. He reckoned that
this was because of the "new Soviet-British rapprochement" and that
the decision would be "rather damaging to the reputation of the Soviet
Government in India."[52] Oblivious to Stalinist terror, Nehru had been
euphoric about what he had seen of social transformation in the Soviet
Union. Bose's critical remarks on communism in *The Indian Struggle*
may have had something to do with the unwelcoming attitude of the
Russians. His disappointment with the Soviet Union, however, was
more than offset by the permit he was granted to visit the Irish Free
State. Emilie conducted some of the correspondence with Irish friends
on his behalf. Subhas was still under the mistaken assumption that he
was not allowed to visit England, and so made plans to go directly from
the Continent to Ireland.[53]

In the second week of January 1936, Bose set off from Vienna for his
final swing through Europe, before his planned return to India in time
for the annual session of the Indian National Congress in Lucknow. His
first stop was Prague, where he had a conversation with President Edouard Benes on January 13. It was a time of hectic diplomatic activity
in Czechoslovakia, with German demands for the Sudetenland threat-
ening the government of Benes. Bose found that Benes's meeting with
him was preceded by one with the French ambassador and followed by
one with the Austrian envoy. In the midst of European conflicts that
clearly had to take precedence for Benes, Bose battled on to keep the
subject of Indian independence on the political agenda. He left the

same night for Berlin; there he had a meeting with expatriate Indians who were planning a Congress jubilee celebration. He described Germany as "now very pro-British," sensing that the Nazis wished to avoid riling the British Empire while trying to build an imperial system of their own. He found the economic situation to be very bad. *Hausfrauen* as a class felt discontented because essential commodities were scarce, but the government could "not put these women into prisons so easily!" The trip to Belgium was pure holiday; Bose spent it sightseeing with his friends Kantilal Parekh and Nathalal Javeri, though he also gave an interview to the Antwerp paper *Le Matin.* Next on his itinerary was Paris, where he met the writer André Gide, the pacifist Félicien Challaye, and leaders of the women's movement, Mme. Drevet and Mme. Duchêne. With Europe in turmoil, he was able to interest French intellectuals—but not the French government—in Indian affairs.[54]

Ireland's shared history of colonization ensured a much more enthusiastic reception for an Indian seeking freedom from British rule. With great excitement and anticipation, Bose boarded the American ship S.S. *Washington* at Le Havre on January 30, 1936, for Ireland. His first act on disembarking at Cork was to leave a floral tribute at the grave of Terence MacSwiney, the former mayor, who had died as the result of a hunger strike against the British authorities. Bose regarded his two weeks in Ireland as the political high point of his European sojourn. President Eamon de Valera warmly received him upon his arrival in Dublin. De Valera accorded Bose the status of a high dignitary from a friendly foreign country, and held three meetings with him: a formal exchange of views in the government buildings, an informal tea reception hosted by his Fianna Fáil party, and a private dinner at his home outside Dublin. Bose looked up to the older anticolonial revolutionary, and sought his advice. They discussed the possibilities and limits of external help for a country that was struggling for freedom against its colonial rulers. De Valera would have known a good deal about this issue: in 1916, Ireland had counted on arms from the Continent to aid the Easter Rising, but these had not arrived in time and the failure had led to the execution of Roger Casement. De Valera's own experiences of trawling for support in the United States for the Irish cause had been mixed. The conversations with de Valera may have steeled Bose's resolve to return to India, whatever reception the British might have in store for him.[55]

Bose also had one-on-one meetings with most of the Fianna Fáil ministers, whom he found "exceedingly sympathetic, accessible and humane." "Most of them had been on the run when they were fighting for their freedom," he remarked, "and would be shot on sight if they had been spotted." He was glad to see that they had not yet become "hardened bureaucratic ministers" and that they did not put on official airs. He talked with the minister of lands about the abolition of land-lordism and the redistribution of land among the peasantry. With the minister of agriculture, he exchanged views on the balance between food and commercial crops, including the way the cultivation of jute was restricted in India to drive up the price during the Depression. The role of private and state enterprise in bringing about industrial genera-tion figured in his conversation with the minister of industries. Overall, the work of the Fianna Fáil ministers seemed to him interesting and valuable as India prepared for the task of economic reconstruction in an independent future. He thought that W. T. Cosgrave's opposition party had many fine debaters, but its pro-British reputation ensured that Fianna Fáil, along with its Labour ally, would have majority sup-port. He met with the president of Sinn Féin, and some of its other of-ficials, even though he "could not wholly support" many features of that organization. He would have "liked to see a more cordial relation-ship" between Fianna Fáil and the Republicans—the sort of relations that had prevailed when de Valera had first come to power in 1932. He was saddened to see how those who had fought together for freedom were drifting apart after winning state power.[56]

The rivalry between different strands of the anticolonial movement, the conflict between religiously defined majorities and minorities, and the agrarian question were all features that Ireland and India shared. Despite the special relationship between Ireland and Bengal, Bose had to correct a journalist who described him as a leader from Bengal; Bose said firmly that he was an Indian leader and not at all provincial. In a corridor of Dublin's Shelbourne Hotel, he was vividly reminded of the fact that the Irish were both supporters and opponents of empire:

he came face to face with Colonel J. H. Smith, whom he had known as a superintendent in Mandalay Jail. Before departing for Cork, he gave a reception at the Shelbourne for all of his Irish friends, including Maud Gonne McBride. The days he spent in Dublin were, he said, "like a dream" because he was able to vent his deepest passions and concerns about independence among people who understood them. He was especially grateful to Mrs. Woods, of the Indian Irish Independence League, whose entire family had been splendid hosts. "I do not know when we shall meet again," he wrote to her. "Bhavabhuti, one of our ancient poets, once wrote, 'Time is eternal and the earth is a vast expanse,' so may be we shall meet again—but perhaps not so unexpectedly as when I knocked against my prison-superintendent in Shelbourne Hotel."[57]

On February 12, 1936, Bose sailed for France on the American liner *President Harding.* In Paris, he once more engaged intellectuals like André Gide and André Malraux, and found the minister of education, M. Guernut, "kind but slightly official."[58] It is hardly surprising that India was not uppermost in the mind of French officialdom. On February 17, addressing a conference in Paris under the auspices of the League against Imperialism, Bose analyzed two aspects of the Indian movement: the struggle for national liberation and the endeavor to create a new social order. Since India occupied a crucial place in the British empire, the anti-imperialist movement in India concerned the "whole of humanity." He noted that many were concerned about Japanese imperialism in Asia. "If tomorrow China could be strong and unified, if tomorrow India could be free," he argued, "I am sure it would influence the balance of power in Asia and serve to check the spread of Japanese imperialism." On the question of "social freedom," he noted that there was popular pressure on the Indian National Congress to "declare itself more explicitly on the side of the masses."[59]

On February 26, 1936, Bose set off from Paris to see Nehru in Lausanne and Romain Rolland in Villeneuve, on his way to Badgastein. He was held up in Lausanne, where Kamala Nehru was very ill; she breathed her last on February 28. Subhas was present at the end, along with Jawaharlal and his daughter Indira, and he helped with arrangements for the funeral.[60] Bose and Nehru's personal bond deepened during this period of loss and mourning in Jawaharlal's life. After reaching the Kurhaus Hochland in Badgastein on March 3, 1936, Bose at last found a moment of peace after his whirlwind tour of the Continent, which had lasted more than six weeks. "The landscape here is beautiful," he wrote, "exactly like the Himalayas. There is snow all around and the mountain ranges stand firm and unshakable."[61] The next day he wrote a warm and supportive letter to Jawahar, who was soon to leave for India to preside over the Lucknow session of the Congress. He wished his friend could have had some rest in Europe before plunging into the vortex of Indian politics. In a strong endorsement of Jawaharlal's leadership, Subhas wrote:

> Among the front-rank leaders of today—you are the only one whom we can look up to for leading the Congress in a progressive direction. Moreover, your position is unique and I think that even Mahatma Gandhi will be more accommodating towards you than towards anybody else. I earnestly hope that you will fully utilize the strength of your public position in making decisions. Please do not consider your position to be weaker than it really is. Gandhiji will never take a stand which will alienate you.

He was very pleased that Jawaharlal intended to set up a foreign department of the Indian National Congress that was entirely consonant with Subhas's views.[62]

After three years in Europe, Bose was ready to give his own assessment of Italy and Germany in public and private, prior to his departure for India. Late in 1935, he had already published an article on Italy, after the launch of its imperialist expedition against Ethiopia. He condemned Italian aggression and British hypocrisy. The lesson that he drew from Ethiopia's predicament was that in the twentieth century a nation could "hope to be free only if it is strong." For that to happen, it was necessary to harness all the knowledge that modern science could offer. He tried hard to find something positive in the rather sorry and sordid state of affairs in East Africa. "Abyssinia will go down fighting," he wrote, "but she will stir the conscience of the world." This would happen in two ways: a new awakening among people of color, and a

questioning of the legitimacy of colonial conquest in the imperial metropolis. Imperialism could be overthrown through an anti-imperialist
struggle of the colonized or through an internecine conflict among rival imperialists. If the rise of Italian imperialism strengthened the latter
tendency, "then Abyssinia will not have suffered in vain."[63]

To an Indian nationalist, German policy rankled even more deeply
than Italy's misadventure. "Against Germany, we [Indians] have many
complaints," he wrote to the poet Amiya Chakravarty, Tagore's former
secretary. "The other day [in January 1936], I made known my protest,
when I was in Berlin. They worship strength, not weakness. Against Italy there are complaints from other standpoints—not from the standpoint of India's interest or prestige. But, against Germany, we have
many accusations from India's standpoint." He urged the Federation of
Indian Students to issue a "sharp refutation" of Hitler's recent speech in
Munich, where the Führer had spoken of the destiny of the white races
to rule the world. He himself had sent a statement to the Indian press
supporting a trade boycott against Germany. He could see, however,
that there was "no early possibility of the fall of Hitler's government."
"If war breaks out some day," he wrote presciently, "and the war weak-
ens Germany, then such a fall is possible, otherwise not." Noting the
clout wielded in Germany by the army and the business lobby, he
hoped that an Indian trade boycott would lead German businessmen
to put pressure on Hitler.[64]

These were his views expressed in private to an Indian friend—but
he was equally forthright in his communications on this subject with
his principal German interlocutor, and with the Geneva press. He told
Franz Thierfelder of the Deutsche Akademie that he was returning to
India with "the conviction that the new nationalism of Germany" was
"not only narrow and selfish but arrogant." He was aware that the German government had issued a diplomatic explanation to Japan and
India relating to Hitler's offensive speech, but he refused to give it cre-
dence, since the British and German press had not published it. He was
still prepared to work for an understanding between Germany and India, but only if it was consistent with India's "national self-respect."
"When we are fighting the greatest Empire in the world for our freedom and for our rights and when we are confident of our ultimate suc-

cess," he declared, "we cannot brook any insult from any other nation or any attack on our race or culture."[65] He was even more blunt during an interaction with the press in Geneva. He had been "greatly disturbed" by the insulting remarks of the German Führer, designed to curry favor with Britain. "I can have no objection if the Germans desire to lick the boots of the Britishers," he said sarcastically, "but if they think that in the year 1936 an insult hurled at India will be quietly pocketed by us, they are sadly mistaken."[66]

For his European friends who ran the risk of falling foul of the Nazi regime, Bose had deep concern. "I often wonder why you stay in Berlin," he had written to Kitty Kurti in December 1935. "Don't you find the atmosphere suffocating?"[67] The Kurti couple suffered a double jeopardy: they were Czech and Jewish. Bose called on Kitty Kurti during his January 1936 visit to Berlin, and advised her to leave Germany. On being assured they planned to return soon to their home country, Bose said that Czechoslovakia was "far too close and far too weak." He had just come from Prague, and wanted the Kurtis to leave for the United States as soon as they could obtain a visa. "All this was said with great reticence," Kitty Kurti remembered after she had emigrated to the United States, "in the extraordinary way that was his. But beneath it all, I felt his concern and I was grateful for it. I was also glad to note his deep contempt for the Nazis, a feeling which he did not attempt to hide from me."[68]

As Bose prepared to return to India in March 1936, he was given a stern warning by the British foreign secretary, communicated through His Majesty's consul in Vienna: "The Government of India desire to make it clear to you that should you do so you cannot expect to remain at liberty."[69] A new constitution embodied in the Government of India Act of 1935, granting provincial autonomy, had just been inaugurated with great fanfare. New elections to the provincial legislatures were scheduled for 1937. On receiving the warning, Bose could not help wondering if this was "a foretaste of the expanded liberty which the new constitution will usher in."[70] He was inclined to defy the warning and go home, but wrote to Nehru seeking his advice: "My only excuse for troubling you on such a matter is that I can think of no one else in whom I could have greater confidence."[71]

Even before the explicit warning, the odds were that he would be jailed in India. Yet there had been at least a small chance of his being allowed to attend the Lucknow Congress, over which Nehru would preside, in the second week of April. That prospect had now been firmly shut down. Well before Jawaharlal could reply, advising Subhas to follow his intuition and not submit to indefinite exile, Bose had made up his mind.[72] Romain Rolland sent his "sympathetic affection" and asked him to consider postponing his return. Bose replied that he felt it was his duty to return to India at once. "It is, of course, a tragic thing," he wrote, "that the best and most creative years of one's life should be spent behind prison walls, but that is a price which enslaved people always had and always will have to pay in this world."[73]

Unbeknownst to the world, the greatest difficulty for Bose in leaving Europe was not the certainty of imprisonment in India, but the pain of separation from the woman he loved. As he prepared to go home, he wrote Emilie a letter that was a forthright confession of his feelings. "Even the iceberg sometimes melts," he began, "and so it is with me now." He had "already sold" himself to his "first love"—his country—to whom he had to return. As usual, it was an adventure into the unknown:

> I do not know what the future has in store for me. May be, I shall spend my life in prison, may be, I shall be shot or hanged. But whatever happens, I shall think of you and convey my gratitude to you in silence for your love for me. May be I shall never see you again—may be I shall not be able to write to you again when I am back—but believe me, you will always live in my heart, in my thoughts and in my dreams. If fate should thus separate us in this life—I shall long for you in my next life.

He had "never thought before that a woman's love could ensnare" him. And he mused:

> Is this love of any earthly use? We who belong to two different lands— have we anything in common? My country, my people, my traditions, my habits and customs, my climate—in fact everything is so different

from yours. . . . For the moment, 1 have forgotten all these differences
that separate our countries. I have loved the woman in you—the soul
in you.[74]

Subhas spent March 17 to March 26, 1936—the last few days before
his departure for India—with Emilie in Badgastein. "Can you please
come here for a week?" Subhas had implored on March 15. "Please
ask your parents if they will allow you to be away from home for one
week or so."[75] The hills and valleys of Badgastein had enchanted Franz
Schubert in 1825, inspiring him to compose his Piano Sonata in D
and a missing symphony, perhaps his great Symphony in C Major.
Those magic mountains had cast a spell on Subhas as well. From the
Kurhaus Hochland, where they stayed, Subhas and Emilie took long
walks together—all the way to Grüner Baum to have coffee. Together
they enjoyed the quiet beauty of snowy Badgastein, with its invigorating thermal waters, and created for an ephemeral moment their own
symphony of life.[76]

On March 17, Subhas wrote a letter from Badgastein congratulating
a young colleague in India who had recently married. It was very revealing of his priorities and philosophy of life. "Personal and family
happiness," he wrote, "has hardly any value to me unless personal and
family life is dedicated to the well-being of the country. I shall therefore
particularly pray that your lives may be devoted to the good of your
country and countrymen—you will certainly find true happiness and
bliss only in this."[77] On March 26, Emilie took the train to Vienna and
Subhas commenced his journey back to India. "I am now on a pilgrimage," he observed that day, "so there is no worry."[78] Subhas wrote to
Emilie from Villach and Naples, before boarding the Italian ship *Conte
Verde.*[79]

"There are many things I want to write to you about," he wrote from
the boat on March 29, 1936, "but I shall write in a disconnected way—
so please read this letter carefully."[80] From now on, Emilie would have
to learn to read between the lines to decipher the full import of Subhas's messages. At the end of March 1936, while aboard ship, he wrote
her three letters on three consecutive days; they marked the beginning
of nearly twenty months of geographic separation. At Port Said, police

officers came in search of him, seized his passport, and placed him under guard. In January 1935, he had gone to meet the Egyptian nationalist leader Mustafa el Nahas Pasha.[81] It was clear that the British would
not let him disembark or meet anyone in Egypt on this occasion.

"Just one thing more before I close this long letter," Subhas wrote to
Emilie on March 30, 1936, before leaving the Mediterranean for the
Indian Ocean. "For your life, never pray for any selfish object or aim.
Always pray for what is good for humanity—for what is good for all
time—for what is good in the eyes of God. Pray in a *nishkama* (disinterested) way."[82] This allusion to the *Gita* was all he had to offer to the
woman he loved, as he prepared himself for the trials ahead.

Leader in Waiting

As soon as his ship docked in Bombay on April 8, 1936, Bose was
greeted by the police and taken away to the city's Arthur Road Prison.
The government was unmoved by the public outcry against his imprisonment. After a few days, he was moved to Yeravda Central Prison in
Poona, and kept in the same yard where Gandhi had been lodged in
1932.[83] Jawaharlal Nehru, the Congress president, called on the entire
country to observe All-India Subhas Day on May 10, 1936, in an attempt to bring pressure to bear on the British. "We who know him
also know how frivolous are the charges brought against him," Nehru
wrote. "He did me the honor to ask me for advice and I was puzzled
and perplexed, for it is no easy thing to advise another in such a matter, when such advice might mean prison. Subhas Bose has suffered
enough at the cost of his health."[84]

Subhas was finding the heat very oppressive in western India, where
the temperature had soared to 43 degrees Celsius—nearly 110 degrees
Fahrenheit. "You cannot even imagine how hot it is here," he wrote to
Emilie on May 11. "I often think of the thick snow that was lying all
around in Badgastein when I left Europe." After another ten days, the
government decided to "intern" Subhas in a bungalow belonging to
Sarat in a place called Kurseong, in northern Bengal. It was situated
more than five thousand feet above sea level, on the way to the famous
hill station of Darjeeling. "It is delightfully cool here," he informed

Emilie on May 22, "and the villa commands a nice view of the plains."[85]
He was left there to lead a mostly solitary existence until December.

Subhas was back in Bengal after more than four years, but he was
being kept out of action so far as Bengal politics was concerned. His
years of exile had contributed much to the development of his personality and qualities of leadership. His forced absence from Bengal and
India, however, was much to the detriment of nationalist politics—all
the more so, since his elder brother and closest political comrade, Sarat,
had likewise been in prison from 1932 to 1935. Sarat assumed the leadership of the Congress in Bengal from 1936 on, but Subhas was not
permitted by the British to play any active role in the run-up to the
elections of 1937.

Not only had the brothers' boldness of vision been sorely missed
during the second phase of the civil disobedience and revolutionary
movements, from 1932 to 1934, but no other leader had the generosity
and foresight to stem the deterioration in Hindu-Muslim relations
during these critical years. Several setbacks in this regard had already
been suffered by the time they returned to the center stage of Indian
politics and tried to turn things around. "Can you tell me what is
wrong with Bengal?" Subhas had asked the mayor of Calcutta from
Vienna in January 1936. "We shall have to begin again at the very beginning."[86] The 1935 constitution had given Muslims 119 seats in the
Bengal legislative assembly, under a system of separate electorates, and
had given 80 to Hindus, of which 50 were in general constituencies
and 30 were reserved for the scheduled castes. In addition, another 39
seats had been given to Europeans, Anglo-Indians, and special-interest
groups. Muslim support was drifting away from the Congress to a
peasants' and tenants' organization called the Krishak Praja party and
to the Muslim League. "The future of the Bengal Congress," Subhas
wrote in 1937, "lies in converting it into the one organ of the Bengal
peasantry."[87] He had the theory right, but was not around to translate
theory into practice.

In early June, Subhas was delighted to be permitted a two-day visit
by Sarat and an opportunity, after a long interval, to catch up on family
and political news. Later that month, two of his nephews, Sarat's sons
Amiya and Sisir, were allowed to come for a fortnight. Subhas enjoyed

their company and gave them a few lessons in European etiquette. Seeing that they tilted their soup bowl away from them at the dinner table,
he pointed out that this was the British custom. He turned the bowl
toward himself, as was done on the Continent—a simple lesson in not
blindly following the manners taught by their colonial masters.[88] Once
the nephews had returned to the plains, Subhas was once again left
alone with his books and correspondence. On June 30, 1936, he wrote
to the chief secretary of the government of Bengal that Mahatma Gandhi had "expressed a desire to correspond" with him on "non-political
topics like *Khadi, Harijan* movement and village reconstruction." The
governments of Bengal and India deemed these subjects to be "public
affairs" and denied Bose and Gandhi permission to correspond with
each other.[89] A letter dated July 8, 1936, from Nehru to Bose regarding
the formation of the Indian Civil Liberties Union was withheld by the
police.[90] Members of the central legislative assembly, such as S. Satya-
murti and V. V. Giri, kept up a steady barrage of questions about Bose's
health during his continued detention without trial. In reply to a question from Lord Kinoullin in the House of Lords, Lord Zetland said that
"nothing was more distasteful for any administrator than to have to
resort to measures of this kind," but "in India it was unavoidable." Describing Bose as "a man of great ability and possibly of genius," the
secretary of state thought it a pity that "he had always directed his ability to destructive rather than constructive purpose."[91]

From July, Bose was granted special permission to go for walks
within a one-mile radius of the bungalow. "It is of course not much to
be allowed only one mile radius," Emilie commented, "but better than
nothing." He wanted to take photographs of Pagla Jhora, or the "Mad
Waterfall," which was within his walking radius. He acquired a gramo-
phone to keep him company, and asked Emilie to recommend some
good recordings of European music.[92] He requested a long list of political writings and other works from Nehru, including *An Historical Geography of Europe,* by Gordon East; *The Clash of Culture and the Contact of Races,* by George Pitt-Rivers; *A Short History of Our Times,* by
J. A. Spender; and *Daedalus; or, Science and the Future,* by J. B. S. Haldane.[93] In July he was reading Freud's *Interpretation of Dreams* and trying to apply what he read to his own dreams. In Europe he had learned

from Kitty Kurti about Jung's shift of emphasis to the soul from Freud's focus on the sexual instinct, and about Jung's theory of the collective unconscious. He eagerly asked her if she had gone to meet Jung in Switzerland, and what she could tell him about his recent works. He also inquired about her impressions of Freud and his family in Vienna.[94]

All of Bose's letters had to pass through police censors and bear the stamp of approval of the superintendent of police in Darjeeling. Subhas and Emilie used formal modes of address—"Fräulein Schenkl" and "Mr. Bose"—when writing to each other, but still managed to exchange fairly detailed news. Each of Emilie's long letters could cause a welcome break in his "monstrous life" and could take his "thoughts away to Vienna for a while." The letters they exchanged between April and December 1936 touched on a variety of topics—Austrian politics, books, music, the charms of Budapest and Prague, jokes in Viennese cafés, spirituality, and concern for each other's fragile health. In the closest thing to a love letter, he asked Emilie to find the German original of an English translation he sent her of Goethe's poem inspired by Kalidasa's drama *Shakuntala*:

> Wouldst thou the young year's blossoms and the fruits of its decline,
> And all whereby the soul is enraptured, feasted, fed;
> Wouldst thou the heaven and earth in one sole name combine,
> I name thee, oh Shakuntala! And all at once is said.

Subhas noted that Emilie was becoming interested in matters spiritual and received assurances that she was not going to give up the world completely. She reported a funny dream that she was in the Himalayan Mountains, "somewhere high up near the highest summits." Subhas told her that the most important chapter in the *Gita* was the second one, on *karma yoga*, or worship or union with the Beloved through work. Emilie had "not so much affection for Austria" as she should, while Subhas was more of a nationalist and hoped that India, which was doing badly in the 1936 Olympics, would "be able to retain the championship in hockey at least." She enclosed in one of her letters a *Glücksklee*, a four-leafed clover, which would bring him luck. He replied that he had thought there were no superstitions outside India, "because we have bagged the whole lot of them." Subhas wanted to hear the latest jokes in Viennese cafés from Emilie. The new schillings in Austria, Emilie reported, were being made of rubber—they could be stretched, and "if the schilling falls you do not hear it." The two exchanged photographs—or "snaps," as they put it—of their natural surroundings. It was clear that Emilie was the better photographer. As winter enveloped the Himalayas, Subhas's health began to fail again. "I was not at all well and the weather was very disagreeable," Subhas wrote to Emilie on December 15, 1936.[95] Two days later, he was transferred to Calcutta's Medical College Hospital—as a prisoner, of course.

Subhas was glad to be in Calcutta, where the winter was pleasant. The large hospital was located between Calcutta's busy College Street and Central Avenue. The buses, trams, and other motley forms of transport caused a tremendous racket, and patients in pain tended to be noisy in the general ward. After "a long period of isolation," however, Subhas welcomed the proximity of human beings "even when they are noisy."[96] Close relatives were permitted to visit him regularly. He was very happy to receive Rabindranath Tagore's blessings in his own hand, along with a gift of the poet's new collection, *Sanchayita*.[97] Subhas ushered in the New Year, 1937, as an ailing prisoner in the familiar surroundings of his home city.

Meanwhile, the ritual of *Bleigiessen*, performed in Vienna on New Year's Eve, foretold with uncanny accuracy the future of a young Austrian woman whose destiny seemed inextricably linked with the fate of a country she would never see. As Emilie narrated the incident to Subhas: "Then suddenly I had the foolish idea of *Bleigiessen*. It is done in this way. You melt on a spoon some metal (lead) and when it is melted, you pour it into cold water. At once it becomes hard and gets shaped. According to the shape, you foretell the future of the one who has poured this spoonful of metal. I had a very funny thing, looking like the map of India."[98]

Indian newspapers and Subhas's letters were Emilie's only connections with the subcontinent. Another Viennese friend, Hedy Fülöp-Miller, was staying as a guest at Sarat's Woodburn Park home at that time, and visited Subhas in hospital. In a letter from Medical College

Hospital, on February 3, 1937, to Naomi Vetter in Vienna, Subhas wrote: "Lest I forget, may I ask one question. The Indian papers published the news some time ago that Chancellor Schussnig was secretly married at Mariazell some months ago. The news did not come through the regular news agency—so I do not know if it is idle gossiping. Nowadays there is so much idle gossiping going on in Europe about people who are prominent in the public eye."[99] This was not just an innocent query about some idle gossip. The matter of a secret marriage was clearly something that Subhas was weighing in his own mind.

By early March 1937, it was becoming increasingly untenable for the British authorities to continue holding their ailing prisoner in detention. There was some disagreement among Bose's doctors as to whether the source of his health problems was his liver or his lungs. The doctor in charge, Lieutenant Colonel Vere Hodge, was of the opinion that it was an enlarged liver.[100] On the political front, there had been new provincial elections in which the Indian National Congress had done remarkably well with clear majorities in six out of the eleven provinces, and it was well positioned to be able to form governments in two more. In Bengal, the Congress under Sarat Chandra Bose's leadership had won most of the general constituencies, but the constitutional arrangements had provided for many more Muslim reserved seats that were shared by the Krishak Praja party, the Muslim League, and independents.

Prior to the elections, radicals within the Congress—including Jawaharlal Nehru and Subhas Chandra Bose—had been opposed to accepting office in the provinces. After the good showing in the elections, however, the majority opinion within the Congress swung toward forming governments where the party had won the majority of the seats. The Congress was still implacably opposed to the federal part of the Government of India Act of 1935, which had counterposed representatives of the princely states in a future federal assembly, in order to deny elected nationalists from the eleven British Indian provinces a majority at the all-India level. As the British mulled over the possibility of releasing Bose, they were anxious not to let him strengthen Nehru's hand at a Congress meeting slated for March 1937. They also did not want him to influence the formation of the ministry in Bengal.[101] Even though Subhas was opposed, in principle, to accepting office at the provincial level, the Bose brothers soon came to believe that if Congress was going to form governments in provinces where the party had won majorities, then it had to form coalition governments in provinces like Bengal for the sake of Hindu-Muslim unity. Once the stage had been set for a Krishak Praja–Muslim League coalition government in Bengal, with the Congress led by Sarat Chandra Bose cast into the role of the opposition, the governor of Bengal, John Anderson, saw no reason to delay the release of Subhas Chandra Bose.

Around ten o'clock at night, on March 17, 1937, Bose was suddenly released and came home from Medical College Hospital. He promptly informed Emilie of this new development the next day. "My freedom means," he wrote, "that I can move about freely and that my correspondence will not be *officially* censored—though, of course, it will always be secretly censored." In his letter of March 25, 1937, he promised to "try to write a few lines every week," a promise he kept during the next few months, corresponding with Emilie regularly from Calcutta, Lahore, Dalhousie, and Kurseong. His doctors allowed him to attend one public meeting in Calcutta, before sending him off to the hills once more to recoup his health. "Tomorrow there will be a public reception for me," he wrote on April 5, 1937, "and it will be a very big gathering."[102]

The size of the gathering on April 6 probably exceeded Subhas's fondest expectations. Six hundred different associations offered him garlands and bouquets at a huge meeting at Shraddhananda Park in Calcutta, and a message of welcome from Tagore was read out. Subhas felt like "a political Rip Van Winkle." Nevertheless, he visualized a bold strategy of forging "a broad anti-Imperialist front of workers, peasants and middle class" under "the aegis of the Indian National Congress for effecting the political and economic liberation of our hungry and enslaved millions." He sought the forbearance of his supporters, since he needed time "to pick up the old threads, to find my bearings and then to look into the future."[103]

When his friend Dilip had come to see him at his Elgin Road home in late March, Subhas had embraced him and "wept like a child." A misunderstanding that had arisen between them over Sri Aurobindo's renunciation of the world was removed. Dilip was "shocked to see his emaciated frame, though he looked more spiritual than ever."[104] Subhas decided that he would spend a few months with Dr. and Mrs. Dharmavir, whom Subhas and Dilip had known during their student days in England, at the hill resort of Dalhousie in Punjab. En route to Dalhousie from Calcutta in late April, Bose stopped for a few days in Allahabad to meet Mahatma Gandhi, and spent another ten days in Lahore, the capital of Punjab. By May 12, he was ensconced in Dalhousie, where he felt completely at home with the Dharmavirs, just as he had in their Lancashire home years before.[105] He was very affectionate toward their daughters Sita and Leila, and supported Sita in her plans to marry a fellow doctor named Santosh Sen, whom he had known in Austria. In his letters to Sita, who was away from Dalhousie, he gave full vent to both his lighthearted humor and his profound humaneness, as he skillfully persuaded her parents to nurture the young woman's aspirations in her personal life and professional career.[106]

Dalhousie, situated high in the Himalayan range, did not allow Subhas to forget the Austrian Alps. On May 27, he urged Emilie to write a few lines to him every week. "Have you forgotten me?" he asked in German in the middle of this letter in English. "Why do you write so seldom? I wait for your letter—don't you know?" At about this time, he expressed his emotions in a letter written in block letters:

> I have been longing to write to you for some time past—but you can easily understand how difficult it was to write to you about my feelings. I just want to let you know now that I am exactly what I was before, when you knew me. Not a single day passes that I do not think of you. You are with me all the time. I cannot possibly think of anyone else in this world. . . . I cannot tell you how lonely I have been feeling all these months and how sorrowful. Only one thing could make me happy— but I do not know if that is possible. However, I am thinking of it day and night and praying to God to show me the right path.

He asked Emilie to reply in simple German. On June 3, 1937, he asked her in German: "Gracious lady, what will you do in the future?" A week later, he wrote with a sense of relief that he had received her letter the day before and had "understood everything."[107]

"I believe in God," Subhas wrote from Dalhousie to the younger brother of an old college friend, who had asked for advice. "I also believe in prayer," he added, "though I do not do much of it myself." He had been practicing self-assertion, self-analysis, and self-surrender. Self-assertion in the form of peaceful meditation served as an aid to "overcome the human frailties"—lust, anger, temptation, and fear. Self-analysis preceded self-assertion as an effort to inquire into his own mind and identify any weakness. Since the mind was a subtle thing and often deceived itself, continual self-analysis was required as "a daily mental exercise." His study of abnormal psychology and psychopathology had helped him to analyze himself. The practice of self-surrender involved trying to think of "a mighty stream of Divine Energy, something like Bergson's 'élan vital'" and merging his existence in it: "I try to feel that as a result of this merging (or self-surrender), the Divine Energy flows through me and that I am but an instrument in the hands of the Divine. I never consciously pray for anything material. It is mean and sordid. On the contrary, I try to repeat to my mind—'Thy will be done,' in a spirit of self-surrender." The "greatest joy" he had felt, he told his young interlocutor, was in living "a life of uncertainty and adventure—and a life devoted to a cause"; the "greatest pain" had been inflicted by "the behavior of human beings," often friends who had been less than noble. He did not have enough time anymore to pursue his interest in philosophy, but had kept up with psychology. He was now devoted to the study of "political philosophy and international politics."[108]

Upon arrival in Dalhousie in May 1937, Bose had been reading Robert Briffault's *Europa* and Aldous Huxley's novel *Eyeless in Gaza*. He noted the erotic passages in both, and commented that the popularity of Huxley's book in England showed that "even English society is not as prudish and hypocritical as it was before."[109] This was a somewhat odd charge to lay at the door of the English, given Subhas's own prudish past. Leaving novels behind, he focused his reading and writing, during the later months of his sojourn in Dalhousie, on analyses of global politics. In particular, he wrote two very substantial essays on contemporary developments in Europe and East Asia. His article "Europe: Today and Tomorrow," completed in August 1937 and published in the September issue of the *Modern Review,* was an incisive, realist analysis of the shifting configuration of power on the Continent. "If war comes," he argued, "it will come as a result of a German challenge to the status quo in Central and Eastern Europe." "But will it come?" he went on to ask. The answer to that question, he reckoned, rested mainly with Britain. He calculated that Germany was unlikely to repeat "the errors of 1914" and would not launch a war if it knew that Britain would definitely oppose such a belligerent course of action. He conceded, however, that Germany might be "trapped" into a war, as in 1914, "thinking that Britain would keep out of it." His final comment in this essay, on the enigma of the "Russian Colossus," had an uncanny quality about it: "It baffled Napoleon—the conqueror of Europe. Will it baffle Hitler?"[110]

As early as 1934, Subhas Chandra Bose had described Japan as "the British of the East."[111] Japan's invasion of the Chinese mainland in 1937 showed that Asia was as prone to nationalist wars as Europe. In its October 1937 issue, the *Modern Review* carried a long essay by Bose titled "Japan's Role in the Far East," which he had completed in Dalhousie on September 21. In some ways, it offered a remarkably dispassionate analysis of power relations in East Asia. Toward the end of the article, however, Bose did not hesitate to reveal where his sympathies lay. Japan, he conceded, had "done great things for herself and for Asia." He recalled how Japan had been a beacon of inspiration for all of Asia at the dawn of the twentieth century. He welcomed Japan's stance against the Western imperial powers. But, he asked, could not Japan's aims be achieved "without Imperialism, without dismembering the Chinese Republic, without humiliating another proud, cultured and ancient race?" "No," he replied, "with all our admiration for Japan, where such admiration is due, our whole heart goes out to China in her hour of trial." He then went on to draw some ethical lessons for India from the conflict in East Asia. "Standing at the threshold of a new era," he wrote, "let India resolve to aspire after national self-fulfillment in every direction—but not at the expense of other nations and not through the bloody path of self-aggrandizement and imperialism."[112]

These lengthy commentaries on European and Asian affairs were coming from a man who was soon to be at the helm of India's premier nationalist organization. "I shall probably be elected the President of the Indian National Congress early next year," Bose had written to Mrs. Woods in Ireland on September 9, 1937. "The elections (by the party branches) take place early in January, 1938."[113] Gandhi had clearly broached the subject with him by this time. A Gandhian connection to Bose during the summer of 1937 was provided by Miraben (or Madeleine) Slade, the Mahatma's English disciple, who spent two months in Dalhousie as a guest of the Dharmavirs at the same time as Subhas.[114] The Bose brothers offered to host Gandhi and Nehru during an important meeting of the All-India Congress Committee at Calcutta, in late October 1937. Subhas therefore left Dalhousie on October 5, 1937, and after briefly seeing his mother and other relatives in Calcutta, went up to join Sarat in Kurseong to discuss plans for the future.[115] The five months in Dalhousie with the Dharmavirs had done Subhas a world of good. He was now in fighting trim and ready to take on the challenges ahead. At the crack of dawn, he would awaken his nephew Sisir to join him on his six-mile morning walks in Kurseong. The seventeen-year-old Sisir struggled to keep pace as his uncle marched in his majestic swaying gait down from the bungalow on Gidhapahar to Mahanadi—and did an about-face, without a moment's rest, to head back to Kurseong.[116]

From Kurseong, Bose corresponded with Nehru and Tagore about a delicate question touching on Hindu-Muslim relations that was slated to come up at the Congress meeting in Calcutta. In the 1937 provincial elections, the Congress had done remarkably well, while the Muslim League had performed poorly. Even though the two parties had contested the elections on similar platforms, the Congress did not need the League's support to form ministries in areas like the United Provinces. The Congress success on the hustings had emboldened its president, Jawaharlal Nehru, to claim that there were only two parties in India—the British and the Congress—much to the chagrin of Mohammed Ali Jinnah, the leader of the Muslim League. With Congress holding office in seven of the eleven provinces of British India, the League raised the bogey of "Islam in danger." The Congress response was to emphasize the common economic needs and interests of the Hindu and Muslim masses. In addition to material factors, including the relative economic deprivation of Muslims in Bengal, a number of symbolic issues contributed to tensions between religious communities. One of these was the singing of "Bande Mataram," an ode to the motherland, by the Congress on formal political occasions.

The great Bengali writer Bankim Chandra Chattopadhyay had composed this song in 1875 to fill a blank page in his journal, *Bangadarshan*. It began with a lyrical evocation of Bengal's scenic beauty and went on to compare the mother country with the mother goddess Durga. The song was inserted into Bankim's 1882 novel *Ananda Math*, which was thick with anti-Muslim prejudice. Nehru acquired an English translation of the novel, and needed little time to figure out that this background of the song was "likely to irritate the Muslims." Bose could see the element of triumphalism in the singing of "Bande Mataram" in the legislatures, "thereby demonstrating Congress victory." Yet this problematic cultural icon had been sanctified between the late nineteenth century and the 1930s through sacrifice, as Gandhian agitators had withstood baton charges and revolutionaries had gone to the gallows with "Bande Mataram" on their lips. Bose suggested to Nehru that it would be a good idea to seek Rabindranath Tagore's advice on this fraught question, before trying to resolve it at the meeting of the Congress.[117]

In a private letter to Bose, Tagore wrote that the song containing adoration of Durga was hardly appropriate for a national party that aspired to welcome members of all religious communities. "Bengali Hindus have become restless at this debate," he wrote, "but the matter is not confined to the Hindus. Where there are strong feelings on both sides, what is needed is impartial judgment. In our national quest we need peace, unity, good sense—we do not need endless rivalry because of one side's obstinate refusal to yield." Tagore issued a measured press statement explaining his admiration for the feelings of devotion and tenderness, as well as for the evocation of the beauty of *Bharatmata* ("Mother India"), in the first verse of the song. He had no difficulty in detaching this verse from the whole song and the book in which it appeared. He acknowledged that once "Bande Mataram" became a national slogan, many noble friends had made immense, unforgettable sacrifices while uttering it as a *mantra*. At the same time, the entire song and the literary history with which it was entwined were sure to offend Muslims. Tagore argued that the first verse of the song stood on its own and had an inspirational quality that was not offensive to any religious community.[118] The Congress accepted Tagore's sage advice and resolved that only the first part of the song would be performed from now on at national gatherings. Bengal's two luminaries, Rabindranath Tagore and Subhas Chandra Bose, courted a great deal of unpopularity in Bengali Hindu literary and political circles for their decision to abridge the song. Bose did his best to shield Gandhi from this controversy and protected the Mahatma from the ire of Bengali Hindu zealots. "Bande Mataram" lived on as a slogan, but Bankim Chandra Chattopadhyay's equation of mother-nation with mother-goddess was banished from the platform of India's premier nationalist organization.[119]

In late October 1937, the Bose brothers were the cynosure of the anticolonial movement, as the top leadership of the Indian National Congress gathered in Calcutta. At his mother's insistence, Subhas lived at 38/2 Elgin Road, in his late father's room; but he entertained his guests at Sarat's home, 1 Woodburn Park, where Nehru was lodged in his usual room on the ground floor of the three-story house. He and Sarat were exact contemporaries and had developed a good rapport: Sarat had served on the Congress Working Committee during Nehru's presidency in 1936 and 1937 and the two had campaigned together during the 1937 elections. Nehru was an easy guest, though he was heard to complain half in jest: "Sarat Bose's dinners are a nuisance—they never end." A spare eater, he shared his small portions with the children of the family. The entire top floor of the house was given over to Mahatma Gandhi and his entourage. The choicest fruits and vegetables were garnered from Calcutta's markets for the Mahatma's diet, and a large number of goats with jingling bells around their necks were brought to the house every morning so that his secretary could choose the one which would provide Gandhi's milk for the day. The large terrace was used for Gandhi's prayer meetings. In Calcutta, the music was not restricted to his favorite hymns to the god-king Rama, but had a more eclectic range, with the presence of Dilip Kumar Roy and the young sensation Uma Basu, whom Gandhi described as the "nightingale of India." Dilip had often sung devotional and patriotic songs in this house, and the Bose brothers had listened with tears flowing down their cheeks. For Gandhi, one evening, he sang "Abide with Me" and other English prayer music; the Mahatma was deeply moved. Another evening, a troupe from Orissa performed the "Chhow" dance for Gandhi's entertainment. Gandhi signed heaps of autograph books, taking a fee of five rupees per signature for his Harijan Fund for the uplift of the "untouchable" castes. With Gandhi, Nehru, and Bose present in the house, this residential mansion was transformed during the Congress meeting into a public place, with throngs gathered outside and forcing their way inside seeking to catch a glimpse of their beloved leaders.[120]

Beyond the symbolic issue of "Bande Mataram," the question of Bengali political detainees was another explosive political matter that had to be addressed by the Congress leadership. Even though all Gandhian votaries of *satyagraha* had long since been released from jail, thousands of prisoners with alleged revolutionary connections were still being held in detention. Talks between the Bengal Congress and the Krishak Praja party exploring the possibility of a coalition government in Bengal had collapsed in March 1937, because of disagreements over whether to give precedence to the release of political prisoners or to the implementation of a pro-peasant agrarian program. After the breakdown of negotiations with Bengal's Congress leaders, the peasant leader Fazlul Huq had formed a ministry in alliance with the Muslim League. The Congress opposition, led by Sarat Chandra Bose, had been hammering away against the government in the legislature demanding a general amnesty for all political detainees, as well as radical agrarian reforms. In late October 1937, Subhas addressed a large and enthusiastic peasants' rally in Shraddhananda Park in Calcutta, along with N. G. Ranga, the leader of the All-India Kisan Sabha ("Peasants' Association") in the chair. Subhas was helped on the peasant front by the Bengali leader Ashrafuddin Ahmed Chaudhuri, of Tippera district in east Bengal. Bose promised an end to all exploitation, whether by the British or by Indian vested interests. He also presided over a trade union congress being held in Calcutta. On the question of political prisoners,

Gandhi lent a helping hand by taking up their cause with the British governor of the province. From the prisoners, he sought assurances of a commitment to nonviolence, something that Subhas urged his Bengali compatriots to accept. Gandhi's exertions made him very ill; on November 1, his blood pressure rose to dangerously high levels, and his doctors had to struggle to stabilize his condition. A concerned Rabindranath Tagore came to visit. He himself was quite frail, and had to be carried upstairs in a chair by Sarat, Subhas, Jawaharlal, and Gandhi's secretary Mahadev Desai, to see the Mahatma.[121]

"It was utterly impossible for me to think of myself in Calcutta when Gandhiji was there," Subhas wrote, "especially after his own collapse on the 1st of Nov. because we had invited him to tackle the case of about 2,000 imprisoned détenus and political prisoners." By this time, Gandhi had decided—despite the reservations of many Gandhians, including Vallabhbhai Patel—that there really was no one other than Subhas who deserved to become the next president of the Indian National Congress. Gandhi encouraged the stormy petrel of Indian politics to take a break in Europe, before taking up his onerous responsibility in January 1938.[122] On November 4, 1937, Subhas sent a letter to Emilie in German, saying that he would probably travel to Europe in the middle of November. "Please write to Kurhaus Hochland, Badgastein," he instructed her, "and enquire if I (and you also) can stay there." He asked her to mention this message only to her parents, not to reply, and wait for his next airmail letter or telegram. On November 16, he sent a cable: "Starting aeroplane arriving Badgastein twentysecond arrange lodging and meet me station."[123]

On November 18, 1937, the next president of the Indian National Congress boarded a KLM flight in Calcutta, heading for Europe. The Italian police questioned him and searched his luggage once his plane landed in Naples. He lodged a complaint and received an apology from the Italian government.[124] He spent a month and a half—from November 22, 1937, to January 8, 1938—with Emilie at his favorite resort of Badgastein. "It is awfully nice here now," he wrote to Mrs. Dharmavir on December 6, "all white with snow and with it, sunshine. A dry cold, which is so bracing. I have been taking the baths and shall continue with treatment till the end of the month."[125] In ten days, during early

December of 1937, Subhas wrote ten chapters of his unfinished biography, which he wanted to title *An Indian Pilgrim*. Influenced by his reading of psychoanalysis, it was an elegantly written, introspective work which illuminated the process of individuation that was inherent in the phenomenon of anticolonial nationalism. It supplied insights into the roots of his rebellion against all forms of patriarchal authority, and described his search for an ethics founded on the principles of service, self-respect, and sacrifice.[126]

Bose used three notebooks for the manuscript, which he wrote in pencil. This narrative of the first twenty-four years of his life ends abruptly with his resignation from the Indian Civil Service in 1921. Even though he had a contract with a British publisher, his inability to complete the work because of the call of duty meant that his account of the pilgrim's progress would not be published in his lifetime. The outline he made on the first page of his original manuscript makes clear that he had intended to take the story of his life all the way to 1937.[127] He was quite candid as he related the inner struggle he endured in seeking the right path and in identifying the mission of his life. In his adolescence and youth, he had tried very hard to sublimate or transcend the sexual impulse. "As I have gradually turned from a purely spiritual ideal to a life of social service," he clarified in a footnote, "my views on sex have undergone transformation."[128] His admirers' overemphasis on values and attitudes he held very early in his life has contributed to misconceptions about Subhas's asceticism.

In addition to a chronologically arranged analytical narrative, Bose had planned to discuss his fundamental beliefs in three chapters titled "My Faith—Philosophical," "My Faith—Political," and "My Faith—Economic." These were to form the final chapters of his autobiography; he completed only the first of them during his stay in Badgastein. "Why do I believe in Spirit?" he asked in his essay on his philosophical faith. He answered that for him it was a "pragmatic necessity," demanded by his nature, his vision of purpose and design in nature, his growing perception of his mission in life, and his feeling that he was "not a mere conglomeration of atoms." Reality, too, seemed to him more than a "fortuitous combination of molecules." He was interested in the ultimate nature of reality because, when analyzing experience, one had to posit the self—"the mind which receives"—and the nonself—"the source of all impressions." The nonself—"reality apart from the self"— was there underlying human experience, and on "our conception of it depends much that is of theoretical and practical value to us." It was important to try to fathom reality's meaning, even if one could aspire only to relative knowledge of it, falling well short of absolute truth.

For Subhas, "the essential nature of reality" was "Love," which he regarded as "the essence of the Universe" and "the essential principle in human life." He had arrived at this faith through a combination of rational study, intuition, and pragmatic considerations. "I see all around me," he wrote, "the play of love; I perceive within me the same instinct; I feel that I must love in order to fulfill myself and I need love as the basic principle on which to reconstruct life." He explained the existence of much in life that was opposed to love by invoking a dynamic process of the unfolding of reality. "Reality, therefore, is Spirit," he concluded, "the essence of which is Love, gradually unfolding itself in an eternal play of conflicting forces and their solutions."[129]

It was more than just love in the abstract that pervaded his life during the six weeks Subhas and Emilie spent in Badgastein during the bright winter of 1937. His friend and colleague A. C. N. Nambiar, the singer Hedy Fülöp-Miller, and nephew Amiya came for brief visits. The photographer and filmmaker A. K. Chettiar, then making the first documentary on Gandhi, spent a week in snowy Badgastein, ensuring that there would be a visual record of a key moment in Subhas's personal life. Like so many Indians, Chettiar was starry-eyed in his admiration of Bose, and could hardly believe his good fortune in meeting the charismatic leader at such close quarters. He was touched by Bose's kindness in looking after him when his fingers became cold and numb as he was trying to take pictures. Chettiar described a sleigh ride they all took to a neighboring town, to buy his return ticket to Rome. Bose insisted on walking back by himself in the snow. His companions were worried, but held him in such awe that they dared not question his decision. They waited anxiously until he returned hale and hearty to Badgastein, well after dark.[130]

On December 26, 1937, Subhas Chandra Bose secretly married Emilie Schenkl. Despite the obvious anguish, they chose to keep their rela-

tionship and marriage a closely guarded secret. Emilie's explanation
was simple. "Country came first" for Subhas, and any public announcement at that stage would have caused unnecessary "upheaval."[131] Badgastein was more important in Bose's life than simply the place where
he wrote his autobiography. It was the place where he forged a relationship of rare beauty, high purpose, and, in the end, deep tragedy. In the
Austrian mountains outside Salzburg, he was making a private commitment to the woman he loved, a commitment he could only redeem
in public once he had done his duty by his country, his "first love."
Emilie brought to the relationship her qualities of enormous courage,
utmost dignity, and spirit of high sacrifice. Did the fact that Emilie was
European have anything to do with the decision to keep the marriage a
secret? She had once called him *pranadhik*—a Bengali term meaning
"more precious than my own life"—tutored no doubt by Subhas in the
nuances of selfless love. Europeans have a "different tradition," he had
said, and asked, "Why should you love me more than your own life?"
Yet he had chosen to transcend the differences of countries and traditions, habits and customs, in order to love the woman in her, the soul
in her. He had quoted to her Goethe's translation of the ode to Shakuntala, by the ancient Indian poet Kalidasa. Their love was all about
translation. Goethe was the one German poet who evoked "die ewige
Weibliche"—"the eternal feminine"—and its uplifting qualities. In *The
Merchant of Venice* (Act 5, scene 1), Shakespeare had depicted a marriage that would not be allowed to fail in the act of translation between
black and white, two cultures, Lorenzo and Jessica, Christian and Jew:

> Sit Jessica: look how the floor of heaven
> Is thick inlaid with patines of bright gold;
> There's not the smallest orb, which thou behold'st.
> But in his motion like an angel sings,
> Still quiring to young-eyed cherubins:
> Such harmony is in immortal souls;
> But whilst this muddy vesture of decay
> Doth grossly close it in, we cannot hear it.

To a literary scholar eavesdropping on their conversations, there could
be no doubt that Subhas and Emilie "heard the music of the Spheres."

"You are the first woman I have loved," Subhas had written to her. "God grant that you may also be the last. Adieu, my dearest." His prayer was granted.[132]

"I am now having coffee at this Munich station with some Indian friends," Subhas wrote to Emilie on January 8, 1938. "All well." He had come by train from Salzburg to Munich, and was waiting to take the train to Brussels. On January 9, in Antwerp, he went with friends to see a film on Charles Parnell, the late-nineteenth-century nationalist leader of Ireland, and afterward he recommended it to Emilie. His friends took him by car to Ostend for the Channel crossing to England.[133] On November 25, 1937, Bose had written from Badgastein to Lord Zetland, the British secretary of state for India, asking him to lift the ban on his entry to England.[134] The British government had obliged by quietly withdrawing the legally nonexistent ban on the man who was soon to become the Congress president. Sixteen and a half years after he had left the shores of Britain, following his resignation from the Indian Civil Service, Bose returned to a warm and enthusiastic welcome. Representatives of a wide array of Indian associations gave him a reception at Victoria Station. The stationmaster personally escorted him from the train to the waiting car, which was flying the Congress's tricolor flag. A hundred journalists had gathered at a West End hotel for a press conference. Bose fielded their questions "coolly, adroitly and with the greatest good humor."[135]

"I have been frightfully busy these days," Subhas informed Emilie on January 16, 1938, "and so could not write."[136] In all his meetings, Bose urged the British to drop their scheme of future federation with the princes. India wanted and deserved to frame its own democratic constitution. If the British allowed that to happen, he saw "no reason why India and Britain should not be the best of friends." At a reception held in his honor at the Saint Pancras Town Hall on January 11, he told his audience that "India's destiny" was "bound up with the rest of humanity," and that the Congress was beginning to realize that "India's struggle for freedom, democracy and socialism was part of the world struggle." In his address, he specifically mentioned China, Abyssinia, and Spain, where a civil war was raging.[137] "My personal view today," Bose said in an interview to Rajani Palme Dutt, a leftist Indian intellectual, "is that the Indian National Congress should be organized on the broadest anti-imperialist front, and should have the two-fold objective of winning political freedom and the establishment of a socialist regime." Dutt pressed him on his references to fascism and his criticisms of communism in the closing part of his book *The Indian Struggle.* Bose explained that what he really meant was that, having won national freedom, India should "move in the direction of Socialism." He conceded that perhaps the expression he used—"a synthesis between Communism and Fascism"—was "not a happy one." At the time he wrote his book, "Fascism had not started on its imperialist expedition" and "Communism as it appeared to be demonstrated by many of those who were supposed to stand for it in India" seemed to him to be "antinational." It was clear to him that the situation had "fundamentally altered," and he always understood and was quite satisfied that the writings of Marx and Lenin, as well as the official statements of policy of the Communist International, gave "full support to the struggle for national independence."[138] If the communists were ready to support the forces of socialism in Europe and nationalism in the colonized world, he was prepared to welcome them.

Lord Zetland, the secretary of state for India and a former governor of Bengal, pursued Bose's views on communism during their one-on-one meeting. Bose dismissed the possibility of a communist form of government in India and told Zetland that "the actual number of genuine communists was small." "He was himself a socialist," Zetland noted, "but that was a very different thing from being a communist." Bose's meeting with Zetland was quite cordial, and the Congress leader appeared to have made a favorable impression on the cabinet minister in charge of India, even though Zetland believed Bose had some "fixed ideas." This was to be expected, as Bose was staunchly opposed to the federal part of the Government of India Act of 1935, denounced reactionary princes, and objected to Britain's exclusive control over India's defense. He also felt that provincial autonomy was hedged with too many emergency powers in British hands, and he was critical of British divide-and-rule tactics.[139]

In addition to Lord Zetland, Bose met Lord Halifax, the Conservative leader of the House of Lords, who as Lord Irwin had served as viceroy of India. He also held talks with Clement Attlee, then leader of the Labour opposition in the House of Commons, and other Labour party leaders, including Stafford Cripps, George Lansbury, and Arthur Greenwood. He was clear, however, that India would have to win independence and could not expect it as a gift from a future Labour government. In London, he exchanged views with a range of prominent political philosophers and constitutional experts, such as Harold Laski, J. B. S. Haldane, and Ivor Jennings. In those discussions, he consistently pointed out the deficiencies of the 1935 constitution that had to be remedied. He made a day trip to his alma mater, Cambridge, where he had lunch and tea with Masters and Fellows of a number of Cambridge colleges, and addressed a well-attended meeting of faculty and students. To maintain bipartisanship in his dealings with political leaders and academics, he visited Oxford the next day. He discussed politics with G. D. H. Cole and had dinner with Gilbert Murray, seeking to create a broad constituency of support among British intellectuals for rapid progress toward Indian self-rule. He was diplomatic and tactful in his conversations about the path forward, while being firm in his demands for complete independence.[140]

On his arrival in London, Bose had been described by one newspaper as "India's de Valera."[141] From Badgastein he had written to Mrs. Woods expressing his wish to make a flying visit to Dublin from London in order to see de Valera.[142] As it happened, the Irish leader was in London to hold negotiations with the British government about certain outstanding issues following the transformation of the Irish Free State into the Republic of Eire. At midnight on January 15–16, 1938, Bose met de Valera and had a "long talk" in which they reportedly "discussed the political destinies of India and Eire in detail."[143] When to fight and when to negotiate was something that Bose was constantly trying to learn from the example, both positive and negative, of Irish history.

As he concluded his visit to Britain, on January 18, 1938, Acharya J. B. Kripalani, general secretary, announced in India that Subhas Chandra Bose had been duly elected president of the Indian National Congress. Bose's own assessment, as he communicated it privately to Naomi Vetter on January 21, was that his visit was "a great success from every point of view."[144] His British hosts were pleasantly surprised when they encountered the man whom they had been taught for a decade and a half to regard as a dangerous revolutionary. "English people who met Bose for the first time," wrote the *Manchester Guardian,* "were impressed alike by his pleasant, quiet manner and the decisiveness with which he discussed Indian affairs."[145]

On January 19, Bose left London for Prague, where he had a meeting with President Edouard Benes. "Please buy the two watches in steel about which you enquired," Subhas had written to Emilie on January 16 from London, "the Diplomat no. C.K. 124 and the doctor's watch no. 651 Square—both Omega. The lady's watch (Longines) you cannot get there—I understand." These were their wedding gifts, which they would exchange before he returned to India. He asked her to meet him at the Vienna airport on the morning of January 20, during his brief stopover from Prague to Rome. He cabled again from Prague on January 19: "Buy two watches meet aerodrome." After their airport rendezvous, he wrote to her from Rome on January 20 saying that he had arrived safely and was on the verge of leaving for Naples. He wrote again the next day from Athens: "I am writing to you again today because I have a little time in hand and because I shall have no time when I reach India." Asking her not to worry about "imaginary things" if he was unable to write regularly from India, he continued on his eastward flight.[146]

After a night stop in Basra, Bose arrived in Karachi on January 23, 1938, his forty-first birthday. Upon arrival, he was "curiously asked" by someone whether he was thinking of "entering into matrimony"; he reportedly replied, "I have no time to think of that."[147] Another night halt in Jodhpur, and he was back in Calcutta on the morning of January 24. He sent two telegrams in quick succession to Emilie that day. "Safe," said the first; "heartfelt condolence," said the second—Emilie's father had suddenly passed away. "I am terribly grieved," Subhas wrote to her on January 25, "to have the sad news of your father's death. Please let me know at once how this happened. It is so sudden! So awful!"[148] By this time, Subhas was in the tumult of India's anticolonial politics. He could do no more than express his sympathy from afar. The call of public duty left little time for either private joy or private grief.

5

The Warrior and the Saint

Your strength has been sorely taxed by imprisonment, banishment and disease, but rather than impairing, these have helped to broaden your sympathies—enlarging your vision so as to embrace the vast perspectives of history beyond any narrow limits of territory.

—RABINDRANATH TAGORE on Subhas Chandra Bose, January 1939

In February 1938, the revolutionary leader from Bengal came to preside over the fifty-first session of the Indian National Congress in Gujarat. His arrival in the home province of the apostle of nonviolence carried powerful symbolic meaning. It represented the meeting of two generations and the merging of two strands of the anticolonial movement that had been often at odds with each other. Subhas Chandra Bose was taken to the Congress venue, located in the rural setting of Haripura, in a chariot drawn by fifty-one white bulls. The spectacle connected agrarian and urban India and evoked an idyllic past portending a dynamic future. Seeing Gandhi and Bose in earnest conversation on the dais, at the plenary session of the Congress, warmed the hearts of millions of Indians looking forward to a united nationalist stand against the British raj. As Aurobindo Ghose had argued in his essay "The Morality of Boycott" three decades before, in the pursuit of justice and righteousness the saint's holiness had to be complemented by the warrior's sword.[1] Much like Aurobindo, Bose had agreed to eschew violence as a strategic necessity, though not on grounds of political morality. The warrior and saint were thus able, for the time being, to share a platform against the British raj.

The differences of perspective between Bose and Gandhi were not limited to what each considered legitimate methods of anticolonial struggle. Bose's dream of a modern industrial future for free India was at variance with Gandhi's utopia: a *Ramrajya,* an earthly kingdom of the righteous epic hero Ram based on self-governing and largely self-sufficient village communities. Yet it was quite possible that their commonalities in the anti-imperialist effort, and a sense of mutual respect and affection despite their differences, would enable them to work together in relative accord. The situation was complicated, however, by the followers of Gandhi in the upper echelons of the Congress party organization, the Congress ministries in the provinces, and the party's financial supporters from India's capitalist class. Even if Bose made every effort to accommodate Gandhi and abide by his deeply held wishes, the Mahatma's loyal lieutenants could never quite accept the Bengali radical leader as one of their own. Much depended on which way Jawaharlal Nehru would lean—toward the left, with his political principles in Bose's support, or toward the right, out of deference to Gandhi. For some time, Nehru and Bose had been representing the broad radical tendency within the Congress, though they had refrained from forming a group of their own. Others, including Jai Prakash Narayan, had set up a Congress socialist party in 1934 to act as a lobby within the larger nationalist organization. M. N. Roy had been disillusioned with communism and represented another leftist force preaching radical humanism. The Communist party of India, founded in 1920, was from the mid-1930s working in concert with the Congress under the "National Front" rubric, much the way communist parties in Europe were forging popular fronts with their social democratic allies. The possibilities were numerous.

Gandhi Maharaj ("Great King Gandhi") had wisely decided not to play King Canute to the rising leftist tide within the Congress. Instead, he hoped to contain, control, and channel it by anointing first Jawaharlal Nehru and then Subhas Chandra Bose as Congress president. The chief of the premier nationalist party was by now called Rashtrapati ("Head of State") and accorded the reverence due that august post by the nationalist public. In 1936 and 1937, Nehru had experienced many conflicts with members of the fifteen-member Congress Work-

ing Committee, the top decision-making body of the Congress. He had
on occasion threatened resignation, but ultimately fell into line at Gandhi's behest. Unquestioning obedience to patriarchal authority of any
kind was anathema to Bose; he had rejected it over and over again since
he was fifteen years old. The Mahatma would find it much harder to
tame the fiery spirit of this rebellious son.

India Freed Means Humanity Saved

On January 28, 1938, soon after his return from Europe, Bose had to
rush to the Bengal provincial conference being held at Bishnupur, in
Bankura district. It was a star-studded gathering, at which Bose was
joined by M. N. Roy and his wife, Ellen Roy, as well as by Sarojini
Naidu. On January 31, he left for Gandhi's abode in Wardha for a
meeting of the Congress Working Committee, in preparation for the
annual session.[2] After coming back to Calcutta, he had barely a couple
of days to write his presidential address, before boarding the train for
Haripura on February 11. Closeted in his bedroom at 38/2 Elgin Road
for two days, he wrote out his mammoth speech in a single draft. The
pages were couriered to Sarat Chandra Bose's secretary at 1 Woodburn
Park, to be typed up. Once Sarat's talented assistant Nirad C. Chaudhuri had cast an eye over the typescript, it was sent to the printer. The
printed version was not yet ready when Subhas left Calcutta, and it had
to be dispatched to Haripura the next day. Bose's entourage included
his elderly mother, a number of other close relatives, and several political associates.[3] Subhas had very much wanted his second mother, Basanti Devi, to come with him, but she was unable to make the trip.
"The man at whose feet I learnt politics is not with us today," he wrote
to C. R. Das's widow. "How happy he would be if he was with us."[4] For
the first time since the Deshbandhu had presided over the Gaya session
of the Congress in 1922, a leader from Bengal had been elected president of the Indian National Congress.

After crossing the entire subcontinent from east to west, Subhas
Chandra Bose alighted from the train at Bardoli, which had been a
storm center of peasant agitation in Gujarat. From there, he traveled by
car to Haripura and was carried in a ceremonial chariot to the complex

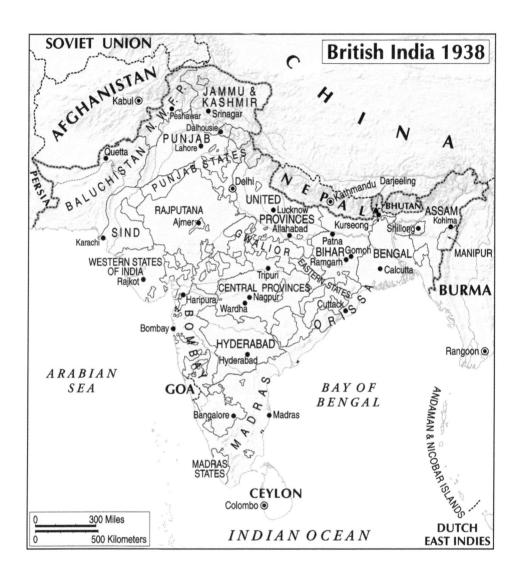

that had been built to host the Congress session. It took two hours for
the procession to travel the distance of two miles as the- rural folk of
Gujarat gave Subhas a rapturous welcome. The temporary complex,
designed to accommodate 50,000 residents and 200,000 daily visitors,
had been named Vithal-nagar after Vallabhbhai Patel's elder brother,
with whom Subhas had worked closely in Europe. The structures made

of bamboo, wooden rafters, and date mats were supplied with all the modern amenities: water, drainage, electricity, telephones, and postal service. The public and private spaces of the Congress venue were embellished with a couple of hundred painted posters depicting Indian rural life, eighty-six of them by the famous painter Nandalal Bose. This was a creative display of the popular culture of mass nationalism. "Following the *pat* style," Nandalal Bose later recalled, "we did a large number of paintings and hung them everywhere—on the main entrance, inside the volunteers' camps, even in the rooms meant for Bapuji [Mahatma Gandhi] and Subhasbabu [Netaji Subhas Chandra Bose], the President."[5] On reaching Vithal-nagar, Bose hoisted the Indian tricolor flag and proclaimed: "There is no power on earth that can keep India enslaved anymore. India shall be free."[6]

Subhas Chandra Bose assumed the post of Congress president as soon as his predecessor, Jawaharlal Nehru, placed around his neck the Rashtrapati's green cloth garland with saffron and white stripes. He gave several formal and informal speeches in fluent English and halting Hindustani, and conducted the open session of the Congress with aplomb. His lengthy and weighty presidential address articulated his vision of the climactic phase of the freedom struggle and the socioeconomic reconstruction of free India. It was the most important, most detailed political speech that he would ever deliver in India. He began with an incisive analysis of the strengths and weaknesses of Britain's global imperialism. For someone who had suffered grievously at British hands, his address was remarkably devoid of rancor toward the colonial masters. He challenged them to transform their empire into a "federation of free nations," not unlike the Commonwealth that eventually came into being after 1947. Quoting Lenin on how "reaction in Britain is strengthened and fed by the enslavement of a number of nations," he claimed that those who were battling for India's freedom and that of other countries enslaved by the British Empire were "incidentally fighting for the economic emancipation of the British people as well." "Once we have real self-determination," he argued, holding out an olive branch, "there is no reason why we should not enter into the most cordial relations with the British people."[7]

While cautioning his compatriots against accepting colonial consti-

tutional devices designed to divide and deflect the anticolonial movement, Bose was perceptive enough to see that "the policy of divide and
rule" was "by no means an unmixed blessing for the ruling power." He
believed the "principle of partition" was ingrained in the "juxtaposition
of autocratic princes and democratically elected representatives of British India." He therefore called for uncompromising opposition to the
federal part of the Government of India Act of 1935, even while urging
the Congress provincial ministries to "change the composition and
character of the bureaucracy." If the scheme of federation with the 565
princely states got rejected, he suspected that the British would "seek
some other constitutional device for partitioning India and thereby
neutralizing the transference of power to the Indian people." At the
same time, however, he could see Britain getting "caught in the meshes
of her own political dualism" flowing from divisive policies based on
religious and sectarian affiliations in India, Palestine, Egypt, Iraq, and
Ireland. It was important, then, for Indian nationalists to address the
minorities question in India. Bose urged a policy of "live and let live in
matters religious and an understanding in matters economic and political." He did not, interestingly enough, use the term "secularism" in
his broad-minded approach to the problem of religious difference. He
knew that religious faith was important to most Indians and advocated
equal respect for all communities, rather than a hard separation of religion and politics. He also wanted justice for the "depressed classes"—
India's erstwhile untouchable castes.

While advocating "cultural autonomy for the different linguistic
areas," Bose suggested accepting Hindustani—a blend of Hindi and
Urdu—as the lingua franca. He wanted to allow "the fullest latitude"
for the use of both the Devanagari and Arabic-Persian scripts, but considered the adoption of the Roman script as "the wisest solution in the
long run." He had been converted to this idea during his visit to Turkey
in 1934. The ambition of unifying India through "a strong central government" had to be balanced, in his view, by the need "to put all the
minority communities as well as the provinces at their ease, by allowing them a large measure of autonomy in cultural as well as governmental affairs."[8] This vision was a stretch removed from the monolithic
nationalism insisted on by some of the other leaders of the Congress,

including Nehru and Patel, who from their different ideological stand-points increasingly evinced scant respect for the expression of cultural difference. Bose, from the beginning, believed that India's future depended on ensuring the dignity of all minorities: multiple identities were not an obstacle to achieving an overarching national unity.

If Indians were prepared to fight for freedom, Bose was convinced that it would come in the foreseeable future. In anticipation of the winning of independence, he outlined, in the course of his Haripura address, his "long-period program for a Free India." The "first problem to tackle," he believed, was the "increasing population."⁹ He was the first among the front-ranking political leaders of India to advocate a policy of population control. The previous year, he had commented to the young doctor Sita Dharmavir: "What you wrote about the babies interested me greatly. I also think that Indians bring too many babies into the world, and all for what? To die because few of them grow up as adults. That brings us to the question of population control, which is absolutely essential for India. Mahatma Gandhi says self-control is very good indeed, if people will oblige him by being so reasonable."¹⁰ At Haripura, he did not want to get into "the theoretical question as to whether India is over-populated or not." He simply thought it "desirable to restrict our population until we are able to feed, clothe and educate those who already exist." This was an issue that he wanted to make the focus of public attention and an educational campaign.¹¹

So far as "reconstruction" after colonial rule was concerned, the "principal problem" would be "how to eradicate poverty from our country." That would "require a radical reform of our land system, including the abolition of landlordism." The drying up of rural credit during the Depression decade had compounded the problem of peasant debt. "Agricultural indebtedness," in Bose's view, would "have to be liquidated and provision made for cheap credit for the rural population." There were limits, however, to focusing on agriculture. In order to "solve the economic problem," agricultural improvement would "not be enough" and an ambitious plan for state-led industrial development would have to be crafted. "However much we may dislike modern industrialism and condemn the evils which follow in its train," Bose declared, alluding to Gandhi's concerns, "we cannot go back to the preindustrial era, even if we desire to do so." The state in independent India would, "on the advice of a planning commission," be called upon "to adopt a comprehensive scheme for gradually socializing our entire agricultural and industrial system in the spheres of both production and appropriation."[12]

Bose visualized a key role for the Congress in the task of national reconstruction and believed, unlike Gandhi, that the party could not be expected to wither away after freedom was won. The "existence of multiple parties and the democratic basis of the Congress Party," he said trustingly, would "prevent the future Indian state becoming a totalitarian one." Intra-party democracy would serve to "ensure that leaders are not thrust upon the people from above, but elected from below."[13] Subsequent developments would soon reveal that Bose's views regarding the Congress party's commitment to internal democracy were overly optimistic. His clear opinion in favor of the Congress's granting collective affiliation to peasants' and workers' organizations was not shared by several of his colleagues, who represented the interests of landowners and industrialists in the Congress leadership.[14]

Bose and Nehru were the only two leaders to take a genuine interest in international relations. Toward the end of his Haripura address, Bose dealt with the foreign policy of a subject nation and urged the Congress to be poised to take advantage of the international situation. India's foreign policy should not, he argued, "be influenced by the internal politics of any country or the form of its state." Every country had men and women sympathetic to the cause of Indian freedom, and he wanted to mobilize their support systematically. He made a strong case for extending India's soft power through vigorous cultural diplomacy. He did not like the word "propaganda," because of the "air of falsity" about it; but he insisted on spreading knowledge about India across the globe. He wished to see trusted representatives of the Congress appointed in all continents, near and distant, and felt it was a pity that Central and South America, where there was deep interest in India, had been neglected so far. He concluded by underscoring the global significance of India's freedom: "Ours is a struggle not only against British Imperialism but against world Imperialism as well, of which the former is the keystone. We are, therefore, fighting not for the cause of India alone but of humanity as well. India freed means humanity saved."[15]

Bose's performance at Haripura was a triumph. Clad in the traditional spotless white Bengali *dhoti* and *punjabi* made of *khadi,* and swathed in a white Kashmiri shawl with a delicate embroidered border, he exuded confidence and impressed everyone with his quiet authority. On formal occasions, he donned a white Gandhi cap. At Badgastein he had told A. K. Chettiar that he did not smile on demand when asked to pose for the camera; at Haripura he smiled spontaneously. When he asked the poor and obscure to come forward with their poverty and obscurity for the service of the motherland, they heard a voice of sincerity and were ready to respond.[16] Bose and the ordinary foot soldiers of the Indian struggle carried the message of freedom from Haripura across the subcontinent. After leaving Haripura on February 23, Bose's first crowded stop was the great metropolis on India's west coast, where he paused for about ten days. "Bombay gave me a magnificent reception," he reported happily to Emilie.[17] For the rest of the year, Bose was constantly on the move, traversing the country by train and plane. The Congress Working Committee usually met every couple of months in Wardha, for Gandhi's convenience. The Congress's permanent secretariat, run by J. B. Kripalani, was located in Allahabad, Nehru's hometown. Bose was based in Calcutta, but the whole of India was his political stage.

Bose's international stature at this time was high. He was well known on the continent of Europe and in Ireland, and had impressed his interlocutors in England on the eve of taking up the Congress presidency. He had never visited the United States, though he appeared on the cover of *Time* magazine on March 7, 1938. Below his garlanded form, which was photographed in color, ran a caption quoting from his speech: "Britain has ruined India economically, politically, culturally and spiritually." The story, titled "Chariot of Freedom," struck a rather supercilious tone in discussing both Gandhi and Bose. "Alumnus Bose" of Cambridge University was so impressed reading an appeal by "Saint Gandhi," *Time* reported, that he had given up his civil service post seventeen years before and had spent most of his time in jail. Upon his release from jail, he had made a "clearly seditious" speech to an audience of Indian students in London, but "His Majesty's Government were not going to add to their present worries by having a London bobby arrest the Indian President just before his Congress of 200,000 met." There followed a description of his arrival at the Indian National Congress venue—the fifty-one bulls adorned with gold leaf and bells drawing "a single chariot in which, beaming through his horn-rimmed glasses, rode Congress President Subhas Bose." "Among the slick, top handful of Congress politicians, most of them obviously enjoying the incense of power and prestige," the *Time* story conceded, "Subhas Bose stands out."[18]

Throughout 1938, Subhas Chandra Bose worked tirelessly to implement most of the items on his Haripura agenda. In May, as a first step toward drawing up a blueprint for the socioeconomic reconstruction of India, he convened in Bombay a conference of the heads of the seven Congress provincial ministries. In addition to these leaders, several ministers and members of the Congress Working Committee were in attendance. The meeting discussed the challenges of industrial reconstruction, development of power resources, and coordination among the Congress-ruled provinces. Bose's own priorities were made clear in a speech he gave to the Bombay municipality at the same time as the conference. While the better and richer parts of Bombay compared well with the most advanced cities of the world, he wanted to train a spotlight on poverty and the slums inhabited by the poor. A modern municipality, in his view, had to provide primary education and health care, with particular attention to the problems of infant mortality and maternal health. While battling to wrest power from British hands at the center, Bose urged the Congress governments in provinces and cities to do their best for the underdogs of society.[19]

Bose was also keen to plan ahead for the time when Indians would wield power at the all-India center. He held meetings with leaders of the scientific community and sought the advice of the renowned scientist Meghnad Saha, who was a regular visitor at his Calcutta home. In August 1938, during a conversation with Saha at a meeting of the Indian Science News Association, Bose called for "far-reaching cooperation between science and politics." Saha tried to put him on the spot by asking a loaded question: "May I enquire whether the India of the future is going to revive the philosophy of village life, of the bullock-cart, thereby perpetuating servitude, or is she going to be a modern industrial nation which, having developed all her natural resources, will solve the problems of poverty, ignorance and defense and will take an honored place in the comity of nations and begin a new cycle in civilization?" Bose answered truthfully: there was some difference of opinion in the Congress on this question, but "the rising generation" were in favor of industrialization. It was deemed essential for solving the problem of unemployment, establishing socialism, competing with foreign industries, and raising the standard of living of the populace. Bose admired Saha's journal *Science and Culture* for its articles on electric power supply, flood control, and river physics. He recognized the need for a permanent National Research Council and a thorough economic survey to generate data for the National Planning Commission.[20]

After further consultation at Congress Working Committee meetings, Bose organized a conference of industries ministers from Congress-ruled provinces in Delhi on October 2, 1938—Mahatma Gandhi's birthday. The goal he set for the Congress was to see that "everybody—man, woman and child, is better clothed, better educated and has sufficient leisure for recreation and for cultural activity." India, Bose noted, had "resources similar to those of the United States of America." What was required was the intelligent and equitable utilization of these resources in the best interests of the nation. He did not see any inevitable conflict between cottage industries and large-scale industries. He reassured Gandhi and Gandhians that he firmly believed in developing cottage industries, but felt it was necessary to embrace the idea of industrialization.[21] Bose's potential ally in this endeavor, Jawaharlal Nehru, was away in Europe for six months during 1938. "You cannot imagine how I have missed you all these months," Subhas wrote to Jawahar on October 19, 1938, in Spain. He recognized the valuable work Nehru was doing in Europe—the sort he himself had done to win supporters of Indian independence abroad. Bose needed Nehru in India, however, as he moved to announce the formation of the National Planning Committee. "I hope you will accept the Chairmanship of the Planning Committee," Subhas wrote. "You must if it is to be a success."[22]

After Nehru's return from Europe in November, Bose was ready to launch the National Planning Committee. Its first meeting was held in Bombay on December 17, 1938. Inaugurating the work of the committee, Bose argued that there could be symbiosis between state planning for heavy industries and private entrepreneurship in setting up light industries and stimulating the revival of cottage industries. He wanted the committee to pay urgent attention to the building of infrastructure, especially in power and communications. He was quite ecumenical in the composition of the committee, choosing representatives of industry and labor and eminent persons from different walks of life. He picked his good friend the scientist Meghnad Saha, but also accommodated J. C. Kumarappa, a Gandhian purist opposed to large-scale industrialization. "The work of the National Planning Committee which you entrusted to me last year grows bigger and bigger and takes up a great deal of time and energy," Jawahar wrote to Subhas months later. "It is exhausting business."[23] Both Nehru and Bose clearly found this kind of constructive work exhilarating, if exhausting. Bose showed far-sightedness during his term as Congress president in pioneering an institutional innovation that became the foundation for India's economic-development efforts for decades to come.

"I have some important work in Bombay," Subhas had written on May 9, 1938. "(1) To discuss with Mr. Jinnah the proposal for Hindu-Muslim understanding, (2) to preside over the Conference of the Prime Ministers of seven provinces, (3) to preside over the meeting of the Congress Working Committee."[24] An improvement in relations between religious communities was an issue high on Bose's list of priorities in 1938. Bose had long believed that Hindu-Muslim unity was not only vital for the anticolonial struggle but that in free India there should be an equitable dispersal of power among religious and linguistic communities. On May 14, 1938, Subhas Chandra Bose, president of the Indian National Congress, called on Mohammed Ali Jinnah, president of the All-India Muslim League, at his elegant Malabar Hill residence in Bombay. Seated on a sofa in front of a book-lined shelf, Bose in his

Bengali garb presented a contrast to Jinnah, attired in his Savile Row suit and Oxford shoes. The meeting was cordial enough, as Bose began a fresh attempt to negotiate a settlement of the Hindu-Muslim question.

In this instance, Bose discovered that his friend Jawaharlal Nehru had complicated the negotiations for him. His predecessor as Congress president had arrogantly proclaimed after the 1937 elections that there were only two parties in India: the British and the Congress. Nehru had looked "through the telescope," the Muslim League leader had been told, for a Hindu-Muslim problem—but "if there is nothing, what can you see?"[25] Jinnah now aspired to be the "sole spokesman" of India's Muslims.[26] He insisted that the Muslim League be recognized as the authoritative and representative organization of the Muslims of India: this had to be the basis for any substantive negotiations between the Congress and the League. The Congress felt it could not possibly accept the implication that it was merely a "communal" organization. "Is it not enough," Bose pleaded with Jinnah on July 25, 1938, "that the Congress is not only willing but eager to establish the friendliest relations with the League and come to an honorable understanding on the much vexed Hindu-Muslim question?" On August 2, Jinnah replied that while the League was "equally anxious" for a settlement, it felt the need to "inform the Congress of the basis on which negotiations between the two organizations should proceed" since the "very existence" of the League had been called into question by Nehru. The exchanges of 1938 foundered on the inability of the Congress and the League to agree on the "basis" for negotiations. After the Congress Working Committee had considered the issue at Wardha, from December 11 to December 16, 1938, Bose wrote to Jinnah abandoning the effort he had commenced on May 14.[27] This was a great pity. Had substantive talks been held, Jinnah might have found in Bose a Congress president willing to share power with the League in key provinces and at the all-India level in the future. As it happened, the two parties were at odds about who they represented and who could speak for the Muslims of India.

As Congress president, Bose tried hard to work in cooperation with Gandhi and sought to carry the Congress Working Committee with him on important matters. Despite Bose's ideological sympathy with the socialists, he tried to maintain a stance of neutrality and fairness in dealing with the left and right wings of the party. The two sides had a serious argument at a meeting of the All-India Congress Committee in late September 1938. The followers of Gandhi proposed a resolution saying that some left-leaning Congressmen were fomenting class war in the name of defending civil liberties, and reaffirmed the Congress's unequivocal support of life and property. Bose, in his presidential role, allowed everyone full freedom of expression, as even Gandhi acknowledged. The radicals, who believed in the equitable redistribution of property, brought amendments to the conservative resolution. Upon being defeated in the voting on these amendments, the members of the Congress socialist party staged a dramatic walkout. Gandhi was mightily annoyed, and said that those who had walked out should permanently leave the Congress if they could not abide by basic principles accepted by the majority. Bose stayed with Gandhi on this occasion, even though later the Congress right wing did not appreciate the middle ground that he had occupied as president.[28]

Bose had also sided with Gandhi in dealing with a ministerial crisis in the Central Provinces in July and August of 1938. This large administrative unit in the middle of India had Marathi-speaking and Hindi-speaking areas. A Marathi-speaker, N. B. Khare, had become the Congress premier in 1937, and he accused the Congress's central leadership of backing the rival Hindi-speaking faction led by D. P. Mishra in 1938. What seems to have influenced Bose in taking Gandhi's side in this dispute was Khare's decision to hobnob with the British governor in seeking to outdo his rivals. Khare later claimed that Bose had sympathized with him. The records of the time, however, make clear that Bose as Congress president worked with Gandhi and the Congress Working Committee to discipline Khare and install a new Congress ministry under a new premier. Whatever his commitments to regional rights, Bose would have no truck with the official representatives of the British Empire in India's provinces.[29]

It was his staunch opposition to British constitutional maneuvering to retain power that led Bose to issue a couple of stiff statements warning against any compromise on the scheme of federation with the princely states. The British media had been reporting back-channel negotiations between the Congress and the British government on this question. Bose said that he did not believe any influential Congress leader was negotiating behind the back of the Congress. He added that weakness shown by any section of the Congress would "amount to treachery of the first magnitude to the cause of India's freedom." He stood for "open, unmitigated and unrelenting opposition to the monstrous Federal Scheme," and would relieve himself of "the trammels of office" if "the unthinkable contingency" of a majority in the Congress accepting that scheme ever came to pass. Members of the right wing of the Congress questioned the need to issue such an aggressive statement, and criticized what they described as a threat to walk out of the Congress. Bose insisted that his statement was issued not a day too soon and was "nothing more than a forceful exposition of the Congress view on federation." Nothing would ever make him give up the Congress, which was like the "very breath" of his life, and he hoped Congressmen would not reduce themselves to "parliamentary busybodies" and do nothing to "whittle down our national demand." He was confident that British imperialism could no longer ignore the national demand of a united and renascent India.[30]

In order for the Congress to be able to present a united national demand to the British, Bose believed at least one of two conditions had to be met: a settlement with the Muslim League at the all-India level, or coalition governments with Congress participation in most, if not all, of the Muslim-majority provinces. When Bose assumed the presidency of the Congress, the party governed seven of the eleven provinces of British India. The four exceptions were Punjab and Sind in the northwest, and Bengal and Assam in the east. Bose had been opposed in principle to office acceptance in 1937; but in the absence of a mass *satyagraha* campaign, and given the decision to form ministries in seven provinces, he felt that coalition provinces in the remaining provinces would improve Hindu-Muslim relations and strengthen nationalist resistance to British rule. As Congress president, Bose was instrumental in ousting the Muslim League ministry headed by Muhammad Saadullah and installing the Congress-led coalition government led by Gopinath Bardoloi in Assam. That gave the Congress party control of government ministries in eight out of the eleven provinces. In Punjab, the pro-British government of the Unionist party was well ensconced based on the electoral support of landlords and rich farmers, and there was little that the Congress could do to dislodge it. Neither the Congress nor the Muslim League had done well in Sind. Here, Bose determined that the best bet was to lend Congress support to a government led by a regional political leader Allah Bux.

The problems attendant on forming provincial coalitions can be seen more closely in the Bose brothers' efforts to work out an arrangement in their home province of Bengal. Subhas and Sarat Chandra Bose were thwarted in their attempts by the Congress central leadership, popularly referred to as the Congress High Command, and by Gandhi himself, acting under the dubious influence of the industrial magnate Ghanashyam Das Birla and a political broker named Nalini Ranjan Sarker, who represented the interests of big business. When Fazlul Huq, in 1937, had formed a government of his Krishak Praja party (KPP) allied with the Muslim League, he had included as many as eight landlords in his eleven-member ministry. There was only one KPP representative other than Huq himself, contending with four Muslim Leaguers, three non-Congress caste Hindus, and two non-Congress scheduled caste nominees.[31] The Bengal Congress, led by Sarat Chandra Bose, kept bringing radical amendments to tenancy legislation that would give rights to those at the bottom of the agrarian hierarchy and prepared the ground for an alliance with the bulk of the Krishak Praja party, which enjoyed strong support among the Muslim peasantry. In August 1937, Sarat wrote to Jawaharlal Nehru indicating that as many as twenty to twenty-five KPP legislators were on his side. All that he needed from the then Congress president was an announcement that the Working Committee would authorize alliances with like-minded groups. He complained about the mischief being done by Nalini Ranjan Sarker, a minister who had "sedulously spread the report that the Working Committee will, in no event, sanction alliances and that has had the effect of isolating the Congress party."[32] By March 1938, as many as thirty-four out of the original thirty-six KPP members of the Bengal legislative assembly sat with the Congress opposition led by Sarat Chandra Bose. The government survived divisions in the assembly during voting on several occasions during 1938, only with the support of twenty-three European members.[33]

Toward the close of the year, a nod from Gandhi was required for the Bose brothers to attempt the formation of a broad-based coalition government in Bengal with Hindu and Muslim support. Thus, a letter to Subhas on December 18, 1938, which Gandhi dictated in the presence of Birla, Sarker, and Abul Kalam Azad, came as a bombshell. Birla carried the letter from Wardha to Calcutta. In it, Gandhi claimed that "we shall lose much by including Congressmen in the ministry" and made it clear that he wanted the status quo in Bengal to continue. "Your letter has given rise to a crisis," Bose wrote in reply, "in which it is necessary for me to speak very frankly and I crave your pardon at the outset for doing so." Even in early December 1938, Gandhi had given the clear impression that he supported the idea of a coalition ministry for Bengal. Bose was furious that he attached "more value and importance to the views of those three gentlemen [Azad, Birla, and Sarker] than to the views of those who are responsible for running the Congress organization in Bengal." Birla was a financial patron of the Gandhian Congress, and carried clout. "It has astonished me," Bose wrote in reply to Gandhi, "that you did not feel it necessary to even consult me before you arrived at a decision on such a serious matter." He urged Gandhi to reconsider the matter, and refused to be party to a policy he described as "suicidal" for Bengal.[34]

Congress participation in coalition governments in the Muslim-majority provinces, Bose believed, would strengthen the party in speaking with the British. He clearly spelled out to Gandhi what he saw as the need of the hour:

> While endeavoring to bring about a Coalition Ministry in the remaining three provinces, we should lose no time in announcing our decision on the various Hindu-Muslim problems that would have come up for discussion if negotiations had taken place between the Congress and the Muslim League. Simultaneously, we should hold an enquiry into the grievances of the Muslims against the Congress Governments. These two steps will help to satisfy reasonable Muslims that we are anx-

ious to understand their complaints and to remedy them as far as hu-
manly possible.[35]

A proposal to launch an inquiry into the conduct of Congress ministries in the Hindu-majority provinces was a red flag to the right wing
of the party comfortably enjoying the fruits of office. In addressing the
intertwined challenges to the construction of an all-India nationalism
presented by affiliations of religious community and linguistic region,
Bose's approach was significantly different from that of most others in
the Congress leadership, as well as substantially more generous.

As Congress president, Bose pursued the deep interest in international affairs he had developed during his European exile. He sent a
Congress medical mission to China as a symbol of solidarity against
Japanese aggression. He encouraged cultural troupes, such as the danc-
ers Uday Shankar and Amala Shankar, to visit Europe and disseminate
Indian arts. He closely monitored political and military developments
in Europe as the Third Reich spread its tentacles, and he sharply criticized the British and French betrayal of Czechoslovakia in 1938. On the
death of Kemal Atatürk in November 1938, he held up the father of
modern Turkey as "a magnificent example of the dictum that those
who strive for liberty and win it should also put into effect the program of post-war reconstruction."[36] By the end of the year, he had
come to the conclusion that the international situation was favorable
for launching another mass movement against colonial rule. As rising
tensions in Europe kept Britain off balance, Bose believed India should
press its own national demand for independence.

Amid hectic political activity at the helm of the Indian National
Congress, Bose seemed to be both healthy and happy during 1938. In
mid-year, at Wardha, the Mahatma found Subhas "looking a picture of
health." "All he needed was work of the type he loves," Gandhi wrote.
"He has got it and he is happy."[37] This was a partially accurate assessment of Bose's state of mind. He was certainly in better health than he
had been since the mid-1920s, even though he had a bout of influenza
and was struck down by malaria in October. In March, he had served as
an advocate for Sita Dharmavir with her parents, so that she could
marry the man of her choice.[38] Yet his own emotional life left behind in

Austrian exile was cause for a measure of wistfulness. He wrote regularly to Emilie on trains as he traveled across the subcontinent. He repeated in a series of letters that he thought of her day and night. The more personal comments and endearments for his "Liebling" tended to be in German, tucked away inside letters written in English. "I feel completely lonely all the time," he wrote from Wardha on October 17, 1938, "even though I work hard day and night." On December 26, 1938, he was in Bombay, but surely could not forget Badgastein. "Today is your birthday," he wrote to Emilie. "I wish you all the best in the world and pray that you may have happiness and peace in the service of mankind—as well as the fulfillment of your heart's desires."[39]

While Bose was in the foreground of Indian nationalist politics, Emilie and his love for her were relegated to the background. There was never any question of priorities for the man. Indian independence came first. Only after that could Bose pursue his own emotional longings. By December 1938, he reported to Emilie the possibility of an impending political crisis.

The Parting of the Ways

In late November and early December 1938, Bose had been touring the United Provinces, Punjab, and Sind. "It is doubtful if I shall be reelected President for the coming year," he wrote to Emilie during a night halt in Jodhpur on December 6, 1938, as he flew from Karachi to Calcutta. "Many people," he explained, "are jealous of me."[40] Besides the personal factor, Bose's political program of uncompromising anticolonialism and socialist reconstruction of free India placed him at odds with Gandhi and the majority of his colleagues on the Working Committee. Led by Vallabhbhai Patel, they found him too aggressive and arrogant. He was obstinate about rejecting the federal part of the 1935 Act in its entirety, and completely stubborn in opposing any compromise with the British raj. So the Congress right wing vehemently opposed his reelection as Congress president. Rabindranath Tagore wrote to Gandhi and Nehru urging them to reelect Subhas Chandra Bose. As Tagore saw it, there were only two "modernists" among the Congress leaders: Nehru and Bose. Since Nehru was serving as the chairman of the National Planning Committee, Tagore wanted to see Bose once more as Congress president.[41] Gandhi was unimpressed by the poet's foray into politics and chose to ignore his recommendation.

Abul Kalam Azad was the old guard's first choice as the next president, but Azad wisely considered discretion to be the better part of valor. Since he was unwilling to enter the fray against Bose, a small coterie within the Working Committee, in consultation with Gandhi, set up another member of the High Command, Pattabhi Sitaramayya of Andhra, as their nominee. Bose remained insistent that a leftist, such as Acharya Narendra Dev, should be Congress president; but as he could not find anyone unanimously acceptable, he decided to run for election himself. Gandhi had been quite satisfied with Bose's fairness when the socialists had walked out of an AICC meeting in September. Patel, however, seemed to nurse a grievance about the episode and complained that Bose had favored the unruly leftists. Bose—differing sharply with Gandhi on this point—had advocated a coalition government in Bengal; this was opposed by G. D. Birla, a powerful financial backer of the Gandhian Congress who was wary about taking too radical a stance against the British raj. The socialist agenda of the National Planning Committee incensed leaders of the right wing of the Congress. K. M. Munshi, a close friend of Patel, complained to Gandhi that Bose was seeking German help against the British. A conversation with some German businessmen in December was misreported as a conspiratorial meeting with the German consul aimed at fomenting anger against the British. As it happened, Bose had been critical of German policies in the course of that conversation.[42]

In his private correspondence, Bose sounded remarkably detached about the prospects of his reelection as Congress president. "Though there is a very general desire for my re-election," he wrote on January 4, 1939, "I do not think I will be again President. In a way, it will be good not to be President again. I shall then be more free and have more time to myself."[43] In December 1938, Rabindranath Tagore had written about his wish to honor Bose at a public reception in Calcutta. He was delighted when Subhas decided to visit him in Santiniketan during a quiet moment after the "din and bustle" of the traditional winter fair.[44] Subhas had been doing something unthinkable since 1920: challenging the unquestioned authority of Gandhi in Congress affairs. This did not worry Tagore. On January 21, 1939, the poet welcomed the rebel president of the Congress in the mango grove at his abode of peace. In reply to his welcoming address, Subhas said: "Those of us who spend most of our time in the political life of the country feel very deeply about the poverty of the inner life. We want the inspiration of the treasure that enriches the mind without which no man or nation can rise to great heights. We seek that inspiration from you."[45] For the next year and half, Tagore would continue to be a rock of support for Bose during his travails. Bose enjoyed the brief respite from Congress politics in the idyllic setting of Tagore's university, and mingled happily with Nanda-lal Bose's art students.

The presidential election debate turned quite nasty in late January. Patel cabled Sarat Chandra Bose, his Working Committee colleague for the previous three years, saying that Subhas's reelection was unnecessary and that members of the Working Committee would issue a statement supporting Sitaramayya. Sarat replied that Working Committee colleagues ought to avoid taking sides, and expressed the view that Sitaramayya would not inspire confidence in the coming fight against the British raj. Patel responded saying that Subhas's "re-election is held to be harmful to country's cause," much to the chagrin of the Bose brothers. The press statements and counter-statements, as part of the election campaign, dealt primarily with two issues: the attitude toward the British scheme of federation with the princes, and the question of intra-party democracy within the Congress. When Bose pointed out the widespread belief in the "prospect of a compromise on the Federal Scheme between the right-wing of the Congress and the British government," he was accused of casting an "aspersion" on his colleagues. He was correct in suspecting that informal talks were being held between top British officials and a number of congressmen close to Patel on possibly accepting an amended version of the federal part of the Government of India Act of 1935. G. D. Birla, the industrial tycoon close to the Congress right wing, had been hinting that such a deal was possible. Since Bose was unable to supply hard evidence at the time to substantiate his charge, the "aspersion affair" was not allowed to die down even after the election was over. Bose claimed that Patel wanted the Congress president to be a mere tool in the hands of the Working Committee. On the question of intra-party democracy, he was of the opinion that "to have a proper election of the delegates and not nomination by a group within the Working Committee," it was "essential that the delegates have a free and unfettered choice." "If this freedom is not guaranteed to them," he warned, "then the constitution of the Congress will cease to be a democratic one."[46]

The democratic verdict of the delegates from the provinces, after an unprecedented electoral contest, was delivered on January 29, 1939. Subhas sipped tea in a relaxed mood at a party to celebrate the wedding of Sarat's eldest son, and commented on the early trends as the results from different parts of the country started pouring in. As the outcome became clearer, he moved to 38/2 Elgin Road. "We are winning" rather than "I am winning" is what he told visitors and callers on the telephone.[47] The final tally showed that Subhas Chandra Bose had emerged victorious by 1,580 votes to Pattabhi Sitaramayya's 1,375. As was to be expected, Bengal had voted decisively for Bose, while Gujarat and Andhra had gone Sitaramayya's way. Among the major provinces, Bose had carried the United Provinces, Punjab, and Assam in the north, and Karnataka, Kerala, and Tamil Nadu in the south.[48] The regional spread of his support was impressive. The Bose headquarters were flooded with congratulatory telegrams from all parts of the country.[49] For the first time in two decades Gandhi's authority had been successfully challenged within the Indian National Congress.

The Mahatma was not pleased at this turn of events. Since he had been "instrumental in inducing Dr. Pattabhi not to withdraw his name as a candidate," he acknowledged on January 31 that "the defeat is more mine than his." It was clear to him that the delegates did "not approve of the principles and policy" for which he stood. "I rejoice in this defeat," proclaimed Gandhi. And then with uncharacteristic peevishness, he added: "After all, Subhas *babu* is not an enemy of his country. He has suffered for it." Bose, in his public response on February 4, said he was pained to see that Mahatma Gandhi had taken the election result as "a personal defeat," and he would "respectfully differ" on that point. Though he had occasionally disagreed with Gandhi on public questions, he would "yield to none" in his respect for the Mahatma. "It will always be my aim and object," he promised, "to try and win his confidence[,] for the simple reason that it will be a tragic thing for me if I succeed in winning the confidence of other people but fail to win the confidence of India's greatest man."[50]

Bose wanted to bury the recent past and shake hands after a vigorous, sportsmanlike contest. He seemed to believe that the controversies during the heat of the electoral battle could be left behind and an understanding reached with Gandhi, whom he distinguished from Gandhi's lieutenants. M. N. Roy had a more acute reading of the Mahatma's mood. He wrote to Bose that he looked upon Gandhi's statement as "a declaration of war which may be waged in true Gandhian fashion, namely, non-cooperation[,] which, under the given relation of forces inside the Congress, can only be willful sabotage for discrediting yourself and your supporters." Gandhi had clearly implied that there was no room at the helm of the Congress for both Bose and those who had opposed him. In Roy's view, the "logical conclusion of that unreasonableness" was that Bose must sacrifice himself for the cause: the unity of Congress under Gandhi's leadership.[51]

"Did you rejoice over my victory?" Subhas asked Emilie on February 11, 1939. Gandhi and his lieutenants had "opposed" him and Nehru had been "indifferent." "The result of the election is a great victory for me," he wrote. "The whole country is full of excitement over the election, but a terrible responsibility has come on my shoulders." He wanted to deliberate carefully on how best to shoulder that responsibility. He did not wish to split the Congress if he could possibly avoid it, and was reluctant to move ahead without Gandhi's support. For someone who was usually decisive and sure of his course, he now evinced great uncertainty: "I don't know what I should do in the future," he wrote to Emilie. "Please tell me what I should do."[52]

Bose headed to Wardha for a meeting with Gandhi. He hoped that a face-to-face meeting would clear the air, but no breakthrough was achieved during their talks on February 15. On his way back by train to Calcutta the next day, Bose fell ill with a high fever. When he asked for a slight postponement of the Congress Working Committee scheduled for February 22, Vallabhbhai Patel led all the members—except for Jawaharlal Nehru and Sarat Chandra Bose—to resign. Nehru issued an ambiguous separate statement, which led many to believe that he too had joined Patel in leaving the Working Committee. The battle lines were now being drawn, to determine who should form the new Congress Working Committee—the elected president or the Mahatma, whose word had been law in the party until very recently.

Though he had pneumonia in both lungs, Bose decided to defy his doctors' orders and attend the annual session of the Congress at Tripuri in the Central Provinces. He traveled by train from Calcutta to Jubbulpore, where on March 6 he was taken by stretcher to an ambulance and transported to the Congress venue. His political opponents had so assiduously spread the rumor that he was faking his illness that even the doctors at Tripuri were surprised to find him genuinely ill.[53] Despite his fever of 103 degrees, Bose managed to welcome a fraternal delegation from Egypt and preside over a meeting of the Subjects' Committee. He was too ill to deliver his presidential address, which had to be read by Sarat. The speech was much shorter than the one he had delivered at Haripura.

In his Tripuri address, Bose called upon the Congress to submit its national demand in the form of an ultimatum to the British government and to incite mass civil disobedience if no satisfactory reply was forthcoming. He anticipated war in Europe in about six months. He wanted the Congress to guide the popular movements in the princely states "on a comprehensive and systematic basis," rather than making efforts that were of a "piecemeal nature." Gandhi had absented himself from the Congress session at Tripuri and was occupying himself with the politics of Rajkot, a tiny princely state in western India; he even went on a fast in support of civil liberties in that autocratic enclave. He wanted the British viceroy, Linlithgow, to introduce a semblance of representative government, which was being fiercely resisted by the ruler and the minorities. Bose deplored Gandhi's focus on one small princely fiefdom, where Patel's followers were angling for power. Bose believed in a coordinated policy to promote democracy in the 565-odd states that acknowledged British paramountcy. He was as unequivocal as before on the need for "close co-operation with all the anti-imperialist organizations in the country, particularly the *Kisan* [peasant] movement and the Trade Union movement."[54]

At Tripuri, the right wing of the Congress struck a calculated politi-cal blow in their campaign to avenge their defeat in the presidential election. They proposed a resolution—put forward by Govind Ballabh Pant, the Congress premier of the United Provinces—that "the Con-gress executive should command [Gandhiji's] implicit confidence and requests the President to nominate the Working Committee in accor-dance with the wishes of Gandhiji." The bulk of the Congress left wing, including M. N. Roy's radical democratic party and the communists using the "National Front" label, opposed the Pant resolution. The Congress socialist party, however, dithered and abstained, and so the resolution passed. It left the Congress president shackled to the wishes of the Mahatma, if the latter agreed to give expression to them. Quite apart from the specific resolution, the atmosphere at Tripuri was so suffused with the spirit of vendetta that Bose left the place with "a loathing and disgust for politics."[55]

From Tripuri, Bose left for a place called Jamadoba (near Dhanbad, in Bihar) for a period of convalescence. "At the last Congress session," Tagore wrote to the Mahatma on March 29, 1939, "some rude hands have deeply hurt Bengal with an ungracious persistence[.] Please apply without delay balm to the wound with your own kind hands and pre-vent it from festering." Gandhi replied that the poet had set before him a difficult problem.[56] Gandhi at this time was living in Birla's house in Delhi and was engrossed with the Rajkot affair. "I suggest your coming here and living with me," Gandhi wrote to Bose. "I undertake to nurse you to health while we are slowly conferring." Bose did not accept the offer to reside in Birla's house, and in any case Gandhi left for Rajkot after a few days. The task of consulting him on the formation of a new Working Committee was carried out by correspondence in late March and early April of 1939. "I am temperamentally not a vindictive per-son," Bose explained to Gandhi, "and I do not nurse grievances. In a way, I have the mentality of a boxer—that is, to shake hands smilingly when the boxing bout is over and take the result in a sporting spirit." All he wanted was to see the Mahatma renew the struggle for *swaraj*. If he could give the British an ultimatum over Rajkot, why couldn't he do the same with India's national demand? Gandhi disagreed with Bose's view that the country was more nonviolent than ever before; he could "smell violence in the air." He conceded that he was "an old man, per-haps growing timid and over-cautious," while Bose had the "reckless optimism born of youth." Yet he believed that Congress "cannot offer civil disobedience worth the name." If Bose was right about the coun-try being ready for a new struggle, then Gandhi felt that he himself was "a back number and played out as the generalissimo of Satyagraha."[57]

Not ready to be turned back so easily, Subhas thought it was a "mag-nificent idea" to have a "heart-to-heart talk" between the leaders of the two wings of the party, as the Mahatma had suggested to Sarat. Their points of agreement, in Bose's view, outweighed their points of dis-agreement. Besides, Bose suggested to Gandhi, "there is a world of dif-ference between yourself and your lieutenants, even your chosen lieu-tenants. There are people who will do anything for you—but not for them." He added innocently, "There was no quarrel between yourself and myself." He was glad Gandhi had written that their "private rela-tions will not suffer," whatever else happened. Bose believed in the Deshbandhu's saying: "Life is larger than politics."[58]

So far as politics was concerned, Bose preferred a "composite" cabi-net drawn from the various strands of nationalist politics. Gandhi went on asking him to go ahead with a "homogeneous" cabinet of those who happened to be in a majority. In a classic maneuver of noncooperation, Gandhi refused to suggest any names for the Working Committee and urged Bose to form his own executive. This, as Bose pointed out, might be acting "in accordance with Gandhiji's wishes," but could not result in an executive that commanded Gandhi's "implicit confidence," as the Pant resolution demanded. "The more I study it [Pant's resolution]," Gandhi replied disingenuously, "the more I dislike it." Although Bose's own predilection was to include half of the members from each of the two wings of the party, he was prepared by mid-April to let Gandhi nominate the entire Working Committee in an attempt to resolve the crisis. If Gandhi refused to do so, Bose wondered whether the All-India Congress Committee might elect the Working Committee.[59] A call for more democracy within the Congress was certain to leave Gandhi's fol-lowers unmoved at this critical moment, when their standing had been undermined through an election.

While showing utmost respect toward the saint, the warrior took up his pen and used it like a sword against his leftist comrade Jawaharlal Nehru. On March 28, 1939, Subhas wrote a "brutally frank" letter that strongly reproached his friend and that ran to twenty-seven closely typed pages. Ever since being released from internment, he had treated Nehru "with the utmost regard and consideration, in private life and in public," and looked upon him "as politically an elder brother and leader" whose advice he often sought. But the "elder brother" had taken up the cudgels on behalf of his political opponents when the election result was not seen in a sporting light, and "the spirit of vendetta set to work." Throughout the crisis Nehru had sought to play a mediating role, keeping at least a slight distance from the joint machinations of members of the Working Committee led by Patel. "When a crisis comes," Bose wrote to Nehru in a sharp rebuke, "you often do not succeed in making up your mind one way or the other—with the result that to the public you appear as if you are riding two horses." The "devil" who had been reelected president—despite the opposition of the biggest leaders, including Gandhi, and of several provincial governments—must have some "saving grace" and must have served the country well as president "to be able to draw so many votes." Nehru had accused him of using the political language of left versus right in the Congress, but had used the same terminology throughout his years as president. Bose had a clear policy to "force the issue of Swaraj with the British Government," while Nehru had none. Nehru had said that autocracy in Rajkot and Jaipur would cast every other issue into the shade. In Bose's view, if the Congress pursued a "piecemeal, tinkering and nibbling policy" in relation to the princely states, it would take 250 years to win civil liberty and responsible government for them. If Nehru was vague about internal policy, Bose described Nehru's views on international affairs as "nebulous." "Frothy sentiments and pious platitudes," Subhas told Jawahar with disdain, "do not make foreign policy." He charged the "elder brother" with holding a doctrinaire view on coalition governments and advised him to tour Assam before pronouncing on that question again. "Regarding Bengal," Bose commented, "I am afraid you know practically nothing." In the upper echelons of the Congress, Patel and others had a technique of dealing with Nehru: "They would let you talk and talk," Bose charged, "and they would ultimately finish up by asking you to draft their resolution." Bose was relentless in his critique. "The unity that we strive for or maintain," he said in conclusion, "must be the unity of action and not the unity of inaction."[60] Bose was certainly too harsh and perhaps unfair in his criticism of Nehru's vacillation at this decisive moment. But years later, Nehru was to confess in his interviews with Taya Zinkin that in 1939 he had "agreed with" what Subhas was trying to do but had "let him down."[61]

For the moment, Subhas's plain speaking with Jawahar produced better results than his pleading with the Mahatma. After being hit by the long missive, Jawahar hastened to reply on April 3. Regarding the many failings that Subhas had listed, he had little to say. "I plead guilty to them," he wrote, "well realizing that I have the misfortune to possess them." He appreciated the "truth of the remark" that Subhas had treated him well, and he was grateful for it. Personally, he professed "regard and affection" for Subhas, though sometimes he did not at all like what the younger colleague did or how he did it. Nehru took pains to explain his various statements and actions. He ended on a rather melancholy note: he was an "unsatisfactory human being" who was "dissatisfied with himself and the world, and whom the petty world he lives in does not particularly like."[62] Subhas's withering attack did seem to have shaken him up. Soon after this exchange, Nehru argued Bose's brief with Gandhi. "Subhas has numerous failings," Nehru urged Gandhi, "but he is susceptible to a friendly approach." He clearly expressed the view that the Mahatma should accept Subhas as president. "To try to push him out," Nehru felt, with his concern for democratic norms, "seems to me to be an exceedingly wrong step." He accepted that the composition of the Working Committee was for Gandhi to decide, but the "idea of homogeneity" on which the Mahatma was insisting would "not lead to peace or effective working."[63]

If Nehru was riding two horses, Rabindranath Tagore had evidently decided which horse he wanted to bet on. He had been to Calcutta in late March and early April, and had been able to gauge the "mental attitude" of his countrymen. On April 3, he wrote to Subhas with some earnest political advice:

The whole country is waiting for you—if you lose this favorable chance through hesitation you will never get it back. You will be deprived of the strength that you may get from Bengal, on the other hand the other side will all the time try to sap your strength. Do not by any means commit this big mistake. I am saying this not for your own sake but for the sake of the country. Please demand firmly of Mahatmaji to let you have his final answer at an early date. If he procrastinates then you may give up your post on that ground.[64]

On April 15, Subhas wrote to Jawahar that he planned to make "a last effort at settlement through a personal talk with Gandhiji." Their recent duel via marathon letters notwithstanding, Bose wanted Nehru's advice on how to proceed. "Will it be possible for you to run up here for a few hours?" he asked Jawahar from Jamadoba. "I cannot say no to you," Jawahar replied on April 17; and when the two met on April 19, there was no bitterness. "Jawahar was here yesterday," Subhas wrote to the Mahatma on April 20. "We had a long discussion on the present situation. I was glad to find that our views concurred."[65]

Gandhi's obduracy could not be broken, however. The Mahatma arrived in Sodepur near Calcutta on April 27, after suffering a political defeat at Rajkot. He held two days of direct talks with Bose. Gandhi had sensibly asked Patel to stay away from Calcutta. Nehru, who as usual was staying at 1 Woodburn Park as Sarat's guest, joined the conversations. Gandhi continued to refuse to suggest names for the Working Committee, saying that would mean an "imposition" on Bose.[66] Once it was clear that an impasse had been reached, Bose submitted his resignation as Congress president, "in an entirely helpful spirit," at the meeting of the All-India Congress Committee in Calcutta on April 29, 1939.[67] Nehru brought a resolution asking the AICC not to accept Bose's resignation; he called upon Bose to renominate the old Working Committee and nominate two new members of his choice to fill vacancies. Since Bose wanted a more representative Working Committee than that, Nehru withdrew his resolution and Bose's resignation took effect. A Gandhian, Rajendra Prasad, was asked to serve as interim president. Tension was running high outside the meeting venue in Wellington Square, in central Calcutta. Bose had to escort his colleagues out of the meeting and protect them from the ire of the crowd that had gathered in his support.

Bose was comprehensively outwitted and outmaneuvered by Gandhi in Congress politics during the spring of 1939. Tripuri and its aftermath clearly represented a defeat for Bose, who—notwithstanding his personal popularity—was temperamentally and organizationally incapable of matching the political cunning of Gandhi and his lieutenants. Yet Gandhi emerged from the tussle of 1939 with his aura tarnished. He had appeared petty and vindictive in the face of a youthful challenge. Bose's conduct, by contrast, won the approbation of no less a figure than Rabindranath Tagore, who sent a warm message: "The dignity and forbearance, which you have shown in the midst of a most aggravating situation, has won my admiration and confidence in your leadership. The same perfect decorum has still to be maintained by Bengal for the sake of her own self-respect and thereby to help turn your apparent defeat into a permanent victory."[68]

Robbed of the presidency by the Mahatma, the Deshbandhu's political disciple had been, unbeknownst to him, given the appellation "Deshnayak" ("Leader of the Country") by "Gurudev," the "Revered Teacher," as Tagore was called by his admirers, including Gandhi. Even though the public reception Tagore had planned for Bose in February was postponed, the poet had already composed his "Deshnayak" address in January 1939. "As Bengal's poet," Tagore wrote with his usual literary flair: "I invite you to the honored seat of the leader of the people. We have the sacred assurance of the Gita that from time to time the Divine champion of the good arises to challenge the reign of the evil. When misfortune from all directions swarms to attack the living spirit of the nation, its anguished cry calls forth from its own being the liberator to its rescue." Tagore confessed he had felt "misgivings" in the uncertain dawn of Subhas Chandra's "political *Sadhana* [quest]." But now that he was revealed in the "pure light of midday sun," there was no room for any doubt. Tagore was not setting up the warrior in counterpoise to the saint. "Let nobody make such a grievous mistake as to think," he cautioned, "that, in foolish pride of narrow provincialism, I desire to see Bengal as an entity separate from the rest of India, or dream of setting in my own province a rival throne to the one on which is seated a majestic figure representing a new age in the political history of the world." Yet he saw Subhas Chandra as the "deliverer" who would claim of his countrymen "the resoluteness, the unyielding will to live and to conquer strengthened by the inspiration" of his own life. "I may not join him in the fight that is to come," the seventy-eight-year-old poet wrote in conclusion. "I can only bless him and take my leave knowing that he has made his country's burden of sorrow his own, that his final reward is fast coming as his country's freedom."[69]

Besides earning Tagore's blessing, Bose had also inspired a "genuine feeling of sympathy and affection" in a very large number of common people. In an article titled "My Strange Illness," he mentioned the letters, telegrams, parcels, packets of medicine, flowers, and amulets he had received:

> I was trying to analyze the above writers and senders according to their religious faith, and I found that every religious denomination was represented. And not only every religious denomination, but every system of medicine (all the "pathies," if I may use the word) and both the sexes! Hindus, Muslims, Christians, Parsis, etc.—Allopaths, Homeopaths, Vaids, Hakims, Naturopaths, Astrologers, etc.—men and women —all have been writing to me, giving me their advice and sometimes also samples of medicines and amulets.

It was this outpouring of love and concern that restored Bose's faith after he had been subjected to the "morally sickening atmosphere of Tripuri." "This is the India," he reassured himself, "for which one toils and suffers. This is the India for which one can even lay down [one's] life. This is the real India in which one can have undying faith, no matter what Tripuri says or does."[70]

My Conscience Is My Own

"India is a strange land," Subhas wrote to Emilie in June 1939, "where people are loved not because they have power, but because they give up power. For instance, at Lahore I had a warmer welcome this time than when I went last year as Congress President." He was confident that he had lost nothing by resigning and had, in fact, gained in popularity. As a price of his popularity, his wallet—containing Emilie's recent letter and photograph—was picked from his pocket while he was surrounded by a big crowd at Lahore.[71]

Within a week of resigning, Bose had proposed the formation of the "Forward Bloc" within the Congress to serve as a forum for the more radical elements in the party. He considered this bloc to be an integral part of the Congress, and his political aim was to convert the majority within the Congress to a radical point of view. He sought to provide the Indian people with an alternative leadership at the national level in place of the old guard, represented by the Congress High Command. This alternative was based on a commitment to uncompromising anti-imperialism in the current phase of Indian politics and undiluted socialism once freedom was achieved.

In trying to bring the Indian National Congress round to a more militant program, Bose differed from some leftist leaders such as M. N. Roy, who wanted a clean break with the Congress. His position was also at variance with other self-proclaimed leftists, who in the name of unity would not risk putting pressure on the existing Congress leadership to move in the direction of greater democracy. Bose's initial hope had been that all left-leaning political forces would gather under the umbrella of the Forward Bloc. Soon it became apparent that the Congress socialist party, with its two factions headed by Jaiprakash Narayan and Minoo Masani; the Radical League, led by M. N. Roy; and the communists, using the cover of the National Front, were not of a mind to shed their distinct identities. All that they agreed to form was a Left Consolidation Committee, with Subhas Chandra Bose as chairman. The sectarian ideological disagreements among the various leftist groups prevented them from operating as a truly cohesive force.

In these circumstances, Bose decided to go straight to the people preaching his radical program. He consolidated his political base in Bengal with a quick tour of Dacca district. From May to July 1939, he embarked on an extensive tour of the United Provinces, Punjab, the North-West Frontier Province, the Central Provinces, Bombay, and Karnataka. Wherever he went, large crowds greeted him at wayside stations and capital cities, and enthusiastic audiences came to hear him speak. The stalwarts of the Congress stayed away, but Bose was able to obtain the services of some able lieutenants, such as Sardul Singh Caveeshar in Punjab, Mian Akbar Shah in the Frontier, and K. F. Nariman and Hari Vishnu Kamath in Bombay. He also received the backing of peasant leaders, including Swami Sahajanand Saraswati of Bihar (president of the All-India Kisan Sabha), N. G. Ranga of Andhra, and Indulal Yagnik of Gujarat. In Karnataka, he was pleasantly surprised when S. K. Hosmani, the incumbent president of the Congress party in that province, crossed over to his Forward Bloc.[72]

At a meeting of the All-India Congress Committee (AICC) in late June 1939, the right wing—in order to tighten its control over the party apparatus and the provincial ministries—passed two resolutions prohibiting Congress members from offering *satyagraha* without the permission of the party brass and freed the Congress provincial ministries from the need to follow the directives of the provincial parties. The Left Consolidation Committee, led by Bose, responded by calling for demonstrations across the country on July 9 against what they saw as the stifling of intra-party democracy. Meetings denouncing the two resolutions were held in many places, and Bose himself addressed a large crowd that had gathered inside and outside the Franji Cowasji Hall in Bombay.[73] The Congress Working Committee charged him with violating party discipline and banned him from holding any elective office in the Congress for three years, beginning in August 1939.

This disciplinary action by the Congress High Command had serious repercussions in Bengal. Even after resigning as Congress president, Bose had been serving as president of the Bengal Provincial Congress Committee, and the overwhelming majority of Bengal's congressmen and congresswomen were on his side. As soon as Rajendra Prasad had taken over as Congress president, two men belonging to the anti-Bose minority in Bengal, Bidhan Chandra Roy and Prafulla Chandra Ghosh, had been appointed to the Working Committee. If anything, Bose's removal from the chair of the Bengal Provincial Congress Committee solidified support for him in the region. Since the elected Bengal Provincial Congress Committee continued to side with Bose by a large majority, the Congress High Command appointed a small ad hoc

committee for Bengal headed by Abul Kalam Azad. In doing so, the
Congress central leadership alienated itself from the bulk of the nationalist forces in Bengal. The move precipitated a split in the Congress
legislative party as well. Sarat Chandra Bose now led the Bose group in
the Bengal legislative assembly while Kiran Sankar Roy was appointed
leader of the group owing allegiance to the ad hoc Congress. Disciplinary action was taken against Sarat as well for siding with his younger
brother.[74]

Subhas Chandra Bose resisted being expelled from the party he had
joined in 1921. Reacting to the news of disciplinary action against him
by the Congress High Command, he wrote on August 19, 1939:

> I shall cling to the Congress with even greater devotion than before and
> shall go on serving the Congress and the country as a servant of the na-
> tion. I appeal to my countrymen to come and join the Congress in their
> millions and to enlist as members of the Forward Bloc. Only by doing
> so shall we be able to convert the rank and file of the Congress to our
> point of view, secure a reversal of the present policy of Constitutional-
> ism and Reformism and resume the national struggle for Independence
> with the united strength of the Indian people.[75]

On the same day, in Calcutta, he welcomed Rabindranath Tagore at
the foundation-laying ceremony of Mahajati Sadan ("House of the
Great Nation"), which he hoped would become "the living center of
all those beneficial activities for the emancipation of the individual
and the nation." This edifice had been conceived as the home of the
Indian National Congress; to finance its construction, benefactors had
contributed liberally to the Subhas Fund started in March 1937. Bose
visualized it as a memorial for the martyrs who had laid down their
lives in the freedom struggle, and as an active venue for planning the
nation's future. Introducing Tagore as the "poet of humanity," Bose
asked him to perform the "sacred ceremony" as the "high priest of today's national festival."[76]

In giving enlightened and dignified expression to the idea of a "great
nation," Tagore distinguished the strength of the nation they were try-

ing to invoke from the type of state power that instilled fear and doubt in the minds of friends and foes alike. As part of his speech on the occasion, he recited a Bengali prayer he had composed in the Swadeshi era during the antipartition movement of 1905:

> The Bengalis' faith, the Bengalis' hope,
> The Bengalis' work, the Bengalis' language,
> Bless them with truth, O Lord.
> The Bengalis' heart, the Bengalis' mind,
> All the brothers and sisters in Bengali homes,
> May they be one, O Lord.

After a short pause he said, "And let this word be added: may Bengal's arm lend strength to India's arm, may Bengal's message make India's message come true."[77]

As poetry and patriotism mingled in Calcutta, war clouds were gathering over Europe. A week before the outbreak of hostilities, Bose wrote that "if war broke out between Germany and Poland the sympathy of the Indian people would be with the Poles." But he then asked: "Whatever our subjective reactions in this international conflict may be, what are we to do as a nation?" He wanted the Congress to emulate the practice of Europe's national cabinets in wartime and establish a composite rather than a homogeneous Congress Working Committee. Bose was clear about the role of the national leadership in the event of war:

> Great Britain and her apologists are now talking of self-determination for the Poles and if she goes to war, she will do so with the word "Self-determination" on her lips. Is not this the time to remind our British rulers that east of the Suez Canal there is a land inhabited by an ancient and cultured people who have been deprived of their birthright of liberty and have been groaning under the British yoke? And is not this the time to tell the British people and their Government that those who are slaves at home cannot fight for the freedom of others?

He urged Mahatma Gandhi to adopt a bold policy, so that he could become one of Gandhi's humble camp followers.[78]

Even as the prospect of a European war loomed, Bose considered taking a vacation at his favorite resort in Austria. "I wish I could go to Badgastein," Subhas had written to Emilie on April 19, 1939, even before he had resigned as Congress president. He asked her to inquire from the proprietress of Kurhaus Hochland how much a visit would cost. "And can you come there if I come for change?" he had asked. On June 21, during his political tour, he wrote that it was time to work and not to rest. "Please wait till August," he wrote to Emilie, "probably I will come then to Gastein." He also asked when she would come to India. He had to work because there was "so much public enthusiasm." "I must take a month's holiday at least," he wrote to Emilie on July 6, as he traveled by train from Jubbulpore to Bombay, "but I do not know if the holiday will begin in the middle of August or the beginning of September." He thought of her all the time, he assured her, sending his love.[79]

At the beginning of September, he was still in India. On the evening of September 3, 1939, he was addressing a massive public meeting of two hundred thousand people on the Marina Beach in Madras when someone thrust an evening newspaper into his hands. Britain had responded to Germany's invasion of Poland by declaring war. Bose immediately described the European war as an opportunity that was rare in the history of a nation—a chance that India could not afford to lose.[80] He analyzed the unfolding international situation from the strategic point of view of India's freedom struggle alone. At any crucial moment of decision, Bose felt a need to combine intuitive perception with rational understanding. "Where reason fails," as he put it, "instinct can guide us. Where instinct misleads by creating a mystical haze, reason can put us on the right path." From September to November 1939, Bose traversed the length and breadth of the country to bring together what he called the "individual-mind" and the "mass-mind."[81]

The outbreak of war changed all of the political calculations in India. The viceroy, Lord Linlithgow, declared India a belligerent in the war against Germany without bothering to consult the Indian National Congress, which held office in eight of the eleven provinces of British India. Though disciplinary action had been taken against him just over a month before, Subhas Chandra Bose was specially invited to attend a three-day meeting of the Congress Working Committee at Wardha, beginning on September 9. He urged the Congress to launch a mass movement to wrest India's freedom from Britain.[82] But the Congress leadership was not quite ready to do this, and instead asked the British to clarify their war aims. Its resolution expressed sympathy for Poland, stated that it had no quarrel with Germany, and asked the British how the principles of freedom and democracy would apply to India.

As a preeminent political leader, Bose was invited to an audience with Viceroy Linlithgow on October 10. After the meeting, Bose made it plain that he did not speak with two voices, one in public and another in private. He had communicated India's national demand to His Majesty's representative. Linlithgow's response to the call to define Britain's war aims came as a huge disappointment to the Congress. The viceroy was authorized to convey His Majesty's government's willingness to consult representatives of parties and communities in British India and the princely states, to bring about appropriate constitutional modifications—but such consultations should take place only at the war's end. The reply deeply embarrassed the Congress leadership, which had been saying it did not want to embarrass the British during their difficulty. In frustration and anger, the Congress High Command directed all of its provincial ministries to resign office. These eight provinces would be administered by British governors and their civil servants for the duration of the Second World War.[83]

During the war crisis of 1939, the rest of the Congress leadership behaved like His Majesty's Opposition; having shed all the inhibitions of colonial subjecthood, Bose alone stood forth as His Majesty's Opponent.[84] In December 1939, Tagore urged Gandhi to withdraw the disciplinary action against Bose and cordially invite his cooperation in the "supreme interest of national unity." Gandhi would not be persuaded. He had C. F. Andrews convey the message that the matter was "too complicated for Gurudev to handle." Tagore was offended by the tenor of the response, even though Gandhi added: "Let him trust that no one in the Committee has anything personal against Subhas. For me, he is as my son." Subhas could only console himself that Bapu's treatment of him came nowhere close to the harshness of the discipline that Gandhi imposed on his own eldest son, Harilal. As Gandhi explained in one of his columns: "The love of my conception, if it is as soft as a rose petal, can also be harder than flint. My wife has had to experience the hard variety. My eldest son is experiencing it even now. I had thought I had gained Subhas *Babu* for all time as a son. I have fallen from grace. I had the pain of wholly associating myself with the ban pronounced on him."[85] The rebellious son refused to bow to the quintessential patriarch.

By December 1939, Bose was denouncing the vacillating policy of the Congress leadership. He issued a stern warning against the Congress proposal of a "Constituent Assembly under the aegis of an Imperialist Government," which he likened to the Irish Convention of Lloyd George. It was a "stunt" to "stave off a struggle," since "behind the façade of a party-struggle within the Congress there was in reality a class-struggle going on all the time."[86] The nationalists could convene a genuine Constituent Assembly only after the seizure of power. In his presidential address to the All-India Students' Conference at Delhi, in January 1940, he commended the Ahrars, a Muslim group in Punjab, for acting while the Congress leaders were deliberating. "Nevertheless," he declared, "there are people—and stay-at-homes at that—who do not scruple to cast aspersions on the patriotism of Indian Muslims as a body." The Congress High Command, he charged, could "think of a compromise with the Fascist British Government" but was hell-bent on "war to the bitter end" against their leftist compatriots. Alluding to Mahatma Gandhi's stirring call issued at the time of the noncooperation and Khilafat movement, he reminded his student audience of a "message once given to 'Young India' by one of our erstwhile Leftist leaders," who had said: "Freedom comes to those who dare and act."[87]

Though Subhas Chandra Bose used the adjective "fascist" to denounce the British raj, he was certainly aware of the menace that Britain's fascist enemies posed to the entire world. His elder brother Sarat attempted an answer to this moral dilemma in the course of a speech in December 1939. Imperialism, Sarat argued, even more than totalitarianism, had "darkened the prospects of human freedom" across the globe. He conceded that, being older, imperialism had lost some of its virility, while the adherents of totalitarianism had the "zeal and energy of new converts." From the perspective of India and Indians, both -isms had "wreaked havoc." "If we hate totalitarianism," he proclaimed, "we hate imperialism more." Adding a Shakespearean touch, he declared his refusal to beg "with bated breath and whispering humbleness" to subsist in his own homeland. "If to demand our birthright is to be a rebel in act and deed," he concluded, "quoting the words of a great Irishman I shall say 'I am proud to be a rebel and shall cling to my rebellion with the last drop of my blood.'"[88]

Subhas, for his part, held up the examples of the Sinn Féin rejection of Lloyd George's Irish Convention, and the Bolshevik withdrawal from the Russian Constituent Assembly in 1917, for Indian nationalists to emulate.[89] One obstacle in the path of compromise, Bose noted, was the British penchant for using the minorities "as a lever against the Congress." But he felt that if a compromise with the Congress High Command could be worked out, the British "would be prepared to let down the Muslim League." Although Bose glimpsed what was to transpire in 1947, when the British would forsake their Muslim and princely allies, it was premature on his part to anticipate splits in both the Congress and the Muslim League in the event of a compromise with the British by the Congress right wing. In such an eventuality, he expected the loyalist elements in the Muslim League to side with the compromisers and break away "from Mr. Jinnah and the progressive sections who are influential in the League Council today." In the event the Congress High Command struck a deal with British imperialism, Bose hoped for "the voluntary withdrawal or expulsion from the Congress of the compromise-wallahs." "Why should we secede from the Congress," he asked, "and allow the backsliders to inherit the name and the traditions of that body?"[90]

No compromise with British imperialism: this was Bose's theme and motto during 1940. When the Indian National Congress met for its annual session under the presidency of Abul Kalam Azad at Ramgarh in March, Bose held his own mammoth Anti-Compromise Conference close to the site of that meeting. His parallel conference compared favorably with the official gathering in size and enthusiasm, despite some inclement weather. The peasant volunteers of Swami Sahajanand Sara-swati provided the organizational backbone of Bose's conference at this Bihar venue. "The age of Imperialism," he declared, "is drawing to a close and the era of freedom, democracy and socialism looms ahead of us. India, therefore, stands at one of the crossroads of history." His Ramgarh address contained a blistering attack on the indecisive nature of the existing leadership at that fateful moment. He issued a call for a political consolidation of all genuine leftists. "In the present phase of our movement," he explained, "Leftists will be all those who will wage an uncompromising fight with Imperialism. In the next phase of our movement, Leftism will be synonymous with socialism."[91]

Bose interpreted the Second World War as a conflict between rival imperialisms. From April 1940 onward—as the "old imperialist power," Britain, seemed to be discomfited by the "new imperialist power," Ger-many—Bose turned his attention more specifically to ways of forging unity among the religious communities.[92] March 1940 had witnessed not just the rival Ramgarh meetings, but also the momentous Lahore session of the All-India Muslim League. Mohammed Ali Jinnah, the leader of the League, claimed the Muslims of India were not just a mi-nority seeking safeguards, but a nation deserving an equitable sharing of power with the Hindus. The Muslim League passed a resolution at Lahore, stating that the Muslim-majority provinces in the northwest and east of the subcontinent should be grouped to constitute inde-pendent states. The resolution also spoke of a "constitution" (in the singular) that would cover all-India arrangements and protect minor-ity rights. Not quite a secessionist demand, the Lahore resolution men-tioned neither Pakistan nor partition. It sought to balance the needs and aspirations of Muslims in both majority provinces and minority provinces, in the face of Congress majoritarianism and quest for power in a unitary state.[93]

While being sharply critical of "communalism"—a word which by now had acquired a clear pejorative connotation, that of being a nar-row, religiously based particularism—Subhas Chandra Bose did not seem to have been entirely persuaded by the mainstream Congress dis-course on a singular nationalism exemplified by Jawaharlal Nehru. A Bengali Muslim leader, Abul Mansur Ahmed, had explained to Bose that the Lahore resolution was not necessarily secessionist in its import.[94] In a key essay published on May 4, 1940, Bose recalled that not so long before, "prominent leaders of the Congress could be members and leaders of communal organizations like the Hindu Mahasabha and the Muslim League." Lala Lajpat Rai, the redoubtable nationalist of Punjab, had been a leader of both the Congress and the Mahasabha, just as the Ali brothers, Shaukat and Mohammad, had at one time been leaders of both the Congress and the League. In the pre-1920 period, Bose might have mentioned Jinnah himself as a prominent leader of both parties. He did cite the case of Akram Khan, who had served as president of the Bengal Provincial Congress Committee even while he was a leader of the Muslim League. Bose, therefore, did not wish to treat the "communal organizations" as untouchable.[95]

Bose then went on to explain how his group within the Congress had reached a pact with the Muslim League in the Calcutta Corporation, a pact which had infuriated "a certain number of communally-minded Hindus." After negotiations with the Muslim League leader M. A. H. Ispahani, Abdur Rahman Siddiqui of the Muslim League had been installed as mayor of Calcutta with the support of the Bose group. Bose observed that for the previous three years, there had been futile attempts to foster an understanding between the Congress and the Muslim League. His own attempts to negotiate with Jinnah and the Muslim League in 1938 had been blessed by the Congress Working Committee and Mahatma Gandhi. "Those who had not objected to that attempt which failed ultimately," he wrote, "now strongly object to the present attempt, because it has succeeded." His overall assessment of the Bose group's pact with the Muslim League in Calcutta was as follows:

We regard the present agreement with the Muslim League as a great achievement not in its actuality, but in its potentiality. During the last three years, we have been groping in the dark, but without success. Every time we have come up against a dead wall of communal prejudice and passion and we have been frustrated in our efforts. This time we have broken through the wall and through the fissure, a ray of light has poured in. There is now some hope that we may ultimately succeed in solving a problem well nigh insoluble to many. Great achievements are often born out of small beginnings.[96]

Bose met Jinnah in Bombay, to see if an understanding could be reached on a broader basis. The Muslim League leader reportedly told the Congress rebel that he needed to take control of the Indian National Congress before he could effect a Hindu-Muslim settlement.[97]

In May 1940, as Britain suffered reverses in the war, Bose noted that the problem of "fighting British Imperialism" was likely in the future to give way to the more pressing problem of "internal unity and consolidation." "There is today dark uncertainty before us as to our future fate," he wrote. "But all this will vanish in no time, if we can achieve two things—unity among Congressmen and a Hindu-Muslim settlement."[98] Bose saw no prospect of an enslaved India coming to the rescue of Britain. "India," he asserted, "has first to save herself. And she can save herself only if the Hindus and Muslims put forward a joint demand for a provisional national government to whom all powers should be immediately transferred." Only after India was "strong enough to save herself" could she "lend a helping hand to other friendly countries." He wondered if the Congress and the Muslim League could agree on this issue of presenting a joint Hindu-Muslim demand to the colonial masters.[99] He felt that India, at this critical moment, needed Deshbandhu Chitta Ranjan Das's "unbounded love which made him a friend of the people and which drew the Muslims and the backward classes so close to him."[100]

Subhas Chandra Bose provided his most elaborate statement on the duty of anti-imperialists in the context of the "war between rival Imperialisms" in his address at Nagpur, as president of the second All-India Forward Bloc Conference, in June 1940. He stressed the need for national unity and solidarity. "National unity," he declared, "will presuppose unity within the Congress on the basis of a dynamic program of struggle and at the same time unity between the Congress and other organizations like the Muslim League." He called upon all parties to join together in establishing a citizens' defense corps aimed at preserving internal peace, harmony, and goodwill. Defense of subjugated India against any foreign power should concern the government only, and

not the people. "What interest can we have in fighting for the perpetu-
ation of our own slavery," he asked, "for that is exactly what is implied
in fighting to defend an enslaved India."[101] At the end of June 1940, he
reiterated his demand for national cabinets at the center and in the
provinces, which "will ensure internal peace and harmony during the
transitional period and will pave the way to a lasting Hindu-Muslim
settlement." India, much as Britain did, faced a wartime emergency requiring rival parties to come together. If it proved impossible to set up
a national cabinet at the center straightaway, Bose was in favor of trying the experiment of national cabinets in the provinces. He was, in
effect, calling for a reversal of the Congress policy, which in 1937 had
left the Muslim League out in the cold in places like the United Provinces. He wanted broad-based national coalitions in Hindu-majority
and Muslim-majority provinces alike. "In the present dynamic situation," he believed, "national cabinets in the provinces will be a great
help not only in maintaining internal harmony, [and] not only in establishing Hindu-Muslim unity[,] but also in winning power at the
center—should there be obstacles in the path of attaining Swaraj."[102]

In his pursuit of Hindu-Muslim unity in Bengal, Subhas Chandra
Bose called for the observance of Siraj-ud-daula Day on July 3, 1940,
to honor the memory of Bengal's last independent Nawab. That day,
he proposed to launch a movement for the removal of the Holwell
monument from Dalhousie Square, in front of the Writers' Building in
Calcutta. The edifice, according to Bose, was both "an unwarranted
stain on the memory of the Nawab" and "the symbol of our slavery and
humiliation."[103] Although the movement was successful and the government removed the offending monument from public view, the British seized this opportunity to place Bose behind prison bars even before the agitation began. July 2, 1940, turned out to be the last day that
Bose spent as a free man in India. During the day, he went to see Rabindranath Tagore at his home in the Jorasanko neighborhood of
Calcutta. A couple of hours later, the police arrested Bose at his home
and took him away to Presidency Jail.[104]

During this, his last spell in prison, from July 3 to December 5, 1940,
Bose wrote a number of letters and essays. In his private letters to Sarat
Chandra Bose, he criticized the moral failings of the Congress leader-

ship in a frank and forthright manner. In one letter, he condemned Gandhism for its "sanctimonious hypocrisy" and "outrage on democracy." In another, he wrote: "The more I think of Congress Politics, the more convinced I feel that in future we should devote more energy and time to fighting the High Command. If power goes into the hands of such mean, vindictive and unscrupulous persons when Swaraj is won, what will happen to the country. We should concentrate on fighting the Congress High Command now[,] and to that end, we should make alliances with other political parties wherever and whenever possible."[105] He was especially scathing about Abul Kalam Azad, who was taking disciplinary action against the Bose brothers. If discipline in a democratic organization meant rule by the majority, then the Congress leadership was playing a game of double standards. They wanted the leftist minority to blindly obey the dictates of the rightist majority at the all-India level, yet demanded that the overwhelming majority, who were loyal to the Boses in Bengal, should submit to a minority that formed the ad hoc committee. By this token, it was Azad who was indulging in indiscipline, not the Boses.[106]

It was Bose's determination to fight British Imperialism rather than the Congress High Command that led him to make the decision to go on a hunger strike, in an attempt to force the government to release him. He was keen to take advantage of the international war crisis to fight for India's freedom and not waste the war years in prison. The day before Bose began his fast, Gandhi sent a telegram to a friend on the question of disciplinary action: "Regret inability even unwillingness to interfere notwithstanding my regard and friendship for the brothers. Feel bans cannot be lifted without their apologizing for indiscipline." Public protests against the democracy deficit within the Congress constituted lack of discipline. Subhas responded by wishing to keep personal relations above political differences, and by professing deep personal regard and love for Mahatma Gandhi. He then quoted J. H. Gurney's poem on William Tell, the greatest hero of Switzerland, which summed up the warrior's attitude toward the saint:

My knee shall bend, he calmly said,
To God and God alone,

My life is in the Austrians' hands,
My conscience is my own.

"I am not aware of any wrong that I have committed in my political career," he said defiantly. "Consequently, my reply to the Mahatma will be on the above lines, with a few verbal changes."[107]

6

One Man and a World at War

This is the technique of the soul. The individual must die, so that the nation may live. Today I must die, so that India may live and may win freedom and glory.

—SUBHAS CHANDRA BOSE, "My Political Testament," November 26, 1940

When the Battle of Britain was raging over London in 1940, India's colonial masters had their most uncompromising opponent safely behind bars in the Presidency Jail of Calcutta. Having resigned the Congress presidency, Subhas Chandra Bose was calling for a final showdown with the British raj. His concern for Hindu-Muslim unity led him to launch a movement urging that the Holwell Monument be removed from the public square in front of the seat of the British government in Bengal. The monument commemorated the legend of the Black Hole of Calcutta, where British prisoners-of-war allegedly died in cramped conditions—a legend that Hindus and Muslims alike considered a slur on the honor of Nawab Siraj-ud-daula, the last independent king of Bengal, whom Robert Clive had defeated at Plassey in 1757.[1] On July 2, 1940, the day before he was to lead the civil disobedience campaign in the streets of Calcutta, Bose was arrested under the Defence of India Rules and charged with two counts of sedition. The fury of the resulting agitation by both Hindus and Muslims alike forced the government to dismantle the monument and discreetly remove it from public view. But that was a small price to pay if Subhas Chandra Bose and his inflammatory words and actions could be put out of circulation for the duration of the war.

Bose had other ideas, however. On November 29, 1940, he started a hunger strike in prison, challenging the government: "Release me, or I shall refuse to live." Three days before that, he had composed a thirteen-page handwritten letter, addressed to the British governor of Bengal, which he described as his "political testament." It opened and closed with two requests. At the outset, Bose asked that his letter "be carefully preserved in the archives of the Government, so that it may be available to those of my countrymen who will succeed you in office in future." The message to his countrymen was clear: "One individual may die for an idea—but that idea will, after his death, incarnate itself in a thousand lives." The long statement gradually rose to a crescendo, lyrically describing the search for the fulfillment of an idea through an "ordeal of suffering and sacrifice":

> What greater solace can there be than the feeling that one has lived and died for a principle? What higher satisfaction can a man possess than the knowledge that his spirit will beget kindred spirits to carry on his unfinished task? What better reward can a soul desire than the certainty that his message will be wafted over hills and dales and over the broad plains to distant lands? What higher consummation can life attain than peaceful self-immolation at the altar of one's Cause?

The "Cause" that he held dear was his country's freedom, based on unity among its diverse religious communities. He demanded that the government cease trying to divide Hindus and Muslims, and exhorted his compatriots never to "compromise with injustice and wrong." It was evident to him that "nobody can lose through suffering and sacrifice": "If he does lose anything 'of the earth, earthy,' he will gain much more in return by becoming the heir to a life immortal."[2]

Bose's second request came toward the end of his letter: he asked the government not to interfere with his fast. He reminded the government of others who had fasted from political conviction—Terence MacSwiney of Ireland, Jatin Das, who died in Lahore Jail in 1929, and

Mahatma Gandhi—and he mentioned his own fast of 1926. In a separate letter, he appealed to the chief minister to refrain from force-
feeding and warned that his was no ordinary fast, but one resorted
to after "several months' mature deliberation, finally sealed by a vow
prayerfully taken by me on the sacred day of Kali Puja"—a day devoted
to worship of the mother goddess Kali.[3]

The government of Bengal did not wish to have Bose's death on its
hands. Since July 1940, Viceroy Linlithgow had been instructing the
governor, John Herbert, to keep Bose in prison at any cost. A coalition
government of the Krishak Praja (Peasants and Tenants) party and the
Muslim League was ruling the province at that time. In August, Sarat
Chandra Bose had written to the premier, Fazlul Huq, demanding the
release of political prisoners, including his brother. Herbert "had advised Huq to send a very guarded acknowledgement (if he sends one at
all) as he is capable of making the wildest statements when he puts pen
to paper."[4] If such was his opinion of Bengal's redoubtable peasant
leader, he was even more derisive of Khwaja Nazimuddin of the Muslim League, who was the province's home minister in charge of law and
order. Nazimuddin, Herbert reported to Linlithgow, was "frightened to
face facts" regarding the prosecution of Bose. The viceroy likewise
found Nazimuddin, who had gone to see him in Simla, "in a very wob-
bly condition and afraid of everything," including the handling of Bose.
The viceroy and the governor agreed that Bose must be kept in detention. While in prison, Bose had been elected to the Central Legislative Assembly from a Dacca constituency, though the government had
done its best to have him disqualified. On September 20, 1940, Herbert
sent a bizarre report that Subhas Bose had "lost 24 pounds since he was
admitted into jail, in spite of the fact that he continues to eat gargan-
tuan meals." Once Bose stopped taking food on November 29, Herbert's confidence and resolve faltered.

On December 5, 1940, exactly a week after Bose had begun his fast
unto death, Herbert decided to send him home in an ambulance to
preclude his death in prison. The governor intended to rearrest Bose as
soon as he had recovered his health. Herbert had acted with the greatest reluctance, but "there seemed to be no other alternative in view of
the report of the Jail Superintendent," who refused to take responsibil-

ity for the consequences of force-feeding the ailing prisoner. On December 6, Viceroy Linlithgow informed the secretary of state for India in London that he expected Bose to be out of action for three weeks; afterward, they could rearrest him by implementing a "cat and mouse" policy devised by the governor of Bengal.[5] "If he resorts to hunger strike again," Herbert blithely wrote to Linlithgow on December 11, "the present 'cat and mouse' policy will be continued, and its employment will serve both to render him innocuous and to make him realize that nothing is to be gained from a series of fasts."[6]

On December 5, a frail and exhausted Subhas had been transported by stretcher to his three-story ancestral home at 38/2 Elgin Road. Janaki Nath Bose had died in 1934, and Subhas was lodged in his father's erstwhile bedroom on the middle floor near the front of the house. But Janaki's grand four-poster bed remained vacant, as Subhas preferred to sleep on a cot. The room was airy and bright; it had seven large windows on three sides, with traditional glass-and-wood shutters. In addition to oil paintings of family elders and a picture of the divine mother Kali, Subhas adorned the walls with some photographs taken in his favorite Austrian hill resort, Badgastein.[7] A tiger-skin prayer mat was spread in one corner on the marble floor. A low wooden bookcase held the *Bhagavad Gita*. Subhas's elderly mother, Prabhabati, lived in the adjoining room, although since her husband's death the connecting door was kept shut. A niece, Ila, had a room on the same floor and helped to take care of her uncle while he recuperated. Several other members of the extended Bose family lived on the upper floor of the house, which was constantly abuzz with a curious mixture of domestic and political activity.

The government's "cat and mouse" policy required enveloping 38/2 Elgin Road with a ring of security, while at the same time penetrating its inner recesses. Herbert was at pains to explain that the government "did not intend to withdraw either the order under section 26 of the Defence of India Rules, or the two cases at present pending." Subhas was "neither in custody nor on bail." He would be rearrested soon—all the government had done was to "suspend temporarily the order for his detention."[8] In addition to stationing plainclothes policemen outside to keep a close watch on the house, the government engaged at least a dozen intelligence agents employed by the central and provincial governments to ferret out information on what might be going on inside. One such agent dutifully reported that Subhas, upon his return home on December 5, had oatmeal porridge and vegetable soup, and his voice sounded quite normal. From that day onward, all his visitors were monitored and his correspondence was intercepted, copied, and read at the post office before being dispatched or delivered. During the week following Bose's return home, the agents mostly reported that he was discussing affairs of the Congress parliamentary board and planning an all-India protest calling for the release of detainees. On December 12, he reportedly formed a council of action for that movement.[9]

Unbeknownst to those who imagined they had him under strict surveillance, Bose had by that time taken a decisive step for action of a very different sort. On the afternoon of December 5, Subhas had warmly clasped the hand of his nephew Sisir for an unusually long time. Sisir, the third son of Sarat Chandra Bose, was a twenty-year-old student at Calcutta Medical College. The following week, once the stream of visitors of the first few days had ebbed, Subhas sent for Sisir at Sarat's three-story mansion, 1 Woodburn Park—another premier political address in early twentieth-century Calcutta. Sarat's home had spacious rooms with high ceilings, an impressive marble staircase, curved southern verandahs, and sophisticated Western furnishings. Mahatma Gandhi and Jawaharlal Nehru stayed there as Sarat's guests during visits to the city. Gandhi held his prayer meetings on its terrace, and the house had served as the venue for important political conferences of the Indian National Congress. Having received his uncle's summons, Sisir walked immediately from one Bose house to the other.

The Wanderer

Sisir had always been in awe of his *Rangakakababu,* his radiant uncle. Looking pale and thin, with a bushy half-grown beard, Subhas was reclining on his pillows when Sisir entered his bedroom that December afternoon. Subhas bade his nephew take a seat on the bed, to his right.

After looking at Sisir intensely for a few minutes, Subhas asked, "Amar ekta kaj korte parbe?"—"Can you do some work for me?"[10] Without knowing what sort of *kaj* ("work") he was being asked to do, Sisir nodded. The task, as it turned out, was to help plan and execute Subhas's escape from India. Sisir would have to drive his uncle, in the dead of night, to a railway station quite a long distance from Calcutta. Subhas stressed that they needed to draw up a "fool-proof" plan of escape. No one must know, except for Sisir's sister Ila, who would make sure people thought Subhas was still at home. This encounter between uncle and nephew closed with Subhas asking Sisir to return the next evening with clear-cut ideas. Sisir walked back to 1 Woodburn Park "in a state of wonder and subdued excitement."[11]

The next evening, Subhas and Sisir had the first of many daily confabulations to perfect their plan. Though it was quite normal for a nephew to visit an ailing uncle, they found an additional excuse to account for the frequency of the visits: Sisir, who was good at operating the radio, was ostensibly helping Subhas listen to foreign radio broadcasts. In fact, Subhas was closely following the course of the war by listening to news and analysis from London, Berlin, Moscow, and Rome. After the German *Blitzkrieg,* France lay prostrate, Britain was reeling under bombing raids by the Luftwaffe, and the German-Soviet pact signed by Joachim von Ribbentrop and Vyacheslav Molotov in 1939 was still holding fast. Bose saw Britain's difficulty as India's opportunity to break free, but his first challenge was to figure out how, exactly, to take advantage of the international crisis.

After discussing various possible ways of exiting from 38/2 Elgin Road, Subhas and Sisir decided to drive out, in the most natural fashion, through the main driveway and gate. There were two cars to choose from: an American Studebaker President registered in the name of Sisir's mother, Bivabati, and a German car called the Wanderer registered in Sisir's name. The American vehicle was larger and more powerful, but too easily recognizable as Sarat's car. Subhas and Sisir deemed the Wanderer more suitable for their journey. They decided that Subhas would be in disguise and that the exact date of the escape would depend on arrangements to be made in the North-West Frontier Province (NWFP).

On December 16, 1940, one of the government's agents reported that Mian Akbar Shah was coming from the frontier to meet with Subhas Chandra Bose. Akbar Shah hailed from Nowshera in the NWFP and was the provincial head of the Forward Bloc, formed by Bose in 1939 to pressure the Indian National Congress toward a more radical confrontation with the British raj. Bose had cabled Akbar Shah, inviting him to visit Calcutta, and the police agent had seized upon the government's first useful and potentially dangerous piece of information. As a young man, in 1920, Akbar had crossed the tribal territories and Afghanistan to reach the Soviet Union. Bose now asked him to help plan the escape route from Peshawar to Kabul. As a cover, they spread the word that Bose wanted Akbar Shah to organize a major Forward Bloc conference, and this falsehood was what the intelligence operative reported to the authorities.[12]

Sisir was introduced to Mian Akbar Shah, and the two went together to Wachel Molla's department store in central Calcutta, where Akbar Shah purchased some baggy *shalwars* (trousers) and a black fez for Bose's disguise. Sisir then dropped him off at the Howrah railway station, where he caught a train back to the frontier. In the following days, Sisir bought a suitcase, an attaché case, and a bedroll, as well as two flannel shirts, toiletries, pillows, and quilts. Dressed in European attire, with a felt hat on his head, he went to a printing shop and ordered a set of calling cards, which read: "Mohd. Ziauddin, B.A., LL.B., Traveling Inspector, The Empire of India Life Assurance Co. Ltd., Permanent Address: Civil Lines, Jubbulpore."[13]

On Christmas Day 1940, Sisir went through an endurance test: he drove from Calcutta to Burdwan, a railway junction, in the morning; had lunch at the station; and returned the same day. In early January he visited his eldest brother, Asoke, near Dhanbad, on the pretext of fetching his mother and other members of the family, and took the opportunity to scout out the area. On the return journey, his parents' Studebaker President (in which he was traveling as a passenger) broke down, and he, along with other family members, had to return to Calcutta in a ramshackle taxi. About the same time, Sarat came back to Calcutta from a three-week vacation in the hill station of Kalimpong, and was immediately informed of the plan by Subhas. The elder brother suggested some changes to the escape plan. He was not happy that a young woman, namely Ila, might have to bear the brunt of the police *zulm* ("crackdown") after the escape; he wanted a male cousin, Dwijen, to help with the cover-up at home after Subhas's departure.

In all his conversations and correspondence with friends, relatives, and political associates, Subhas spoke of his impending return to jail. His excellent contacts enabled him to obtain a confidential government file on British officials' plans for dealing with him, and to return the file after perusing its contents. Meanwhile, Sisir observed the behavior of the police assigned to watch the house. They had set themselves up on a *charpoi* (four-legged platform) at the corner of Elgin Road and Woodburn Road, where they could keep an eye on both Bose houses. They paced up and down the streets during the day, but tended to prefer the comfort of their blankets on their *charpoi* during the cool winter nights. Not even the letters exchanged between Subhas Chandra Bose and Mahatma Gandhi could evade the prying eyes of the colonial state. On December 23, 1940, Bose wrote to Gandhi offering his unconditional support to any movement the Mahatma might lead in the cause of India's independence. On December 29, Gandhi replied that until one of them could convert the other on the question of the best way to pursue Independence, they must "sail in different boats": "You are irrepressible whether ill or well," *Bapu* wrote to his rebellious son. "Do get well before going in for fireworks."[14] On January 3, 1941, the government censors opened and read this letter.[15] Little did they know that the rebel had already completed preparations for his "fireworks" and was simply waiting for the right moment to light the fuse.

Respectful of all religious traditions, Subhas, in his personal life, was especially devoted to the Supreme Being in the form of the mother goddess. One evening, on Subhas's instructions, Sisir drove Ila to the Kali temple at Dakshineswar, where she was to seek the divine mother's blessings for their endeavor. Subhas gave Sisir just over two days' notice of the date of the escape. Sisir delivered the bedroll to Elgin Road; he took back two editions of the Holy Quran and some medicines, to pack into the attaché case at Woodburn Park. On the night before the escape, he discovered that the suitcase he had bought was too big for the Wanderer and he had to replace it with a smaller one. This involved rubbing off the initials "SCB" and inscribing "MZ" on it with Chinese ink. On January 16, he had the car serviced and returned home early from medical school. That evening, he had a conversation with his father on the lit-up terrace of Woodburn Park: Sarat was worried that Subhas and Sisir might be stopped by the police in the French enclave of Chandernagore. Sisir had dinner early, with his mother sitting quietly by. She gave him some money for the journey and said with a faint smile, "God knows what you people are up to." After managing to load the luggage unnoticed, Sisir drove across from Woodburn Park to Elgin Road at about 8:30 P.M. and parked the car near the rear entrance of the house.[16]

In order to deceive the British, Subhas and Sisir unfortunately had to deceive family members as well, including Subhas's elderly mother. Sisir found his *Rangakakababu* changing into a silk *dhoti* and *chaddar,* in preparation for a ritualistic dinner that would be served on a marble plate and bowls and eaten in the presence of his mother and other family members. Subhas had told them of his pious resolution to go into religious seclusion for a period of time, and he was not to be disturbed. Henceforth, food was to be served from behind a screen. Meanwhile, Subhas had scribbled various notes on small pieces of paper, to be handed to visitors depending on the nature of their business. He had also written a number of postdated letters, mostly to comrades in prison, to be mailed in sequence after his departure. "I shall be back in jail very soon, because there are two cases going on against me," he wrote to Hari Vishnu Kamath, expecting that the letter, dated January 18, 1941, would be opened by police censors. The departure from the house was delayed until the younger members of the family had retired for the night. Earlier in the day, Sisir's cousin Aurobindo had grown suspicious and had been let into the conspiracy, but Subhas was unwilling to expand the circle of confidants any further.

At last, around 1:35 A.M., the coast was deemed clear. Subhas had changed into his disguise as "Muhammad Ziauddin." Dressed in a long, brown, closed-collar coat, baggy *shalwars,* and a black fez, he wore the gold wire-rimmed glasses that he had stopped using more than a decade before. He felt uncomfortable in the *Kabuli chappals* (Afghani sandals) that Sisir had bought for him, so he chose to wear his own laced European shoes for the long journey. Once Dwijen signaled from a room upstairs that there were no government agents or passers-by in front of the house, Subhas kissed his niece Ila goodbye. It was a moon-lit night. Aurobindo, carrying the bedroll, was followed by Subhas and Sisir; they hugged the inner wall of the long corridor as they tiptoed their way down the back stairs to the car. Subhas sat quietly in the left rear. Sisir took the driver's seat (on the right), started the engine, and drove the Wanderer BLA 7169 away from 38/2 Elgin Road, as he had done on so many past occasions. The lights in Subhas's bedroom were kept burning for another hour.[17]

The Wanderer went through the gate, turned right, then took an-other immediate right southward onto Allenby Road, avoiding the cor-ner between Elgin Road and Woodburn Road. Soon, Sisir turned left to join Lansdowne Road and began their northerly journey. As Calcutta slept, uncle and nephew sped along Lower Circular Road, Sealdah, and Harrison Road, then crossed Howrah Bridge over the River Hooghly. Now they were beyond the city's precincts. The conversation between uncle and nephew turned to the Irish anticolonial struggle, from which Subhas had taken inspiration. Pouring Sisir hot coffee from a thermos, Subhas asked whether his nephew knew about Eamon de Valera's es-cape from Lincoln Prison in 1919. Sisir knew that de Valera had made a wax imprint of the key to his cell, and that a key had been delivered to him hidden in a cake. But he also knew that Michael Collins, the other great hero of the Irish struggle, had thought he had lost the key to the outer gate at a critical moment. Fortunately, the key was retrieved and Collins was able to help his friend "Dev" to break free.[18] In the midst of the discussion of de Valera's escape, Sisir had to brake to a sudden stop at a closed railway crossing. An overflow of petrol stalled the engine, and there were a few anxious minutes before the Wanderer started up again.

Sarat's fears proved groundless: the drive through the French enclave of Chandernagore was uneventful, and no policemen barred the car's progress. Had uncle and nephew been stopped anywhere, Subhas was to pretend to be the Muslim chauffeur who was allowing the young owner to drive the car. But the trip was unimpeded by any sort of hu-man interference. As Sisir was dashing along at high speed through the

Durgapur forest beyond Burdwan, he came upon a large herd of buffalo crossing the road and again had to bring the Wanderer to an abrupt halt. Dawn broke as they reached the outskirts of Asansol; their late start in Calcutta meant that the drive along the undulating road from Asansol to Dhanbad had to be done in the bright morning light. At around 8:30 A.M., Sisir dropped off his passenger a few hundred yards from his brother Asoke's house in Bararee, near Dhanbad.

Sisir had barely finished telling Asoke what was going on and what had to be done, when a north Indian Muslim named Muhammad Ziauddin (Subhas in disguise) arrived on insurance business. Asoke told the gentleman that since he was about to leave for work, a conversation would have to wait until the evening. The domestic staff were instructed to make up the spare room for the visitor and in their presence Sisir was formally introduced to Ziauddin in English. At the end of the day's work for Asoke and a good day's rest for the travelers, the visitor and Asoke had a discussion, ostensibly on the hazards of work in the coalfields. Subhas communicated his decision that Gomoh in Bihar, rather than Asansol in Bengal, was the railway station where he preferred to board the train. As Sisir was not quite sure of the route to Gomoh, he wanted his brother to serve as navigator. Asoke was reluctant to leave his wife alone late at night in that locality, and so it was decided that Sisir's sister-in-law Mira would also join the party. After an early dinner, Muhammad Ziauddin left, bidding the Boses goodbye as they prepared to go out to visit friends. Some distance from the Bararee house, Ziauddin was picked up in the Wanderer, and they all took the road to Gomoh.[19]

The Delhi-Kalka Mail was not due at Gomoh Station until much later that night. So the Wanderer stopped twice on the way. The Boses sat under a tree listening to the bells jingling on the necks of bullocks as a procession of carts passed by. Closer to Gomoh, they stopped amid an expanse of rice fields, where they could see the silhouette of Pareshnath Hill in the moonlight. At Gomoh Station, a sleepy porter came and picked up the luggage. "I am off—you go back," *Rangakakababu* said as he took his leave. Sisir watched him "mount the overbridge slowly after the porter and walk across it with his usual majestic gait till he disappeared into the darkness toward the platform on the opposite side." The Delhi-Kalka Mail rumbled in from the direction of Calcutta. After a while, Sisir "heard the train steam off and then saw a garland of lights moving away and away to the rhythmic clatter of moving wheels."[20]

Muhammad Ziauddin

Late on the evening of January 19, the Frontier Mail from Delhi trundled into Peshawar cantonment station. Mian Akbar Shah, hovering near the exit gate, spotted a distinguished-looking Muslim gentleman coming through it. Confident that this was Bose in disguise (and it was), he walked alongside and asked him to get into a waiting *tonga*. He instructed the *tongawallah* to take the gentleman to Dean's Hotel, and got into another carriage to follow. Akbar's *tongawallah* asked why he was taking such an obviously devout Muslim, who looked like an *alim* (a learned Islamic scholar), to a hotel for infidels; he suggested going to the Taj Mahal Hotel, where the guest would be provided with a prayer mat and water for ablutions. It struck Akbar that the Taj Mahal might well be the safer place, since Dean's Hotel was likely to be crawling with police agents—and so the two *tongas* changed course. The manager of the Taj Mahal was as impressed with Muhammad Ziauddin as the *tongawallah* had been, and found the visitor a nice room with a working fireplace and a *jai namaz* (prayer rug). Akbar had intended to shift Bose, the next morning, to the home of a well-to-do friend. But on the way back from the Taj Mahal Hotel, he encountered Abad Khan, a close political associate from a humble background, who insisted on playing host to Subhas Chandra Bose. Before dawn, Muhammad Ziauddin was shifted to Abad Khan's home, where in the next few days he underwent a transformation from a north Indian Muslim gentleman to a deaf-mute Pathan. This was necessary, since Bose did not speak the local language, Pushto.[21]

Prior to his leader's arrival, Akbar had already identified two possible escorts—Muhammad Shah and Bhagat Ram Talwar—for the next stage of Bose's journey, across the border of British India. Both were at that time active members of the Forward Bloc. Akbar yielded to Bhagat Ram's eagerness and entrusted him with the task of accompanying

Bose to Kabul. Bhagat Ram, under the assumed name "Rahmat Khan," would be taking his deaf-mute elder relative Ziauddin to the shrine at Adda Sharif, in an attempt to cure him of his affliction. Abad Khan taught Ziauddin how to drink water from a *kandoli* and partake of food from a common plate with his fellow Pathans. With a new set of clothes, complete with the local headgear, Subhas Chandra Bose fully looked the part but had to be careful not to utter a word.[22]

January 26 was observed all over the country as India's Independence Day. On that day in 1930, by the side of the River Ravi in Lahore, the Indian National Congress had ceremonially made a pledge to strive for *purna swaraj,* or "complete independence." On the morning of January 26, 1941, Muhammad Ziauddin and Rahmat Khan set off from Peshawar with Muhammad Shah and an Afridi guide, in a car arranged by Abad Khan. Muhammad Shah returned after dropping them off about half a mile from the actual border. By the afternoon of Independence Day, Subhas Chandra Bose had crossed the territorial limits of Britain's Indian empire and begun his trek across the rugged terrain of the tribal territories beyond the North-West Frontier. The travelers negotiated this difficult route—involving strenuous climbs—during the day, and accepted tribal hospitality in remote villages for the first two nights. They traveled mostly on foot and occasionally rode on a mule, which once slipped on a snowy downward path, leaving its rider bruised but not badly injured. It was well past midnight on January 27–28 when they reached the first village in Afghanistan. At that point, the tribal guide was sent back. The next morning, Ziauddin and Rahmat Khan continued their journey toward the Afghan capital. Eventually they reached the Peshawar-Kabul highway, near the village of Garhdi. The travelers managed to hitch a ride on a truck loaded with tea-chests, and arrived in Jalalabad late on the night of January 28. The next day they visited the shrine in Adda Sharif, near Jalalabad, and made contact with a political associate, Haji Muhammad Amin. On January 30 they started out toward Kabul in a *tonga,* then switched to a truck, reaching the checkpoint at Bud Khak the next morning. Another *tonga* ride brought them to Kabul late on the morning of January 31, 1941.[23]

Meanwhile, in Calcutta, a drama was enacted at Bose's Elgin Road home on Independence Day, January 26. Sisir had returned to Calcutta on the evening of January 18 and had accompanied his father to the wedding of a granddaughter of Subhas's political guru, Deshbandhu Chitta Ranjan Das. There he had dutifully answered questions about the poor state of his uncle's health. The niece and nephews in the know consumed their uncle's food, to keep up the pretense that he was still confined to his room. Subhas had told Sisir that if they could only hold out for four or five days, he would have enough time to get away. Since a court hearing was scheduled for January 27, in connection with one of the sedition cases, the conspirators in Calcutta decided to report that they could not find Bose, rather than cede the initiative to the police. After leaving clear instructions on how Subhas's disappearance should be disclosed, Sarat and Sisir left for their garden house in Rishra, outside Calcutta. Subhas's food, consumed by his niece and nephews during the previous few days, was now left uneaten; and the cook, upon discovering this, naturally raised a hue and cry. Two anxious nephews hurried to Rishra to inform Sarat that Subhas had disappeared. Sisir drove his father back to the Elgin Road home in Calcutta, to hear family members and domestic staff give their version of events and to take stock of the situation. Subhas's mother, Prabhabati, was distraught. Seeing her in distress, Sarat tried to reassure her and moved the headquarters of his cover-up operations to Woodburn Park. Sisir was sent in his Wanderer to search the areas around the Keoratala burning ghat and the temple at Kalighat. A holy man, who believed Subhas had renounced the world, promised to wake the goddess at night to seek further information.[24]

The news of Subhas's disappearance was published in two friendly newspapers, the *Ananda Bazaar Patrika* and the *Hindusthan Standard,* on the morning of January 27. It was then picked up by Reuters and transmitted to the world, leaving British intelligence officers embarrassed and bewildered.[25] The police arrived in force at the Elgin Road home and started questioning everyone. Sisir observed them as they looked at all the wrong points of possible exit from the house. One agent reported that Subhas Chandra Bose had left his home on January 25 for Pondicherry, to join his old friend Dilip Kumar Roy in religious seclusion.[26] Sarat and Sisir made subtle efforts to propagate the renunciation theory. An anxious telegram from Mahatma Gandhi elicited a three-word reply from Sarat: "Circumstances indicate renunciation." But he would not deliberately mislead Rabindranath Tagore, who had stood by Subhas during his political battles with Gandhi in 1939. "May Subhas receive your blessings wherever he may be," was the cable the poet received from Sarat in response to his query.[27]

The police could see that Prabhabati was genuinely disconsolate. While most of the police officers and intelligence agents floundered and blamed one another, the most astute among them, J. V. B. Janvrin, deputy commissioner of police of the Special Branch in Calcutta, believed there were "grave reasons to doubt" that sudden religious fervor was the "true explanation" for Subhas's disappearance. On January 27, Janvrin forwarded to Delhi an intercepted letter dated January 23 from the amateurish Aurobindo to a colleague, saying the reason he could not accept an invitation to travel outside Bengal would become evident on January 27. But this error brought the police no closer to fathoming what had really taken place. One report from Punjab claimed to know of a plot to fly Subhas toward Russia. Another conjectured that Subhas's friend Nathalal Parikh, who had visited from Bombay in December, may have got him a false passport to travel to Japan. There was serious speculation that Bose may have left Calcutta on January 17 on a ship called the *Thaisung,* which had sailed for Penang, Singapore, and Hong Kong.[28]

All this bungling made Viceroy Linlithgow furious with Governor Herbert, who had ventured to suggest that if their inveterate opponent had indeed left India, this might not turn out to be such a bad thing. Linlithgow believed that Bose's escape reflected very poorly on those who were responsible for keeping him under surveillance; and if he had left so easily, he might just as easily return to torment them.[29] Richard Tottenham, of the Home Department in Delhi, was categorical that the government had "wanted to prevent Bose from doing harm within India or abroad," but that "Bose had hoodwinked the police." "How he arranged to escape and where he now is," he wrote on February 13, "is still a mystery," and he told Linlithgow that Herbert "was by no means proud of the performance." Janvrin, in Calcutta, may have been outmaneuvered, but his assessment of Subhas Chandra Bose was on the mark. Even if Bose had left home to become a *sannyasi* (an ascetic), this police detective was certain it was not for religious reasons, but to plot a mass revolution. The other alternative was that Bose had gone abroad to seek foreign help for his country's freedom. "He would never, I think," Janvrin concluded, "cease to strive his utmost to achieve what has been his life's aim—the complete independence of India."[30]

In Kabul, a hub of international espionage in the Second World War, Subhas Chandra Bose faced an agonizing wait in the pursuit of his life's aim. Upon arrival in the Afghan capital on January 31, Rahmat Khan and his deaf-mute relative Ziauddin had found lodging in a *serai* (inn) near the Lahori Gate. But what was to be the wanderer's next destination? After seeing their uncle off at Gomoh Station, Asoke had remarked that Subhas seemed to be blazing the trail of Indian revolutionaries toward Russia. Sisir had agreed with the bit about the revolutionary trail but was convinced that, in the wartime context, it led to Germany.[31] During the first few days in Kabul, Bhagat Ram alias Rahmat Khan made a couple of futile attempts to establish contact with the Soviet ambassador.[32]

Bose then decided to take matters into his own hands; he barged into the German Embassy. It was Germany and not the Soviet Union that was at war with Britain, and there were Indian prisoners-of-war in German and Italian custody. All that the Soviet Union had was a non-aggression pact with Germany. The German minister in Kabul, Hans Pilger, cabled the German foreign minister in Berlin on February 5: "Advised Bose urgently about the local Afghan security system after he had visited me rashly at the embassy, asked him to keep himself hidden amongst Indian friends in the bazaar and contacted the Russian Ambassador on his behalf." The Russian envoy had expressed a rather bizarre suspicion that there might be a British plot behind Bose's wish to travel through Russia—a plan to engender conflict between Russia and Afghanistan. Pilger therefore thought it was "indispensable to take up the matter with Moscow as a follow-up for making journey possible." He added that the Italian ambassador in Kabul had already informed Rome.[33] On February 8 the Italian chargé d'affaires in Berlin spoke to Ernst Woermann of the German Foreign Ministry, offering Italy's good offices in Moscow to facilitate Bose's journey to Germany via Russia. If the German foreign minister permitted that step, Woermann wrote that the Italian ambassador "should get in touch with Count Schulenburg," the German ambassador in Moscow.[34]

Until clearance was obtained from the highest levels in Berlin and Moscow, Bose was to stay in touch with the Germans in Kabul through Herr Thomas of the Siemens Company. Life in the *serai* was becoming increasingly hazardous for Ziauddin and Rahmat Khan. A suspicious Afghan policeman had been frequenting the inn and had to be bribed, first with money and then reluctantly with Bose's gold wristwatch, a present from his father. In the second week of February, Bhagat Ram sought out an old acquaintance from Peshawar, Uttam Chand Malhotra, who now ran a shop in the Indian neighborhood of Kabul and agreed to give Bose refuge in his home. Uttam Chand's nervousness about having raised suspicions in a neighbor led Bose to leave this shelter briefly, but poor health forced him back again once it was deemed safe to do so. The delay in getting a clear signal from Germany led Bhagat Ram in desperation to consider sending Bose across to the Soviet Union, with the aid of an absconder from Peshawar who lived near the Afghan-Soviet border.[35]

At this crucial moment, a message was received from Herr Thomas of Siemens that Subhas Chandra Bose should meet the Italian ambassador, Pietro Quaroni, if he wished to take his plans forward. Bose arrived at the Italian legation on the evening of February 22, 1941, and held discussions with Quaroni through the night. Quaroni was deeply impressed by the man he would soon describe as "intelligent, able, full of passion and without doubt the most realistic, may be the only realist among the Indian nationalist leaders."[36] They considered alternative ways of getting out of Afghanistan. Quaroni was shortly expecting a couple of Italian diplomatic couriers; one of them could give Bose his passport to use, if the Russians agreed to provide a transit visa. Or Bose might travel to Europe through Iran and Iraq. The idea that Bose could try to travel on his own across the Afghan-Soviet frontier was rejected outright.[37]

The Italians were trying to be helpful to Bose. On February 27, 1941, the British intercepted and decoded an Italian telegram dated February 23 that suggested their elusive enemy might be in Kabul. On

March 7, Britain's Special Operations Executive (SOE) informed its representatives in Istanbul and Cairo that Bose "was understood to be traveling from Afghanistan with vital information to Germany via Iran, Iraq and Turkey" and asked them "to wire what arrangements they could make for his assassination."[38] In the event, Bose did not take the Middle Eastern route. On March 3, Count Schulenburg, the German ambassador, cabled Berlin from Moscow: "The Commissariat for External Affairs informs that the Soviet government is ready to give Subhas Bose the visa for journey from Afghanistan to Germany through Russia. The Commissariat has been requested to instruct the Soviet Embassy in Kabul accordingly."[39]

Subhas Chandra Bose was at this time keeping himself busy writing a lengthy political tract justifying his political choices. Drawing on Hegelian dialectics, he argued that in each phase of history, there was a need for a leftist antithesis to a rightist thesis, and that the melding of the two would result in a higher synthesis. Interestingly, he suggested that Gandhi in his "Young India" phase (1920–1922) represented the leftist antithesis to the rightist thesis embodied in moderate constitutionalism. He reiterated his two criteria for "genuine leftism" in Indian politics: uncompromising anti-imperialism in the current phase, and socialist reconstruction once political independence had been won. Having abandoned his fledgling pressure group within the Congress—the Forward Bloc—to raise an army of liberation abroad, he expressed a pious hope that "history will separate the chaff from the grain—the pseudo-Leftists from the genuine Leftists." He claimed that his Forward Bloc had "saved the Congress from stagnation and death," helped "bring the Congress back to the path of struggle, however inadequately," and "stimulated the intellectual and ideological progress of the Congress." He asserted that, "in fullness of time," it would succeed in "establishing Leftist ascendancy in the Congress so that the future progress of the latter (the Congress) may continue unhampered." The "pseudo-Leftists," he charged, "conveniently forget the imperialist character of Britain's war and also the fact that the greatest revolutionary force in the world, the Soviet Union, has entered into a solemn pact with the Nazi Government."[40]

The Germans, Russians, and Italians had come together to clear

Bose's path out of Afghanistan, enabling him to avoid the ambush being plotted by British assassins. Around March 10, 1941, Mrs. Quaroni,
the aristocratic Russian wife of the Italian ambassador, came to Uttam
Chand's shop with a message for Subhas Chandra Bose. He had to be
photographed and needed a new set of clothes. His photograph would
be pasted onto the passport of Orlando Mazzotta, an Italian diplomatic
courier, and Ziauddin would soon have a new identity. On the night
of March 17, Bose was shifted to the home of Signor Crescini, one of
the Italian diplomats. He handed over his political thesis, postdated
March 22; a message to his countrymen from "somewhere in Europe";
and a personal letter in Bengali, to be delivered by Bhagat Ram to his
brother Sarat or his nephew Sisir in Calcutta. Having acquired the
passport of Orlando Mazzotta, he set off from Kabul by car before
dawn, accompanied by a German engineer named Wenger and two
others. He traversed the mountain passes of the Hindu Kush range and
crossed the Afghan frontier at the River Oxus, before driving on to the
historic city of Samarkand. From there, Bose and his companions traveled by train to Moscow. "Bose possessing an Italian passport under
the name of Orlando Mazzotta dropped in at the embassy today,"
Count Schulenburg cabled from Moscow on March 31, 1941, adding
that Bose intended "to call immediately at the Foreign Office" on arrival in Berlin.[41]

   "You will be surprised to get this letter from me," he wrote to Emilie,
"and even more surprised to know that I am writing this from Berlin."[42] He had flown into the German capital the previous afternoon, on
April 2, 1941. It was ironic to find Subhas Chandra Bose, the man who
had espoused left-wing socialist views as president of the Indian National Congress in 1938 and 1939, in wartime Berlin. But the reason lay
in the prisoner-of-war camps of Germany and Italy. Bose had joined
the Indian freedom movement led by Gandhi in 1921, after his resignation from the Indian Civil Service. For two long decades, he had seen
how the soldiers in Britain's Indian Army had remained untouched by
anticolonial mass movements. They gladly did the bidding of their colonial masters, working to extinguish the fires of anticolonial revolts
across the globe. The British Empire could count on Indian soldiers'

loyalty to the king-emperor. Yet Bose wondered: Could a larger cause—that of Indian independence—be broached to them as an alternative to the oath they had taken to buttress the Empire? The question had occurred to anticolonial revolutionaries, but attempts to wean soldiers away from imperial service had achieved limited success during World War I. The crisis of an even bigger international war provided another opportunity to do so. Once Indian soldiers began to fall into the hands of Britain's enemies, it was possible to imagine a concerted effort to turn them against their rulers. An army of liberation raised outside India could potentially serve as a catalyst for another mass movement within the country. Bose was convinced that an armed struggle in aid of the nonviolent agitation at home was imperative to bring the British raj to its knees.

While immersed in his escape plans to fulfill his political mission in Europe, Bose also desired to see his Emilie. In June and July 1939, he had written to her saying that by early September he would probably come to Badgastein, their favorite hill resort near Salzburg.[43] The outbreak of the Second World War on September 1 had upset these travel plans. Now, in April 1941, Subhas asked Emilie to come and join him in Berlin. "Please write at once to Orlando Mazzotta, Hotel Nürnberger Hof, near Anhalter Bahnhof, Berlin," he urged. "Please give my best regards to your mother and greetings to your sister."[44] In a short while, they were reunited in Berlin.

Yet, for Bose, the personal was always subordinate to the political. For Indian anticolonial activists, Berlin was not just the capital of Germany, but a strategic diasporic space they had inhabited since the Swadeshi era at the beginning of the twentieth century, in their efforts to undermine the British raj.[45] For the moment it was Bose's destination, as Germany was once again at war with Britain. He would not hesitate to leave, however, if he could not extract the right terms for India's independence or if circumstances changed. Bose had succeeded in his dramatic escape from British India. Instead of languishing in prison, he had thrown himself into the vortex of the mighty upheavals that were convulsing the entire globe. Once Subhas had safely reached Europe, Sarat Chandra Bose, during a visit to the ailing Rabindranath

Tagore in Santiniketan, had told the poet the true nature of his broth er's mission. In perhaps his last short story, written before his death in August 1941, Tagore described the journey of a lonely traveler making his way across the rugged terrain of Afghanistan in search of freedom.[46] The travails of one man in the midst of a world at war were far from over.

11

In this mortal world, everything perishes and will perish — but ideas, ideals and dreams do not. One individual may die for an idea — but that idea will, after his death, incarnate itself in a thousand lives. That is how the wheels of evolution move on and the ideas, ideals and dreams of one generation are bequeathed to the next. No idea has ever fulfilled itself in this world except through an ordeal of suffering and sacrifice.

What greater solace can there be than the feeling that one has lived and died for a principle? What higher satisfaction can a man possess than the knowledge that his spirit will beget kindred spirits to carry on his unfinished task? What better reward can a soul desire than the certainty that his message will be wafted over hills and dales and over the broad plains to every corner of his land and across the seas to distant lands? What higher consummation can life attain than peaceful self-immolation at the altar of one's Cause?

Hence it is evident that nobody can lose through suffering and sacrifice. If he does lose anything of the earth earthy, he will gain much more in return by becoming the heir to

Political Testament: A page from a letter written by Bose to the governor of Bengal prior to Bose's hunger strike, Calcutta, November 26, 1940. Courtesy: Netaji Research Bureau.

Before the Escape: Bose in his bedroom at 38/2 Elgin Road with Mayor A. R. Siddiqui, eldest brother Satish, and mother Prabhabati, Calcutta, December 1940. Courtesy: Netaji Research Bureau.

Planning the Escape: Sisir Kumar Bose at 1 Woodburn Park, Calcutta, 1941. Courtesy: Netaji Research Bureau.

Orlando Mazzotta: Subhas Chandra Bose disguised as an Italian, 1941. Courtesy: Netaji Research Bureau.

In Wartime Germany: Bose in the garden of his house on Sophienstrasse, Berlin, 1941. Courtesy: Netaji Research Bureau.

Nucleus of an Army: Bose with the first officers of the Indian Legion in Europe, 1942. Courtesy: Netaji Research Bureau.

The Submarine Voyage: Subhas Chandra Bose with Captain Werner Musenberg, 1943. Courtesy: Netaji Research Bureau.

The Submarine Voyage: Subhas Chandra Bose with Abid Hasan, 1943. Courtesy: Netaji Research Bureau.

The Submarine Voyage: Bose being transferred in a rubber raft from the German vessel to the Japanese submarine, April 1943. Courtesy: Netaji Research Bureau.

The Submarine Voyage: Bose with the crew of the Japanese submarine, May 1943; Abid Hasan and Bose in the front row on the left. Courtesy: Netaji Research Bureau.

In Wartime Japan: A portrait of Subhas Chandra Bose, Tokyo, June 1943. Courtesy: Netaji Research Bureau.

India's Army of Liberation: The Indian National Army (INA) in Singapore, July 5, 1943. Courtesy: Netaji Research Bureau.

The INA and Its Netaji: Bose reviewing his troops in Singapore, 1943. Courtesy: Netaji Research Bureau.

On to Delhi: INA soldiers marching past as Netaji takes the salute, Singapore, 1943. Courtesy: Netaji Research Bureau.

On to Delhi: Netaji reviewing a mechanized unit of the INA, Singapore, 1943. Courtesy: Netaji Research Bureau.

A Call to Women: Bose addressing a women's meeting, Singapore, 1943; photograph of Gandhi in the background. Courtesy: Netaji Research Bureau.

Women's Regiment: Bose reviewing the Rani of Jhansi Regiment with Lakshmi Swaminathan, Singapore, 1943. Courtesy: Netaji Research Bureau.

Proclaiming Freedom: The announcement of the Provisional Government of Free India, Singapore, October 21, 1943. Courtesy: Netaji Research Bureau.

Head of State: Netaji Subhas Chandra
Bose outside the Imperial Hotel, Tokyo,
November 1943. Courtesy: Netaji
Research Bureau.

Head of State: Bose in a car on the way to see Emperor Hirohito of Japan, Tokyo, November
1943. Courtesy: Netaji Research Bureau.

Lighting Up: Bose in Tokyo, November 1943. Courtesy: Netaji Research Bureau.

Raising a Toast: Subhas Chandra Bose with Ba Maw of Burma and José Laurel of the Philippines, Tokyo, November 1943. Courtesy: Netaji Research Bureau.

Kadam Kadam Barhae Ja: Soldiers marching toward Delhi with Netaji's portrait held aloft, 1944. Courtesy: Netaji Research Bureau.

Freeing the Bastille: Bose walking out of the Cellular Jail, Andaman Islands, December 1943. Courtesy: Netaji Research Bureau.

Supreme Commander: Bose at the front, 1944. Courtesy: Netaji Research Bureau.

Ref.

SADAR DAFTAR
ARZI HUKUMATE AZAD HIND
(THE PROVISIONAL GOVERNMENT OF FREE INDIA)

16. 4. 44

Jai Hind,

I have an opportunity of sending mail to Rangoon and I am taking this opportunity of scribbling a few lines before crossing the frontier. Once I do so, I do not know when I shall be able to communicate with you again.

Things are going on very well at the front — on the whole — and the spirits of all are high.

Please convey my respectful namaskars to Swamiji and accept same yourself.

Besides our troops, many many men of the Reconstruction Department from Azad and Rangoon have gone forward. We shall soon be meeting them in Free India. Azad Hind.

Jindabad!

Jai Hind
Subhas Chandra Bose

To
Brahmachari Kailasam
Syam.

Toward Free India: A letter from Bose to Brahmachari Kailasam, April 16, 1944. Courtesy: Netaji Research Bureau.

Freedom's Battle: Bose reviewing an anti-aircraft battery of the Indian National Army, Burma, 1944. Courtesy: Netaji Research Bureau.

INA Officers: Netaji with A. C. Chatterji, M. Z. Kiani, and Habibur Rahman, 1944. Courtesy: Netaji Research Bureau.

Unity, Faith, Sacrifice: Bose laying the foundation stone of the INA Martyrs' Memorial, Singapore, July 8, 1945. Courtesy: Netaji Research Bureau.

Signing Off: Autographed photo of Bose in Bangkok on August 17, 1945. Courtesy: Netaji Research Bureau.

The Last Salute: Bose at Saigon airport, August 17, 1945. Courtesy: Netaji Research Bureau.

Trying to Be Brave: Sisir Kumar Bose just after his release from prison, September 1945. Courtesy: Netaji Research Bureau.

Wife and Daughter: Emilie and Anita, November 1948. Courtesy: Netaji Research Bureau.

Looking Back: Prime Minister Nehru visits the Netaji Museum, Netaji Research Bureau, Calcutta, 1961. He is being shown around by Sisir Kumar Bose; the child at Nehru's feet is the author. Courtesy: Netaji Research Bureau.

Offering Incense: Indira Gandhi pays homage to Netaji's memory at the Renko-ji Temple, Tokyo, June 25, 1969. Courtesy: Netaji Research Bureau.

7

The Terrible Price of Freedom

My allegiance and my loyalty has ever been and will ever be to India and to India alone, no matter in which part of the world I may live at any given time.

—SUBHAS CHANDRA BOSE, in a broadcast from Berlin, May 1, 1942

The exigencies of the Second World War gave rise to strange alliances, none stranger than the ones that led the arch-imperialist Winston Churchill to make common cause with Josef Stalin, and the uncompromising anti-imperialist Subhas Chandra Bose to shake hands with Adolf Hitler. When Bose escaped from India, Germany and the Soviet Union still had a nonaggression pact. Fascism and communism were entwined in a cynical and awkward embrace. The internal politics of European states had little to do with international alliances. Britain and France, the countries that held sway over the two largest colonial empires, had entered the war in September 1939 in defense of Poland, which at that time had a dictatorial regime. Their slogans of freedom and democracy sounded hollow to their colonial subjects. By June 1940, the German *Blitzkrieg* had overrun France. Paris had fallen to Hitler's army, and the German *Luftwaffe* was conducting relentless bombing raids on London, the first city of the British Empire.

"When the Nazi hordes crossed the German frontier into Holland and Belgium only the other day with the cry of 'nach Paris' on their lips," Bose wrote on June 15, 1940, "who could have dreamt that they would reach their objective so soon?" He went on to "make a guess" about the terms of agreement that the Soviet Union might arrange with Germany and Italy: Germany would be given a free hand on the Continent, minus the Balkans; Italy would have preeminence in the Mediterranean region; and the Russian sphere of influence would include the Balkans and the Middle East.[1] Though this was an accurate assessment of what the Russians and even the German military brass might find acceptable, Bose miscalculated on the predilections of the German Führer. Hitler was not prepared to cede the Balkans to the Russian sphere of influence.

During the first six months of 1940 the chief of the German High Command, General Alfred Jodl, had drawn up plans for coordinated German and Soviet action in Afghanistan and India. The Germans were already funding the Faqir of Ipi and inciting his tribal followers on India's northwest frontier to harass the British in Waziristan. When Germany, Japan, and Italy signed a tripartite pact on September 27, 1940, India was deemed to be within the Russian zone of influence. The Soviet Union, however, was less interested in India and more concerned about retaining its traditional upper hand in Eastern Europe and the Balkans. Molotov may have signed the German-Soviet pact with Ribbentrop in 1939, but on a November 1940 visit to Berlin the Soviet foreign minister refused to yield on Europe. Faced with Molotov's determined effort to undermine his designs, Hitler made up his mind to invade the Soviet Union. By contrast, Japan's relations with Russia improved as the "strike north" strand in Japanese strategic thinking lost out to the advocates of striking south against Britain in Southeast Asia and the United States in the Pacific.

By the time Bose escaped from India, in January 1941, the German war machine might have seemed unstoppable in Western Europe, but he did not know that the German-Soviet pact was hanging by the most tenuous thread. In addition to wanting to get first-hand information on the course of the war and mobilizing Indian soldiers and civilians abroad for a final assault on the British raj, Bose gave one other reason to his followers for coming to Germany: in the event Germany signed a separate peace with a battered but undefeated Britain, he wanted a strong Indian voice to defend India's interests at the negotiating table. Otherwise, he feared that India would become a mere pawn in the struggle between the new imperial powers and the old. "In the early part of his stay in Europe," his deputy A. C. N. Nambiar has written, "he had more fears of German victory than doubts regarding it."[2] Hitler's admiration for Britain was undiminished, and he greatly preferred forging solidarity among the "Nordic races" to aligning with those he had derided as "Asiatic jugglers." Bose's single-minded absorption in the cause of India's independence led him to ignore the ghastly brutalities perpetrated by the forces of Nazism and fascism in Europe. By going to Germany because it happened to be at war with Britain, he ensured that his reputation would long be tarred by the opprobrium that was due the Nazis. A pact with the devil: such was the terrible price of freedom.

Orlando Mazzotta

In Kabul, Bose had discussed his plan of an Indian revolution with Pietro Quaroni, the Italian ambassador. On April 2, 1941, the day Bose arrived in Berlin, Quaroni sent a favorable report to Rome on Bose's proposals about India. As a "first step," Bose wanted "to constitute in Europe a 'Government of Free India,' something on the lines of the various free governments that have been constituted in London." Quaroni had asked Bose about "the possibilities in the field of terrorism." According to Quaroni's report, Bose had replied that "the terroristic organization of Bengal and other similar ones in different parts of India still exist," but he was "not much convinced of the usefulness of terrorism." He was, however, prepared to consider sending instructions about "large-scale sabotage" to impede Britain's war effort. The encounter with Bose had convinced Quaroni about the value of using the "revolution weapon" with regard to India, "the corner-stone of the British Empire."[3]

Just a week later, on April 9, Bose submitted a detailed memorandum with an explanatory note to the German government, setting out the work to be done in Europe, Afghanistan, the Tribal Territory, and India. He pointed out that the "overthrow of British power in India can, in its last stages, be materially assisted by Japanese policy in the Far East." He wrote with prescience: "A defeat of the British Navy in the Far

East including the smashing up of the Singapore base will automatically weaken British military strength and prestige in India." Yet he felt that a prior agreement between the Soviet Union and Japan would both pave the way for a settlement with China and free up Japan to move confidently against the British in Southeast Asia.[4]

At a meeting with the German foreign minister, Joachim von Ribbentrop, at the Imperial Hotel in Vienna on April 29, 1941, Bose was disappointed to hear that the German government felt it would be premature to accept his plan. He suggested that significant numbers of Indian prisoners-of-war captured in North Africa could be organized into an effective fighting force against the British. Ribbentrop responded that the time for such action had not yet come and he refused to make a public statement in support of Indian independence. When Bose probed further, saying the Indians were concerned that Britain might accept defeat in Europe but hold on to its empire in India, the German foreign minister expressed the opinion that the British, having refused Hitler's olive branch, had doomed their empire. Asked about the Indian attitude toward Germany, Bose "wanted to admit in all frankness that feeling against National Socialists and the fascists had been rather strong in India," because they were seen as "striving to dominate the other races." The foreign minister "interjected at this point that National Socialism merely advocated racial purity, but not its rule over other races."[5] Bose's first encounter with a senior German minister was not a happy one.

Undeterred, on May 3 Bose submitted a supplementary memorandum in which he asked the Axis powers to make a clear declaration of policy regarding the freedom of India and the Arab countries. The anti-British revolt in Iraq had just occurred, and he urged the Germans to support the Iraqi government. "For the success of the task of exterminating British power and influence from the countries of the Near and the Middle East," he wrote, "it is desirable that the status quo between Germany and the Soviet Union should be maintained." He also discussed four possible routes for opening up a channel of communication between Germany and India; of those four, he favored the one going through Russia and Afghanistan. An invasion spearheaded by an Indian legion from the traditional northwesterly direction, he believed, would greatly help India's unarmed freedom fighters at home.[6] Before implementing any of his plans, Bose demanded that the tripartite powers make an unambiguous and unequivocal declaration recognizing Indian independence. In the latter half of May, he wrote up a draft of such a declaration and tried his best to get the German and Italian governments to issue it publicly.[7] The Germans and Italians gave various excuses for delaying it. One reason for this prevarication was that the tripartite powers had tacitly agreed that India was within the Russian sphere of influence, and they could not at this stage publicly repudiate that position.

Bose was on a visit to Rome when he received news that on June 22, 1941, Germany had invaded the Soviet Union. He was utterly dismayed. The international scenario "looked gloomy."[8] Bose's strategy had been critically dependent on the continuance of the German-Soviet pact. He had even indulged in some wishful thinking that a rapprochement between Japan and China could be facilitated through Soviet mediation. Hitler's Operation Barbarossa, which had been secretly in the works even as Bose passed through Moscow, upset all his plans. He decided to be characteristically frank, forthright, and fearless in speaking his mind to the Germans. He told the German Foreign Office in clear terms: "The Indian people felt definitely that Germany was the aggressor." The Germans thought Bose was "strongly influenced by the Soviet thesis on the question of the origin of the German-Russian conflict." They tried to reassure him that they remained "firm" in their "intention regarding a proclamation for a free India," but were waiting for a "suitable time."[9]

Bose returned to Berlin on July 17. On that day, his instructor in German, Gieselher Wirsing, found him seated in a lotus position with a grave look on his face and a world map in front of him. He railed against Hitler's decision to invade the Soviet Union and warned that it would have very bad consequences.[10] In a letter to Ribbentrop on August 15, Bose stressed that without a declaration regarding Indian independence, "the nearer the German armies move towards India, the more hostile will the Indian people become towards Germany." "The march of the German troops towards the East," he warned Ribbentrop, "will be regarded as the approach not of a friend, but of an enemy."[11]

Yet perseverance in adversity was a quality that Subhas Chandra Bose possessed in full measure. He gradually shook off the deep depression that had descended on him on June 22. With the help of Indian exiles—including students—in various parts of Europe, he set up a Free India Center; and from among Indian soldiers, he raised an Indian legion. He sought out talented young Indians who, though of different ideological persuasions, were all committed to the goal of India's freedom, and he asked them to join him in crafting in microcosm the future free India of his dreams. Indians of many religious and linguistic backgrounds—A. C. N. Nambiar, Abid Hasan, N. G. Swamy, N. G. Ganpuley, K. M. Bhatt, M. R. Vyas, P. B. Sharma, Pramode Sengupta, J. K. Banerji, A. M. Sultan, Habibur Rahman, and Girija Mookerjee—were drawn into the movement by Bose's magnetic pull.

"Where is Nambiar?" Subhas had asked Emilie as soon as she joined him in Berlin in April 1941. The staunchly anti-Nazi Arathil Candeth Narayanan Nambiar, from Kerala, had been a close friend since 1933. After being arrested by the Nazi government in 1933, he had relocated to Prague, where he helped Bose strengthen Indo-Czech ties. The Munich Pact of 1938 and the ensuing German occupation of Czechoslovakia in March 1939 forced him to leave Prague for Paris. In mid-1941 Bose tracked him down in Foix, France, where Nambiar was living quietly with his newfound love, Madame de Saussure. In August they met in Paris, and Bose tried to persuade Nambiar to join him in Berlin. He laid out three possible outcomes of the war. He was worried about an outright German victory, and hoped that an understanding with Italy on the winning side might be to India's benefit. If the Allies and the Axis powers fought each other to a draw or a truce, Nehru and he working together could improve the terms for India. If Germany was defeated, he would still have advanced the cause of Indian independence internationally. Nambiar's ideological qualms and personal life stood in the way of an immediate move to Berlin. But eventually, in January 1942, Nambiar came to Berlin and took charge at the Free India Center as Bose's deputy.[12]

N. G. Swami of Tamil Nadu and Abid Hasan of Hyderabad had joined much earlier, in August 1941. Swami had come to the attention of Bose in 1934, when he made strong protests from Vienna against the

German government's treatment of Indians. On another occasion, as a student, he had been expelled from class by a German professor for expressing sympathy with the Jews. In 1941, when he was working for the German engineering company Siemens, he was invited to meet an Indian leader of known political standing and was astonished to find himself face to face with Subhas Chandra Bose. He soon brought along his friend Abid Hasan, an engineering student, and they became Bose's close aides.[13] Girija Mookerjee, who came with Nambiar from France in January 1942, found that during the preceding six months the Indians in Berlin had fallen under "the spell of Subhas's charm." M. R. Vyas found Bose, who was "basically an introvert," to be "a very pleasant talking partner, quite patient, tolerant and appreciative." When Bose was asked the hostile question why he, a socialist, had come to Berlin, he "displayed no annoyance" and "seemed to understand" and share the questioner's reasoning. Bose explained to Vyas "how Lenin, though fundamentally opposed to German 'Kaiserism,' had used Germany as a base of operation during World War I to fight Czarism, which he considered to be the root of all evils in Russia." He "never sounded pedantic or overbearing," and Vyas noted with "amazement and admiration" that Bose, even when conversing with common soldiers, never showed the slightest trace of "I know better than you" superiority.[14]

The circle of Indians Bose gathered around him interacted with the special India division of the German Foreign Office headed by the Oxford-educated Adam von Trott zu Solz and his deputy, Alexander Werth. A Rhodes scholar at Oxford, the aristocratic Trott was a skilled international lawyer and had traveled widely in China, Britain, and the United States. After the outbreak of the war, he had been assigned to the Foreign Office desk dealing with the United States, Britain, and the British Empire. He used this position as a cover for his anti-Nazi activities, and was later executed for his part in Claus von Stauffenberg's failed plot, in July 1944, to assassinate Hitler. As a result of his political opposition, Werth had already suffered imprisonment at the hands of the Nazis in 1934 and subsequently went to Britain, where he was called to the bar at the Middle Temple. He was permitted to return to Germany in 1939, on condition that he join the army; he was recruited in 1940 by the Foreign Office because of his knowledge of the Anglo-

Saxon world. These diplomats shielded the Indians, many of whom had left-leaning political beliefs, from what might have been rougher encounters with the Nazi party hierarchy. Werth believed that without Trott and his devoted team of workers at the Foreign Office, Bose would "probably not have remained in Berlin." From the spring of 1941 onward, they met often with Bose. They "felt the strength of his will power, the honesty of his intentions and the inexorability of his personal dedication to India's cause."[15]

In June 1941, long after Bose had safely reached Europe, the Special Operations Executive (SOE) in Istanbul sought confirmation of the continuing validity of the March order from London to assassinate him. In late May, Delhi had informed London that they had thought Bose "would be used for Radio Propaganda from Russia, Italy or Germany, but nothing of the sort has eventuated." They believed, therefore, that Bose might still be in Afghanistan, and wondered "whether demand should be presented to Afghan Government to deal with him under rules of practice."[16] It was on June 13 that SOE in Istanbul inquired whether the assassination order was still in effect. Sir Frank Nelson, the chief of SOE, was reported to be "in a minority of one at that morning's meeting in insisting that it should be referred to the Foreign Office. He said he was sure the Secretary of State for India [L. S. Amery], who was also interested in this question, would not take kindly to Sir Hughe Knatchbull-Hugessen [the British ambassador to Turkey] objecting to Bose being liquidated on Turkish territory."[17] Reconfirmation of the assassination decision having been obtained, London cabled SOE in Istanbul telling their operative Gardyne de Chastelain that "the Foreign Office agreed to the liquidation of Chandra Bose being carried out on Turkish territory," but that Gardyne de Chastelain should tell no one about this.[18]

By now, Bose was well beyond the reach of his potential assassins. Following his return from Rome and Vienna in July 1941, Subhas lived with Emilie in a mansion at Sophienstrasse 7 in the Charlottenburg neighborhood of Berlin. The house had been previously occupied by the American military attaché. Here, amid the tumult of war, Bose spent a period of home life that his hectic political career in India had denied him. Yet the trappings of status accorded to him, such as the form of address "Your Excellency," could not relieve his frustration with the Germans and Italians. In September, he went to Badgastein and had to be coaxed back to Berlin with promises of forward movement in implementing his plans.

Bose's Indian followers held him in awe. Respected Indian leaders were generally granted honorific titles—Gandhi was "Mahatma" ("Great Soul"); Bose's political mentor Chitta Ranjan Das was "Deshbandhu" ("Friend of the Country"). Tagore had hailed Bose as "Deshnayak" ("Leader of the Country") in 1939, but it was the simpler "Netaji" ("Revered Leader"), used by Indians in Europe and later in Southeast Asia, that caught the popular imagination. A soldier had referred to Bose as "Hamare Neta" ("Our Leader"), and from that it was a small step to "Netaji." Far from smacking of the fearsome connotations of "Führer," it was a very Indian form of expressing affection mingled with honor. The man being so honored expressed his disapproval, but his followers had their way.[19]

Both N. G. Swami and Hasan had volunteered to join the military wing of the movement. Swami became the leading figure among ninety young men who received sophisticated training as members of an elite commando force at Meseritz, near Hamburg. The commander in charge of the training camp was a very capable German officer named Walter Harbich. Indian members of this unit wore a German-style uniform with a silk emblem—the Indian national tricolor with a springing tiger in the center—stitched on their left sleeve. While most wore a German field cap or helmet as headgear, Sikh soldiers wore green cloth turbans and Sikh officers were distinguished by turbans made of light-blue silk. A veteran of World War I, Harbich had the political sophistication to implement Bose's ideas about mingling members of the different religious and linguistic communities, instead of keeping them separate, as the British had done. Bose wanted Indians to be united in the smallest tactical unit, regardless of their religious affiliation. "Contrary to the original doubts," Harbich reported, "the result was surprisingly good."[20] According to a British intelligence officer who later interrogated the Meseritz recruits, "Morale, discipline and Indo-German relations were excellent" and "the German officers first-rate."[21]

Hasan's primary role was to make the initial overtures to Indian prisoners-of-war being held since early 1941 in a camp at Annaberg, near Dresden, before Netaji himself came to persuade them to switch their allegiance to the cause of free India. The actual recruitment had to await the transfer of the majority of the prisoners taken in North Africa, who were being held in Italy, and a formal decision by the German war office to permit the raising of an Indian legion. Once this permission came, toward the end of 1941, a second and larger training camp was established at Frankenberg, later moved to Königsbruck, in Saxony. The Legion at Frankenberg was under the Reserve Forces headed by General Fromm, who, like Trott, would later be executed for his involvement in the July 1944 plot to assassinate Hitler.

Recruitment into the Indian Legion was entirely voluntary. The process began slowly, in December 1941 and January 1942, with the noncommissioned officers among the prisoners doing their best to prevent the ordinary soldiers from enlisting in the legion. The call of patriotic duty met with obstacles: the soldiers had taken an earlier oath to serve their British masters, and they were concerned about the well-being of their families in India. It required all of Bose's powers of persuasion to create the nucleus of India's army of liberation.[22] The fact that the Indian civilian population in Europe was quite small also made it difficult to bridge the gap between anticolonial politics and the military mentality. In the end, no more than four thousand of the nearly seventeen thousand Indian prisoners-of-war in German and Italian captivity agreed to join the Indian legion.[23]

The Free India Center was formally inaugurated on November 2, 1941, at Liechtenstein Alee 2, in the Tiergarten area of Berlin. The green, saffron, and white tricolor of the Indian National Congress was adopted as the national flag. The image of a springing tiger, reminiscent of the eighteenth-century anti-British warrior Tipu Sultan of Mysore, replaced the *charkha* ("spinning wheel") in the middle, though Bose would revert to the Gandhian symbol in Southeast Asia. After independence, both the *charkha* and the tiger would give way to the Asokan *chakra* ("wheel"), evocative of the ancient Maurya Empire. A Tagore song—"Jana Gana Mana Adhinayak Jaya He," seeking divine benediction for India—was chosen by Netaji as the national anthem; this choice would be ratified by the Indian government after independence was achieved in 1947. Bose had played a key role in resolving the controversy surrounding the other song, "Bande Mataram," in 1937—he had opted not to use it, since he was keen to win Muslim support. He was open to accepting Muhammad Iqbal's song "Sare Jahan se achha Hindustan Hamara"—proclaiming the excellence of India compared to the whole world—as the national anthem, but in the end the collective decision was in favor of Tagore. Bose asked his followers to find a common national greeting that would have a nice ring to it and would be acceptable to all religious communities. One day, Abid Hasan heard some Rajput soldiers greet each other with "Jai Ramji Ki"—a phrase that had a musical quality. Hasan changed it to "Jai Hindustan Ki." This did not quite work, but the abbreviated form "Jai Hind" ("Victory to India") sounded perfect, and Netaji enthusiastically embraced it as India's national greeting.[24] These words became India's national slogan in 1947, and continue to reverberate across the length and breadth of India. The decisions regarding the national anthem and greeting were examples of Bose's well-honed political intuition, and would be among his lasting legacies to independent India.

During 1941, Bose used two channels of communication to stay in touch with family and friends in India: one went via Kabul, the other through Tokyo. On March 31, Sisir, sitting at Woodburn Park in Calcutta, had received a visitor's slip saying, "Bhagat Ram—I come from frontier." Bhagat Ram handed over letters and documents from Subhas to Sarat and Sisir, and arrangements were made to send a young Bengali revolutionary, Santimoy Ganguli, to Peshawar and Kabul. The Kabul conduit, however, became compromised once Bhagat Ram revealed his German and Italian contacts to the Russians in September 1941 and began to play the role of a consummate multiple agent. The German invasion of the Soviet Union transformed the war, in the eyes of many communists and their fellow travelers, from an imperialist war to a people's war. Bhagat Ram shed his old Forward Bloc connections to join a local organization known as the Kirti Kisan party, and thus moved close to the communist line on the war. Much later, in November 1942, he would be arrested and immediately released by the British, on condition that he supply intelligence about Bose's moves through the Communist party of India.[25]

Subhas Chandra Bose was also able to send wireless messages from Berlin to Tokyo that were delivered to his brother Sarat by diplomats of the Japanese consulate in Calcutta. Sisir would drive the Japanese consul-general, Katsuo Okazaki, to his father's garden house in Rishra. After Okazaki's departure, another officer named Ota, along with his wife, wearing an Indian sari, would come to Rishra for ostensibly social visits. While the British police in Calcutta were aware that these meetings were taking place, they could do no more than speculate on the content of the conversations. The vulnerability of the Japanese telegraphic code at the highest governmental level eventually undermined the security of the messages the Bose brothers exchanged via Tokyo. A telegram from the Japanese foreign minister in Tokyo to his ambassador in Berlin—a message containing one of Sarat's communications with Subhas, dated September 1, 1941—landed on Winston Churchill's desk on September 5. The prime minister was assured that "the Government of India were awaiting an opportunity to arrest Sarat and the prominent members of his group."[26]

Toward the end of the year, Sarat Chandra Bose was able to bring about a major change in the provincial politics of Bengal. The coalition of the Krishak Praja party and the Muslim League was replaced by a new formation headed by the Krishak Praja leader, Fazlul Huq, in alliance with Sarat's followers in the Bengal legislature. Sarat himself was slated to become the home minister in charge of police and law and order in Bengal. On December 11, 1941, as the new ministry of the Progressive Coalition party took office, J. V. B. Janvrin arrived at Woodburn Park to arrest Sarat. The detainee was to be held as a prisoner in distant south India for the duration of the war. His Japanese contacts were seen to present "a very real and definite danger" to security, and Richard Tottenham of the Home Department in Delhi was clear "that it would be impossible to contemplate having Sarat Chandra Bose as a Minister." On December 10 a telegram had arrived from L. S. Amery, secretary of state for India, addressed to Viceroy Linlithgow and calling for the arrest of Sarat Bose "without delay."[27]

Meanwhile, in mid-December, the Germans gave the green light to shift Indian prisoners-of-war from Italy to Germany and to try recruiting them into an Indian legion.[28] But this tardy policy decision was overshadowed by more momentous events in East Asia. Japan's entry into the Second World War on December 7, 1941, and the rapid advance of Japanese troops across Southeast Asia against the Western colonial powers, opened up new strategic possibilities for Subhas Chandra Bose. The fall of Singapore, on February 15, 1942, provided the occasion for Bose to discard his identity as Orlando Mazzotta: he made his first open broadcast to India on February 19, 1942. "The fall of Singapore," he declared, "means the collapse of the British Empire, the end of the iniquitous regime which it has symbolized and the dawn of a new era in Indian history. Through India's liberation will Asia and the world move forward towards the larger goal of human emancipation." More than a year after his dramatic escape from India, his countrymen heard his voice: "This is Subhas Chandra Bose speaking to you over the Azad Hind [Free India] Radio."[29]

The Voice of Free India

The broadcasts on Azad Hind Radio usually began with stirring English lines—"To arms, to arms,/ The Heavens ring,/ With the clarion call,/ To Freedom's fray"—and ended with "Our cause is just!"[30] When Japanese forces took Rangoon from the British, Bose hailed the prospect of Burmese freedom. He derided the propaganda of the British viceroy Archibald Wavell: that India was under threat of enemy attack and that its frontiers, therefore, were at Suez and Hong Kong, which had to be defended with Indian troops. India, Bose pointed out, had "no imaginary Wavellian frontiers," only "a national geographical boundary determined by Providence and nature." Having brought "India into the war" in September 1939, the British were now trying to bring "the war into India."[31]

Mahatma Gandhi now shared this perspective on the war. Though Bose had failed to persuade Gandhi to issue an ultimatum to the British in 1939, the British debacle at the hands of the Japanese in Southeast Asia emboldened the Mahatma to prepare for a final showdown with the British raj. Gandhi believed that India could be spared the devastation of war if the British left India. He was confident of his ability to negotiate with the Japanese, who would have no reason to enter

India if it was rid of the British presence. He regarded the "ordered anarchy" represented by the British raj to be worse than "real anarchy." In the spring of 1942, the apostle of nonviolence was even "prepared to take the risk of violence" to end "the great calamity of slavery."[32]

Since October 1941, the Japanese ambassador in Berlin, Lieutenant General Oshima Hiroshi, and the military attaché, Colonel Yamamoto Bin, had been holding meetings with Subhas Chandra Bose. The Japanese military victories in Southeast Asia, Bose's activities abroad, and Gandhi's increasingly militant mood combined to cause great nervousness among British war leaders. Winston Churchill came under pressure from the U.S. president, Franklin D. Roosevelt, and from his own Labour party colleagues in the British government, to do something to conciliate Indian nationalist opinion. Stafford Cripps had returned from a successful stint as British ambassador to Moscow, and had joined the cabinet a few days after the fall of Singapore. The British viceroy in India, Lord Linlithgow, was a hard-liner opposed to any concessions to Indian demands. In late January he had reported the existence of "a large and dangerous 5th column in Bengal, Assam, Bihar and Orissa," and said he regarded the "potential of pro-enemy sympathy and activity in Eastern India" to be "enormous." "Sarat Bose has been a lesson," the viceroy told L. S. Amery, the secretary of state for India. "India and Burma," Linlithgow wrote in prose that would have done Macaulay proud, "have no natural association with the empire, from which they are alien by race, history and religion, and for which as such neither of them have any natural affection, and both are in the empire because they are conquered countries, which have been brought there by force, kept there by our controls, and which hitherto it has suited to remain under our protection."[33] After the British surrendered at Singapore and fled from Rangoon, Linlithgow's candid observations sounded like obduracy in London. With the utmost reluctance, the British prime minister agreed to send Cripps on a mission to India, hoping both that it would placate his ally across the Atlantic and that it would fail.

Having shed his Italian disguise, Bose was ready to take full advantage of the military and psychological repercussions of the fall of Singapore. On February 26, 1942, he submitted an ambitious eleven-point plan to the tripartite powers. He had made his first broadcast on February 19 from Berlin, but that was not where he wanted to be. He had to go to Rangoon—the capital of Burma, soon to be freed by the Japanese—and make it the base for Indian nationalist propaganda and the springboard for Indian nationalist action. His friends in the German Foreign Office, including Adam von Trott, supported his efforts, and a declaration in support of Indian freedom seemed on the anvil. The draft declaration produced by the German Foreign Office on February 22 contained everything Bose could have asked for:

> Germany, Italy and Japan are convinced that the Indian nation will break the political and economic bonds of British Imperialism and then as master of its own fate will carry out a sweeping transformation of its national life for the lasting benefit of its own people and as contribution to the welfare and the peace of the world. It is no concern of the Tripartite Powers what form the Indian people, after their liberation, will in future give to their interior political organization. It is a matter to be decided upon by the Indian people themselves and their leaders what constitution is the most suitable for their country and how it is to be put into practice. The Tripartite Powers are concerned to end—on a basis of social justice—the misery and poverty of the Indian people, and to see the exploited masses assisted to a proper standard of living as well as to employment and prosperity.[34]

The lack of trust and coordination between Japan and Germany ensured that the moment was lost. The presence of someone of Bose's stature on its soil gave Germany a lever not just in relation to Britain, but also in its negotiations with Japan.

The Japanese had launched their war without caring to inform either their enemies or their allies, and did not intend to follow German directives in matters to do with Asia. Japan wanted Germany to give up its obsession with the Soviet Union and instead concentrate its military might on the British in the Suez. The naval commands of both Japan and Germany wished to establish a link across the Indian Ocean. If this could be done, "the war would be practically won and the British Empire would be finished." This breakthrough, according to the naval strategists, had to "occur soon in order to bring the war to a speedy and happy conclusion." The Japanese even advocated a separate peace between Germany and the Soviet Union, to facilitate Germany's ability to focus on the Mediterranean and link up with the Japanese in the Indian Ocean. Hitler, however, would not entertain the possibility of a truce on the Eastern Front and was determined to wrestle once more with the Russian bear during the summer.[35] With Germany and Japan out of sync, Ribbentrop turned down Bose's request that he be permitted to travel to Asia. Bitter at being let down yet again, Bose left Berlin in a huff for Badgastein. When the Germans sent an emissary to persuade him to return, Bose denounced their lack of seriousness about Indian independence and suggested that he and the Indian cause were being used as a bargaining chip for a possible German compromise with the British.[36]

An Indian compromise with the British raj, however, was something that Bose was not prepared to allow without having his say on the matter. He came back to Berlin to wage a propaganda battle against the Cripps mission. On March 24, 1942, British news agencies reported that Subhas Chandra Bose had been killed in an air crash on his way to attend an important conference in Tokyo. Having heard the news of his own death on the BBC News, Bose was very concerned about what effect it would have on his old and ailing mother. Before Bose could contradict the false news by making a statement on Azad Hind Radio, Gandhi sent a condolence message to Prabhabati: "The whole nation mourns with you the death of your brave son. I share your sorrow to the full. May God give you courage to bear this unexpected loss." Fortunately, Prabhabati suspected that the news of her son's death was not true, and Sisir was able to reassure her and other family members. Subhas himself made a radio broadcast on March 25: "My death is perhaps an instance of wishful thinking." He could imagine that the British government would like to see him dead, since they were trying to win India over for "the purpose of their imperialistic war." He warned the Indian people to be wary of Britain's divisive policies—the sort that had been deployed with such damaging effect in Ireland and Palestine. Gandhi wired Prabhabati again, expressing his joy and relief. The reaction in India to the fabricated news had only confirmed Bose's high standing among his people, at a time when the British were eager to brand him a quisling. In a series of broadcasts in late March and early April 1942, Bose excoriated Stafford Cripps for donning the imperialist mantle and urged the Indian people and leaders to contemptuously reject the offer of dominion status after the war's end.[37]

Bose need not have worried. Gandhi was not of a mind to accept a postdated check on a bank that was obviously failing. Nehru and Azad may have been open to a compromise, if the defense portfolio in the central government could be handed over to the Congress. But Cripps had nothing to offer in the here-and-now: he could only hold out promises for the future. Linlithgow worked closely with Churchill and Amery to make certain that Cripps did not concede anything of substance. Gandhi was not prepared to accept anything less than full independence. Abul Kalam Azad found that "Subhas Bose's escape to Germany had made a great impression on Gandhiji." "He had not formerly approved many of Bose's actions," Azad explained, "but now I found a change in his outlook. Many of his remarks convinced me that he admired the courage and resourcefulness Subhas Bose had displayed in making his escape from India. His admiration for Subhas Bose unconsciously colored his view about the whole war situation."[38]

While deriding the Cripps offer, Bose had welcomed the assurances of Japanese premier Hideki Tojo, who promised "India for the Indians." On April 11, 1942, as the Cripps mission teetered on the brink of failure, the Japanese sent a draft declaration to Germany and Italy, advocating freedom for the Indians and Arabs. The German Foreign Office deemed the draft "too journalistic," but produced an amended draft of its own; on April 16, Ribbentrop presented it to Hitler and urged that it be accepted. The German foreign minister suggested that "peace-favoring circles in Britain" would welcome such a move. Hitler did not take the bait, and rejected the declaration the following day. He saw no reason to accept the declaration just when the Japanese sought it. He was wary—and not a little envious—of Japan's spectacular successes against the European colonial powers in Asia. Italy was more inclined to go along with the Japanese; but at a meeting on April 29 at Klessheim Castle, near Salzburg, Hitler persuaded Mussolini not to issue the declaration.[39] Only when the world was collapsing around him, in the spring of 1945, did Hitler regret his decision not to back the struggle of the colonized peoples of Asia and the Arab world.[40]

The tenacity of Bose now came into play. He thought he could get Italy on his side. On April 19, the renowned Italian journalist Luigi Barzini had published an interview with him in *Il Popolo d'Italia,* describing him as "a Buddha, vivacious and dynamic, though peaceful in his speeches and gestures." Bose had spoken "with devotion and admiration of the Mahatma" and his "composure and self-control" Barzini interpreted as "a sign of Asian nobility."[41] On May 5, putting all his persuasive powers to the test, Bose went to Rome to meet Mussolini in an attempt to get the Salzburg decisions reversed. Galeazzo Ciano, Italy's foreign minister and Mussolini's son-in-law, recorded what transpired in his diary: "I go with Bose to the Duce. A long conference without any new developments, except the fact that Mussolini allowed himself to be persuaded by the arguments produced by Bose to obtain a tripartite declaration in favor of Indian independence. He has telegraphed the Germans, proposing—contrary to the Salzburg decisions—proceeding at once with the declaration. I feel that Hitler will not agree to it very willingly."[42] Ciano was right. Hitler turned down Mussolini's proposal.

While seeking the tripartite powers' endorsement of Indian independence, Bose was keen to distance himself from the ideologies of their totalitarian regimes. In a candid broadcast on May 1, 1942, he made it clear that he was "not an apologist of the Tripartite Powers" and did not see it as his task "to defend what they have done or may do in future." He rebutted "Britain's paid propagandists," and justified his own wartime strategy in the quest of India's liberation in these terms:

> I need no credentials when I speak to my own people. My whole life, which has been one long, consistent and continuous record of uncompromising struggle against British Imperialism, is the best guarantee of my bona fides. If the Britishers[,] who are the past masters in the art of diplomacy and political seduction, have in spite of their best efforts failed to tempt, corrupt or mislead me, no other power on earth can do so. All my life I have been a servant of India and till the last hours of my

life I shall remain one. My allegiance and my loyalty has ever been and will ever be to India and India alone, no matter in which part of the world I may live at any given time.[43]

He had absolutely no doubt where he should be at that particular moment in world history. "Now the time has come," he wrote to Ribbentrop on May 22, 1942, "when the final effort should be made for achieving India's political emancipation. For this purpose, it is absolutely essential that I should be in the East. Only when I am there, shall I be able to direct the revolution along the right channels."[44]

On May 29, 1942, Bose found himself face to face with the German Führer. The official record filed by Paul Schmidt, Hitler's interpreter, gave the date of the meeting as May 27 and the venue as the "Führer's Headquarters." But it is clear from other sources—including the supreme command of the Wehrmacht, the Führer's diary, and the report of the German News Bureau (DNB)—that Bose's one and only encounter with Hitler took place in Berlin on May 29 at the Reich Chancellory. According to Schmidt's detailed account of the conversation, Bose raised the issue of his "journey to East Asia," "motivated by the desire to find a point as close to India as possible, from where the Indian revolution could be directed." Fortunately, the Führer agreed with this proposal and promised logistical support for Bose to travel by submarine from Europe to Asia. Hitler warned Bose against taking the risk of a journey by air, which might entail a forced landing in British territory—he was "too important a personality to let his life be endangered by such an experiment." Either he could travel in a Japanese submarine, or the Führer would "place a German submarine at his disposal, which would take him to Bangkok." Later in the conversation, Bose brought up the matter of Hitler's anti-Indian racist remarks in *Mein Kampf* and sought a clarifying statement for the Indian nation. Hitler evaded the question, saying that he had not wanted "passive resistance for the Reich of the Indian pattern." Bose was lucky not to have the offer of the submarine withdrawn.[45]

A German declaration supporting Indian independence still eluded Bose. Hitler launched into a long monologue on the virtues of political and military realism. He gave the example of Egypt, where Erwin Rommel had launched an offensive the day before. If his general achieved only limited success, a declaration supporting Egyptian independence would be premature. A decisive defeat inflicted on the British forces, on the other hand, would be the occasion for Hitler to goad the Egyptians to throw off the British yoke. India, Hitler pointed out, was "endlessly far" from Germany. Japan, by contrast, "had practically advanced to the borders of India." Revealing the yawning communications gap between the Axis powers, Hitler confessed that "Japan's aim was not known to him." He did not know whether Japan's priority was "to relieve their flanks from being threatened by Chiang-Kai-Shek or to seek a rapprochement with him" or "to turn to Australia or India." Britain's military defeats in Asia "would possibly lead to the collapse of the British Empire." In the prevailing war situation, "Bose should negotiate with the Japanese, not only for influencing events in his motherland, but also for restraining the Japanese themselves from committing psychological mistakes by appropriate advice." Withholding a clear declaration in support of Indian independence, the Führer instead "extended his best wishes to Bose for the success of his journey and plans."[46]

What did Bose make of Hitler at their only face-to-face encounter? Even though Bose got the Führer's nod for his plan to travel to Asia, most of his associates report that the meeting was not a comfortable one. The German foreign minister, Ribbentrop, had escorted Bose to the interview with Hitler. Alexander Werth has reported that Bose bristled at being lectured by Hitler, and that Adam von Trott had to tone down some of Bose's responses into diplomatic language. The official record of the conversation, however, does not say that Trott was present to interpret for Bose. According to Paul Schmidt, the only other people at the meeting were secretary of state Wilhelm Keppler and ambassador Walther Hewel. Girija Mookerjee has written that the meeting was "a disappointment for Subhas" and that he "did not like very much to speak about it." To his aides at the Free India Center, who were curious to hear his opinion of Hitler, he described the Führer as "a sort of German version of the Fakir of Ipi" and declared that "a logical discussion with him of any topic even for a few minutes was practically impossible." Bose dubbed Hitler "baddha pagal" ("raving mad," in Bengali) to his compatriots, but the record of their conversation reveals the Führer to be quite rational, if rather long-winded, in his comments and analyses.[47]

Bose certainly was aware of the pernicious character of the regime he was dealing with, though in May 1942 he could not have known how much worse things would get. It is doubtless difficult to reconcile Bose's ethics, sensibilities, and friendships since the 1930s with his political choice of allies in the 1940s. But he was not alone in accepting as political and strategic allies those whom he would not dream of having as friends. "I am glad to see you," Roosevelt would say to Stalin, when they met in November 1943. In fact, the U.S. president was not pleased to meet a totalitarian dictator who had presided over campaigns of mass murder; but Stalin was a necessary ally in the effort to protect American national interests during World War II. Bose's passionate commitment to the goal of Indian independence determined his wartime alliances with unsavory regimes and their leaders. Gandhi, in his inimitable fashion, had addressed Hitler as "Dear Friend" in a letter he had written on July 23, 1939. "It is quite clear," the Mahatma wrote, "that you are today the one person in the world who can prevent a war which may reduce humanity to its savage state."[48] Once war and savagery did break out, both Gandhi and Bose, in their different ways, tried their best to protect and promote the interests of India.

Bose seemed even more anxious than before to stress his ideological distance from the Axis powers during the weeks following his meeting with Hitler. He had boldly condemned the German invasion of the Soviet Union in 1941, but had remained silent about Germany's domestic policies. He now kept repeating that once freedom was won, it would be "the duty of the Indian people to decide what form of Government they desire and who should guide the future Indian state." "In this fateful hour in India's history," he proclaimed in a key broadcast on June 17, 1942, "it would be a grievous mistake to be carried away by ideological considerations alone. The internal politics of Germany or Italy or Japan do not concern us—they are the concern of the people of those countries." He wanted Indians to "differentiate between the inter-

nal and external policy of Free India." "While standing for full collaboration with the Tripartite Powers in the external sphere," he asserted, "I
stand for absolute self-determination for India where her national affairs are concerned, and I shall never tolerate any interference in the internal policy of the Free Indian State." Insofar as socioeconomic problems were concerned, his views were "exactly what they were when I
was at home—and no one should make the mistake of concluding that
external collaboration with the Tripartite Powers meant acceptance of
their domination or even of their ideology in [India's] internal affairs."
Once his task of liberating India was complete, he would once again
call on Mahatma Gandhi, as he had promised in his farewell talk with
him in June 1940.[49]

During the spring and summer of 1942, Gandhi and Bose drew
closer in their aims and tactics in relation to World War II and the final
struggle for Indian freedom. In late April 1942, Gandhi had drafted a
radical resolution for the Congress Working Committee, calling upon
the British to quit India. "Japan's quarrel is not with India," Gandhi
wrote. "She is warring against the British Empire. India's participation
in the war has not been with the consent of the representatives of the
Indian people. It was a purely British act. If India were freed her first
step would probably be to negotiate with Japan." The Mahatma was
prepared to tell the colonial masters to leave India to anarchy or God.
"Rivers of blood" may have to flow, he told journalists, for India to pay
the "price of freedom."[50] Under the influence of the more cautious
among the leaders, including Nehru and Azad, the Congress Working
Committee adopted a watered-down version of the resolution at its
meetings in the second week of July.

Bose still had a fine intuitive grasp of Indian anticolonial politics,
even though he was located thousands of miles away. "In view of the
internal developments in India," he urged Ribbentrop on July 23, 1942,
"I would like to be in the Far East in the first week of August, if possible."[51] On August 4, Adam von Trott wrote to one of his colleagues that
Bose was expecting a major conflagration in India after the meeting of
the All-India Congress Committee (AICC) on August 8. He was right.
That evening, the AICC delegates gathered on the sprawling Chow-

patty Beach of Bombay and passed the Quit India resolution by a massive majority. Gandhi exhorted his followers to "do or die" in what he envisaged as the final mass movement to expel the British from India. Viceroy Linlithgow had by now perfected his plans to repress the Quit India movement with a heavy hand and crush the Congress organization as a whole. Though he did not act on a suggestion from London to deport Gandhi, the British government imprisoned Gandhi, Nehru, and the entire top leadership of the Congress party in the early morning hours of August 9.

The Quit India movement began in the second week of August 1942 as an urban uprising in which students, other young people, and workers took the most prominent part. The police opened fire in the major cities of Bombay and Calcutta—causing, by their own admission, more than a thousand deaths—and reestablished their control over the major urban centers by the end of the month. From late September, the movement took the form of an agrarian rebellion in certain districts of Bihar, the United Provinces, Bengal, Orissa, and Bombay Province. Mass fury was directed against all visible symbols of government authority. Railway lines were torn up, police stations looted, and revenue and post offices set afire. Orchestrated by middle-ranking leaders, the 1942 movement was the biggest civilian uprising since the 1857 revolt, and was similar to it in its varied, multiclass character. The rebels had perceived British power to be vulnerable, after the hard knocks it had taken in the early years of the war. Yet the British had established a formidable military presence to counter the Japanese threat from Southeast Asia. The weakly organized rebels were overwhelmed by the armed might of the British raj, which was unleashed against them. The government counted more than sixty thousand arrests and some four thousand rebels killed; the Congress claimed that nearly twenty-five thousand Quit India rebels had been martyred. By March 1943, the back of the resistance would be broken.

Bose gave unstinted and enthusiastic support as Gandhi moved toward launching the Quit India movement. Once the rebellion began, Bose broadcast detailed instructions to the insurgents on how to sustain the uprising and make it more effective. Having taken part in all the Congress-led movements since 1921, he was disappointed not to be at home with his people in 1942. There was wistfulness in his tone when he promised that it would "not be long before" he was at their side again. On August 17, 1942, he correctly noted that British colonial rule had been forced to rest on its ultimate coercive foundation:

> The whole world now sees that the velvet glove, which ordinarily hides the mailed fist of Britain, has now been cast away and brute force— naked and unashamed—rules over India. Behind the thick screen of gas, underneath the heavy blows of police batons, amid the continual whistle of bullets and the angry defiance of the injured and the dying— the soul of India asks—"Where are the four freedoms?" The words float over the seven seas to all corners of the globe—but Washington does not reply. After a pause, the soul of India asks again—"Where is the Atlantic Charter, which guaranteed to every nation its own Govern- ment?" This time Downing Street and White House reply simultane- ously—'That Charter was not meant for India.'[52]

In his broadcasts, Bose made a distinction between the American peo- ple and their government. "We thankfully recognize the fact," he said, "that a large section of the American people have sympathy for Indian independence, but unfortunately they are powerless to influence their own Government. So far as American official policy towards India is concerned, it is as imperialistic as that of Britain."[53]

Despite his support for Gandhi, Bose knew that the Congress-led movement of 1942 had failed to inspire all of India's religious commu- nities and regional peoples. He therefore called upon the "progressive elements" of the Muslim League, the Majlis-i-Ahrar, the Jamiat-ul- Ulema, the Azad Muslim League, the Akali Dal, and, last but not the least, the Krishak Praja party of Bengal to form a broad-based patriotic front. He also underlined the key role of the peasantry in the guerrilla war being waged by mostly unarmed rebels in India.[54] Bose may have wondered in August 1942 whether he had made a mistake in traveling to Germany in 1941, but the last thing he wanted was to have been locked away in prison and thus have wasted the opportunity presented by the war. He was also convinced that the quest for Indian freedom was a global struggle. In June 1942 he had sent a message to a conference in Bangkok stressing the need "to link up Indian nationalists all over the world in one all-embracing organization." During the August crisis, he yearned to be close to the eastern borders of India—but despite his best efforts, he had been trapped in Europe since February.

The radio was the only weapon Bose could use to fight alongside his compatriots at home. Azad Hind Radio had been broadcasting since October 1941; and from February 1942 onward, Bose himself was the leading voice calling for a free India. Every day, broadcasts lasting 230 minutes were transmitted in English and seven South Asian languages: Hindustani (a blend of Hindi and Urdu), Bengali, Tamil, Telegu, Gujarati, Persian, and Pushtu. A powerful Philips transmitter at Huizen, in the Netherlands, was used to beam the broadcasts to India, where there were an estimated 120,000 radio sets and where listening to the voice of Azad Hind became a favorite clandestine activity. During the visit of Stafford Cripps, a second broadcasting service—called National Congress Radio—was established, to align the movements within and without to a common purpose. Once the Quit India movement began in earnest, a third service—Azad Muslim Radio—hit the airwaves, urging the Muslims of India to join the struggle for independence. Talented scriptwriters and speakers in Urdu, Habibur Rahman and A. M. Sultan, were put in charge of broadcasts on this channel.

The concern about Hindu-Muslim unity animated Bose's efforts as he went about the task of recruiting soldiers for the Indian Legion. Even though he wanted to be in Asia, he did not let up on his endeavor to wean Indian soldiers in European prisoner-of-war camps from their loyalty to the British. From a modest beginning in December 1941, the Indian Legion grew to four battalions by December 1942. At his very first encounter with Indian soldiers, in the German POW camp at Annaberg, some noncommissioned officers had tried to disrupt the recruitment process. Deeming fully committed recruits to be preferable to vacillating ones, Bose relied entirely on his powers of persuasion in the battle for the hearts and minds of soldiers who had once served the British king-emperor. "In his long dark robe," N. G. Ganpuley has observed, "he looked more like a priest preaching his sermon than a military leader addressing soldiers."[55] Girija Mookerjee has described a rally

near Dresden, where a crowd of Indian soldiers from peasant backgrounds came to hear Bose speak on an autumn afternoon in 1942. He
addressed them in Hindustani for nearly an hour and a half:

> Standing very erect under the shadow of a huge plane tree, Subhas be-
> gan to speak to them. He spoke in Hindustani and we circled round
> him, and as he warmed up I saw how the whole audience was coming
> under his spell and how they were listening with the greatest attention
> to every word that fell from his lip. When he finished, this audience of
> about four hundred men had almost acquired a new life, a new anima-
> tion, and there was a new excitement among the men, who had mostly
> come to the meeting out of sheer curiosity. Dozens of Jats, Sikhs, and
> Pathans, many of them veterans of frontier wars, came crowding to-
> wards us and asked us to enroll them.

According to Mookerjee, Bose "liked the German form of military discipline, although he was never a militarist at heart."[56] He had entrusted
the work of military recruitment to N. G. Swamy and Abid Hasan.
When M. R. Vyas offered to join the two, Bose humorously turned him
down saying: "I have enough to explain to Mahatmaji, but how can I
ever justify to him that I converted a Gujarati to non-violence?"[57]

Bose spoke from the heart to his soldiers, but also strove to make
members of all religious communities feel a shared sense of belonging.
Vyas remembers that during their journey by car to the Annaberg
camp, Bose would ask A. M. Sultan "the proper Hindustani word or
expression for this and that." He appreciated Abid Hasan's efforts to
ensure that Hindu, Muslim and Sikh soldiers dined together instead of
eating in separate messes. Gradually, Muslims and Sikhs gave up their
insistence on being served meat separately that accorded with the appropriate method of slaughter—*halal* or *jhatka*. The overenthusiastic
Hasan even came up with a common prayer that addressed neither the
Hindus' Ishwar nor the Muslims' Allah, but was directed to Duniya-ki-
Malik ("Lord of the Universe"). Bose suggested that he drop the idea,
arguing that if religion was resorted to in the name of unity, it could be
equally redeployed to divide the communities.[58]

An attempt to divide the religious communities was in fact made by another Indian political activist, Iqbal Shedai, who was based in Italy. Shedai's "Radio Himalaya" sided with the All-India Muslim League, rather than with the Indian National Congress. In April 1942, the Italians had permitted him to form the Centro Militare India and to raise a small military force of about 350 soldiers, drawn from prisoners-of-war in transit camps. Shedai was an irritant to Bose. He accused Bose of harboring a nest of communists in the heart of Nazi Germany. Bose, for his part, was certain that Shedai's operation would implode. He was proved right when the Centro Militare India had to be disbanded after a mutiny in November 1942.[59]

Meanwhile, Bose's Indian Legion was gathering strength under German auspices. At first, Bose insisted that it could be deployed only in or near India against British forces. On the eve of the battle of El Alamein, he changed tactics and suggested sending it to take part in the fight to take Alexandria from British imperial control. Rommel, who was disinclined to mix politics with military matters, turned down the offer. Bose was adamant that the Indians would never battle against the Soviet Union on the Eastern Front. During his time in Europe, the Indian Legion received training but did not take part in any military action. After his departure, Nambiar would successfully keep the legion away from deployment in the East. In late 1943 and 1944, it fought on the French coast against the Allied landings.[60]

While waiting for his travel plans to materialize, Bose kept himself busy thinking and writing about the postwar reconstruction of free India. In an essay titled "Free India and Her Problems," published in the Free India Center's bilingual monthly journal *Azad Hind* in August 1942, Bose wrote that it would be "wrong to dogmatize from now about the form of the future Indian state." He did say, however, that to begin with there would be "a strong Central Government" and "a well-organized, disciplined all-India party." The state would "guarantee complete religious and cultural freedom for individuals and groups." "When the new regime is stabilized and the state-machinery begins to function smoothly," he explained, "power will be decentralized and the provincial governments will be given more responsibility."[61] In addition to Bose's own speeches and articles, *Azad Hind,* edited by Pandit K. A. Bhatta, carried quite fascinating articles about India's future, written by a number of talented young men Bose had gathered around him. Most espoused left-leaning socialist views, even if they were located in wartime Berlin. When an opportunity presented itself, as it did at the founding of the Indo-German Society in Hamburg on September 11, 1942, Bose spoke of the bonds of poetry and philosophy between the two countries. On that occasion, a German orchestra played Tagore's song as India's national anthem—the first time the song was presented for that purpose. Perhaps Bose was invoking the past world of Goethe and Schopenhauer, Friedrich Rückert and A. W. Schlegel, Max Müller and Paul Deussen, as a refuge from the oppressive present of Nazi Germany.[62]

More than poetry and philosophy, it was his passionate relationship with Emilie that had sustained him through the stresses and strains of his European sojourn. She was constantly by his side in Berlin, from April 1941 to July 1942. On their visits to Rome, she took him to her favorite quiet churches; and Badgastein was a rejuvenating retreat for them, as it had been in the 1930s. Some of Bose's habits changed in wartime Europe, but he was unchanged as a human being and in his single-minded devotion to the mission of his life. He had dropped some of his earlier inhibitions. His first alcoholic drink was a glass of vodka in Moscow, following his escape from India. "It burnt me," he confessed to Emilie.[63] In Europe he learned to enjoy a glass of wine, usually red. Beef was no longer forbidden for this devout Hindu. He also took to smoking cigarettes, to soothe his nerves. The sustained period of time he and Emilie spent together at their Sophienstrasse home resulted in Emilie's pregnancy. In July 1942, when she was five months pregnant, Emilie left Berlin for Vienna to be with her mother and sister. Subhas was in any case scheduled to leave for Asia as soon as travel arrangements could be made. Emilie chose to give birth to their child in her home city, while Subhas pursued his ultimate mission to deliver his nation from its occupiers.[64]

Since the Germans and the Japanese were unable to make swift arrangements for his submarine voyage to Asia, Bose explored the possibility of seeking Italian help once again, to go by air. He was encouraged by a successful nonstop Italian flight from Rhodes to Rangoon. While Bose was in Königsbruck inspecting the Indian Legion in early

October 1942, Alexander Werth arrived with the good news that arrangements for his flight from Rome were ready. Bose rushed back to Berlin to say his farewells. He then flew to Ribbentrop's field headquarters in Ukraine, and introduced Nambiar as the man he would leave in charge of the Free India Center in Europe. The October flight had to be abandoned, however, because of an intelligence leak by careless Italian authorities, much to Bose's dismay. To keep their angry guest occupied, the German Foreign Office arranged a trip to Czechoslovakia for Bose and Nambiar in late October 1942. Accompanied by Keppler and Trott, the two Indians met Vojtech Tuka, the Slovakian prime minister, in Bratislava, and were received by the president and other ministers. Bose also intervened with the German authorities on behalf of his friend Professor V. Lesny. He returned to Berlin by way of Vienna, where he saw Emilie.[65] They continued to keep in touch by phone, though Bose had to seek the intervention of the German Foreign Office to allow them to speak to each other in English.[66]

On November 6, 1942, Bose left for Rome to take the much-delayed flight to Asia, but he was in for yet another bitter disappointment. The Italians and the Japanese could not agree on the flight path. The first flight had used Soviet air space, but the Japanese did not want that route used again, as they were not at war with the Soviet Union. The Italians objected that a more southerly route, recommended by the Japanese, would be too risky. A thoroughly dejected Bose returned to Berlin after cooling his heels in Rome for a week.[67]

Perhaps the hand of destiny was at work in Bose's failed attempts to depart from Europe. Had his flight from Rome materialized, he would have missed a joyous event in his personal life. On November 29, 1942, Subhas and Emilie's daughter, Anita, was born in Vienna. According to Nambiar, when Subhas received the news, this great champion of women's rights was a bit disappointed that he had not been blessed with a son. But the brief disappointment gave way to pride and joy once Subhas saw Anita in December. Subhas, Emilie, and Anita spent a quiet Christmas together in Vienna.[68]

Domestic bliss could have no more than a fleeting presence in a revolutionary's life. Emilie herself was back at work, translating the updated version of Subhas's book *The Indian Struggle* into German.[69]

On his return from Rome in mid-November, Bose had already started negotiations with Ribbentrop and the Japanese ambassador, Hiroshi Oshima, to find an alternative way of traveling to Asia. The military attaché, Colonel Yamamoto Bin, left for Japan by air across Turkish and Soviet territory in late November, to make the necessary arrangements. The courtesy extended by the Soviet Union to a Japanese diplomat, allowing the use of its airspace, did not extend to India's anticolonial revolutionary.[70] "I could do much more for my country," Bose wrote to Ribbentrop on December 5, 1942, exactly a week after his daughter's birth, "if I could be somewhere near India." He continued his urging: "I believe it is technically possible for the German Government to help me to travel to the Far East—either by aeroplane or by submarine or by ship. There is a certain amount of risk undoubtedly in this undertaking, but so is there in every undertaking. That risk I shall gladly and voluntarily take. At the same time, I believe in my destiny and I therefore believe that this endeavor will succeed."[71]

By mid-January 1943, the plans for Bose's submarine voyage to Asia were finalized. Emilie came to Berlin on January 20, so they could spend a few days together. A small party was held at the Sophienstrasse home on January 23, to celebrate Subhas's forty-sixth birthday. There was much work to be done. Speeches were recorded that were to be broadcast during Bose's journey. The one berating the BBC as the "Bluff and Bluster Corporation" of British imperialists was not especially well done, as it contained a long passage from an earlier speech. There was an unanticipated difficulty by the time it was broadcast: a fast by Gandhi coincided with Bose's departure, and Bose had not been able to make any mention of this key development. Another speech, commemorating the Amritsar Massacre on April 13, could be broadcast without references to recent military and political developments.[72]

Bose made his final public appearance in Berlin on January 26, 1943, at a big ceremony to observe Independence Day. The independence pledge of the Indian National Congress was read out. According to the *Azad Hind*, the "very colorful and eminent gathering" of some six hundred guests included the Grand Mufti of Jerusalem and Rashid Ali El-Gilani of Iraq. The hall was decorated with red tulips and white lilacs. Netaji entered, dressed in a black *sherwani,* and addressed the assembly in German. An English recording of his speech was beamed simultaneously to India. In a wide-ranging address, he made a philosophical digression:

> To us, life is one long unending wave. It is God manifesting himself in
> the infinite variety of creation. It is *Leela*—an eternal play of forces. In
> this cosmic interplay of forces—there is not only sunshine, but there is
> also darkness. There is not only joy, but there is also sorrow. There is
> not only a rise, but there is also a fall. If we do not lose faith in ourselves and in our divinity—we shall move on through darkness, sorrow
> and degradation towards renewed sunshine, joy and progress.[73]

Subhas Chandra Bose was now ready to ride the wave toward the fulfillment of his destiny and that of his country.

The Path of Danger

Seven years earlier, in March 1936, Subhas had left Emilie to go back to his "first love—my country." So it was to be again, but now in far more difficult and dangerous wartime conditions. On February 8, 1943, just before embarking on his perilous journey from Europe to Asia, he wrote a poignant letter in Bengali for his elder brother Sarat, and left it in Emilie's hands:

> Today once again I am embarking on the path of danger. But this time
> towards home. I may not see the end of the road. If I meet with any
> such danger, I will not be able to send you any further news in this life.
> That is why today I am leaving my news here—it will reach you in due
> time. I have married here and I have a daughter. In my absence please
> show my wife and daughter the love that you have given me throughout your life.[74]

Emilie lingered for a few more days at Sophienstrasse in Berlin, to give the impression that nothing was amiss. Then she returned to Anita in Vienna.

Always conscious of the need to foster unity among religious communities, Bose had toyed with the idea of taking a Hindu, a Muslim, and a Sikh on his journey to Asia. Once the German naval authorities told him that he could take only one aide, he picked Abid Hasan to be his companion. N. G. Swami, and four others with advanced training in wireless telegraphy, secret inks, and sophisticated radio transmitters, were to follow on a blockade-runner in March.[75] Hasan was simply told to pack his bags for a long journey, and had no inkling of his destination. He feared that he might be sent to Mecca as part of a scheme to find anticolonial recruits during the haj. Only when he met Netaji at the Lehrter train station did he realize that he would be accompanying his leader. On the train from Berlin to Kiel, Bose asked Hasan: "Now do you know where you're going?" "Yes, sir," Hasan replied, "I know where we're going." "Where are we going?" Bose inquired. "We are both going to perform Haj," the aide commented wryly, eliciting peals of laughter from his leader.[76]

Bose and Hasan arrived at the north German port city of Kiel on February 8, 1943. Before dawn on February 9, Werner Musenberg, captain of the German submarine U-180, welcomed them aboard. As soon as the two Indians had boarded the vessel, the submarine set off. "In one respect," historians Christopher Bayly and Tim Harper write of the war situation in early 1943, "the British had much to fear. Subhas Chandra Bose, their most resolute and resourceful Indian enemy, was on the move."[77] They were apprehensive despite the fact that Rommel had been stopped in his tracks at El Alamein on November 4, 1942, and the Soviets had defeated the Germans at Stalingrad on February 2, 1943, barely a week before Bose's departure. The historical significance of Bose's submarine voyage is underscored by the British response to another crucial development in India on February 9, 1943. This was the commencement of Mahatma Gandhi's fast, which was to keep Indians on tenterhooks for three weeks.

The British cabinet had decided that if Gandhi fasted, he would be allowed to die. Flush with the victories at El Alamein and Stalingrad, Churchill was of the clear opinion that "this our hour of triumph everywhere in the world was not the time to crawl before a miserable old man who had always been our enemy."[78] In the event of Gandhi's death, Linlithgow expected "six months' unpleasantness steadily declining in volume; little or nothing at the end of it."[79] The prime minister and the viceroy, along with L. S. Amery, the secretary of state for India, were keen to expose Gandhi as a fraud: they hoped to find evidence that he was taking glucose with his water. The Americans were alarmed at the prospect that Gandhi might die in British custody, but the British brushed aside their advice that it would be wise to be conciliatory. Linlithgow thanked Churchill for refusing to yield to "the world's most successful humbug" who was engaged in a "wicked system of blackmail and terror."[80]

At a time when the Quit India movement was nearly crushed and the Mahatma was being treated with scant respect, Bose alone was showing grit and a determination to fight the colonial masters. Though the Allies knew from intercepts and decodes of Japanese and German telegraphic communications that their inveterate opponent was again on the move, they did not have the precise intelligence or military resources to strike at him under the sea. The U-180 navigated through the small belt of the Danish waters toward Kristiansand on the Norwegian coast, and then entered the North Sea. It passed through the strait north of Scotland and south of Iceland, successfully avoiding British depth charges, whose booming could be heard in the distance. The journey south through the Atlantic Ocean included a refueling off the Spanish coast. The U-boat, of the 9D type, surfaced at night to recharge its batteries. It had a speed of 18 knots per hour on the surface and up to 7.7 knots when submerged.[81]

"I was quite fascinated by the romance of having to travel by the submarine," Abid Hasan recalled. "But the moment I entered the submarine, all the romance of it went away." The atmosphere inside the U-boat was "suffocating." The stench of diesel oil permeated the air, the food, and the blankets. Bose was given a bunk in a small recess along the passage, which served as the officers' quarters. Hasan's heart sank when they were served their first meal, consisting of tough greasy chunks of beef and damp bread. He rushed to the kitchen and found a bag of rice and some lentils. Fortunately, Bose's political and military aide knew how to cook, and fed him a simple Indian diet that he could consume. The only difficulty was Bose's penchant for generously offering a share of his food to the German officers, depleting the limited supply of rice on board.[82]

If Hasan had thought of passing his time lying on his bunk reading books, he was soon in for a rude shock. Bose asked him to bring out his typewriter and get down to work. The first few weeks were spent completing revisions for a new edition of *The Indian Struggle*. That manuscript was sent back to Germany at the time of the refueling rendezvous with a U-tanker near Spain. Bose then turned his attention to careful preparation for the challenges he would face in Asia. Hasan was asked to play the role of Tojo and ask him difficult questions. After formulating his negotiating strategy vis-à-vis the Japanese, Bose discussed ways to win the trust of the officers of the British Indian Army, who might be prepared to join the Indian National Army. He dictated or wrote out in longhand the speeches he would make to soldiers of India's army of liberation, and he had Hasan type them out for him. His review of India's struggle for independence since 1857 would have been, in Hasan's opinion, an excellent history textbook on the subject. He made elaborate plans for the formation of a women's regiment of the INA, and discussed the psychology of women from different regional and class backgrounds. When he broached the idea of putting women in uniform, Hasan was of the view that he would get Indian women to fight but never to abandon the sari and the *shalwar-kameez* for pants and bush shirts. Bose was convinced of his ability to persuade Indian women to don military uniforms.[83]

The long submarine voyage gave Hasan some unique insights into the qualities of his leader. When they were up on the bridge of the vessel and Bose could not dictate speeches to him, Hasan asked Netaji questions. On being asked to name the worst fate that he might suffer, Bose answered without a moment's hesitation: "To be in exile." Hasan came to admire his leader's courage and composure in the face of great danger. The U-180 had a mandate to attack enemy ships, even though it had an important political personality on board. On April 18, in the southern Atlantic off the West African coast, the submarine sighted the British merchant ship S.S. *Corbis*. Torpedoes were fired from the U-180, and the ship went down in flames. Hasan noticed that the Indian

and Malayan sailors were put on flimsy rafts, while the only real life-
boat was filled with European crew. The color line was as ubiquitous as
the Equator. A couple of days later, another cargo boat was sighted, but
on this occasion the U-180 surfaced by mistake. The British vessel tried
to ram the submarine as the captain gave the order to dive. In the midst
of the crisis, Hasan heard Bose's voice: "Hasan, I have dictated the
matter to you twice and you have not taken it down!" Once the submarine had steadied itself under the sea, after a close shave with the enemy
ship, Captain Musenberg instructed his sailors to emulate the unflap-
pable demeanor of the Indian leader and his secretary when in danger.[84]

Following its adventures in the Atlantic, the submarine rounded the
Cape of Good Hope and entered the Indian Ocean. Meanwhile, on
April 20, 1943, the Japanese submarine I-29 had left Penang with the
flotilla commander Captain Masao Teraoka on board. Local Indians
had been intrigued by the crew's decision to buy supplies for the on-
board preparation of Indian meals. On April 26, the German and Japanese submarines spotted each other at approximately 25 degrees south
latitude and 60 degrees east longitude, in the Indian Ocean, some four
hundred nautical miles off the coast of Madagascar. After they surfaced
at their prearranged rendezvous point, the crews discovered the sea
was very rough, making a transfer of passengers virtually impossible.
The two submarines sailed alongside each other for what seemed to
Teraoka to be an eternity. Late in the afternoon on April 27, a German
officer and a signalman swam across to the Japanese vessel. At dawn
on April 28, though the waves were still high, it was decided to attempt
the transfer, since continuing the surface maneuver was riskier. The
two Germans rode a rubber dinghy back to their submarine, dragging
a strong hemp rope. Bose and Hasan climbed down from the U-180
into the raft and made their way through the surging sea toward the
I-29. Drenched to the bone, the Indian leader and his adjutant clam-
bered aboard the Japanese submarine to a very warm welcome. An as-
tonishing military feat had been accomplished: the only submarine-to-
submarine transfer of passengers in the annals of World War II, in
waters where the enemy was superior in air and naval power. The mortality rate on German U-boats was greater than 80 percent, and the risk

had been immense. The German seaman who took the photographs of this daring voyage and transfer was killed on his next mission. He left his pictures with his mother, saying that someone from India would one day ask for them.[85]

The German officers and crew had been friendly and courteous to their Indian guests throughout the arduous journey, in the most cramped conditions. Yet on boarding the Japanese submarine, Bose and Hasan felt "something akin to a home-coming." "Immediately we had that feeling," Abid Hasan remembered. "Netaji had that feeling. We could be less formal, although we had to be more formal." The Japanese submarine was also more spacious than the German one. The flotilla commander, Masao Teraoka, vacated his cabin for Bose. The captain of the submarine, Juichi Izu, organized a party on April 29 to celebrate the unique achievement of successfully transferring Bose and his aide, and to honor the Japanese emperor on his birthday. The Indians felt they had "come back to an Asian nation," and the food prepared by the Japanese cooks with Indian spices obtained in Penang suited their taste. Four meals a day were, however, a little too much for Bose. "Do we have to eat again, Captain Teraoka?" he asked with a smile as he was overwhelmed with Japanese hospitality.[86]

The I-29 passed to the south of India on its way to Southeast Asia. Outside the British patrolling radius, it picked up a radio message from Penang with instructions to detour and take the passengers to Sabang, a tiny islet off the north Sumatran coast. Swirling rumors in Penang about Bose's impending arrival made this diversion necessary. On May 6, 1943, the I-29 safely docked in the harbor at Sabang. It had played its part in the history of World War II. Juichi Izu was soon transferred; he became the skipper of I-11, which went missing in the central Pacific early next year. An American submarine eventually sank the I-29 near the Philippines, in July 1944. Subhas Chandra Bose posed for a photograph with the entire crew of the Japanese submarine before disembarking at Sabang. He autographed this picture with a heartfelt message: "It was a great pleasure to sail aboard this submarine. I believe this will mark a milestone in our fight for victory and peace."[87]

Bose's friend Colonel Yamamoto, the former military attaché in Berlin, was on hand to greet him at the pier in Sabang. After a few days' rest, Bose boarded a small Japanese combat aircraft on his way to To-kyo. The plane made several stops in Penang, Saigon, Manila, Taipei, and Hamamatsu, eventually arriving in the Japanese capital in mid-May. Arrangements had been made for Bose to stay at the Imperial Hotel, designed by the American architect Frank Lloyd Wright, just across the moat from the Imperial Palace. He checked in under the as-sumed Japanese name "Matsuda"—but the days of having to pretend to be Ziauddin, Mazzotta, or Matsuda were soon to be left behind. In less than a month, Indians would once again hear his familiar voice: "This is Subhas Chandra Bose speaking to his countrymen in East Asia."[88]

8

Roads to Delhi

There, there in the distance—beyond that river, beyond those jungles, beyond those hills lies the promised land—the soil from which we sprang—the land to which we shall now return.

—SUBHAS CHANDRA BOSE, Order of the Day, March 1944

Around midday on July 2, 1943, Subhas Chandra Bose, accompanied by Abid Hasan, landed in Singapore in a twin-engine Japanese aircraft. He was greeted with a Hindustani song composed by Mumtaz Hussain: "Subhas-ji, Subhas-ji, woh jaan-e-Hind aagaye, woh naaz jispe Hind ko, woh shan-e-Hind aagaye." Set to music by Ram Singh Thakur (the melody was a European marching tune), the song joyfully welcomed the beloved leader who was the pride of India. "Asia ke Aftab"—"the light of Asia"—had now arrived in Asia, the song proclaimed. As early as December 1941, General Fujiwara Iwaichi had noted in Thailand and Malaya that "all the Indians" he encountered "had a great admiration for Bose, amounting almost to a religious devotion."[1] A conference of Indian expatriate patriots in Bangkok on June 15, 1942, had issued him an invitation to lead them in Southeast Asia. At the time, he had been able only to send them a message underscoring the need to "link up Indian nationalists all over the world."[2] A year later he was at last among them, providing that link in person.

During the long delay—from June 1942 to July 1943—in the implementation of Bose's travel plans, the relative fortunes of the warring powers had changed. The Soviet Union had decisively turned the tables on Germany in Europe, and the United States was steadily gaining on Japan in the Pacific, gaining control of one island after another. Japan, however, still occupied the erstwhile European colonial territories in Southeast Asia. The presence of well over two million—if not three million, as claimed by Bose—Indian civilians in that vast region gave his planned movement in Asia potentially a very large social base of support. The millennia-old ties between South and Southeast Asia had grown stronger in the modern era. Since the middle of the nineteenth century, Indian capitalists, laborers, and professionals had been migrating in large numbers across the eastern Indian Ocean. Most of the financiers, as well as the laborers working on Southeast Asian plantations, came from the southern Indian region of Tamil Nadu. Indian novelists, poets, artists, missionaries, mystics, soldiers, and anticolonial visionaries had circulated across Southeast Asia in the early decades of the twentieth century. Rabindranath Tagore, for example, had made a well-publicized voyage to Southeast Asia in 1927, to retrace the footprints of "India's entry into the universal."[3]

The first Indian National Army was formed on February 17, 1942, two days after the British surrendered to Japanese forces in Singapore. But it was in disarray by December. Bose possessed the stature, vision, and organizational ability to rekindle the spirit of anticolonial nationalism among the soldiers and weld them into an effective fighting force. If he was to achieve his dream of leading an army of liberation into India, however, he had to win a desperate race against time. Could he lead the Indian National Army into Calcutta, which he had left secretly in the dead of night on January 16–17, 1941? Bengal, his home province, was being devastated by a gigantic man-made famine just as he assumed leadership of the Azad Hind ("Free India") movement in Southeast Asia. For years he had been keeping a handwritten calendar of important landmarks in his life: "Began work" was all he wrote next to the date "July 1943."[4] It was a euphemism for a concentrated spell of tireless, frenetic activity pitting an individual's will against the formidable current of global military trends.

The crescent stretching from Singapore to Calcutta was the setting for some of the most dramatic developments of the Second World War in the years 1943–1945. During Bose's first year in the region (mid-

1943 to mid-1944), there was hope, bordering on euphoria, that his Indian National Army, allied with the Japanese forces, might well succeed in breaking through the British defenses in northeastern India and ignite an anticolonial uprising within the country. After that daring gambit failed, the second year (mid-1944 to August 1945) sorely tested the mettle of the army of liberation and its leader, who continued to display dogged determination in retreat while searching for alternative routes to freedom. Delhi still remained the ultimate goal, even if only an example of heroism in military defeat would pave the political path to that imperial metropolis.

The Blood of Freedom-Loving Indians

After his arrival by submarine in Sabang, Bose flew to Tokyo to garner support for his armed struggle and Japanese recognition of Indian independence. He arrived in the Japanese capital on May 16, 1943, but his first meeting with Hideki Tojo, the prime minister, did not take place until June 10. Some Japanese sources suggest that India did not figure very prominently on Tojo's list of priorities at this time, distraught as he was because of the military setbacks in the Pacific. Abid Hasan contends that Bose did not insist on a very early meeting with the Japanese prime minister. He understood that Tojo's position—as the first among equals—was quite different from that of the European dictators. While Hitler and Mussolini had frequent contact with each other, Tojo had never met either of them in person. Before meeting with Tojo, Bose wanted to create a lobby in support of Indian independence among the political and military elite in Tokyo. If a Bose file was being prepared by Tojo's subordinates, he wanted indirectly to be its author. Thus, for the first few weeks he was quite content to meet with the top military commander, Hajime Sugiyama; the foreign minister, Mamoru Shigemitsu; various other Japanese military officers, such as General Seizo Arisue; and a number of political leaders. He took it upon himself to educate them about India and its freedom struggle, in the manner of a tutor. Having never visited Japan before, he was also willing to spend about ten days touring Japanese factories, farms, hospitals, and schools.[5]

A special effort at reaching mutual understanding was required, because of a breakdown in communication between the Indians and the Japanese in Southeast Asia that had preceded Bose's arrival. Indo-Japanese relations had been off to a good start in October 1941: a young idealistic Japanese major, Fujiwara Iwaichi, made contact in Bangkok with an Indian anticolonial activist, Giani Pritam Singh, of the Indian Independence League, the premier nationalist organization for the large population of Indian expatriates. Fujiwara headed a small liaison unit known as the Fujiwara Kikan, charged with winning Indian support for Japan's military effort. During the campaign in north Malaya during December 1941, Fujiwara and Pritam Singh befriended Captain Mohan Singh of the 1/14 Punjab Regiment of the British Indian Army—a regiment that had been decimated by Japanese forces. They took him to the town of Alor Star and assured him that the Japanese had no intention of holding Indian soldiers as prisoners-of-war. Japan wanted "Asia for the Asiatics" and was prepared to help form an Indian National Army to wrest India's freedom from British rule. They would try to get a man of the highest caliber and political integrity, Subhas Chandra Bose, who had already escaped the clutches of the British, to lead them in Southeast Asia. By the end of December 1941, Mohan Singh was persuaded and helped the Japanese to win over Indian soldiers to their side as the military campaign moved swiftly southward down the Malay Peninsula.[6]

After the fall of Singapore on February 15, 1942, the Indian soldiers were separated from their British counterparts and handed over to the Japanese by the British commanding officer. On February 17, Indian soldiers of all ranks gathered at Singapore's Farrer Park, while the British officers and their men were assembled at Changi, an area in the eastern part of the city. Colonel J. C. Hunt curtly announced that Indian soldiers should conduct themselves from now on according to Japanese directives, and left Farrer Park. Fujiwara then rose to deliver a carefully prepared speech. Lieutenant Kazunori Kunizuka translated his Japanese words into English, and Colonel N. S. Gill, an Indian soldier, rendered them in Hindustani. "The Japanese Army will treat you not as POWs," Fujiwara declared with sincerity and passion, "but as friends." Japan was prepared to help the Indian soldiers in their freedom struggle if they would voluntarily pledge their loyalty to Mother India and join the Indian National Army (INA). Fujiwara's speech was received with great enthusiasm. As he finished, the Indian soldiers gave him a standing ovation and "thousands of caps were tossed into the air." Fujiwara reckoned that he had swayed an overwhelming majority of the fifty thousand soldiers who heard him speak.[7] British intelligence sources gave slightly lower estimates. The British believed that forty thousand of the forty-five thousand Indian troops who surrendered in Singapore volunteered to join the INA. Only five thousand of them, mostly officers, remained in the nonvolunteer category.[8]

After this early success among POWs in Singapore, the Indian inde-pendence movement in Southeast Asia suffered a series of setbacks. On March 19, some of the top leaders of the Indian Independence League, including Giani Pritam Singh and Swami Satyananda Puri of Bangkok, were killed in an air crash on their way to a conference in Tokyo. At around the same time, Colonel Hideo Iwakuro replaced Fujiwara as the chief liaison officer with the Indians. Contrary to Fujiwara's advice that Japan needed a diplomatic mission to handle relations with the Indians, the Iwakuro Kikan operated more like an espionage agency dedicated to short-term military objectives.[9] The arrogance and high-handedness of middle-ranking Japanese officers irked the Indian military and civilian leadership. The rift was papered over in June 1942, at the time of the Indian Independence League's Bangkok conference, under the chairmanship of Rashbehari Bose, a veteran Indian revolu-tionary. In 1912, Rashbehari (no relation to Subhas) had hurled a bomb at Charles Hardinge, the British viceroy, as he ceremonially en-tered Delhi, the new British capital, riding on an elephant. The assassi-nation attempt was unsuccessful, but a symbolic point had been made. Since 1915, Rashbehari had lived as a political refugee in Japan.[10] De-spite his efforts to keep Indo-Japanese relations on an even keel, the lack of trust between the two sides became palpable during the latter half of 1942. Finally, in December, an impatient and exasperated Mo-han Singh issued an order to disband the Indian National Army. The Japanese promptly took him into detention. Rashbehari Bose tried to salvage the situation over the next few weeks, and prevented the com-plete dissolution of the INA. Assurances given by him and the Japanese in February 1943 that Subhas Chandra Bose was on his way to assume the leadership of the movement persuaded those who were wavering to remain in—and other officers who had stayed aloof to join—what came to be called the second INA.[11]

Given the history of these tensions prior to his arrival, Subhas Chandra Bose had to summon all his diplomatic skills in Tokyo to assert Indian independence while securing Japanese support. He had prepared the ground well by the time he met with Tojo for the first time, on June 10, 1943, in the prime minister's office. He instantly impressed the Japanese leader with his dignified bearing and the force of his personality. If Tojo had harbored doubts about India's ability to fight for freedom, these were quickly dispelled.[12] A second meeting was arranged, for June 14. Bose asked Tojo whether Japan was prepared to render "unconditional support" to the Indian struggle. On hearing the Japanese prime minister's answer in the affirmative, Bose ventured a further request: he wanted the Japanese leader to sanction a military thrust from Burma into India—an offensive in which the Indian National Army would fight shoulder to shoulder with the Japanese Imperial Army. Tojo was unable to give an immediate answer without consulting his military commanders. Two days later, on June 16, Bose was invited to attend a session of the Imperial Diet as a special guest, and had the satisfaction of hearing Tojo declare that Japan would do "everything possible" to help the cause of Indian independence.[13]

Once such an unequivocal declaration had been made, Bose decided to appear in public. On June 19, he addressed a press conference attended by sixty journalists. The fact that he was standing before them "in the heart of Nippon instead of sitting idly in a prison house in India" was symbolic of the dynamism of the new movement that was sweeping across his country. While seeking assistance from foreign powers, he spoke of the duty "to pay for our liberty with our own blood." "The freedom that we shall win, through our sacrifices and exertions," he argued, "we shall be able to preserve with our own strength."[14] He followed up his media interaction with a series of stirring radio broadcasts from Tokyo. He was quite candid in his analysis of the war between the old and new imperial powers, and urged his countrymen to take advantage of the turmoil to win freedom for India.

He asked his compatriots not to listen to British propaganda but rather to place their trust in him. "If the wily, cunning and resourceful British politicians have failed to cajole or corrupt me," he assured them, "nobody else can do so." He expressed special solicitude for the comrades who were rotting in British jails. He promised to "throw open the prison gates" before long, so that India's worthy sons could "step out of the darkness of prison cells into the light of freedom, joy and self-fulfillment." "The hour has struck," he declared, "and every patriotic Indian must advance towards the field of battle. Only when the blood of freedom-loving Indians begins to flow will India attain her freedom."[15]

Subhas Chandra Bose left Tokyo for Singapore at the end of June, accompanied by the elderly Rashbehari Bose and by Abid Hasan. He had persuaded Tokyo to replace Iwakuro with a man of his choice, Yamamoto, as the head of the Hikari Kikan, Japan's liaison agency. His radio speeches had created an atmosphere of eager anticipation among Indians in Southeast Asia. Upon his arrival in Singapore on July 2, he was given a rapturous welcome. Top military commanders J. K. Bhonsle and Mohammad Zaman Kiani received him at the airport, and the Indian National Army gave him a guard of honor. A week of energetic activity followed. On July 4, 1943, representatives of the Indian Independence League assembled at the Cathay Theater to witness Subhas's acceptance of the leadership of the movement from Rashbehari Bose. Young women sang patriotic hymns to the motherland and showered the leaders with flower petals as they took the stage. "You might well ask what I have been in Tokyo for," Rashbehari told the gathering, "or what present I have brought for you." "Well, I have brought for you this present," he said, turning to Subhas amid thunderous cheers and chanting from the audience. Describing Subhas as symbolizing all that is "best, noblest, the most daring, and the most dynamic in the youth of India," he conducted the generational transfer of leadership with grace and dignity.[16]

Subhas accepted the baton with humility, and prayed aloud that Khuda, the Almighty, would give him the necessary strength to discharge his duty. He spoke in Hindustani, with great eloquence and passion. His audience responded with unbridled enthusiasm, especially

when he evoked the vision of holding their victory parade at Delhi's
Red Fort. He asked his followers to join the movement after careful
consideration, for ahead lay a grim fight requiring great suffering and
sacrifice. He announced his intention of setting up a Provisional Government of Free India "to lead the Indian Revolution to a successful
conclusion." "When the revolution succeeds and Anglo-American imperialism is expelled from India," he told the delegates, "the task of the
provisional government will be over. It will then make room for a permanent government to be set up inside India, in accordance with the
will of the Indian people."[17]

The following day, July 5, at 10:30 in the morning, Bose appeared in
military uniform to address India's army of liberation. Some twelve
thousand soldiers had gathered on the expanse of green in front of
Singapore's municipal building. He insisted that this army had been
formed and would go into battle entirely under Indian leadership. He
gave this Azad Hind Fauj ("Free India Army") their battle cry: "Chalo
Delhi!" ("Onward to Delhi!"). "For an enslaved people," he said with
emotion, "there can be no greater pride, no higher honor, than to be
the first soldier in the army of liberation." He promised his troops that
he would be with them "in darkness and in sunshine, in sorrow and in
joy, in suffering and in victory." The soldiers responded with shouts of
"Long live revolution!" and cries of victory to Mahatma Gandhi and
Subhas Chandra Bose. "For the present," their leader warned them, "I
can offer you nothing except hunger, thirst, privation, forced marches
and death. But if you follow me in life and in death—as I am confident
you will—I shall lead you to victory and freedom."[18] The next day the
INA held another parade, at which Tojo, who was in Singapore for
other reasons, took the salute.

In the months that followed, Bose electrified massive audiences of
soldiers and civilians with his speeches in Hindustani, and elicited an
overwhelmingly positive response to his call for men and matériel for
the final struggle against the British raj. Since the majority of Indian
immigrants in Southeast Asia were from southern India, his speeches
were instantly translated into Tamil. "Indians outside India," he told a
crowd of more than sixty thousand civilians in Singapore on July 9,
1943, "particularly Indians in East Asia, are going to organize a fighting

force which will be powerful enough to attack the British army of occupation in India. When we do so, a revolution will break out, not only among the civilian population at home, but also among the Indian Army, which is now standing under the British flag. When the British government is thus attacked from both sides—from inside India and from outside—it will collapse, and the Indian people will then regain their liberty."[19]

A large majority of Indian expatriates in Southeast Asia responded with great fervor to this patriotic call for a revolution. At least eighteen thousand civilians, mostly Tamils from southern India, deemed nonmartial by the British as part of their mythology about martial races and castes, enlisted in the Indian National Army. They received military training alongside professional soldiers from the northwestern regions of the subcontinent. Some forty thousand soldiers of Britain's Indian Army had forsaken their allegiance to the British king-emperor. Those who had been unconvinced in 1942 were swept off their feet by "Netaji" (as they came to call Subhas Chandra Bose), and swore loyalty to him and the cause of India's freedom. Many tens of thousands of civilians joined the numerous local branches of the Indian Independence League, which provided support functions of various kinds to this newly formed army of liberation.[20]

During his submarine journey, Bose had dictated a speech to Abid Hasan which he planned to deliver to the INA women's regiment that he envisioned.[21] On July 12, he gave that speech to the first recruits of the Rani of Jhansi Regiment, which eventually enlisted a thousand young Indian women from Malaya and Burma—mostly but not exclusively Tamils.[22] The queen of Jhansi had died fighting against the British on horseback during the great rebellion of 1857. Bose cited her as a shining example of female heroism in India, comparable to France's Joan of Arc. Lakshmi Swaminathan, a young medical doctor, took charge as the commander of the women's regiment. She belonged to a distinguished family from Madras which had taken part in the freedom movement since the 1920s. She had caught a glimpse of Bose at the Calcutta Congress of 1928, and now promptly accepted his invitation to raise a regiment of death-defying women. The Japanese were aghast at the idea of a women's regiment, and at first refused to supply ammunition for their training. The head of the Indian Independence League's branch in Singapore, Attavar Yellappa, overcame the Japanese objections and found barracks and equipment for the young Ranis. The first guard-of-honor to their leader was given by sari-clad women bearing weapons of war, but they were soon in military uniform and underwent rigorous military training in their camp. A few came from educated, privileged backgrounds, while the majority were simple rubber-plantation workers in Malaya.[23]

Recruitment into the women's regiment was facilitated to a large extent by Netaji's charisma. Janaki Thevar has described how, as a teenager, she went on her bicycle to hear Bose speak at a rally in Kuala Lumpur. At the end of the meeting, she saw people rushing forward to offer Netaji money, jewelry, and anything else they possessed. Janaki took off her earrings and gold chain and put them in Netaji's hands. Her parents learned of what she had done from a photograph on the front page of the local newspaper the next day. When Lakshmi Swaminathan came recruiting for the women's regiment, Janaki persuaded her father to let her join. In January 1944, after training for six months, she went with the regiment to Burma. Decades later, women of the Rani of Jhansi Regiment—many of whom went on to have distinguished careers—remembered the fatherlike figure of Bose with devotion and regarded the years 1943–1945 as the finest period in their lives.[24]

From July to September 1943, Bose undertook a whirlwind tour of various Southeast Asian countries, galvanizing support for his cause among Indian expatriates. He quickly grasped that Malaya, Thailand, and Burma would be the most important countries from his point of view. He had already visited Saigon, in South Vietnam, en route from Tokyo to Singapore, but the Indian community there was small. Malaya had nearly a million Indians—some wealthy financiers and bankers, as well as a much larger number of poor migrant laborers. The latter, in particular, had their first taste of human dignity and a feeling of equal citizenship by joining the Azad Hind movement. Thailand, with its nominally neutral but effectively pro-Japanese government headed by Phibul Songkhram, supplied the crucial connection between Malaya and Burma. It, too, had an Indian immigrant community, which num-

bered about sixty thousand, and had served as the base of the Indian
Independence League. Burma would be the springboard for the march
into India. Even after the net emigration of Indians from Burma during the Depression decade and the flight of perhaps four hundred
thousand refugees in advance of the Japanese invasion, a varied population of some eight hundred thousand Indians—merchants, bankers,
laborers, and professionals—remained in Burma. Indo-Burmese relations required delicate handling, as the great peasant rebellion of 1930–
1932, led by Saya San, had been directed quite as much against Indian
moneylenders as against British colonial officials.

Subhas Chandra Bose was invited to be an honored guest at the
Burmese independence celebrations on August 1, 1943. He arrived in
Burma on July 29. Over the next two days, he gave rousing speeches to
the Indian expatriates, who welcomed him enthusiastically. After liberating Burma from its British rulers, Japan had agreed, despite some
dithering, to recognize an independent government of Burma led by
Ba Maw, with Aung San as his deputy and defense minister. Ba Maw
had led the legal defense of Saya San (who was executed by the British)
and served as premier between 1937 and 1939 under a new constitution, which had kept real power in the British governor's hands. He was
leader of the Sinyetha, or Poor Men's party, which enjoyed limited
popular support in Burma. Far more influential was the Thakins party,
of which Aung San was a prominent leader. The word *thakin* meant
"master," and the Thakins addressed one another with that title as a
way of refusing to accept the authority of the British colonial masters.
In the late 1930s, the more radical among the Thakins formed the Freedom Bloc, which had a connection with Bose's Forward Bloc. When
the Burmese leaders refused to collaborate with the British war effort,
they were cast into prison. Aung San escaped. After receiving military training in Japan, he and his comrades—known as the "Thirty
Heroes"—returned to Burma with the Japanese invading force that
expelled the British.

Ba Maw had met Bose in Singapore on July 6 and was suitably impressed. "Subhas Chandra Bose was a man you could not forget once
you knew him," he wrote in his memoirs. "His greatness was manifest."[25] On August 1, Bose made a moving speech on the occasion of

Burma's freedom: "From 1925 to 1927, I used to gaze from the verandah of my cell in Mandalay prison on the palace of the last independent king of Burma, and I used to wonder when Burma would be free once again. Today Burma is an independent state and I am breathing the atmosphere of that liberated country."[26] He offered a *nazar* ("gift") of 250,000 rupees—around $76,000—donated by Indians in Southeast Asia to the Burmese government, as a token of India's appreciation of Burmese hospitality.

In the Bengali literary imagination, Burma had been the setting of a romantic battle for freedom. A popular Bengali novelist, Sarat Chandra Chattopadhyay, had published *Pather Dabi* (The Road's Demand) in 1926, when Bose was a prisoner in Mandalay Jail. Bose would have been familiar with this story, about a superhuman Bengali revolutionary organizing India's freedom struggle in Burma. In Rangoon, Ba Maw thought Bose looked "a little sad and wistful," apparently because Bose was thinking of "the long and bloody journey still ahead of him and his forces before India too would be free."[27] The cause of Bose's sadness was more likely to be the terrible man-made famine that was decimating his home province of Bengal, just across the border. More than three million people belonging to the vulnerable sections of society perished in this avoidable calamity. The British, focused on the war, were interested only in feeding their soldiers and in keeping the industrial areas around Calcutta quiet by making rice available to workers at subsidized prices through ration shops. The masses of agricultural laborers, market-dependent sharecroppers, and jute-growing smallholding peasants lost their ability to obtain food as prices soared. The British also instituted a "denial policy" under which they confiscated boats, bicycles, and all modes of transport within fifty miles of the coast, thereby depriving people in those areas of their livelihood. The famine, which began in March 1943, was not acknowledged in the British Parliament until October of that year. The nineteenth century's fabled "famine code," which would have triggered the organization of relief, was not even invoked by the colonial state. External supplies of food were either not sought or not accepted to aid in famine relief. Large injections of food into the public distribution system were needed to break the famine's grip on the economy and society. In July 1943, the

U.S. Board of Economic Warfare estimated that hundreds of thousands of people would die if external supplies of food were not urgently shipped to India. Churchill, however, felt no sympathy for the Indians, whom he regarded as a beastly people; he turned down requests for ships to be made available to carry food to the starving millions.[28]

Subhas Chandra Bose tried to send rice from Burma to Bengal, but the British in India nervously suppressed his offer. On August 20, 1943, Rangoon Radio broadcast his proposal to send one hundred thousand tons of rice to Bengal from a port near India. Bose promised that as soon as the British expressed their willingness to accept the delivery, he would name the harbor that would load the shipment and the authorities who would hand over the rice. He would ask the Japanese for a guarantee of safe conduct for the supply ships. Once the first delivery had been made, further deliveries could be arranged. He expressed his earnest hope that his offer would be accepted, since "hundreds of thousands of men, women and children would be saved from starvation." His words reached the desperate people in his homeland. "The latest Bose rumor," a British intelligence report stated days later, "is to the effect that he has written to the Viceroy asking him to send two ships to enable Bose to send rice to the starving people of Bengal." There was a flurry of activity in the corridors of power in New Delhi to impose the strictest press censorship on Bose's offer. "We are of course particularly anxious to discredit Subhas Bose in every possible way," Richard Tottenham noted on September 1, 1943.[29]

Burma was more than just a potential source of rice. It was a storehouse of rich symbolic resources for India's struggle against the British Empire. The last Mughal emperor had been exiled to Burma in 1858, after his show trial at the Red Fort of Delhi. On September 26, 1943, a ceremonial parade and prayers were held at Bahadur Shah's tomb in Rangoon, to signal the INA's determination to march to the Red Fort of Delhi. Bose paid his respects:

> We Indians, regardless of religious faiths, cherish the memory of Bahadur Shah, not because he was the man who gave the clarion call to his countrymen to fight the enemy from without, but because he was the man under whose flag fought Indians from all provinces, Indians

professing different religious faiths, the man under whose sacred flag freedom-loving Hindus, Muslims and Sikhs fought side by side in the war that has been dubbed by English historians as the sepoy mutiny, but which we Indians call the first war of independence.

That spirit of dynamic faith-inspired unity, not listless secular uniformity, was what he wanted to see emulated in the "last war of independence."[30]

Bangkok, the capital of Thailand, was the usual stopover point as Bose shuttled between Singapore and Rangoon. On August 4 he met Phibul, the prime minister, and, according to Japanese sources, "plenty of goodwill and understanding developed between them." On August 8, the first anniversary of the passage of the Quit India resolution, Bose addressed a public meeting at Chulalongkorn University. The following day he "embraced more than one thousand Indians" who contributed liberally to his war chest.[31] By September, Netaji had reason to be satisfied with the enthusiastic response he had elicited in Malaya, Thailand, and Burma. In addition to the major cities—Singapore, Bangkok, and Rangoon—towns such as Kuala Lumpur, Penang, and Ipoh held rallies that were highly successful. Bose sent his representatives to Vietnam, Indonesia, and China as well, to spread his message. On occasion, he allowed himself to be carried away by the fervor that he aroused. Much to the consternation of his aides, he announced at a public meeting that the Indian National Army would be on Indian soil before the year was out.[32] This was a bit like Gandhi's 1921 promise of *swaraj* within the year, a morale-boosting but unrealistic claim Bose had once criticized. Fortunately, the Japanese formally handed over the Andaman and Nicobar islands to the Provisional Government of Free India on December 29, 1943, enabling Bose to stand on Indian soil before year's end.

By the time Bose arrived in Singapore, the effective strength of the Indian National Army had dwindled to twelve thousand armed men, due to disagreements with the Japanese; but with his presence, the number of volunteers soared. He wanted to raise the troop strength of the INA to fifty thousand, but the Japanese would offer training and equipment for no more than thirty thousand Indian soldiers organized in three divisions. During their first conversation, Field Marshal Count Hisaichi Terauchi, the commander of Japanese forces in Southeast Asia, had told Bose that he wanted the INA's role to be limited to field propaganda units. Bose would have none of that, and insisted that the INA would spearhead the offensive into India. "Any liberation of India secured through Japanese sacrifices," he told Terauchi, "is worse than slavery."[33] The field marshal agreed to the deployment of one INA regiment—the equivalent of a British brigade—as a test of their efficiency and morale, before he would send the rest of the INA into action.

The first division of the INA, some ten thousand soldiers, was put under the command of Mohammad Zaman Kiani. It was divided into three regiments, or brigades, which Bose named after Gandhi, Nehru, and Azad in a deliberate effort to make common cause with the struggle at home. In response to Terauchi's challenge, the INA selected the best soldiers from the three regiments and formed the No. 1 Guerrilla Regiment, intended as the first to be sent into action. This regiment went into training in the northern Malayan town of Taiping in September 1943, under the command of Shah Nawaz Khan, and was sent to Burma on November 20. The soldiers themselves called it the Subhas Brigade. According to Shah Nawaz, Netaji did not approve of this; he "repeatedly issued instructions that no one should call it 'Subhas Brigade,' but the soldiers found it hard to obey the order."[34]

As supreme commander of the INA, Netaji built a close personal rapport with his officers' corps. They had easy access to his home and often joined him for badminton matches in the evenings. He made unannounced visits to the barracks of the ordinary soldiers and frequently shared meals with them. Hindu, Muslim, Sikh, and Christian soldiers dined together—a striking departure from the British custom of having separate mess halls. A warm camaraderie developed among soldiers drawn from the different religious communities and linguistic groups. He urged Hindus to be generous toward the religious minorities. He taught soldiers from martial backgrounds to be welcoming toward civilians who flocked to recruitment centers and joined the liberation army. He sent forty-five handpicked young men for training in Tokyo's elite Military Academy; he also selected thirty-five for the army and ten for a future air force. His success in raising funds enabled him to increase pay and provide decent rations during the training period. He loved music and gave patronage to a talented INA orchestra, which created a repertoire of inspiring songs set to innovative tunes. Music, quite as much as the supreme commander's speeches, was deployed to raise morale—the key asset of any revolutionary army.[35]

Time was of the essence, in view of the overall war situation. Bose worked incredibly hard and slept on average for three hours per night. During the early months at his Meyer Road residence in Singapore, he was often still hard at work, with a glass of brandy and a cup of coffee by his elbow, when Abid Hasan left him at midnight. The next morning, Hasan could tell from the number of cigarette butts in the ashtray how late Bose had worked at his desk. Bose was up at the crack of dawn, which is when he was thought to say his prayers. A rosary of beads and a small copy of the *Gita* were his constant companions, but he never made a public display of his religiosity. "He *never* even once *spoke* his God in public," his colleague S. A. Ayer has written. "He *lived* him." The day would be spent visiting the Indian Independence League headquarters on Chancery Lane and the Supreme Command headquarters and training camps, as well as attending numerous meetings to discuss strategy or build mass support. He refused to discuss work over dinner and instead held forth on the variety of fish recipes or the different ways of cooking spinach and bitter gourd *(karela)*. He was invariably kind to his subordinates (though he sometimes scolded those who were really close to him), and made them feel at ease when they were around him. He loved all animals except cats, a species he had to accept reluctantly in his home, since they were Abid Hasan's favorites. After a long day's work in Singapore, he would sometimes drive to the Ramakrishna Mission, an organization founded by Swami Vivekananda. There he would change from his military attire into a silk *dhoti*, meditate for an hour or two, and emerge rejuvenated. Even though he was the most turbulent figure in Southeast Asia during the war, his closest associates found him serene and Buddha-like in quiet moments.[36]

On October 21, 1943, Netaji proclaimed the formation of the Provisional Government of Azad Hind ("Free India") in Singapore. Sibbier Appadurai Ayer has described how Netaji wrote the proclamation himself on October 19–20, 1943, drawing on Indian history and on elements of the Irish and American declarations of independence. Earlier that evening, Bose had asked whether Ayer knew what had happened to the signatories of the Irish proclamation of independence: they had been shot dead—and the same might happen to those who ventured to sign his proclamation, he added with a laugh. Once the last visitor had departed, well after midnight, he sat down with his coffee to write the proclamation. "Then I witnessed a phenomenon," Ayer has recorded. "I had a glimpse of the great man. He took hold of a bunch of quarter-sheets of blank paper, took a pencil in hand, and started writing." As Netaji delivered each handwritten page, Ayer typed it up to be sent to the printers. "Having goaded Indians to desperation by its hypocrisy," Netaji began, "and having driven them to starvation and death by plunder and loot, British rule in India has forfeited the goodwill of the Indian people altogether and is now living a precarious existence. It needs but a flame to destroy the last vestige of that unhappy rule. To light that flame is the task of India's Army of Liberation." Ayer has described the writing process during that night:

> He did not lift his eyes from the paper in front of him, silently handed to me the first page as soon as he finished it, and I walked out of the room and sat at the typewriter. Abid [Hasan] and [N. G.] Swami went to his room in turn and brought me the proclamation manuscript, sheet after sheet, as Netaji finished it. What amazed me was that he never once wanted to see any of the earlier pages that he had written. How he could remember every word that he had written in the preceding pages, how he could remember the sequence of the paragraphs. In the entire manuscript there was not one word corrected or scored out, and the punctuation was complete.

In the final paragraph came the exhortation to the Indian people: "In the name of God, in the name of bygone generations who have welded the Indian people into one nation, and in the name of the dead heroes who have bequeathed to us a tradition of heroism and self-sacrifice—we call upon the Indian people to rally round our banner and strike for India's freedom." The wording echoed that of the proclamation's Irish predecessor: "The Provisional Government is entitled to, and hereby claims, the allegiance of every Indian. It guarantees religious liberty, as well as equal rights and equal opportunities to its citizens. It declares its firm resolve to pursue the happiness and prosperity of the whole nation equally and transcending all the differences cunningly fostered by an alien government in the past."[37]

The ceremonies surrounding the proclamation of the Provisional Government were held at the Cathay Theater, where Bose had assumed leadership of the movement. As head of state, he held the foreign affairs and war portfolios. His voice choked with emotion as he took his oath: "In the name of God, I take this sacred oath—that to liberate India and the thirty-eight crores [three hundred eighty million] of my countrymen, I, Subhas Chandra Bose, will continue this sacred war of freedom till the last breath of my life."[38] He gave A. C. Chatterjee charge of finance; S. A. Ayer became minister of publicity and propaganda; and Lakshmi Swaminathan was made responsible for women's affairs. Eight representatives of the armed forces—Aziz Ahmed, N. S. Bhagat, J. K. Bhonsle, Gulzara Singh, Mohammad Zaman Kiani, A. D. Loganathan, Ehsan Qadir, and Shah Nawaz Khan—found places in his cabinet, and Anand Mohan Sahay became cabinet secretary with ministerial rank. Rashbehari Bose was designated supreme adviser; and seven others, drawn from Burma, Thailand, and Malaya—Karim Gani, Debnath Das, D. M. Khan, Attavar Yellappa, John Thivy, Sardar Ishar Singh, and A. N. Sarkar—figured on his panel of advisers. What was notable about the composition of his cabinet was the strong representation given to members of religious minorities and the diversity of regional backgrounds.

Bose achieved remarkable success in forging a spirit of unity and solidarity among different religious communities and linguistic groups. He did so without asking his followers to give up their own ethnic affiliations in pledging their loyalty to the Indian nation. Bridging the disparities of class posed a somewhat greater challenge. Poorer Indians initially responded to Netaji's call with greater alacrity. He could barely conceal his exasperation with the niggardliness of a few of the richer Indians, though there were also stunning instances in which millionaires chose to become fakirs. "When the INA is getting trained either to march to victory or to spill its last drop of blood on the way," he said to the Chettiars (the leading Tamil community of financiers) and other merchants on October 25, 1943, "the rich people are asking me whether total mobilization means 10 percent or 5 percent. I would ask these people who are speaking of percentage whether we can tell our soldiers to fight and spill only 10 percent of their blood and save the rest."[39] In the end, the Provisional Government gratefully accepted 100 percent from the enthusiastic and settled for 10 percent from the reluctant. Netaji turned out to be a very successful fundraiser, ensuring receipts of nearly two million Straits dollars a month by the close of 1943. At a particularly successful event attended by fifteen thousand Indians at Penang in August, he raised two million dollars in one day.[40] The Chettiars from Tamil Nadu were among the big contributors to the coffers of the Azad Hind government.

When priests of the main Chettiar temple in Singapore came to invite Netaji to a religious ceremony in October, they were turned away because of their inegalitarian practices. He acceded to their request only after they agreed to host a national meeting open to all castes and communities. He went to that temple gathering flanked by his Muslim comrades Abid Hasan and Mohammad Zaman Kiani. "When we came to the temple," Hasan has written, "I found it filled to capacity with the uniforms of the INA officers and men and the black caps of the South Indian Muslims glaringly evident." He hesitated to enter the inner sanctum, but a priest gently pushed him in. *Tilaks* made of sandalwood paste were put on their foreheads in true Hindu fashion. Netaji wiped his off on leaving the temple and so did his followers. Abid Hasan could not remember the speech that Netaji gave on that occasion. "The memory I retain," he wrote much later, "is one of an invigorating music as that of a symphony dedicated to the unity of the motherland and the common purpose of all Indians to be united in their efforts to establish their identity." The echo of that music was to sustain him during the trials and tribulations on the battlefield.[41]

The Azad Hind government inculcated this spirit of unity with a subtle sense of purpose. "Jai Hind!"—"Victory to India!"—was chosen from the very outset as the common greeting or salutation when Indians met one another. Hindustani, a mixture of Hindi and Urdu written in the Roman script, became the national language; but given the large south Indian presence, translation into Tamil was provided at all public meetings. Even the proclamation of the Azad Hind government was read in Hindustani, Tamil, and English. A simple Hindustani translation of Rabindranath Tagore's song "Jana Gana Mana Adhinayak Jai He" became the national anthem. A springing tiger, evoking Tipu Sultan of Mysore's gallant resistance against the British, featured as the emblem on the tricolor shoulder-pieces on uniforms. Gandhi's *charkha* continued to adorn the center of the tricolor flags that INA soldiers were to carry on their march toward Delhi. Three Urdu words—*Itmad* ("Faith"), *Ittefaq* ("Unity"), and *Kurbani* ("Sacrifice")—encapsulated the motto of the Azad Hind movement.[42]

The spirit of solidarity was infused in the soldiers of the Azad Hind Fauj (literally "Free India Army," the Indian National Army) through a process of political education. Netaji either wrote or influenced the platoon lectures that were delivered to the troops in their training camps. One such lecture given to INA recruits, titled "Unity of India, Past and Present," rehearsed the history of Hindu-Muslim relations on the subcontinent. "Once the Moghul rule was established," the recruits were told, "Hindus and Muslims lived as brothers." In more recent times, Mahatma Gandhi was credited with being "very largely responsible" for inspiring and uniting the masses of India. Bose showered high praise on Gandhi, choosing to forget their differences of 1939. On the occasion of the Mahatma's seventy-fourth birthday, on October 2, 1943, he made a broadcast from Bangkok describing Gandhi's contributions to the Indian struggle as "unique and unparalleled." Gandhi was at this time languishing in British detention. "No single man could have achieved more," Bose said in his eulogy, "in one single lifetime under similar circumstances." The lesson to be learned was that Indians in Southeast Asia "should form one common blood brotherhood for the achievement of Purna Swaraj [complete independence] for India."[43] Bose's and Gandhi's discourses on unity sanctified by the fire of sacrificial patriotism relied more on the language of blood than on the language of rights, even though there was room for both in their formulations. Gandhi's call in 1942 that "rivers of blood" must flow to pay the "price of freedom" was not qualitatively different from Bose's exhortations in 1943. Both were talking about shedding Indian blood, rather than spilling the blood of their enemies.

Secular nationalism in the late colonial era had slid rather easily into forms of religious or ethnic majoritarianism. When it came to bridging differences, rights-based discourses on secular uniformity generally failed, whereas discourses focusing on blood sacrifice and blood brotherhood did not. Perhaps Bose's success was easier to achieve in an overseas context, where there was less obsession with land than in territorial nationalisms, despite references to the sacred soil of India. There were both territorial and extraterritorial features in the INA's anticolonialism. Bose was extraordinarily effective in forging Hindu-Muslim unity at a time when divisions along lines of religion were looming large within India. He blazed an innovative path to a cosmopolitan anticolonialism among expatriate patriots by nurturing a process of cultural intimacy among India's diverse communities. His strategy entailed combating religious prejudice without stumbling into the secularists' pitfall of making religion the enemy of the nation.

Just after midnight on October 23–24, 1943, the Provisional Government of Free India declared war on Britain and the United States of America. The decision to include the United States as an enemy was not uncontested. At a cabinet meeting on the evening of October 23, A. D. Loganathan asked: "Why drag in America, sir?" He had a point. Since Indians had no particular quarrel with the United States, there was something to be said for retaining American goodwill for the future. Bose argued that the presence of American forces on Indian soil was a "grim reality" that would make the INA's task of defeating the British "doubly difficult." The United States should have put pressure on Britain to accede to India's demand for independence immediately. Since the INA would have to fight against British and American troops on Indian soil, he wanted to include the United States in his government's declaration of war.[44] If he had not insisted on this course, his appeals to the American public the following year to support the cause of India's freedom might have carried more weight.

Nine states of the Axis and pro-Axis powers, including Japan and Germany, gave international diplomatic recognition to the Indian Provisional Government. A message of personal congratulations arrived from Ireland. Bose, however, was interested more in legitimacy than in formal recognition of his sovereignty. This he pursued through an interesting combination of claims to Indian territory and the allegiance of India's overseas citizens. Once Indian expatriate patriotism had expressed itself in the form of a government in exile, it felt the need for territory as a mark of its legitimacy. Addressing fifty thousand Indians assembled on the *padang* in Singapore on the afternoon of October 24, Bose reminded them of the determination he had expressed on August 15 to set foot "on the holy soil of India before the end of this year." "Mine was not an empty declaration," he claimed, "or a mere boast."[45] Preparations were well under way for his soldiers to cross into northeastern India and for his government to set up the civilian administration in liberated areas. Before his self-proclaimed deadline elapsed, however, he would have to make do with a group of islands in the Bay of Bengal, much the way Charles de Gaulle's Free French initially declared sovereignty over some islands off the French coast in the Atlantic.

Territory was not the be-all and end-all of sovereignty. People were more important. The Provisional Government gave Indians domiciled abroad the option of accepting Indian citizenship. The Provisional Government of Free India was the first such experiment in conferring citizenship anywhere in colonial Southeast Asia. Indians residing in Southeast Asia were invited to sign the following oath printed on a small blue card:

> I, a member of the Azad Hind Sangh [Indian Independence League], do hereby solemnly promise in the name of God and take this holy oath that I will be absolutely loyal and faithful to the Provisional Government of Azad Hind, and shall be always prepared for any sacrifice for the cause of the freedom of our motherland, under the leadership of Subhas Chandra Bose.

By June 1944, two hundred thirty thousand Indians took written oaths of allegiance to the government in Malaya alone. These oaths were produced after the war during the Red Fort trial as legal evidence that the war had been waged by a duly constituted government.[46]

Toward the end of October, Bose left Singapore for Tokyo. On November 1, as head of the Provisional Government, he parleyed on equal terms with Tojo. He expressed displeasure with the attitude of the liaison agency Hikari Kikan, and of Japanese military officers in Southeast Asia. He wanted to deploy the entire first division of the INA in the Indian offensive and to train two further divisions in Malaya. He demanded full control of intelligence operatives to be sent to India. He asked Japan to hand over the Andaman and Nicobar islands to the Provisional Government, which also had to be in charge of liberated zones within India. He sought acknowledgment of his government's right to issue currency and exercise jurisdiction over abandoned Indian property all over Southeast Asia. Tojo yielded on the political and economic questions and promised to discuss the military matters with his commanders.[47]

On this visit, Bose was hosted at the home of Shibusawa Shakuro, the governor of Japan's reserve bank, whose father had presided over Meiji Japan's financial reforms in the late nineteenth century. Meiji constitution day, on November 3, provided the occasion for a visit to the Meiji shrine and Tokyo's museum of art. The primary purpose of the trip was to enable Bose to attend the Greater East Asia Conference on November 5 and 6, 1943. Bose, according to the Japanese Foreign Office, "chose to be an observer because he was of the opinion that India would not join the Greater East Asia Co-Prosperity Sphere," which was regarded by many as a façade for spreading Japan's economic hegemony. Despite his observer status, Bose's "imposing figure" dominated the proceedings.[48]

Rising to speak on the second day, Bose said that he had visualized the "panorama of the world's history" as he listened to the proceedings:

My thoughts went back to the Congress of Vienna in 1815 after the downfall of the Napoleonic Empire, to the Congress of Paris in 1856 after the Crimean War, to the Congress of Berlin in 1878 after the Russo-Turkish War in the Balkans, to the Versailles Peace Conference in 1919 at the end of the last War, to the Washington Conference held in 1921 for ensuring the Anglo-American domination of the Pacific and the Far East, and to the Locarno Conference in 1925 for ingeniously binding the hands of the German people, once and for all. My thoughts also went back to the Assembly of the League of Nations, that League of Nations along whose corridors and lobbies I spent many a day, knocking at one door after another, in the vain attempt to obtain a hearing for the cause of Indian freedom.

The Tokyo conference, he claimed, was different: it had not been convened for "dividing the spoils among the conquerors," "hatching a conspiracy to victimize a weak power," or "trying to defraud a weak neighbor." India had by now learned to distinguish between false and real universalism and favored a true internationalism "which did not ignore nationalism, but is rooted in it." An "international society of nations" could be created, in his view, only on the basis of "regional federations."[49] This was not said for the benefit of his hosts but was something in which he genuinely believed, since he had called upon the British Empire in the past to transform itself into a federation of free nations. Though the Japanese sponsorship of the document was less than altruistic, the five principles adopted in the joint declaration— justice, national sovereignty, reciprocity in international relations, mutual aid and assistance, and racial equality—predated by a dozen years the Panchsheel ("Five Principles") resolution adopted by Afro-Asian nations at Bandung in 1955.

Bose's speech, according to the Japanese record, "held the entire assembly in awe." His emotions, foresight, vast knowledge, and obvious strength of character combined to produce an "admirable effect." As soon as he ended his address, Tojo rose to reiterate his full support for Indian independence and announced his intention to transfer the Andaman and Nicobar islands to Bose's Provisional Government "in the near future." In the following days, Bose was invited to address a mass meeting held in Hibiya Park and a smaller gathering in Hibiya Hall. He persuaded the army chief, General Sugiyama, to regard the INA as an allied army and to accept his plans regarding the second and third divisions of the INA. He put in requests for equipment to build a navy and an air force. All Japanese support he treated as loans to be repaid after independence, and he undertook to pay for civilian recruits in the INA from funds contributed by India's overseas citizens. Bose visited Indian students at their hostel. "Like a mother," the Japanese narrative states, "he showered his heartfelt affection on them and inspired them by his words to devote themselves to the future well-being of their motherland." He decided to leave all the gifts he had received, including a Japanese sword, with the Shibusawa family, saying he would take them only when India was free. He had charmed the entire Shibusawa family, especially the children, and their staff who felt "in the whole wide world they would not find many lovable personalities like Bose."[50] He had clearly made a profound impression, in both public and private, on his Japanese hosts.

The conflict between Japan and China had troubled Bose since the 1930s. He had wanted to visit China in 1940 following Nehru's trip to that country, but the British had not allowed it. On November 18, 1943, Bose left the shores of Japan for occupied Nanjing at the invitation of Wang Jing Wei, the pro-Japanese Chinese leader, though he intended to communicate with the Chungking government of Chiang Kai-shek. He paid homage to Sun Yat-sen, the father of the 1911 Chinese Republic, at his memorial in Nanjing. In a broadcast from Nanjing on November 20, he described Sun Yat-sen as "a sincere believer in the liberation of Asia and in Asian unity." On November 21, 1943, he broadcast a second appeal to Chungking from Shanghai. "The Indian people," he said, "really sympathize with China and the Chinese people." He reminded the Chungking government that, as president of the Indian National Congress, he had sent the first medical mission to China as a gesture of sympathy for the Chinese people. He urged Chungking not to send troops to India "to fight against us on the side of the British." He tried to suggest that 1943 was not 1937 and that East Asia faced "an entirely new situation." He looked forward to the day "not far off" when, by means of an "honorable peace," Japan would "withdraw her troops" from China. Given the recent history of Japanese atrocities in China, this wishful thinking about a rapprochement between China and Japan was unrealistic but showed a lingering faith in an Asian universalism, despite the rifts caused by nationalist rivalries. Bose mentioned Gandhi's statement the previous year: had India been free, the Mahatma would have embarked on a mission to foster peace between China and Japan. He left Abid Hasan behind for a number of days to hold talks with representatives of the Chungking government. By now, however, Chiang Kai-shek was being given a seat at the high table of the Allies by Roosevelt and Churchill, and had little incentive to respond to an overture from an Indian freedom fighter allied with Japan.[51]

In a tragic episode of Asian history, the British had used Indian soldiers and police against Chinese protesters in Shanghai and Nanjing in 1924–1925. Tagore protested against this deployment following his visit to Shanghai in 1924. A number of Sikh policemen continued to be employed by the British, and a sizable Indian expatriate community lived in Chinese port cities. Now, in 1943 in Shanghai, Bose recruited a significant number of volunteers, mostly Sikhs, for his Indian National Army. Faced with the difficulty of transporting them to Southeast Asia, he made arrangements to train these troops in China. Bose's next stop was Manila, the capital of the Philippines, whose independence Japan had recognized in October. Though Manuel Quezon and Sergio Osmena had left the Philippines along with the American forces in early 1942, the majority of the Filipino elite and provincial administrators had come to an accommodation with the Japanese occupiers. José Laurel, the prime minster of the Japanese-recognized government, welcomed Bose in Manila. The relatively small Indian community in the Philippines attended a meeting addressed by Bose and contributed funds to the Provisional Government.[52]

Upon his return to Singapore on November 25, 1943, Netaji plunged into the final preparations for the march toward India. In the second week of December, he made a final swing through Indonesia to garner the support of Indians based in Jakarta and Surabaya on the island of Java, as well as those living in Borneo and Sumatra. This tour completed Bose's attempt to reach Indians living in nearly all parts of Japanese-occupied Asia. While Japan was clearly the colonial aggressor in Northeast Asia, with a dark record of oppression in Korea and China, the situation in Southeast Asia was more complex. Even here, the Chinese in Malaya and Singapore felt the brunt of Japan's wartime brutalities. Yet in this vast region Japan had also played an instrumental role in defeating and destroying the mystique of Western imperial powers—the British in Burma and Malaya, the French in Indochina, the Dutch in the East Indies, and the Americans in the Philippines. In Indochina, the Japanese found it expedient to work with the Vichy French; too late, in 1945, they shifted to supporting some Vietnamese nationalists. This enabled the communists in the Viet Minh to adopt the nationalist mantle. Elsewhere, the Japanese supported Asian nationalists, to a greater or lesser degree. The Indians, the Burmese, the Indonesians, and some Malays and Filipinos took advantage of Japan's undermining of Western colonial authority to advance their own independence movements. In Indonesia, Japan had released Mohammad Sukarno and Mohammad Hatta from long years in Dutch prisons. From 1942 to 1945, they accepted Japanese help to build their civilian administration and train their military. Though the Indonesian proclamation of independence did not come until August 1945, wartime developments would make a Dutch reconquest of Indonesia as difficult as the reassertion of British colonial rule in Burma. That Japan had undermined the British and other Western colonial powers in Southeast Asia was what mattered to Bose, despite the deplorable Japanese aggression toward the Chinese and other Asians.

Bose's Provisional Government extended its protective umbrella over Indians living in all these lands. It obtained *de jure* control over a piece of Indian territory when the Japanese handed over the Andaman and Nicobar islands in late December 1943, though *de facto* military control was not relinquished by the Japanese admiralty. Bose redeemed his rash promise of setting foot on Indian soil before the year's end by arriving in Port Blair on December 29 for a three-day visit to these islands. As usual, his visit was steeped in symbolism. The British had imprisoned some of India's greatest revolutionaries in the notorious Cellular Jail on Andaman Island, where many had spent harsh life sentences and not a few had been sent to the gallows. Netaji paid tribute to the revolutionaries who had suffered there, and likened the opening of the gates of Cellular Jail to the liberation of the Bastille. He hoisted the Indian tricolor at the Gymkhana grounds in Port Blair while a chorus sang the national anthem. Before his departure, he renamed Andaman as Shaheed ("Martyrs") Island, and Nicobar as Swaraj ("Freedom") Island.[53] During a visit to Bangkok a few days later, he appointed A. D. Loganathan the chief commissioner of these islands. According to Hugh Toye, the people of Thailand were "at their best, charming, hospitable, generous, eager to do honor to one who, none dared doubt, would soon march invincibly into India."[54]

Before the close of 1943, Netaji's secret agents had already reached Calcutta. Soon after his arrival in Singapore, he had felt the need for a wireless link with Bengal. The spies that the Japanese had sent into India had not been very successful. Bose tried to assert control over intelligence operations based in Penang and Rangoon, and put N. G. Swami in charge of what came to be called the Azad School. In March, four well-trained intelligence operatives—Bhagwan Lu, Harbans Lal, Kanwal Singh, and Kartar Singh—had accompanied Swami on the journey from Europe to Asia on the blockade runner S.S. *Osorno.* On December 8, Bose, Swami, and Hasan put these four together with another four trained in Penang, and dispatched this group of eight under the leadership of S. N. Chopra toward India on board a Japanese submarine.[55]

The group landed with weapons, money, and sophisticated wireless equipment on the Kathiawar coast of Gujarat on the night of December 22–23, 1943. They had been instructed to split into four pairs and head toward Bengal, the North-West Frontier, the United Provinces in northern India, and Bombay. Late in December, Bhagwan Lu—under cover of his pseudonym, T. K. Rao—called at Woodburn Park in Calcutta to see Sisir Kumar Bose, the nephew who had driven Subhas during his January 1941 escape. After a spell in prison for taking part in the Quit India movement, Sisir was sentenced to house arrest with permission to travel to medical college for his studies. The family was in mourning, since Prabhabati, the matriarch, had just passed away. Rao handed Sisir a handwritten message in Bengali from Subhas, on the letterhead of the Indian Independence League at 3 Chancery Lane in Singapore, dated "Sri Sri Kali Puja," October 29, 1943—the day of the worship of the mother goddess Kali. Subhas had told Sarat and Sisir that his messages in Bengali would be genuine, while those in English might be intended to mislead the British. Both Sisir and his mother,

Bivabati, recognized Subhas's handwriting. Sisir then put Rao in touch with those members of the underground organization Bengal Volunteers who had managed to stay out of prison.[56]

In January 1944, radio contact was successfully established between partisans in Calcutta and Subhas Chandra Bose in Burma. One of the earliest messages transmitted did not contain any valuable military intelligence. It conveyed the news of Prabhabati's death. "You look tired," Debnath Das said to Netaji that evening. "No, I am not tired," Bose replied. "I heard today that I have lost my mother."[57]

Freedom's Battle

On January 7, 1944, the advance headquarters of the Provisional Government were moved forward from Singapore to Rangoon. The first guerrilla regiment known as the Subhas Brigade, of the INA's first division, had already arrived in Burma by November 1942. Tokyo approved plans for the offensive into India in January and, at the beginning of February, sent orders for the Imphal campaign to General Mutaguchi Renea, the commander of Japanese forces in northern Burma. The strategic aims of the Japanese and the Indians were quite different. Japan saw the invasion as a preemptive strike to forestall British attempts to reconquer Burma. The INA, on the other hand, saw its role as that of a catalyst for a civilian uprising against British rule. The capture of Imphal and Kohima would open the way for its advance into the rest of Assam and Bengal, where a heroes' welcome awaited them. All that was required for "ultimate success," Bose said on January 8, 1944, was that "action within the country must synchronize with the action from without."[58]

In addition to the three regular divisions of the INA, the intelligence and field propaganda units had been organized since Bose's arrival into three groups: the Bahadur ("Courageous") group would penetrate behind enemy lines; the Intelligence group would subvert the loyalty of British Indian troops on the battlefield; and the Reinforcement group would be in charge of the political education of Indian prisoners before they joined the INA. By December 1943, four units of two hundred fifty men each had been attached for training to the Japanese divisions that would take part in the Arakan and Imphal campaigns. The Subhas Brigade of the first division, however, had been promised an independent role. In January 1944, General Masakazu Kawabe, the Japanese commander-in-chief in Burma, suggested to Bose that this regiment too should be divided into small groups and attached to the Japanese outfits, just as the field propaganda units had been. Bose flatly refused. Since three battalions formed a regiment or a brigade, he insisted that the regular INA regiments must retain their identity and should not be deployed in units smaller than a battalion. The political objective was as important for him as the military one. He wanted the INA to be seen as the spearhead of the entry into India, even if Indians were vastly outnumbered by Japanese forces. "The first drop of blood on Indian soil," he believed, "should be that of a member of the INA."[59]

After tough negotiations in January, Bose agreed to have one battalion of the Subhas Brigade take part in the fight against the British West African division in the Kaladan Valley, and have the other two protect the strategic routes in the Chin Hills. Once these battalions had acquitted themselves with credit in these operations, he planned to send them and the other brigades of the first division toward Kohima, Imphal, and beyond. He envisaged sending the second division into action soon after Imphal was taken, while his third division would be held in reserve in Malaya. He expected to raise five more INA divisions from the Indian prisoners who would fall into his hands in Imphal and Kohima.[60]

In addition to negotiating with Japanese military commanders, Bose spent the month of January 1944 gathering civilian recruits in Burma for the INA and raising resources from wealthy Indians for his war chest. Many Bengali women joined the Rani of Jhansi Regiment in Burma. Lakshmi Swaminathan had come to Burma with several hundred soldiers of her women's regiment, leaving M. Satyavati Thevar in charge of the rear headquarters in Singapore. Men from the Tamil- and Telegu-speaking communities in Burma swelled the ranks of the INA. The civilian response at Netaji's public rallies in Burma was as enthusiastic as it had been in Malaya. Bose devoted most of his time, however, to observing the training of the Subhas Brigade and boosting their mo-

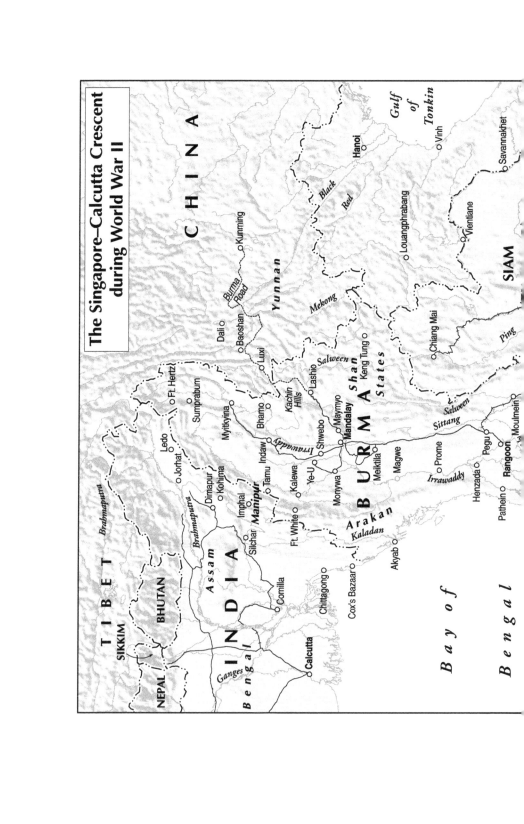

The Singapore–Calcutta Crescent during World War II

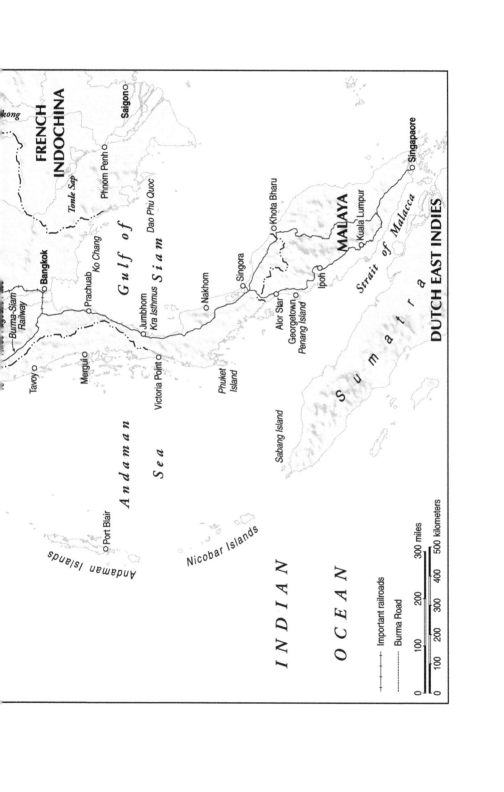

FRENCH
INDOCHINA

Saigon○

kong

Tonle Sap

Phnom Penh ○

Dao Phú Quoc

Gulf of

S i a m

Khota Bharu ○

Singora ○

MALAYA

Kuala Lumpur ○

Ipoh ○

Singapaore ●

Burma-Siam
Railway

Bangkok ●

Prachuab ○

Ko Chang

Kra Isthmus

Jumbhom ○

Nakhom ○

Alor Star ○

Georgetown ○
Penang Island

Strait of Malacca

S u m a t r a

DUTCH EAST INDIES

Tavoy ○

Mergui ○

Victoria Point ○

Phuket
Island

Sabang Island

A n d a m a n

S e a

Port Blair ○

Andaman Islands

Nicobar Islands

I N D I A N

O C E A N

┼──── Important railroads
─ ─ ─ Burma Road

0   100   200   300 miles

0   100   200   300   400   500 kilometers

rale with pep talks. On February 3, 1944, the entire regiment gathered to hear their supreme commander wish them Godspeed in the battles. As the trains carrying his soldiers left Rangoon for Mandalay and Prome on February 4–6, tears streamed down Bose's face.

One Bahadur group of the INA, led by Major L. S. Misra, had already been deployed on the Arakan Front, where the offensive was launched on February 4. The reconnaissance and subversion conducted by Misra's men enabled the 55th Japanese Division to trap the 7th British Indian Division on the eastern side of the Mayu range, cutting it off completely from the 5th British Indian Division and rupturing its communication links with the British 15th Army headquarters. Even though the Japanese were unable to capitalize on this early success, the reputation of the INA as a fighting unit was established. Wireless messages received from Calcutta, sent by the secret agents who had landed on the Kathiawar coast, were further cause for satisfaction. In late March, Bose decorated Misra with a high award for gallantry, and held him up as an example to the officers and men proceeding toward the more important battlefront of Imphal. Misra was killed in action later in the year, but the battalion of the Subhas Brigade sent to the Arakan sector did well against the 81st British West African Division from mid-March onward. From its base in Kyauktaw, the battalion, led by Major P. S. Raturi, moved steadily north up the Kaladan Valley, capturing Kaladan, Paletwa, and Daletme and establishing itself at Mowdok on the Indian side of the Indo-Burmese border.[61]

Just as the three battalions of the INA's Gandhi Brigade, commanded by Inayat Kiani, started arriving in Burma from Malaya, Bose received news that Kasturba, the Mahatma's wife, had died in Poona while in British custody. In a broadcast from Rangoon, Bose paid a moving tribute to the "great lady who was a mother to the Indian people": "Mahatma Gandhi called upon the British to quit India and save India from the horrors of modern war. The insolent reply of the British was to throw him into prison like an ordinary criminal. He and his noble consort would rather die in prison than come out free in an enslaved India." He urged the sons and daughters of India to avenge the death of their mother, Kasturba, by completely destroying the British Empire in India.[62]

The Imphal offensive commenced on March 8, 1944. Bose had drawn up elaborate plans for civilian administration of territories in India that fell to the INA. Civil servants were being trained at the Reconstruction College in Singapore, but few had moved as yet to Burma. Bose hurriedly sent for A. C. Chatterjee, his erstwhile finance minister, and on March 16 he appointed Chatterjee chief administrator of the liberated territories. He quickly created a civil affairs group called the Azad Hind Dal ("Free India Group"), to take charge of administration within India. The initial team of about seventy administrators left Rangoon for the border on March 8. They were to discharge their duties in two phases. The immediate task would be to restore essential utility services, provide relief to refugees, furnish the liberated zones with supplies of food, maintain law and order, and reassure the Indian population of their safety and security. Once military operations ceased in any particular area, a provisional provincial administration would be established reporting to the Provisional Government of Azad Hind until the future, permanent government of Free India could be organized. The work of reconstruction would create, in Bose's words, "a new political, economic and social order by which a better life for the Indians may be secured."[63]

On March 18, 1944, the INA moved into northeastern India, toward Imphal and Kohima. With "Chalo Delhi!" on their lips, the Azad Hind Fauj crossed the Indo-Burma frontier and carried the armed struggle onto Indian soil. They marched singing their battle song, "Kadam Kadam Barhaye Ja"; step by step they would advance until the Indian flag fluttered over the Red Fort of Delhi. On that historic occasion, Netaji issued a lyrical order of the day in which he dwelt on the theme of sacrificial patriotism:

There, there in the distance—beyond that river, beyond those jungles, beyond those hills lies the promised land—the soil from which we sprang—the land to which we shall now return. Hark! India is calling—India's metropolis Delhi is calling—three hundred and eighty eight millions of our countrymen are calling. Blood is calling to blood. Get up, we have no time to lose. Take up your arms. There, in front of you, is the road that our pioneers have built. We shall march along that road.

We shall carve our way through the enemy's ranks—or if God wills, we shall die a martyr's death. And in our last sleep we shall kiss the road that will bring our Army to Delhi. The road to Delhi is the road to Freedom. *Chalo Delhi.*"[64]

The INA soldiers were ecstatic to be on Indian soil, and Japanese journalists reported scenes of jubilation and camaraderie among Indian and Japanese troops as they closed in on Imphal and Kohima.

"The land of India towards which the Azad Hind Fauj is marching," Tojo declared in the Imperial Diet in Tokyo on March 22, "will be placed completely under the administration of the Free India Provisional Government." Even though Bose had the support of the top Japanese leaders in Tokyo, relations with middle-ranking Japanese officers were often fraught with tension. At a meeting on March 24, the two sides met in Rangoon to discuss the formation of joint labor and supply boards, to meet requirements within India. Bose would not countenance the idea of any Japanese chairmen of these boards. The Japanese found him "obstinate" at such meetings; Indians admired the haughtiness bordering on arrogance that he displayed in dealing with the Japanese. He told the Japanese that their banks would not be allowed to operate inside India; the Azad Hind government would set up its own national bank. He discussed the minutest details of the civil administration with Chatterji, approving laws and ordinances to be promulgated and checking the worthiness of the personnel being appointed. He expected the best administrators to be promoted to provincial governorships, as more Indian territory came under his government's sway. The district and village administrative structures were described in detail, government departments defined with precision, and the relations between different layers of government spelled out.[65]

On April 5, 1944, Bose announced the formation of the National Bank of Azad Hind, much to the chagrin of the Japanese in Burma. An Indian millionaire in Rangoon, Abdul Habeeb Saheb, donated all his assets, valued at more than ten million rupees (around $3.03 million); and Shrimati Betai did much the same, earning the decoration of Sewak-i-Hind ("Servant of India").[66] Largely thanks to Netaji's mesmerizing oratory, the Azad Hind Bank was able to raise two hundred million rupees—roughly $60.6 million—from Malaya and Burma.[67] A cabinet reshuffle helped in this regard. Once Chatterji became chief administrator of the liberated territories, Bose appointed N. Raghavan as his finance minister. Raghavan connected better with the wealthy south Indian communities in Malaya and Burma, and ensured a steady flow of resources into the government's coffers. Nambiar, in Europe, was made a member of the cabinet, and the Indian Legion there was declared to be a branch of the INA. G. R. Nagar and Habibur Rahman became the new military representatives in Bose's government. Attavar Yellappa and Ishar Singh were promoted from advisers to ministers, and S. M. Bashir of Rangoon was brought in as an adviser. S. C. Alagappan was given the portfolio of supplies, since that was likely to be of critical importance as the campaign progressed. By early April 1944, the Azad Hind government was issuing postage stamps for use in the liberated zones, and was printing sample currency notes.[68] If anything, Bose's plans for postwar reconstruction in India had run ahead of successful implementation of a war strategy.

On April 7, with the Imphal offensive well under way, Bose moved a small advance headquarters north, from Rangoon to Maymyo, a small hill town near Mandalay. The Japanese general Mutaguchi was based there. It seemed like a good place to get news from the front and establish a base, which would permit a rapid move to Imphal to take charge of the administration. During an earlier conference on strategy, Bose had urged Mutaguchi to avoid cutting the Imphal-Kohima road and to leave a route open for the British to retreat. He reckoned that once the British were forced back from Imphal, the plains of Assam and Bengal would be open to his forces. The next line of defense for the British would be the Chhota Nagpur plateau, after his triumphant entry into Calcutta by the autumn of that year. A consequence of the fall of Imphal might well be "a revolt in Bengal and Bihar against British rule in India on a far larger scale" than the Quit India movement in 1942.[69]

The British kept a tight lid on news regarding the Indian National Army within India, while denouncing Bose as a traitor in broadcasts from London. The threat to northeast India and, by extension, to the strategic road linking China led American journalists to offer their assessment of Bose and his army. On March 11, 1944, *The Saturday Eve-*

ning Post of New York carried a lengthy diatribe on Bose by Alfred Tyrnauer, under the title "India's Would-Be Führer":

> Subhas Chandra Bose, Head of the Japanese-sponsored "Free Indian" government at Singapore, has emerged as the greatest and most sinister Axis figure of the war in Asia. He has been an agent of Hitler and a tool of the Japanese. Yet he is towering far above all other puppets set up by the Axis; he is a Führer, a master intriguer and a war maker in his own right. Shrewd, handsome, intelligent, British-educated, vain and boundlessly ambitious, Bose began his amazing metamorphosis from a revolutionary socialist into an advocate of fascism almost exactly ten years ago.

While condemning Bose as a fascist, Tyrnauer was not above describing his subject as an "Oriental acquisition" of the Nazis and a "brown cavalier" of a "Nordic girl."[70]

John W. Gerber offered a more sober analysis of Bose's strategy in *The Nation*, on April 22, 1944. According to Gerber, Bose had proclaimed in November 1943 that he would march into Bengal and Assam; and when that happened, any hopes Chungking might entertain of a new road from Assam would be dashed. Gerber observed that Bose was "on the verge of achieving his goal," and if he succeeded in doing so, it would be "a major political and military victory." The United Nations could no longer ignore Bose, Gerber argued, since he had "begun to turn his words into action."[71] On April 17, *Time* magazine noted the danger that Bose posed to the Allied cause. "Thoughtful men thought twice," its article titled "Renegade's Revenge" commented, "when they learned that sardonic, myopic Bose, traitor, was with the Japs around Imphal." Yet despite the thick layers of British censorship, news was filtering through about Bose's army. Estimates of its strength, according to *Time*, varied from three thousand to thirty thousand soldiers. Far more significant than the size of his army, the article perceptively remarked, was "one explosive fact: an armed anti-British Indian stands today on Indian soil and calls upon his fellows to rebel against the Raj."[72]

Bose himself reported at this time that things were going "very well at the front" and that spirits were high, as he scribbled a few lines to Brahmachari Kailasam of the Ramakrishna Mission in Singapore on April 16, 1944, "before crossing the frontier." Once he did so, he was not sure when he would be able to communicate with Kailasam again. Besides the INA's soldiers, personnel belonging to the Reconstruction Department from Singapore and Rangoon had gone forward. "We shall be meeting them in Free India," Bose wrote optimistically.[73]

Going against Bose's preferred strategy, Mutaguchi chose to lay siege to Imphal. He obstructed the Imphal-Kohima road, denying the British any chance of escape toward the railhead of Dimapur and the route to Ledo. Mutaguchi had convinced himself that he had caught large fish in his net. Bose decided to make a virtue out of necessity and persuaded himself that a large number of British Indian troops and war matériel captured in Imphal would strengthen his leverage with the Japanese. During the month of April, the Japanese forces and the INA seemed within an ace of capturing both Kohima and Imphal. The Japanese hoped the news of the fall of Imphal could be presented as a gift to Emperor Hirohito, whose birthday fell on April 29. The Bahadur group of the INA, commanded by Shaukat Ali Malik, had fought extraordinarily well in the Bishenpur sector. Netaji had placed his personal faith in this talented and dedicated officer, who had on occasion exhibited an excessive fondness for drink. Malik fulfilled the confidence his leader had shown in him by hoisting the Indian tricolor in Moirang, a few miles short of Imphal.[74]

The Japanese had taken an enormous risk by deciding to travel light with limited supplies across long distances, over difficult and treacherous terrain. A speedy victory was of the essence, if they and the INA forces were not to be stranded on the wrong side of the hills and jungles beyond which Bose could see the promised land. The Japanese counted on capturing "Churchill rations" in Imphal and Kohima, as the supply links connecting Rangoon and Mandalay with the front line were tenuous. On the battlefields of Imphal and Kohima, some eighty-four thousand Japanese troops of the 31st, 33rd, and 15th divisions and twelve thousand INA troops (of whom four thousand were reinforcements) faced one hundred fifty-five thousand British, British Indian, British West African, and American troops. With all escape routes blocked, the British fought with their backs to the wall in Imphal. The Americans organized a continuous airlift of supplies into Imphal throughout the siege, which lasted three and half months. The Allies had a ten-to-one advantage in terms of air power over the Japanese in northeastern India and Burma. Badly overextended in the Pacific, the Japanese found it impossible to provide air cover and to transport adequate supplies to the INA troops as well as their own. Mutaguchi would soon learn, to his dismay, that the large fish he thought he had caught in his net was turning out to be a crocodile.[75]

Mohammad Zaman Kiani, commander of the first division of the INA, had established his base at Chamol, thirty-five miles east of Imphal, on April 17. In late April, M. Z. Kiani asked for the two battalions of the Subhas Brigade deployed in the Chin Hills to rejoin his division, to take part in the assault on Kohima and Imphal. This regiment had seen action on the Haka-Falam front, and a young major, Mehboob Ahmed, had brought credit to it. Its commander, Shah Nawaz Khan, now shifted the main body of this brigade toward Ukhrul, en route to Kharasom and Kohima. By mid-May, the Subhas Brigade had hoisted the Indian flag on the mountaintops around Kohima, but the moment when that town could have been seized had already passed. If the Japanese had bypassed Kohima and taken the railhead at Dimapur, things might have been different. An order to do so was actually issued on one occasion by Mutaguchi, but was countermanded by his immediate superior, Kawabe. General William Slim, in his memoirs, thanked the Japanese commander in the Kohima sector, General Kotoku Sato, for not pursuing this option, which could have brought disaster to the British forces in Imphal. The Nagas, the major tribal community around Kohima, Shah Nawaz Khan reported, were helpful to the INA troops. They did not want to be ruled by either the British or the Japanese. "All that we would like to have," they told Shah Nawaz, "is our own Raja, Netaji Subhas Chandra Bose." The Manipuris around Imphal also aided the INA, and some of them would return with the INA to Burma.[76]

The first division's second regiment, the Gandhi Brigade led by Inayat Jan Kiani, took up its position on April 28 at the village of Khanjol. On May 2, a detachment of about three hundred soldiers from this regiment mounted a daring attack on the British airfield at Palel. The Japanese force under Major-General Yamamoto had advised them to leave all their heavy baggage, including machine guns and grenades, at Kalewa. All that each soldier needed, they had been led to believe, was a rifle and fifty rounds of ammunition and a blanket, since the rest could be acquired in Imphal, which was on the verge of collapse. The lack of supplies proved to be a great handicap for the Gandhi Brigade the following month. The third regiment of the first division, the Azad Brigade commanded by Gulzara Singh, reached Tamu-Moreh on the Burma-India border in the middle of May, and set up its base north of Moreh at a place called Narum. Fierce fighting took place all along the Tamu-Moreh-Palel-Imphal road during the month of May, with hill-tops and villages changing hands more than once. The Gandhi Brigade fought on the left flank of the Japanese forces and the Azad Brigade on the right. Decades later, local residents spoke of encounters with ghosts at these sites of some of the bloodiest battles of the Second World War.[77]

That year, the monsoon broke early—toward the end of the third week of May. On May 21, Bose shifted back to Rangoon from Maymyo, where he was finding it increasingly difficult to get accurate news from the front. If Imphal fell, he could just as quickly fly in from Rangoon using his small aircraft, the *Azad Hind*. He had learned, from both M. Z. Kiani and Shah Nawaz Khan's messages, about the supply short-ages and transportation bottlenecks. The INA soldiers were being rav-aged by malaria and had no medicines. Bose set up a Supply Board in Rangoon and instructed Alagappan, his supply minister, to buy local produce in Mandalay to provision the INA. He then sent Alagappan, Chatterji, and A. M. Sahay to Tamu, to purchase what supplies they could for the INA and bring back for him a precise report of the chal-lenges being faced. Morale in Rangoon was still high, and on May 29 Bose had a successful public meeting where enthusiastic Indians con-tributed nearly five million rupees (around $1.5 million) in cash and kind to help the war effort.[78]

Torrential rains washed away all tracks and turned the entire terrain on the Indo-Burma border into rivers of green mud. The ferocious encounters of May gave way, during the month of June, to anxious patrols by both sides and to skirmishes when they chanced upon each other. Bose made a flying visit to his rear headquarters in Singapore. His presence in Malaya provided another spurt in the inflow of funds. He reviewed the second division of the INA training in north Malayan camps, and asked them to be ready to move to the front in July or August. He paid a visit to the third division being readied in Johore. Since February, he had been able to free intelligence operations based in Rangoon and Penang from Japanese interference, which he detested. In Penang, he was briefed by his intelligence chief, N. G. Swami, about another group of agents he had dispatched to India by sea in May. Bose now saw the possibility of sending his agents over land behind the enemy lines in Imphal. Swami accompanied Bose to Rangoon on his return, toward the end of June.[79]

The news about the Imphal campaign was still positive in Rangoon. The offensive may have slowed or even stalled, but there was no hint of impending calamity. A. M. Sahay gave Bose a report on the administrative difficulties, but they seemed remediable. Planning proceeded on the expectation that victory would be achieved and that northeastern India would be brought under the rule of the Azad Hind government. The mood was optimistic on July 4, when Indians celebrated the first anniversary of Netaji's assumption of the leadership of the Indian Independence League. The Japanese spoke warmly of M. Z. Kiani's leadership of the first division, and were especially appreciative of the tenacity of the Gandhi Brigade.[80]

The Mahatma himself, who was in feeble health, had been recently released from prison in India. In a lengthy radio address to Gandhi on July 6, 1944, Bose offered the most detailed justification of his course of action during the Second World War. He lauded the Mahatma once more for bravely sponsoring the Quit India resolution. If the almighty British Empire could go around with a begging bowl for foreign help, he saw nothing wrong in the decision by an enslaved and disarmed people to seek help in the form of loans from abroad. As one who had stood resolutely for national self-respect and honor all his life, he would be the last person to succumb to any foreign power. Whatever he had done was "for enhancing India's prestige before the world and for advancing the cause of India's freedom." The mission of the Provisional Government he had set up would be over, once India became free. The Indian people would then choose their form of government and decide who should be in charge of that government. He and his coworkers regarded themselves as servants of the Indian people. Freedom of their motherland was the only reward they sought in return for their suffering and sacrifice. "There are many among us," he went on to say, "who would like to retire from the political field, once India is free. The remainder will be content to take up any position in Free India, however humble it may be. The spirit that animates all of us today is that it is more honorable to be even a sweeper in Free India than to have the highest position under British rule."

Bose expressed absolute confidence in "our final victory." By this, he did not mean the victory of the Axis powers or Japan. "His triumph would be the expulsion of the British from India," according to a British intelligence officer who fought against him, "and this he would share with Mr. Gandhi and the Indian people." All that he hoped for from the Japanese was sufficient time for him to ensure that the British could not reassert their authority over their Asian colonies. S. A. Ayer observed Bose intently in the radio studio as he prepared to deliver the last line of his address. "Father of our Nation!" he began. His voice turned hoarse, then quivered, and a solemn look came over his face. His throat cleared and the words came out clear and strong. "In this holy war for India's liberation"—and then came a pause, a lowering of the pitch, and a tone of supplication—"we ask for your blessings and good wishes."[81]

On July 10, 1944, the Japanese informed Bose that their military position had become untenable and they had no option but to order a withdrawal from Imphal. Netaji and his followers gathered once more at Bahadur Shah's tomb on the emperor's death anniversary, which fell on July 11. Their solace on this somber occasion—in addition to a Bahadur Shah couplet about a warrior's faith, composed after the collapse of the 1857 revolt—was a well-known verse from Lord Byron's poem "The Giaour": "Freedom's battle once begun, bequeathed from bleeding sire to son, tho' baffled oft, is e'er won."[82]

Short of food and medicines, the regiments of the INA's first division were in desperate straits by early July. Naga Sundaram, a Tamil civilian in Burma who had joined a field propaganda unit of the INA and fought in Imphal, described how, with supply lines cut, the soldiers of the INA had to subsist on jungle grass and small fish caught in little streams with their mosquito nets.[83] The Gandhi Brigade, which had fought fiercely against the Scottish soldiers of the Seaforth Highlanders, suffered a tragic blow. Unable to bear the hardships any longer, Major B. J. S. Garewal, the second in command of the regiment, deserted to the British side, taking with him details of the positions where the INA soldiers were entrenched. The brigade was in danger of being encircled and decimated. Abid Hasan, Bose's submarine voyage companion, became Inayat Kiani's deputy after Garewal's desertion. Hasan rallied his forces and was able to counterattack and extricate the Gandhi Brigade from a critical situation. Hasan remembered that his Sikh comrades were crestfallen that Garewal, a Sikh officer, had let them down so badly. Soon after war's end, Garewal was assassinated on a street in Lahore.[84]

The military debacle in Imphal was followed by a harrowing retreat back into Burma. On July 18, M. Z. Kiani ordered all the regiments of the first division to withdraw. Japan's decision to suspend the Imphal campaign was made public on July 26, the day Tojo resigned as prime minister for unrelated reasons. The terrain along the Indo-Burmese border has been described by the British commander William Slim as "some of the world's worst country, breeding the world's worst diseases, and having for half the year the world's worst climate."[85] The Japanese armed forces and the INA had dared to cross this two-hundred-mile belt of hills and jungles in their attempt to take Kohima and Imphal. Starvation and disease took an extraordinarily heavy toll as they trudged back, deeply despondent that their march to Delhi had suffered such a tragic fate. August was the cruelest month of all. Their predicament would have been worse, had it not been for the stellar work done by the motor transport company led by Colonel Raja Mohammad Arshad and a civilian, Zora Singh, in ferrying the sick and wounded soldiers from Kalewa to Yeu. By September 1944, the divisional headquarters had been established in Mandalay. The remnants of the Subhas Brigade were based in Budalin, the Gandhi Brigade in Mandalay, and the Azad Brigade in Choungoo.[86]

Netaji publicly acknowledged the failure of the Imphal offensive in a radio address from Rangoon on August 21, 1944. He blamed the setback on the early monsoon, which compounded defects in transport and supply. Until the rains began, the INA had held the enemy in Arakan and Haka and had advanced in Kaladan, Tiddim, Palel, and Kohima. His soldiers and officers had received a "baptism of fire" and hoped to regroup to fight the next round. In September he traveled up to Yeu and Mandalay to meet his retreating forces, the majority of whom had to be hospitalized. Women of the Rani of Jhansi Regiment who had trained in nursing took care of the sick and wounded veterans of the battle of Imphal.[87]

Bose was deeply affected by the suffering of his soldiers, though many showed great stoicism in adversity. Abid Hasan has described how, when Netaji came to see the retreating men from Imphal at Mandalay, the "Sikhs oiled their beards, the Punjabi Muslims, Dogras and Rajputs twirled their moustaches and we the indiscriminates put on as good a face as we could manage."[88] Bose met all the officers individually and embraced them. He pleaded with Abid Hasan to give him a candid description of the terrible hardships they had faced. Hasan simply quoted a Japanese officer who had told him at the front that the situation was "slightly not so very good." Yet the pride of this civilian-turned-soldier, who had trained in Germany and come all the way to Asia with his leader, was undiminished even after the catastrophe in Imphal:

> What a group we were, and ours was but a unit among many of its kind in our army. I felt proud and I feel more proud today that I belonged to it. Baluchis were there among us, and Assamese, Kashmiris and Malayalis, Pathans and Sikhs and Gujeratis, proud members of classes called the martial and those till then denied reputation for martial valor but who proved in battle that they could by their deeds claim equal honor. Every region in India was represented and every religion and every caste, mixed inseparably together not only in bigger formations but even in small platoons and sections, each unit being a living tribute to

the unity of India. We had our different private faiths and we had our different languages, but in our purpose and in our political belief we were a well-knit, determined and indivisible whole.[89]

Their leader had not asked them to give up their distinct regional and religious identities, but had rather inspired them to transcend these for a larger cause. Even Bose's enemies acknowledged that his presence among his soldiers in September was welcomed, "for there was about this dedicated man an awe and a passionate sincerity which could inspire devotion and love." One officer, who was imprisoned and interrogated later, was asked what he had got in return for the suffering he had been through in Imphal. His answer was simple: "Netaji embraced me."[90]

A reconstruction of what actually transpired in Imphal and Kohima is made especially difficult by the contradictory accounts left by the two sides. Some British military memoirs, of which there is a long tradition, disparage the role of the INA and exaggerate the scale of desertions once the prospects of capturing Imphal evaporated. The few reports left by INA veterans recount heroic local actions against tremendous odds. The internal intelligence estimates on the British side in 1944 do not support the self-congratulatory substance and tone of the later memoirs, often written by those who were nowhere on the scene at that time.

A secret British intelligence survey, dated October 2, 1944, of the six months from March to September is instructive. It reckons that by March 1944 there were about twelve thousand INA troops in Burma, of whom about four thousand were in the forward areas. Another seven thousand were believed to be on the way from Malaya to Burma and a third division was under training in Malaya. In Manipur the INA suffered heavy losses, and "this shock, coupled with disease and hard living conditions, soon began to tell": "Several gave themselves up, including a few INA officers of some importance, and still greater numbers were captured. Nevertheless, as in the case of Arakan, there was no question of mass desertion: some 700 of the INA have come into our hands since the end of February 1944, and the rest have retired with the Japanese forces." In September 1944, the numbers of INA troops in

Burma were "still very considerable," and reinforcements from Malaya since March may have raised the total to "something in the neighborhood of 20,000." "If for no other reason," the report stated, "the numbers involved alone would make the INA a major security problem."[91] Desertions from the INA were not only very limited in number; "going over" was a two-way street. More than a hundred Indian soldiers on the British side had crossed over to the INA in the early weeks of fighting in Arakan, and were welcomed by Bose as our "new comrades" in Rangoon. If the early successes had been sustained and if the INA had reached the plains of Assam, "defections by Slim's sepoys might have grown from a trickle to a flood, and destroyed the 14th Army—as Bose was convinced they could."[92] Shah Nawaz Khan may have been too harsh in saying that the Japanese had let them down badly and that but for "their betrayal of the INA, the history of the Imphal campaign may have been a different one." Yet even the British assessment in September 1944 suggested that it was "the Japanese Army which failed the INA," and that the failure of the Japanese to attain their objectives prevented the INA from "being used in the role for which it was designed."[93]

The inability of the Japanese and the INA to break through into Bengal undermined the planned strategy: fomenting an internal revolt to coincide with a military thrust from outside. Over time, the British were able to capture many of the secret agents sent by submarine to India. Even the best-equipped and best-trained group, under S. N. Chopra, had two weak links. The local Gujarati, Ismail Channia, included in the party for his knowledge of local terrain on the Kathiawar coast, gave himself up within two weeks, on January 3, 1944. Since the group had planned to meet in Benares once a month, the others were seized by the British police over the next few months, and five of them were sentenced to death. Three were probably used for counterintelligence operations.[94]

The second vulnerable spot was the northwest frontier, where Bhagat Ram was passing on information received from Bose to the Communist party leadership, for transmission to the British government. The German minister in Kabul, Pilger, recorded in one of his dispatches that secret agents had claimed that Sarat Bose's son Sisir had authenticated a message carried by this group. This information found its way into communist hands. Almost simultaneously with the debacle in Imphal, the British police raided the Calcutta hideout of the revolutionaries who were seeking to support Bose. One of them was killed in the raid. Others were arrested and transported to the Lahore fort, where they were kept in confinement without trial. Sisir, the nephew who had helped his uncle escape from India in 1941, was handed a charge sheet which read as follows: "You, Sisir Bose, are informed that the grounds for your detention are that you were acting in a manner prejudicial to the defense of British India, in as much as in collaboration with members of the Bengal Volunteer Group and others, you were actively engaged in a manner calculated to assist Subhas Chandra Bose and the Japanese."[95] The quaint prose notwithstanding, the charge was clear and accurate enough. Sisir was held without trial, though there were other instances of trials in camera and harsh sentences. Richard Tottenham of the Home Department, who interrogated the secret agents and the Indian revolutionaries, reported a total of seven trials of "enemy agents" during 1944–1945: three in Delhi, three in Madras, and one in Bengal. Altogether, twenty-three secret agents sent from Southeast Asia were sentenced to death, but the sentences of two of them were later commuted to imprisonment for life. One prisoner sentenced to death, Americk Singh Gill, escaped while being transported under police guard in Calcutta.[96]

On October 9, 1944, while Bose was in north Burma tending to his soldiers, an invitation arrived from Japan's new prime minister, General Kuniaki Koiso, asking him to visit Tokyo. Netaji returned to Rangoon and, in mid-October, held a conference with his top military commanders about the INA's future course of action. On October 18, he was nearly killed in Mingaladon, fourteen miles outside Rangoon, while he was reviewing an INA parade. The area was attacked by low-flying Allied fighter jets as Bose stood on a five-foot-high platform, or base, with the women of the Rani of Jhansi Regiment marching past. "This is not the front, Sir, please step off the base," Kiani urged his leader as he ordered the soldiers to disperse and take cover. A splinter from one of the ack-ack guns hit a soldier in the head and killed him within a few feet of where Bose was still standing. Then, according to

S. A. Ayer, "Netaji coolly walked down the steps of the saluting base, strode unconcerned to the edge of the parade ground, and sat under a tree until the duel between the ack-ack guns and the fighters was over."[97] In a radio address later that day, Bose described the war in Burma as "a fight between the human spirit on the one side and steel and armor on the other." "In no revolution in the world's history," he reminded his followers, "have the revolutionaries ever had superiority either in numbers or in equipment. Nevertheless the revolutionaries have, in most cases, succeeded in overthrowing the foreign yoke. This will also happen in the case of India."[98] On October 21, the first anniversary of the formation of his government, he expressed the hope of taking Imphal and Chittagong in a new offensive.

Bose left for Tokyo on October 29, accompanied by M. Z. Kiani, A. C. Chatterji, and Habibur Rahman. The new government—in which Shigemitsu continued to be the foreign minister—received him warmly. He was given an audience with Emperor Hirohito. Bose and his ministers complained about the failure of the Hikari Kikan in maintaining proper liaison with the INA during the Imphal campaign. He wanted full-fledged diplomatic relations to be established with the Azad Hind government through the appointment of an ambassador. Tokyo acceded to this request, but when Teruo Hachiya hurriedly arrived without proper credentials, Bose refused to receive him.[99] Bose agreed in Tokyo to deploy the INA's third division in the defense of Malaya. This was not, as it seemed, a concession to the Japanese. Since people, more than territory, currently formed the basis of his sovereignty, it made sense to defend the million-strong Indian population in Malaya, among whom large numbers had sworn formal allegiance to the Provisional Government.

Away from the battlefield, Netaji found one last occasion to give his views on the fundamental problems of India, when he was invited to address the faculty and students at Tokyo University in November 1944. He argued, in what has come to be called his "Tokyo thesis," that the creative faculty of its people and their determination to resist imperialist domination gave ample proof of India's vitality as a nation. He dwelt skillfully on the theme of Indian modernity, and offered finely etched assessments of Mahatma Gandhi and Rabindranath Tagore. The speech had some glaringly weak points, especially in its discussion of caste in India, which he claimed was withering away in modern India (though it was not). But Bose was able to delineate with clarity for a foreign audience what he thought would be the three most urgent tasks facing free India: national defense, eradication of poverty, and provision of education for all. An international order, he argued, could be built only on the foundation of associations of regional cooperation. Citing the failure of the League of Nations, he urged Japan, as the sponsor-nation of Asian regionalism, to "avoid a selfish and short-sighted policy and work on a moral basis."[100]

Bose desperately wanted to resume his march toward Delhi. Though he continued to hope that Britain's Maginot Line in Imphal could be breached with a second assault, talks with the Japanese, along with American bombs being dropped on Tokyo, appear to have convinced him that he could not expect any further help from that quarter. So in November 1944 he tried to establish contact with the Soviet Union through their ambassador, Jacob Malik, in Tokyo. He anticipated conflicts between the Soviet Union and the Western allies, and wanted to reopen a line of communication with a country which had never really helped him in the past, except to grant him passage though Moscow in 1941. The Soviet ambassador transmitted a message from Bose to Moscow, but there was no reply.[101] From Tokyo, Bose also made a series of broadcasts to the United States. He told his "American friends" that Asia was "surging with revolutionary fervor": "You had an opportunity of helping us, but you did not do so. Now Japan is offering us help and we have reason to trust her sincerity. That is why we have plunged into the struggle alongside of her. It is not Japan that we are helping by waging war on you and on our mortal enemy—England. We are helping ourselves—we are helping Asia."[102] Of the two superpowers on the postwar horizon, he had taken the opportunity of his visit to Japan to make an overture to one and to explain himself to the other.

Netaji's letters from this period reveal his special solicitude and concern for the young cadets he had sent to be trained at the military academy in Tokyo, and for the young women who had joined the Rani of Jhansi Regiment. He made it a point to meet the Tokyo cadets and spend time with them. "My dear boys," he wrote on November 29, 1944 (his daughter's second birthday), "On the eve of my taking off from the soil of Nippon, I want to send you my love and good wishes for the success of your work. I have no son of my own—but you are to me more than my son—because you have dedicated your life to the cause, which is the one and only goal of my life—the freedom of *Bharat Mata* [Mother India]."[103] He returned to Burma to carry on the fight via Taipei, Saigon, and Singapore. Mighty storms over the South China Sea delayed his flights. "Today a gentleman is going from here to Tokyo," he wrote to the cadets from Saigon on December 14, 1944. "I am taking the opportunity of sending a bundle of *papar* for you. I could have sent a few other things, but he could not carry any more weight."[104] His letters to M. Satiavati Thevar were also full of concern, and showed his willingness to deal with the minutest details concerning the organization of the women's regiment.[105]

"It was the battling with no hope along the Irrawady, not the battling with high hope about the Manipur basin," Peter Fay has plausibly argued, "that justified the freedom army and gave it in the end such moral leverage."[106] It was to fight this battle that Netaji returned to Burma on January 10, 1945. On his way there, in early January, he was fêted in Bangkok by the Thai government, which was still friendly toward his movement.[107] Japan's Ichigo offensive in China had gone well, and perhaps the INA could defend Burma at the line of the Irrawady. Indian morale in Rangoon continued to be high, despite the military reverses of the previous year. On January 23, Bose turned forty-eight and his followers celebrated. Much to his embarrassment, he was weighed against gold in grand Mughal style, and more than twenty million dollars was raised for the INA. Young men and women wrote pledges in blood vowing to fight to the death against the enemy. Behind the enthusiasm there was also some careful planning of intelligence activities. Bose devised with Swami an elaborate plan to send agents with wireless sets behind enemy lines. A special group was trained to sabotage the American pipeline in north Burma. The Nehru Brigade of the INA's first division, which had been unscathed in Imphal, was to be joined by two regiments of the second division that had arrived from Malaya. The responsibility for obstructing the advancing British forces at the Irrawady River was given to Gurbaksh Singh

Dhillon, a flamboyant Sikh officer who commanded many Tamil recruits of the Nehru brigade. Bose's military secretary, Prem Kumar
Sahgal, was sent to the front at Mount Popa, while the younger Mehboob Ahmed, who had distinguished himself in the Haka-Falam sector,
took his place at Bose's side.[108]

On February 10, 1945, five waves of American B-29s dropped con-
ventional and incendiary bombs on the INA hospital in Myang, six
miles outside Rangoon, and completely razed it. The hospital was
clearly marked with a large Red Cross sign, but the Japanese had
an ammunition dump in the woods not too far away. Many patients
were killed in this raid by the American flying fortresses, four-engine
heavy bombers, and the survivors with severe burns were evacuated
to the general hospital in Rangoon. Swami and Ayer had rushed in
Bose's car to the site of the attack and narrowly escaped serious injury.
When the attack ended, the supreme commander's car lay upside down
at the edge of a ten-foot by six-foot crater left by one of the bombs.
Aziz Ahmed, the commander of the INA's second division, received a
head injury and was at least temporarily put out of action. For the next
week, Netaji visited the burn victims at the general hospital two or
three times a day, and personally made sure they got the best medical
care available. He came back from these hospital visits feeling mo-
rose.[109]

On February 18, Bose departed Rangoon for the battlefront to the
north. He had given his soldiers an opportunity to leave, if for any reason they did not wish to fight. He wanted only the fully committed
among his followers to make a brave stand against the British advance.
He inspected the Imphal veterans who had taken up a defensive position at Pyinmana, and forged ahead to Meiktila with Shah Nawaz.
Meanwhile, on February 14, the Nehru Brigade under Dhillon had
thwarted the first British attempt at crossing the Irrawady at Nyaungu,
sinking many of the boats and inflicting many casualties on Slim's
South Lancashire Regiment. Initially, the British crossing at Pagan was
blocked as well. These dogged rearguard actions delayed but could not
prevent William Slim's well-planned assault by the 7th British Indian
division on the Japanese and INA defenses on the eastern banks of the
Irrawady.[110]

On February 13, Prem Sahgal had taken leave of Netaji in Rangoon and moved north. He had seen tears flowing down the cheeks of his supreme commander as he bade his erstwhile military secretary good-bye. Sahgal assured his leader that he would be all right. By February 17, he had occupied defensive positions on the western slope of Mount Popa. When Netaji arrived in Meiktila on February 21, the British were reported to be advancing from Nyaungu but the situation on the front appeared confused. Shah Nawaz and Mehboob Ahmed proceeded to Mount Popa with Netaji's instructions, hoping to bring back accurate information. Netaji inspected the INA hospitals at Kalaw and Taunggyi and arranged to remove them to Zeyawaddy, closer to Rangoon. On February 25, Shah Nawaz and Mehboob Ahmed returned to Meiktila and pleaded with Netaji not to travel toward Mount Popa. Finding him stubborn in his determination to risk the journey to Popa, Major Rawat contrived to delay his departure. The morning of February 26 brought news that the British had reached Mahlaing—ten miles north of Meiktila—and obstructed the roads between Meiktila and Mandalay, as well as between Meiktila and Kyaukpadang. The supreme commander of the INA was virtually trapped in Meiktila.[111]

Bose and Shah Nawaz decided to break out of Meiktila and head south toward Pyinmina. Shah Nawaz has described the scene:

> Everyone looked cheerful. One thing was certain, the enemy would never capture us alive. When we entered the car and started off, Netaji was sitting with a loaded Tommy gun in his lap. Raju had two hand grenades ready. The Japanese officer was holding on to another Tommy gun, and I had a loaded Bren gun in my hand. We were all ready to open fire instantaneously. The Japanese officer stood on the footboard of the car to be on the lookout for enemy aircraft. Raju sat next to the driver to locate any roadblocks put up by the enemy, while Netaji and I sat at the back watching both sides of the road.

No sooner had they reached the village of Yindaw, twenty miles south of Meiktila, than enemy aircraft loaded with machine guns strafed the village from the air. The planes did not hesitate to use ten-inch armor-piercing cartridges meant for destroying heavy tanks and railway en-

gines—shells that made "a terrible mess of the human body." After
sheltering in the jungle outside Yindaw for the day, Netaji reached Pyinmina on February 27.[112]

On his arrival at Pyinmina, Netaji put together a new fighting brigade from what remained of his first division. Calling it the "X Regiment," he placed Thakur Singh in command and asked him to take up
defensive positions at Yezin, just north of Pyinmina. He put Raja Muhammad Arshad in charge of the rest of the division. The sick soldiers
were evacuated ten miles to the rear and instructed to surrender if the
British succeeded in breaking through the defenses of the X Regiment.
On March 1, Netaji told Shah Nawaz of his decision to "stop at Pyinmina and fight his last battle against the British there." Shah Nawaz
persuaded him otherwise: there was no immediate prospect of such a
battle until the British consolidated their position in Meiktila. In fact,
the front in Burma remained static throughout the month of March
1945. Slim had taken a risk by sending a flying column under General
Frank Messervy to capture Meiktila, which now found itself isolated.
General Heitaro Kimura, who had replaced Kawabe as the Japanese
commander in Burma, tried to gather his forces to encircle and destroy the British Indian 17th division in Meiktila. Throughout March,
Messervy's forces barely hung on to the town and airfield east of Meiktila. If Kimura's final throw of the dice succeeded, Slim might fall short
of Rangoon before the rains came and evened the odds.[113]

On March 2, 1945, Bose received the dismaying news that five officers of his second division had deserted to the British at Popa. He
rushed back to his headquarters in Rangoon. He gave Shah Nawaz,
who left Rangoon for Popa on March 7, a free hand in choosing the
best and most reliable staff officers to take with him to the front.[114]
March 1945 brought a further complication in the war being fought in
Burma. Now that the fortunes in the war had changed, Aung San
turned against the Japanese and offered his assistance to Slim. The Burmese resistance was being conducted on Burmese soil. The arrogance
of the Japanese had not endeared them to their Burmese allies. The
Indians in Burma were still patriots and would not switch sides: their
objective was to end British rule in India. The Provisional Government
had also to protect the interests of the large Indian expatriate commu-

nity in Malaya. The Indians reached an understanding with the Burmese not to fight against each other. That agreement was adhered to, despite the history of past racial conflicts and a measure of envy in Burmese government circles of the sounder financial basis of the Provisional Government of Free India.[115]

Subhas Chandra Bose was extremely sensitive on the question of Indian soldiers' loyalty to the cause of freedom. He was well aware of the history of Indian treachery at Plassey in 1757 that had enabled the British colonial conquest in the first place. On March 13 he issued a statement on bravery and cowardice and gave an order to "arrest and shoot at the front cowardly and treacherous elements."[116] Despite instances of cowardice and treachery, the INA soldiers commanded by Shah Nawaz, Sahgal, and Dhillon fought courageously around Mount Popa during the month of April. Kanwal Singh and his men distinguished themselves in the battle of Legyi in early April. On April 10, the British bombed the INA field hospital at Kyaukpadaung, killing eighty men and injuring another thirty. Once Mount Popa had to be abandoned, on April 13, the INA struggled toward the south. On April 20, a battalion of Sahgal's regiment led by Captain Bagri perished about twenty miles south of Taundwingyi, fighting against a column of enemy tanks and armored vehicles with rifles and hand grenades. "What did you mean, you people," General Gracey would ask Prem Sahgal after his capture, "by going on fighting? We had armor, artillery. You chaps had nothing. But instead of surrendering, you fought. It was madness." Sahgal conceded it was madness, but of a deliberate, revolutionary sort.[117] Their determination to fight against the odds was "neither light-hearted nor born of hurrah-patriotism." It was a "grim resolve" based on a degree of political education imparted at the camps, perhaps at the cost of military training.[118] By April 1945, the weight of steel was decidedly against the Indians in Burma.

Eventually, on April 29, Prem Kumar Sahgal became a prisoner-of-war near Allanmyo; Shah Nawaz Khan and Gurbaksh Singh Dhillon were captured on May 18, near Pegu.[119] "I have always said that the darkest hour precedes the dawn," their leader had told them. "We are now passing through the darkest hour; therefore, the dawn is not far off."[120]

Adventure into the Unknown

On the eve of his departure from Burma, Netaji addressed his soldiers:

> I have only one word of command to give you, and that is that if you
> have to go down temporarily, then go down fighting with the national
> tri-color held aloft; go down as heroes; go down upholding the highest
> code of honor and discipline. The future generations of Indians, who
> will be born not as slaves but as free men because of your colossal sac-
> rifice, will bless your names and proudly proclaim to the world that
> you, their forebears, fought and suffered reverses in the battles in Ma-
> nipur, Assam, and Burma, but through temporary failure you paved the
> way to ultimate success and glory.[121]

The battle for Burma had been lost, but the war in Southeast Asia, especially Malaya, was far from over. Bose sent some of the best troops
of the Subhas Brigade back to Moulmein, en route to Thailand and
Malaya. He left another 5,000 soldiers in Rangoon under the command
of A. D. Loganathan, who was instructed to negotiate surrender as
prisoners-of-war once the British arrived. N. G. Swami, Bose's intelligence chief, put into operation his stay-behind schemes to keep the
underground revolutionary movement going, before leaving Rangoon
with his leader. Loganathan, with the able assistance of R. M. Arshad
and Mehboob Ahmed, kept perfect order in the city of Rangoon before
handing over authority to the 26th British Indian division on May 4,
1945.[122]

On April 23, Bose told the Japanese that he refused to leave Rangoon
unless transport was provided for about a hundred women of the Rani
of Jhansi Regiment who had to be returned safely to Malaya. The
women who had been recruited in Burma he had already sent to their
homes, after fond farewells. On the night of April 24 he set off from
Rangoon with these women in a ramshackle convoy of trucks. His
ministers S. A. Ayer and A. C. Chatterji, his top military commanders
M. Z. Kiani and J. K. Bhonsle, his intelligence chief N. G. Swami, the
head of the Hikari Kikan Lieutenant General Isoda Saburo, and the
ambassador Teruo Hachiya went with him. Bose had promoted M. Z.

Kiani, J. K. Bhonsle, and A. C. Chatterjee to major-general rank, and Shah Nawaz, Sahgal, and Dhillon had been made colonels. It was Netaji's historic retreat with the soldiers of the INA and the women of the Rani of Jhansi Regiment from Burma to Thailand—a hazardous journey chased by the enemy in late April and early May 1945—that left an indelible imprint on popular memory: these warriors made heroic sacrifices to pay the price of freedom.

"Standing there in the open, in the bright moonlight, with fires and explosions in the distance, and no definite news of the position of the enemy, was a peculiar sensation," S. A. Ayer has written. "We were literally living every moment of our life in those hours. We continued our march through the burning villages of Pegu."[123] With enemy aircraft in full control of the skies, the retreating column could travel only by night. "Not only daylight, we dreaded the moonlight too, only a little less," Ayer remembered. "We felt comparatively safe on pitch dark nights. Rather primitive, do you think? Well, quite so. Otherwise, how can shelters dug 20 or 30 feet underground have such a fascination for man? How else can the sun and moon be objects of horror?"[124] On the night of April 26, the women of the Rani of Jhansi Regiment waded across the River Waw, assisted by Swami and Shaukat Malik. Bose would not cross until his entire entourage was safely on the other side.

With their trucks either destroyed in enemy air raids or stuck in the muddy terrain, Bose and his column covered the last ten miles to the Sittang River on foot. Earlier in the day a young officer, Nazir Ahmed, had been killed by machine-gun fire from the air in a trench next to Netaji. "My girls are wonderful," Janaki Thevar wrote in her diary. "Each one of them is carrying her own pack, containing all their belongings." These packs, weighing thirty-five pounds, included rations, rifles, ammunition, and hand grenades. "Netaji is marching at the head of the column," she recorded, "also carrying his own pack." It does seem a miracle that the retreating column managed to cross the Sittang River without being decimated on that moonlit night. East of the Sittang, three long night marches followed. Bose refused to get into his car or a truck, so long as his companions had to walk. As he sat under a tree and took off his military boots, Janaki Thevar saw that his feet were "a mass of blisters."[125] "We were asked to get ready," Ayer continues the story, "for the trek from Sittang to Moulmein en route to Bangkok. Major General Zaman Kiani was asked to take charge of the party. He ordered us to fall in and gave us instructions as to how our party, including Netaji, should march and how air-raid alarm would be given and how we should immediately disperse on either side of the road and take cover."[126] The Janbaz ("Suicide") unit of the Subhas Brigade had joined the retreating column, and Netaji's group was now nearly a thousand strong. "Such was his spirit of discipline," Mohammad Zaman Kiani confirms, "that, to better arrange the march of the column and deal with related problems, he [Netaji] put me in complete charge and also put himself under my command for the duration of the march."[127]

On reaching Moulmein, the Ranis were put on a train under the charge of A. C. Chatterji and Shaukat Malik. The train could move only at night and had to be kept under camouflage colors on sidings during the day. Bose decided to wait for his X Regiment, which had miraculously extricated itself almost intact from Pyinmina and was headed toward Moulmein.[128] After being assured of the safety of his Imphal veterans, Netaji resumed his journey by road toward Bangkok. "That army is beaten which considers itself to be beaten," he told his followers, quoting Marshal Ferdinand Foch. He and his soldiers had not withdrawn from the fight, but were simply moving from one battlefield to another. Had not Clausewitz said that war has many surprises? There was still reason to fight on.[129]

If General Slim could gloat over turning "defeat into victory" in a military sense,[130] Bose was already considering how the INA could return the compliment on a political plane. In his first public address upon reaching Thailand on May 21, 1945, Netaji drew on examples from the history of Turkey and Ireland in urging Indians to fight on for freedom. "It may be that we shall not go to Delhi via Imphal," he told those he had roused to unprecedented patriotic fervor with his slogan "Chalo Delhi!" "But the roads to Delhi are many," he assured them, "like the roads to Rome. And along one of these many roads we shall travel and ultimately reach our destination, the metropolis of India."[131]

Bose was naturally disappointed that Indian soldiers had once again played a crucial role in the military reconquest of Burma, but he clearly noticed something new that promised a different future:

> There is, however, one silver lining in the cloud that has overtaken us, and that is, the British Indian Army of today is not the British Indian Army of the last war. Soldiers of the Azad Hind Fauj [Indian National Army] have had numerous opportunities of coming into close contact with members of the British Indian Army. Very often our soldiers were told by the latter that if they [i.e., the Azad Hind Fauj] succeed in advancing further, members of the British Indian Army would then come and join them. There is no doubt that at heart large sections of the British Indian Army sympathize with the Azad Hind Fauj and its fight for freedom. But the British Indian Army is not yet prepared to take the risk and line up with the revolutionaries. As a result of foreign rule, members of the British Indian Army have lost their self-confidence and they are afraid that the British might ultimately win, in which case they would be in a difficult situation. Moreover, they have been influenced, to some extent, by the propaganda of our enemies that the Azad Hind Fauj is a puppet army of the Japanese. After coming into Burma, the eyes of the British Indian Army will be opened. They will see for themselves what the Provisional Government of Azad Hind and the Azad Hind Fauj have done and how they have fought for India's freedom. They will hear "Jai Hind," which is the greeting of all free Indians. They will also hear India's inspiring national anthem sung by freedom-loving Indians in Burma. The effect of this experience on the British Indian Army, and all other Indians who have come into Burma alongside of the British, is bound to be great in the days to come.[132]

He said much the same thing in a private letter to Brahmachari Kailasam on June 10, 1945: "The fight goes on, despite what has recently happened in Burma. We shall win and India will be free."[133]

Commenting on the German defeat in Europe, Bose pointed to the blunder committed by the German government in disregarding Bismarck's advice never to fight on two fronts. German foreign policy toward the Soviet Union was the cause of the German disaster. "It is clear by now," he noted, "that the war aims of the Soviet Union are quite different from those of the Anglo-Americans, although they had a common enemy in Germany." He was pleased that at the San Francisco conference, Molotov had refused to accede to Anglo-American demands. In fact, he had gone to the extent of challenging "the puppets of Britain and America who came to represent India and the Philippines."[134]

In Bangkok, Netaji reassembled his civilian administration. Raghavan, his finance minister, brought resources from Singapore, and Ayer negotiated a loan from the Thai government. Chatterji was sent to Saigon, and Sahay to Hanoi, to reconnect with the Indian communities there. After visiting the INA's gunner detachments in Thailand and reaching an understanding with the Thai government, Bose returned to Malaya. The INA's third guerrilla division was stationed in various parts of the peninsula, as were the heavy-gun and tank battalions of the first division that had not been taken to Burma.[135]

Meanwhile, Archibald Wavell, the British viceroy, had invited leaders of Indian political parties to a conference in Simla to discuss political progress after the war. Mohammad Ali Jinnah questioned the right of Abul Kalam Azad, the Congress president, to speak for that party in Simla. Disagreements between Jinnah's Muslim League and the Indian National Congress had in any case doomed the Simla conference from the outset. In late June 1945, Netaji made a series of broadcasts from Singapore urging Indians at home not to compromise with British imperialism. He argued the case for a three-pronged strategy in pursuing the goal of Indian independence: continued armed struggle outside India, resistance rather than compromise inside India, and diplomacy in the international field. Since the almighty British Empire had gone down on its knees to seek American help, he felt he had done nothing wrong as the leader of an enslaved and disarmed nation in allying with Japan. No country had won freedom without some degree of foreign help, he said in his speeches, which now sounded like harangues. Far more important than his analysis of Wavell's initiative were the grounds on which he felt entitled to offer advice to his countrymen at home:

I and my comrades here are engaged in a grim struggle. Our comrades at the front have to play with death. Even those who are not at the front have to face danger every minute of their existence. When we were in Burma, bombing and machine-gunning were our daily entertainment. I have seen many of my comrades killed, maimed and injured from the enemy's ruthless bombing and machine-gunning. I have seen the entire hospital of the Azad Hind Fauj in Rangoon razed to the ground, with our helpless patients suffering heavy casualties. That I and many others with me are still alive today is only through God's grace. It is because we are living, working and fighting in the face of death that I have a right to speak to you and to advise you. Most of you do not know what bombing is. Most of you do not know what it is to be machine-gunned by low-flying bombers and fighters. Most of you have had no experience of bullets whistling past you, to your right and to your left. Those who have gone through this experience and have kept up morale dare not even look at Lord Wavell's offer.[136]

The Fourth of July may be the date of the American Declaration of Independence, but it was no less significant in the history of the Azad Hind movement in East Asia. On July 4, the day he had taken over the leadership of the movement in 1943, Netaji addressed a large gathering in Singapore for two hours in Hindustani; the audience reaffirmed their determination to achieve liberty or death. On July 8, 1945, Netaji laid the foundation stone of a memorial to the martyrs of the INA who had laid down their lives in the cause of freedom. At the end of the month, he traveled north to Seremban and Kuala Lumpur. Even at this stage, he seems to have believed that he would have time, perhaps even up to a year, to determine his future course of action.[137]

The atom bombs dropped on Hiroshima and Nagasaki, on August 6 and 9, 1945, brought the war in East Asia to an abrupt end. By August 9, news of the utter devastation in Hiroshima had spread throughout the world. At midnight on August 10, a phone call came from Inayat Kiani in Kuala Lumpur, informing Netaji that the Soviet Union had entered the war against Japan. The following night he received news of Japan's intention to surrender. "So, that is that," he said with a wry smile. "What next?" He decided to drive down to Singapore the next day, and gave urgent instructions for a car to pick up Raghavan and Swami from Penang and John Thivy from Ipoh, to meet him there. Swami had been devising some stay-behind schemes in Malaya, to keep the flag of independence flying after the Allied landings. A twelve-hour drive down the Malay Peninsula on August 12 brought Bose and his party to Singapore, at about half past seven in the evening.[138]

Bose's cabinet met continuously on the verandah of the upper floor of the bungalow on Meyer Road. Arrangements were made to distribute sufficient money to INA soldiers and civilians affiliated with the Provisional Government, to see them through at least six months. Netaji's most important concerns were the five hundred women in the Rani of Jhansi Regiment camp in Singapore and the forty-five cadets he had sent to Tokyo for training in the army and the air force. He spoke to the commandant of the camp, to get the women safely to their homes with adequate funds and provisions. The commandant, in her turn, invited Netaji to attend a play on the life of Rani Lakshmibai of Jhansi that was being performed by her soldiers on the evening of August 14. Bose was unwell, having had a tooth pulled that afternoon. He sent instructions for the performance to begin, saying that he would join the audience later. "Deafening cheers broke out," Ayer recalled, "when Netaji arrived earlier than expected." At the end of the performance, he stood with three thousand men and women of the INA in the open-air theater as the entire gathering sang the national anthem.[139]

Throughout the cabinet meetings of August 13 and 14, Netaji himself was quite often the focal point of the conversation. He listened to what was being said and took part in the discussion as if someone else were being discussed. He and his staff wondered what the British would dare to do with him in the event he was taken prisoner in Singapore. Not that the British themselves knew this. About that time and a bit later, Wavell and his cabinet were weighing their options and found none of them satisfactory. How could Bose be eliminated? His influence, they had already discovered, powerfully affected "all races, castes and communities," who admired him for forming an army of liberation and standing up to both the British and the Japanese. If he was tried in India, he could not be executed, as "the pressure for his release would be too great." Perhaps he could be tried in Burma or Malaya, or imprisoned secretly without trial on a distant island like the Seychelles. Perhaps they might leave him where he was and not ask for his surrender. There were really no good options for dealing with His Majesty's most inveterate opponent, even in this moment of victory in a world war. Bose's cabinet reckoned that if the British executed him, India would be free that very moment. If they did not, he could continue the freedom struggle. Despite this win-win scenario, the cabinet nevertheless asked whether they should allow the British to take their leader prisoner at all.[140]

In what turned out to be a catastrophic error, Bose's cabinet advised him to choose a course against his own better judgment. The consensus, Ayer tells us, was that he must not be taken prisoner by the British, and "single-handed, Netaji opposed this idea." "He said," according to Ayer, "that he should remain with his ministers and his army in Singapore and face the British. His view prevailed for the time being. But it was not the final decision." After one of his advisers, A. N. Sarkar, arrived from Bangkok and joined the deliberations on the night of August 14, Netaji "showed a slight inclination to reconsider his own decision about staying on in Singapore."[141]

On the morning of August 15, 1945, Cyril John Stracey, an Anglo-Indian officer of the INA (he was of mixed British and Indian descent), accompanied by R. A. Malik, arrived on the verandah with half a dozen models and rolls of paper, containing designs for the memorial to the fallen heroes of the INA. Netaji examined them all and made his choice. "Colonel Stracey, I want this memorial to rise on the sea face of Singapore before the British make a landing there. Do you think you will be able to do it?" he asked. "Certainly, Sir," Stracey replied, and with a smart salute and a "Jai Hind" marched off to build in record time the edifice bearing the words of their motto—*Itmad* ("Faith"), *Ittefaq* ("Unity"), and *Kurbani* ("Sacrifice").[142]

The afternoon of August 15 brought official news on the radio of Japan's surrender. Netaji issued his last order of the day and a special message to Indians in East Asia. "The roads to Delhi are many," he told his soldiers, "and Delhi still remains our goal. The sacrifices of your immortal comrades and yourselves will certainly achieve their fulfillment."[143] And to the Indian civilians who had responded with unprecedented enthusiasm to his call for total mobilization, he had this to say:

> Sisters and Brothers,
>
> A glorious chapter in the history of India's Struggle for Freedom has just come to a close and, in that chapter, the sons and daughters of India in East Asia will have an undying place.
>
> You set a shining example of patriotism and self-sacrifice by pouring out men, money and materials into the struggle for India's independence. I shall never forget the spontaneity and enthusiasm with which you responded to my call for "Total Mobilization." You sent an unending stream of your sons and daughters to the camps to be trained as soldiers of the Azad Hind Fauj and of the Rani of Jhansi Regiment. Money and materials you poured lavishly into the war chest of the Provisional Government of Azad Hind. In short, you did your duty as true sons and daughters of India. I regret more than you do that your sufferings and sacrifices have not borne immediate fruit. But they have not gone in vain, because they have ensured the emancipation of our motherland and will serve as an undying inspiration to Indians all over the world. Posterity will bless your name, and will talk with pride about your offerings at the altar of India's Freedom and about your positive achievement as well.

Urging them never to falter in their faith in India's destiny, Netaji confidently declared that "India shall be free and before long."[144]

At ten o'clock that night, Bose's cabinet gathered once more after dinner on the verandah of his Singapore bungalow. The meeting lasted five hours, until three in the morning. "It did not take us long," Ayer writes, "to persuade Netaji finally that he must get out of Singapore." Kiani remembers disagreeing with this plan. He tried to convince Netaji "that his going to Russia would not be as useful as his staying in Singapore," which had served as the headquarters of his revolutionary government and army. The hopes and aspirations of Indians had been raised there. He suggested that the forces stay together and surrender with dignity. "We had done nothing of which we or our countrymen could ever feel ashamed," Kiani said, "and as the mist of war and censorship lifted and our countrymen back home got to know of our activities in greater detail, they would feel proud of our actions and stand by us." If Netaji stayed in Singapore, his numerous friends and supporters would surround him. The weight of collective opinion, however, was that he should go. The "final decision," according to Ayer, was "out of Malaya definitely, to some Russian territory certainly, to Russia itself, if possible." Netaji conceded that it would be an "adventure into the unknown."[145]

The next morning, August 16, 1945, Subhas Chandra Bose, Head of State, Provisional Government of Azad Hind, signed and issued the following order: "During my absence from Syonan [Singapore], Major General M. Z. Kiani will represent the Provisional Government of Azad Hind." Instructions had been given to protect the interests of the Indian community in Malaya and maintain order in Singapore. Bullion from the Azad Hind Bank, gold bars valued at half a million dollars, was stored in a strong room, to be used in case of emergency.[146] At 9:30 A.M. Bose said goodbye to Kiani, Alagappan, and others and climbed up a steel ladder into a Japanese bomber. Swami, Raghavan, and Thivy had not yet arrived from Penang and Ipoh. Netaji took with him Ayer, Habibur Rahman, and another colonel named Pritam Singh—a Hindu, a Muslim, and a Sikh—and with them went a Japanese interpreter named Negishi. The plane taxied for about five minutes and returned to where it had started. Bose asked to know why and was told there was something wrong with the brakes. The problem was soon fixed, and the plane landed in Bangkok at about three in the afternoon.[147]

From the evening of August 16 until the early morning of August 17, Netaji received an unending stream of visitors, soldiers and civilians alike. There was not an inch of space to sit in the overcrowded house. Walter Mayer, a German intelligence operative based in Bangkok, advised against an attempt to fly in the direction of Russian territory, deeming it too risky. It would be easy for Bose to remain underground for a while in Thailand and reemerge once the dust had settled. Debnath Das, one of the advisers in the Provisional Government, had already made preliminary arrangements for sanctuary in Thailand, with

Bose's express permission. Prince Wan Waithayakon had hosted a tea in honor of Bose in June. He, along with the chief justice of the Thai supreme court and Anuman Rachodhan, president of the Thai-Bharat Cultural Lodge, who were both present on the occasion, had offered help to Bose if Japan lost the war. Anuman Rachodhan was an admirer of both Tagore and Bose. Debnath Das had been in touch with the head priest of the Wat Mahathat temple, who had great reverence for the Buddha-like Indian leader, and with Mahoyang, the priest to the Thai royal family. If Netaji agreed, they would keep him hidden in a Buddhist monastery. The presence of patriotic Indians in Thailand would ensure economic and political support whenever it was needed.[148]

Unfortunately, Bose opted for the riskiest option imaginable. On the morning of August 17, at eight o'clock, he took off from the Bangkok airport for Saigon. He had picked another Hindu-Muslim-Sikh trio in Bangkok: Debnath Das, Abid Hasan, and Gulzara Singh. The group had to travel in two planes. In the first went Netaji, Ayer, Habibur Rahman, Pritam Singh, and the Japanese interpreter. The second carried General Saburo Isoda (chief of the Hikari Kikan), Teruo Hachiya (the Japanese ambassador to the Azad Hind government), Abid Hasan, Debnath Das, and Gulzara Singh. They were met at the Saigon airport by Chandra Mal, secretary of the Transport Department of the Indian Independence League in Indochina, and taken to the home of Naraindas, secretary of the Housing Department, in the outskirts of the city. On arrival in Saigon, Bose must have realized the mistake he had made in leaving the relative security of Singapore and Bangkok. The streets were deserted and rumors were rife about the revenge the French would take against the Indians who had allied with the Japanese.

Isoda and Hachiya dashed off to Count Terauchi's Southern Army headquarters in Dalat, to see what arrangements could be made for the onward journey. They returned in the afternoon and offered Bose a single seat on a Japanese bomber that was ready to leave Saigon. An agonizing conference followed among the Indians, to decide whether Netaji should go alone. After further negotiations, the Japanese came forth with a second seat and Bose asked Habibur Rahman to join him. He might have picked Abid Hasan, his submarine voyage companion, but Habib held the higher military rank and had served as his deputy chief of staff in Singapore. The hope was that the Japanese would provide another plane for the others to follow their leader. There was a mad rush in two cars to the airport, where General Tsunamasa Shidei, a Japanese officer well versed in German and Russian affairs, had been waiting for a couple of hours.[149]

"Well, *Jai Hind,* I will meet you later," Netaji told the five bewildered and confused Indians he was leaving behind. After a round of vigorous farewell handshakes, he "stepped majestically as ever toward the plane, walked up the little ladder and vanished into the plane." At 5:15 P.M. the Japanese bomber took off from Saigon airport, carrying Netaji. The five Indians stood there transfixed and strained their eyes "in the direction of the plane until it grew smaller and smaller and was no more than a speck in the distant horizon."[150]

9

A Life Immortal

Let us all try to be brave at the loss of one of the bravest of men.
His will be done.

—SISIR KUMAR BOSE to Bivabati Bose, August 27, 1945

In late August 1945, Emilie was sitting in the kitchen at her Vienna home with her mother and sister. While rolling some wool into balls, she was as usual listening to the evening news on the radio. Suddenly the newsreader announced that the Indian "quisling" Subhas Chandra Bose had been killed in an air crash at Taihoku (Taipei). Her mother and sister stared at her in stunned silence. She slowly got up and walked to the bedroom where her little daughter Anita was fast asleep. She knelt beside the bed, she recalled many years later, "And I wept."[1]

On the afternoon of Friday, August 24, the superintendent of Lyallpur Jail in Punjab came to see his young prisoner Sisir Kumar Bose in his cell. "I am really very, very sorry," he said, handing Sisir that morning's *Tribune* newspaper. Sisir saw his uncle's photograph and the "terrible news" of his death in an air crash on the island of Formosa (Taiwan). Having used up his week's quota of letters, he waited until Monday, August 27, to write a stoic letter to his mother about trying to be brave at the loss of one of the bravest of men. Throughout the weekend, he had worried about his father. "I shall anxiously await news about you all at home and particularly about father's health," he wrote to his mother. "Please do not be anxious on my account. I shall be all right."[2]

Sarat Chandra Bose was then a prisoner at Coonoor, in distant south India. The newspapers he received—the *Indian Express* and the *Hindu*—were different, but "the heart-rending news" was the same about "Subhas's death as the result of an aeroplane crash." Sarat was utterly distraught. "Divine Mother," he wrote in anguish, "how many sacrifices have we to offer at your altar! Terrible Mother, your blows are too hard to bear! Your last blow was the heaviest and cruelest of all. What divine purpose you are serving thereby, you alone know. Inscrutable are your ways!" Four or five nights earlier, he had dreamed that Subhas had come to visit. "He was standing on the verandah of this bungalow and appeared to have become very tall in stature. I jumped up to see his face. Almost immediately thereafter, he disappeared."[3]

The poet among India's nationalist leaders, Sarojini Naidu, gave eloquent voice to the country's admiration and grief. She recognized that "myriads of men and women" in India felt "a deep personal bereavement" at Netaji's loss. She had not supported his decision to seek Japan's help, but understood what impelled him to do so. "His proud, importunate and violent spirit," she wrote in her tribute, "was a flaming sword forever unsheathed in defense of the land he worshiped with such surpassing devotion. A greater love hath not man than this, that he lay down his life for his country and his people."[4]

Death by War

When Netaji had set off from Saigon airport on the late afternoon of August 17, 1945, the five Indian aides he left behind had badgered the Japanese to put them on another plane immediately so they could follow their leader, but to no avail. Eventually, on August 20, the Japanese offered one seat on a plane flying to Tokyo. The Indians chose S. A. Ayer to be the one among them to take this opportunity. As he was about to board the aircraft, Rear-Admiral Chuda of the Japanese navy blurted out something that sounded to Ayer like "Atherji is dead." Ayer wondered if he meant Chatterji. "No, Netaji," the answer came as the roar of the bomber's engine became louder, "Chandra Bose Kakkaa [Excellency]." Once the plane reached Canton, one Colonel Tada explained further to Ayer what had happened. Netaji had left Saigon on August 17 and his plane had reached Touraine (Da Nang) the same evening. There, Netaji and his fellow passengers had rested for the night. They set off again on the morning of August 18 and reached Taipei safely early in the afternoon. Soon after takeoff from Taipei, the plane crashed.[5]

"Did it crash into the sea?" Ayer asked. If the answer was yes, he could persuade himself it was a contrived story to cover the trail of another great escape. To his disappointment he was told the plane had crashed on land near the airfield. General Tsunamasa Shidei, the Japanese expert on Russian affairs who was the other VIP traveling with Netaji, had been killed instantly. Netaji and Habibur Rahman had been injured, and were taken immediately to the nearest hospital. "Our medical officers did their best for Netaji, but in spite of all that, Netaji . . ." The Colonel's voice choked. "Is Habib alive or is he also . . . ?" asked Ayer, and learned that Habib had survived. Ayer demanded to be taken at once to Taipei so that he could see for himself what had happened. His plane, however, halted at Taichu, not Taipei, on its way to Tokyo, apparently because of adverse weather conditions. "No Indian in India or East Asia," Ayer bitterly told the Japanese, "is going to believe your story of Netaji's plane crash."[6]

On August 23, after a five-day delay, the Domei agency of Japan broadcast the news of Netaji's death. In Tokyo, there was another agonizing wait for more than two weeks for further news from Taipei. Ayer remained in close touch with Rama Murti, the head of the Indian Independence League in Japan, and stayed as the guest of the wife and daughter of Anand Mohan Sahay, a member of Netaji's Provisional Government. On September 8, Ayer and Rama Murti were told at the Japanese imperial army headquarters that Habib had arrived in Tokyo from Taipei with Netaji's ashes, and that he would meet them later in the day. The urn containing the ashes was brought out and handed over to Ayer. "They first put a loop of white cloth, seven or eight inches wide, round my neck," Ayer writes, "and then the Colonel placed the urn in the loop and I held it with both hands." The urn was brought to

Rama Murti's house, where his wife placed it on a high table with incense burning on both sides and a stack of flowers in front. A tiny photograph of Netaji was placed on top of the urn.[7]

Late that night, Habibur Rahman arrived at Mrs. Sahay's home, some two miles from Rama Murti's residence. After exchanging greetings of *"Jai Hind,"* Ayer bombarded Habib with questions. Habib's melancholy narrative corroborated what Ayer had been told by the Japanese colonel. Their plane had halted for refueling at Taipei on August 18. The passengers took the opportunity to have something to eat. Within minutes of takeoff from Taipei, there was a sudden deafening noise. Habib thought at the time that an enemy fighter had taken a pot shot at the Japanese bomber. He learned later that one of the propellers of the port engine had broken. The plane nose-dived to the ground and Habib blacked out. Once he recovered consciousness, he saw that passage to the rear of the plane was completely blocked by luggage while a fire raged in the front. "Aagese nikliye, Netaji!" ("Please get out through the front, Netaji!"), Habib called to his leader. With both his hands, Netaji fought his way through the fire and Habib followed. "When the plane crashed," Habib told Ayer, "Netaji got a splash of petrol all over his cotton khaki, and it caught fire when he struggled through the nose of the plane." He stood outside the plane with his clothes burning and tried to unbuckle the belts of his bushcoat round his waist. Habib's hands were burned in the process of trying to help him. As he was fumbling with the belts, he looked up and his heart nearly stopped when he saw Netaji's face, "battered by iron and burnt by fire." A few minutes later, they lay down exhausted on the ground of Taipei's airfield.[8]

The next thing Habib knew, he was lying on a hospital bed next to Netaji. For the next six hours, Netaji slipped in and out of consciousness. During those hours he never once complained about the wrenching pain he must have been suffering. In a delirious moment, he called for Abid Hasan. "Hasan yahan nahi hain, Sab, main hun, Habib" ("Hasan is not here, sir, I am here, Habib"), Habibur Rahman explained to him. The Japanese doctors made superhuman efforts to save his life. Netaji was convinced that he would not survive. He told Habib in Hindustani that his end was coming very soon. He had fought for his country's freedom till his last breath. Habib should go and tell his countrymen to continue the fight for India's freedom and that India would be free, and before long. At about nine that evening, Netaji's mortal end came, peacefully.[9]

A devastated Habib asked the Japanese to fly Netaji's body to Singapore, or to Tokyo if Singapore was out of bounds. They promised to try, but later reported practical difficulties in doing so. Under those circumstances, Habib had to consent to a cremation in Taipei. The cremation took place on August 20; Netaji's ashes were placed in an urn and kept in the Nishi Honganji temple, close to the hospital. On September 5, Habib boarded an ambulance plane in Taipei with Netaji's mortal remains, on his journey to Japan. Ayer, unable to come to terms with the loss of the leader he adored, put his hands on Habib's shoulders and begged despairingly, "Colonel *Saheb,* for heaven's sake tell me the truth!" With tears in his eyes, Habib replied: "Ayer *Saheb,* I am terribly sorry that all that I have told you is the dreadful truth."[10]

The forty or so Indian cadets whom Netaji regarded as his sons kept continuous vigil over the urn for three days in Rama Murti's house. The urn was then taken to Mrs. Sahay's house, where prayers were offered for another three days. On September 14, the urn was taken to the Renko-ji, a small Buddhist temple in the Suginami district of Tokyo. The priest of that temple, Reverend Mochizuki, conducted a funeral ceremony that was attended by Ayer, Rama Murti, his brother Jaya Murti, Rama Murti's wife, the Indian cadets in Tokyo, and representatives of the Japanese Foreign Office and War Office. Habibur Rahman was unable to attend, since he had been summoned for interrogation by the occupying American forces. The Indians returned to the temple on September 18, a month after Netaji had breathed his last, to offer floral tributes, and again on October 18, to pray for the departed soul.[11]

Ayer, Habib, and the Murti brothers met almost every day during that sad autumn in Tokyo. As he "sat on a bench under the tall trees in the Omiya Park [Tokyo], day after day, with the Bible in hand," Ayer "read and re-read the Acts." "I prayed," he wrote, "for the strength of Peter, and I prayed for an opportunity to bear humble and truthful testimony to Netaji's miraculous achievements." His prayer was answered on November 7, when General MacArthur's headquarters sent him a notice through the Japanese Foreign Office that he was wanted in India by Mountbatten's headquarters, in connection with the Red Fort trial. On November 19, Ayer and Habibur Rahman were flown in an American aircraft from Tokyo to Delhi, to be witnesses at the trial. Upon their arrival in Delhi on November 22, Habib gave Ayer a nudge as the red sandstone ramparts of the fort came into view. That was where Netaji was to have held his victory parade after hoisting the Indian tricolor. They were greeted with shouts of "Jai Hind!" as soon as they entered the wire-netting enclosure inside the fort, called the "cage." Once inside their cage in the Red Fort, Ayer gulped down a cup of tea and then devoured the Indian newspapers from November 5 onward, which were full of stories about the INA. "The INA had literally burst on the country," he discovered, "and the whole country from the Himalayas to Cape Comorin was aflame with an enthusiastic fervor, unprecedented in its history." When he saw the papers in front of him, he felt "sad beyond words that Netaji was not alive and not in Delhi to see for himself how all India had gone mad over his miraculous feats in East Asia."[12]

While Indians reacted with shock, grief, and disbelief, the British authorities in India had received the news of Bose's death with a sense of relief. Now that their most uncompromising opponent was probably out of the way, they approved in mid-September 1945 the release of Sarat Chandra Bose and other members of the Bose family, who were being held long after most political prisoners had been released. Soon after the end of the war, New Delhi had sent two groups of intelligence officers, led by Finney and Davies, to Southeast Asia to conduct inquiries and to arrest Bose, if he was alive. Ironically, these groups included two Bengali police officers named H. K. Roy and K. P. De. Mr. Davies' team, which included H. K. Roy, went first to Saigon and then to Taipei in September 1945. They interviewed the Japanese military officer in charge of the Saigon airport, military officers at the Taipei airport, and the chief medical officer at the Taipei hospital. The team that went to Bangkok seized a telegram dated August 20 from the chief of staff of the Japanese Southern Army in Saigon to the officer-in-charge of the Hikari Kikan in Bangkok; it contained the news of the crash on the afternoon of August 18 and of Bose's death that night. The cable reported that Bose's body had been flown to Tokyo, and Colonel Tada was summoned from Tokyo to Saigon to address this discrepancy. It was due to the fact that the original intention had been to take Bose's body to Tokyo, but this plan could not be implemented. Finney's report reached the definite conclusion that Bose had indeed died as a result of the plane crash on August 18, 1945.[13]

The tumultuous reception given by the Indian public to the INA heroes from November 1945 to February 1946 unnerved the British and made them wonder whether Bose had once again deceived them and escaped. Prem Kumar Sahgal, Shah Nawaz Khan, and Gurbaksh Singh Dhillon had become the symbols of the INA's political triumph inside India, once the British commander-in-chief felt compelled to release them after their trial at the Red Fort. Indian soldiers in Britain's Indian Army, as well as in the Royal Indian Air Force and the Royal Indian Navy, had grown increasingly restive. The letter from the intelligence operative in New Delhi to his counterpart in Singapore dated February 19, 1946, revealing British anxiety as to whether Bose was "actually and permanently dead," was written at the height of the mutiny in the Royal Indian Navy. The British had been worried by Gandhi's assertion in early January 1946 of his belief that Netaji was alive and would appear at the right moment. A week before the naval mutiny, Gandhi insisted on speaking about Bose in the present tense. Congressmen interpreted Gandhi's inner voice to be secret information received from Netaji. There were other rumors making the rounds. According to one, Nehru was said to have received a letter from Bose saying that he was in Russia and wanted to escape to India. He would arrive via Chitral, where one of Sarat Bose's sons would receive him. Gandhi and Sarat Bose were alleged to be aware of these plans. The intelligence assessment deemed this story "unlikely," but "a growing belief in India that Bose is alive" was a cause for concern.[14]

On March 30, 1946, Gandhi clarified his views on the matter in his journal *Harijan*. He referred to the 1942 report on Bose's death, which he had believed but which later turned out to be incorrect. Since then, he had had "a feeling that Netaji could not leave us until his dreams of *swaraj* had been fulfilled." "To lend strength to this feeling," he added, "was the knowledge of Netaji's great ability to hoodwink his enemies and even the world for the sake of his cherished goal." He explained that he had nothing but his "instinct" to tell him "Netaji was alive." He now conceded that no reliance could be placed on "such unsupported feeling" and that there was "strong evidence to counteract the feeling." The British government had access to that evidence. He had also heard the testimony of Habibur Rahman and S. A. Ayer. "In the face of these proofs," the Mahatma wrote, "I appeal to everyone to forget what I have said and, believing in the evidence before them, to reconcile themselves to the fact that Netaji has left us. All man's ingenuity is as nothing before the might of the one God."[15]

Far away in Vienna, Emilie appeared to have accepted her tragic loss. Her home had fallen within the Russian zone of occupation. Bose would have been aware of this development, so his inclination to go to Russia from May 1945 onward may have had a personal as well as a political dimension. Emilie wrote to their Irish friend Mrs. Woods on January 18, 1946, that the Russians had visited their house the previous summer. When the Russians came, the family "had been actually starving." "No milk for the child for many weeks," she wrote. "That was the worst." Mrs. Woods had apparently expressed the view that the news of Bose's death might not be true. Emilie thought otherwise: "Re: what you mention about our mutual friend, I am sorry to say I cannot share your hopes. I have somehow the feeling that he has died. If it were not true, nobody should be more glad than myself. I got such a shock when I heard about this incident that for weeks I was only mechanically doing my duties in household and office. The only consolation being little Anita." Anita was a "real darling" and everyone liked her. "I am still bearing my old name out of certain reasons which I cannot explain here," she told Mrs. Woods. "But perhaps later on I shall have opportunity to write at greater length to you about all this in detail." For now, the body had no strength to resist illness, since they were all "completely undernourished" and had lost a great deal of weight. The warrior's widow provided some poignant reflections on the pity of war: "Would such a war have been necessary at all? What amount of suffering and grieve [sic] it has brought to humanity—and almost every country has had its losses. Everywhere weep mothers, wifes [sic], children and others for the dead ones who fell on the battlefield. And still new means of destructions are sought. The whole world seems to have been plunged into madness."[16]

In 1946, Mountbatten's headquarters at Kandy conducted another inquiry into the fate of Subhas Chandra Bose. The relations of Bose's INA with Mountbatten's forces had been fraught with tension. Cyril John Stracey had kept his promise to his leader and had erected the memorial to the INA martyrs in record time. Mohammad Zaman Kiani, whom Netaji had left in charge at Singapore, performed the inaugural ceremony of this monument with the INA motto "Faith, Unity, Sacrifice" emblazoned on it. It turned out to be a mournful memorial service for Netaji, the first soldier of India's army of liberation, and all others who had perished. When the British landed in Singapore on September 5, 1945, the proud INA memorial on the harbor greeted them. On September 8, Mountbatten's soldiers—Indians under his command—laid dynamite charges and blew the monument to smithereens as INA soldiers watched with helpless rage. This act of vandalism toward the war dead was not forgotten or forgiven by Indians. The specter of Subhas Chandra Bose continued to haunt the British during the winter of 1945–1946. Mountbatten's probe into whether Bose had in fact died was conducted through Colonel J. G. Figgess, who was attached to General MacArthur's headquarters in Tokyo and overseen by an American intelligence officer working under the general headquarters of the Supreme Command Allied Powers (SCAP). On July 25, 1946, Figgess reported that their mortal enemy had indeed met his corporeal death on August 18, 1945.[17]

Yet the matter did not end there. The tension between the feeling that he must be alive and the evidence of his death played itself out for decades to come. One night in 1939, Subhas had been walking along Marine Drive in Bombay with his friend Nathalal Parikh, when he had looked up at the moonlit sky and expressed a wish about how he wanted to die: he wanted to fly as high as the stars and then suddenly come crashing down to earth.[18] But that was not the way his people wanted him to go, and certainly not before India was free. The popular yearning for Netaji to return became even stronger in the immediate aftermath of independence and partition. At the same time, from 1946 to 1956, evidence for the air crash accumulated and became weightier, since there had been six Japanese survivors in addition to Habibur Rahman, and several other direct witnesses at the hospital. In August 1946 an Indian journalist, Harin Shah, visited Taiwan and gathered information on what he described as the gallant end of Netaji. He met among others a Chinese nurse named Tsan Pi Sha, who said she had cared for Netaji at the Nanmon (Southgate) Military Hospital during his final hours on August 18, 1945, and gave correct descriptions of both Netaji and Habibur Rahman. The on-the-spot journalistic inquiries convinced Harin Shah that the news of Netaji's death as a result of the air crash was true.[19]

On October 19, 1946, a British captain named Alfred Raymond Turner recorded a statement by Captain Yoshimi Taneyoshi, the surgeon in charge at the Taipei hospital, inside the Stanley Gaol in Hong Kong. When the injured were brought from the airport to the hospital, a Japanese military officer had pointed out "Chandra Bose" to him. He was urged to make every possible effort and to give Bose "the very best of treatment." His patient had suffered extensive burns. "During the first four hours," according to Dr. Yoshimi, "he was semi-conscious, and practically normal, speaking quite a good deal." The doctor believed that the first words he spoke were in Japanese, asking for water, which he was fed through a hospital cup with a spout. It has been speculated that Bose was unlikely to have used the Japanese word *meju* for water and may have said something about "Mejda," his elder brother Sarat. "As most of his speaking was in English," Yoshimi continued in his statement, "a request for an interpreter was made, and one was sent from the Civil Government Offices named Nakamura. He informed me that he had very often interpreted for Chandra Bose and had had many conversations with him. He appeared to have no doubt that the man he was speaking with was Chandra Bose." His patient began to sink into unconsciousness after four hours, and died later that night. His adjutant, an Indian colonel, who was also under Yoshimi's care, wanted Bose's body to be taken to Tokyo. The doctor therefore injected Formalin into the body and had the coffin partly filled with lime, which was taken to the airport on August 20 by warrant officer Nishi. The officer returned saying that the body, "for some unknown reason," could not be transported to Japan and had to be cremated in Taipei. Apparently, the coffin was too large for the aircraft. The doctor wrote out a death certificate for the crematorium. Bose's ashes were handed over to the Indian colonel.[20]

When the Union Jack was lowered and the Indian tricolor hoisted at the Red Fort on August 15, 1947, the physically absent Subhas Chandra Bose had an uncanny presence in the popular imagination. Calendar art from that period depicted him high in the heavens above the Red Fort observing the independence ceremonies and offering his benediction and protection. The gorier images showed him offering his severed head to Mother India—the ultimate sacrifice to win her freedom.[21] As the euphoria of independence was swept away by the horror of partition violence, a traumatized people lamented the void left by the loss of a unifying leader. Political freedom did not immediately remove deep-seated economic and social injustices. The newly independent nation found it hard to come to terms with Netaji's mortal end.

On a visit to Japan in 1951, S. A. Ayer met two of the six Japanese survivors from the crash—Colonel Nonogaki and Captain Arai—both of whom corroborated what Habibur Rahman had related. He submitted a report dated September 26, 1951, on his investigations in Tokyo, to the prime minister, Jawaharlal Nehru, verifying the circumstances of Netaji's mortal end. In 1952, this report was presented to Parliament.[22] Yet in the India of the 1950s, there was a widespread refusal to accept Netaji's death. Many people longed for him to return and solve the country's myriad problems. In response to insistent public demand, Nehru's government instituted a formal inquiry committee in 1956, to take a comprehensive look at all the evidence. The three members of the committee were Shah Nawaz Khan of Red Fort trial fame, Suresh Chandra Bose, the eldest surviving brother of Netaji, and S. N. Maitra, an experienced civil servant deputed by the government of West Bengal. This committee took depositions in Delhi and Tokyo from a wide range of direct witnesses and also visited Saigon and Touraine (Da Nang). The committee members were unable to visit Taipei, since India had recognized the People's Republic of China and did not have diplomatic relations with Chiang Kai-shek's government in Taiwan.[23]

General Isoda told the Shah Nawaz committee that the plan settled on in Bangkok on August 16 had been for Netaji to go to Tokyo via Saigon and then proceed to Russia via Manchuria. If a move to Russian-held Manchuria proved impossible, there was a general sense that being taken into custody by the Americans in Japan was a better option than falling into the hands of the British. In Saigon, it had been discovered that General Shidei was departing that afternoon for Manchuria to take charge as chief of staff of Japan's Kwangtung Army. Mr. Negishi, the Japanese interpreter attached to Netaji from Singapore, described Shidei as an expert in Russian affairs and "a key man for negotiations with Russia." He also knew German and conversed with Netaji in that language. "Although there was an element of chance in Netaji's travelling by the same plane as General Shidei," the committee found, "it appears that Netaji fell in with the idea that he should go up to Dairen [Manchuria] with General Shidei." The plane in which they traveled was a twin-engine heavy bomber of 97/2 (Sally) type belonging to Japan's Third Air Force Army, based in Singapore.[24]

Habibur Rahman came to Delhi from Pakistan to tell the Shah Nawaz committee about his experiences on the fateful flight. Dr. Yoshimi repeated in 1956 what he had stated to the British in 1946. In addition, the committee heard the testimony of other medical personnel, including Dr. Yoshimi's assistant Dr. Tsuruta, who had treated Bose at Nanmon Hospital. Four of the six Japanese survivors of the plane crash— Lieutenant Colonel Shiro Nonogaki, Major Taro Kono, Major Ihaho Takahashi, and Captain Keikichi Arai—appeared in person before the committee in Tokyo. A fifth—Lieutenant Colonel Tadeo Sakai, who was away from Tokyo in 1956 on a special mission to Taiwan—submitted a written statement. The sixth Japanese survivor, Sergeant Okishta, could not be traced in 1956. The ground engineers who had serviced the plane and saw it come down described what had happened, as did other ground staff.[25]

The most compelling evidence came from the interpreter, Juichi Nakamura, who knew Bose well and had interpreted for him on four previous occasions as he passed through Taipei on his journeys to Tokyo in 1943 and 1944. Bose had stayed at the railway hotel in Taipei during those transits, and Nakamura had dined with him. Upon arrival at Nanmon Hospital on the afternoon of August 18, 1945, Nakamura found a heavily bandaged Netaji lying on a bed and Habibur Rahman on another bed about three feet away. Nakamura asked Habib to come closer to help him decipher what Netaji was saying. Netaji's first words after Nakamura's arrival were: "A few more of my men are coming after me. Please take care of them when they come to Formosa." About half an hour later he inquired, "Where is General Shidei?" Later, he said that he felt blood rushing toward his head. At about nine in the evening, he said, "I want to sleep." "During all this time," Nakamura testified, "not a word of complaint either of pain or suffering came from his lips. The Japanese officers at the other end of the room were groaning with pain and crying out that they may be killed rather than continue to endure their suffering. This composure of Netaji surprised all of us." After Netaji had breathed his last, Nakamura said, the Japanese stood in one line and saluted Netaji's body. Habibur Rahman came and knelt by Netaji's bed and prayed for five or six minutes. He then opened the window and prayed again for about ten minutes, looking toward the sky. He then went back to his own bed and lay down.[26]

Nakamura was present at the cremation, along with Habibur Rahman and one Major Nagatomo, and provided a detailed description of the ceremony. The injured Habib held the incense sticks between the edges of his palms, since he could not hold them in his fingers. When they returned the next day to collect the ashes, Habib, with his bandaged hands, had difficulty holding the ten-inch-long chopsticks used to pick up charred bone fragments. Nakamura helped him to put them in an urn. Major Nagatomo, who also testified, described a similar process of picking up the bone fragments, according to Buddhist custom. The urn was then taken to the Nishi Honganji temple, near the hospital. Another urn containing the ashes of General Shidei was already there. Nakamura explained to the priest that the ashes he had brought belonged to a person of higher status than Shidei. The priest was instructed to place the urn at a higher level and offer fresh flowers every morning. The Shah Nawaz committee also heard from Tatsuo Hayashida, who had carried the urn on the plane journey with Habibur Rahman from Taipei to Japan on September 5, 1945. S. A. Ayer, Habibur Rahman, Rama Murti, Jaya Murti, and Reverend Mochizuki testified on what happened to the urn after it was handed over by the Japanese imperial army, and how it found its final resting place in the Renko-ji temple.[27]

Following the hearings conducted from April to June 1956, the three members of the committee signed a draft of principal findings on July 2. According to this draft, all three members agreed that "the plane carrying Netaji did crash." There was no reason to doubt the witnesses, belonging to various nationalities and walks of life, who all testified that Netaji had met his death as a result of this crash. After putting his signature to this draft, one of the members, Suresh Chandra Bose, changed his mind and wrote a rambling dissent claiming that the crash had not occurred and that his brother was alive. To be sure, there were several minor discrepancies in the versions given by various witnesses eleven years after the event. The time of death, for example, ranged between eight in the evening and midnight of August 18, 1945. Dr. Yoshimi and Dr. Tsuruta did not agree on whether or not a blood transfusion had been given. The original death certificate signed by Dr. Yoshimi could not be found. Nevertheless, the direct witnesses provided evidence that was broadly consistent; Shah Nawaz Khan and S. N. Maitra marshaled it with great skill, and placed it in a cogently argued majority report that was subsequently issued by the government of India.[28]

The report stated categorically that Netaji's mortal end came as the result of the plane crash in Taipei on August 18, 1945. "There is no reason to disbelieve the large number of witnesses, both Japanese and non-Japanese," it said. "There is no evidence before us to show that the plane in question did not crash at Taihoku." The report also noted that there was "no break in the chain" in the depositions regarding the movement of Netaji's ashes from the crematorium to Nishi Honganji temple in Taipei to Minami aerodrome to Tokyo Imperial Headquarters to Mr. Rama Murti's house to Mrs. Sahay's house and finally to the Renko-ji temple. It conceded that "such precautions as were necessary to prove indisputable identity," such as, seals, receipts, and continuous watch, were not taken. Nevertheless, the committee was of the considered view that "in all probability the ashes kept in Renko-ji temple, Tokyo, are the ashes of Netaji Subhas Chandra Bose."[29]

The final recommendation of the Shah Nawaz committee had three unambiguous sentences: "The Committee has come to the conclusion that Netaji Subhas Chandra Bose met his death in an air crash and the ashes now at Renko-ji temple, Tokyo, are his ashes. . . . It is time that his ashes were brought to India with due honor, and a memorial erected over them at a suitable place. . . . If Netaji's mortal remains are honored, and his ideals kept alive, then one could truly ask, 'Where is death's sting, where, grave, thy victory?'"[30]

Nehru's government failed to implement this clear recommendation, even though it agreed with the majority view rather than the dissent. With the matter unsettled, rumors that Netaji was still alive increased in the 1960s. Reports of the unlikeliest sightings were disseminated: people claimed to have spotted him as an ascetic in India, a prisoner in Russia. Some rumormongers hinted darkly at foul play by Nehru himself. In 1970, Indira Gandhi decided to appoint an eminent jurist, G. D. Khosla, as a one-man commission of inquiry to investigate the matter all over again. With the passage of time, fewer direct witnesses were available, and the commission heard testimony from almost anyone with theories to propound. Nevertheless, four of the Japanese survivors of the air crash—Sakai, Nonogaki, Kono, and Takahashi—repeated their testimony before the Khosla commission. Justice Khosla's essential findings, presented in 1974, were the same as that of Shah Nawaz Khan and S. N. Maitra. He concluded that Netaji had been gravely wounded in the air crash and had "succumbed to his injuries" on the night of August 18, 1945. Khosla engaged in a bit of special pleading for Nehru, emphasizing the friendly personal relations between Nehru and Bose, Bose's respect for Nehru, and Nehru's affection for Bose. He was scathing about those who had come to his commission's hearings with improbable tales to tell. "The numerous stories about encounters with Bose at various times and various places after 1945," Khosla wrote, "are completely false and unacceptable. They are the result either of hallucination helped by wishful thinking or have been invented by persons who wanted to draw attention to themselves and advertise themselves as public-spirited men."[31]

The Khosla report, issued in 1974, fell victim to political partisanship in India. Indira Gandhi's government, which had instituted the inquiry, lost the general election of 1977. The Janata party, after assuming power in New Delhi, set aside Khosla's findings. More than two decades later, in 1999, yet another one-man commission was appointed by the government to conduct a fresh inquiry. A retired Bengali judge named Manoj Mukherjee held court for nearly six years, providing a venue for increasingly fanciful stories about Netaji's whereabouts since August 1945. The judge himself harbored a preconceived notion, as he confessed in 2010, that Bose was living as an ascetic in the north Indian town of Faizabad decades after 1945. In October 2002, he sent letters to members of the Bose family asking them to donate one milliliter of blood for a DNA match with "one Gumnami Baba," who "some persons" had claimed was "none other than Netaji Subhas Chandra Bose."[32] The evidence naturally did not support this bizarre theory. Yet by entertaining the most preposterous claims, the judge managed to add to the confusion in the public mind about the life and death of a great leader of the independence movement.

The Mukherjee commission made no distinction between the highly probable and the utterly impossible. In May 2006, after six long years, it submitted a report stating that the air crash on August 18, 1945, had not occurred at all. The basis for this finding was a message from the government of Taiwan saying that it did not possess any records of that crash. It could not be expected to do so, since in August 1945 Taiwan had been under Japanese military occupation. The Japanese had not relinquished control over Taiwan until the spring of 1946, and the Chiang Kai-shek government had consolidated itself on the island only after the communist victory on the mainland of China in 1949. The Manmohan Singh government, quite sensibly, rejected outright the Mukherjee commission's report, while submitting it to Parliament. Yet the government of India has so far neglected to take steps to honor Netaji's mortal remains and to keep his ideals alive, as the Shah Nawaz Khan committee had advocated in 1956.[33]

The mass psychological phenomenon of an initial refusal to accept Netaji's death in the early decades after independence, and the hope that he would one day return as the deliverer of his country, were perfectly understandable in that time of crisis. The recurrent attempts to resurrect him testified to his continuing charisma as a unifying and selfless Indian leader. This popular sentiment, however, came to be exploited by a handful of people and fringe political parties, who used fraudulent claims about Netaji's whereabouts to advance their own interests. The self-selected group that typically came forward to depose before judicial commissions on the question of his death did not represent the vast populace who celebrated the life and work of India's warrior-hero. The strong historical evidence suggests that Netaji died as a result of the air crash in Taipei on August 18, 1945, while attempting to continue his fight for India's freedom at the end of World War II. Stories of his being spotted in various places after that date lie in the domain of rumor and speculation, if not willful fabrication. In particular, there is no evidence to suggest that Netaji succeeded in reaching the Soviet Union or Soviet-held Manchuria.

An overwhelming majority of Netaji's closest political associates, including senior INA officers and leaders of the Azad Hind movement, believed Habibur Rahman's account of Netaji's mortal end. On the leader's birth centenary in 1997, Gurbaksh Singh Dhillon, the sole surviving member of the Red Fort three, made an emotional plea at the historic fort for Netaji's remains to be brought back from Japan to India and for a mausoleum to be built in Delhi. S. A. Ayer, Prem Kumar Sahgal, Shah Nawaz Khan, Mehboob Ahmed, Debnath Das, Lakshmi Sahgal, Janaki Athinahappan, and numerous others had expressed the same view. Prem Kumar Sahgal was one of those who, in the late 1940s, kept hoping that Netaji had managed to escape. After careful examination of the evidence, however, he came to accept the fact of the air crash. Along with his wife, Lakshmi, he strongly advocated that Netaji's mortal remains be returned to India. Sarat Chandra Bose and Sisir Kumar Bose, who had learned of the tragedy while in prison, accepted the news with grief and fortitude. Yet in subsequent years, both allowed themselves to hope that perhaps their worst fears were unfounded. Sarat felt especially deep anguish, and found it hard to accept the loss of his beloved brother. He died on February 20, 1950, long before all the pertinent evidence was gathered in 1956. Sisir Kumar Bose studied all the relevant evidence, and in 1965 made his own investigations in Japan and Taiwan. His doubts were allayed, and he came to the conclusion that Netaji had indeed died a martyr's death in Taipei on August 18, 1945.[34]

General Tsunamasa Shidei's family never questioned the circumstances of his death. His service record, obtained by the Shah Nawaz Khan committee of inquiry, stated the date of death as August 18, 1945, and the place of death as "Taihoku Airfield." The "cause of death" was described as "death by war." "The same was true of Netaji," the 1956 report aptly commented, "only in his case it was a different war, the war for the independence of India. His war was continuing. He was only changing over from one battlefield to another, from Southeast Asia to Manchuria."[35] India's freedom struggle had many noble martyrs, but Netaji was the only front-rank leader of the Indian independence movement who laid down his life in the battle for freedom.

The Legacy

In his political testament, composed on the eve of his hunger strike in November 1940, Subhas Chandra Bose expressed his conviction that nobody could lose through suffering and sacrifice. "If he does lose anything 'of the earth, earthy,'" he wrote prophetically, alluding to Christ's resurrection, "he will gain much more in return by becoming the heir to a life immortal."[36] It is this spirit of sacrifice that has ensured Netaji's transcendence beyond the mere trifle of corporeal death.

Subhas knew that his life had a mission: the freedom of India from bondage. He had cast off all the constraints of colonial subjecthood very early in his life. When he took the momentous decision to resign from the Indian Civil Service at the age of twenty-four, he was already done with the British raj in India. Throughout his long years of incarceration and exile, he was essentially a free man, in the sense that he had rejected submission to the British. That is why he found the slave mentality among some of his countrymen so galling. Having himself refused to owe allegiance to a foreign bureaucracy in 1921, he embarked on a mighty crusade in 1941 to subvert the loyalty of Indians to the armed services of the British Empire and to replace it with a new dedication to the cause of India's freedom. Despite the INA's military failure, he was remarkably successful—if one measures his success by the yardstick of his own aspirations—in fulfilling his life's mission by 1945. On what would have been his fiftieth birthday, January 23, 1947, the Mahatma summed up Netaji's achievements:

> He had sacrificed a brilliant career for the sake of the country's service. He suffered various imprisonments, twice became President of the Congress, and at last by great strategy gave the slip to the guard put over him by the Government of Bengal and by sheer courage and resourcefulness reached Kabul, passed through European countries, and finally found himself in Japan, collected from scattered material an army of brilliant young men drawn from all communities and from all parts of India and dared to give battle to a mighty Government. A lesser man would have succumbed under the trials that he went through; but he in his life verified the saying of Tulsidas that "all becomes right for the brave."[37]

Knocking out the keystone of Britain's worldwide empire was no mean achievement. For this, the old hands of the British raj never forgave Bose. Britain's Indian Army had served for more than a century and a half as the empire's rod of order against recalcitrant and rebellious colonial subjects. Netaji's tireless wartime activities not only hastened the process of Indian independence, but undermined the prospects for reconquest in other parts of the colonial world. The rejuvenation of a flagging freedom struggle at war's end was his signal contribution, aided no doubt by a large dose of British hubris. His friend Dilip Kumar Roy vividly described how Subhas's "suddenly amplified figure, added to the romance of an Indian National Army marching, singing, to Delhi, galvanized a frustrated nation out of its torpor and substantially damaged the insulation of the Indian army from the magnetic currents of popular enthusiasm for immediate independence."[38] Postponement of the burning desire for freedom through palliative measures and a greater Indianization of the colonial administration was now utterly out of the question. Nor could England still conceive of deploying the British Indian Army against Aung San's resurgent Burma or to aid the French and the Dutch against the Vietnamese and Indonesian freedom movements.

Netaji's great wartime achievement had been to unite India's diverse religious communities in a common struggle. The absence of the leader who had inspired this sense of unity did matter in the aftermath of the enthusiasms surrounding the Red Fort trials. When Gandhi visited a group of INA prisoners in the Red Fort, they told him they had never felt any distinction of creed or religion in the INA. "But here we are faced with 'Hindu tea' and 'Muslim tea,'" they complained. "Why do you suffer it?" asked Gandhi. "We don't," they said. "We mix 'Hindu tea' and 'Muslim tea' half and half, and then serve. The same with food." "That is very good," exclaimed Gandhi, laughing.[39] The Mahatma had come a long way since the days when he had refused to dine even with his closest Muslim political comrades, in the era of the noncooperation and Khilafat movements. Yet Gandhi was relevant, so long as another mass movement was needed to force the British to quit India. By the spring of 1946, the British had read the writing on the wall and decided to leave. A three-member Cabinet Mission led by Stafford Cripps had been sent to explore how power might be shared, once the curtain came down on the British raj in India.

Netaji's many admirers passionately believed that, had their leader been on the scene, India would not have been partitioned along religious lines. It is one of those great "ifs" of history to which there can be no definitive answer. What can be said with a measure of confidence is that, based on his record, Netaji would have been generous toward minorities and worked resolutely toward an equitable power-sharing arrangement among religious communities and regional peoples. On the eve of independence, in August 1947, Gandhi was prepared to be more accommodating than other Congress leaders toward the Muslim League and its sole spokesman, Mohammad Ali Jinnah. But the Mahatma's erstwhile political lieutenants, Jawaharlal Nehru and Vallabhbhai Patel, were no longer prepared to listen to his good counsel. The machine politicians of the Congress party were now keen to grasp the helm of the unitary center of the British raj, even if the price to be paid was partition. Gandhi is said to have lamented in 1947 that all his "yes-men" had turned into his "no-men." As the partitioner's axe was about to fall, the Mahatma may have missed the rebellious son whom he had cast aside in 1939 in favor of more obedient followers. Gandhi stood as

a tragic lonely figure during the communal holocaust that accompanied partition. The saint and the warrior acting in concert may have
had a better chance of averting the catastrophe that engulfed the subcontinent in 1947. But this was not to be.

It is clear that, by this time, Gandhi felt genuine admiration for Bose,
though he continued to disagree with the methods the fiery leader had
adopted. According to him, Netaji's final message to the INA was that
even though they fought with arms outside India, they would have to
become nonviolent soldiers of freedom inside the country. Although
Nehru's championing of the INA cause from November 1945 onward
had an element of political opportunism in it, there is evidence that
he was truly moved when he visited the site of the INA memorial on a
trip to Singapore in 1946.[40] Yet under the influence of Lord and Lady
Mountbatten, he was not prepared to integrate the INA raised by his
younger comrade and rival into the army of free India. A number of
talented INA officers were taken into the diplomatic service and served
with distinction as Indian ambassadors abroad. Insofar as the armed
forces were concerned, Nehru opted for postcolonial continuity over
anticolonial rupture. In Jinnah's Pakistan, by contrast, INA officers and
soldiers were accepted into the army after their services had been used
in the war over Kashmir in 1948.[41]

One of the officers who fought on Pakistan's side in the Kashmir war
was none other than Habibur Rahman, Netaji's companion on his final
plane journey. Writing in 1966 to Tatsuo Hayashida, who had carried
the urn containing Netaji's ashes from Taipei to Tokyo, Habib thought
it was a "great tragedy" that Bose had not been able to see for himself
the fruits of his freedom struggle. "How much we wish that he had
come back alive," he wrote. "In that case it is more than certain that he
would have occupied a dominant position in Indian politics." The relations between India and Pakistan would then have been "cordial rather
than embittered," since he was known to be "a most judicious and fair-
minded leader."[42] Fifty years after partition, another of his followers,
Raja Mohammad Arshad, came from Pakistan to India and described
him as "a great exponent of harmony, free of any bias or petty discrimination." "Perhaps with him in the country," he mused, "many problems
that afflict the people of the subcontinent would have been resolved

amicably. Who knows, perhaps there may have been no bloodshed, and no drifting apart."[43]

Bose's critics had charged that he would become a dictatorial leader if he made a triumphant entry into India. His strategic alliance with totalitarian regimes opposed to Britain was seen as evidence of his ideological predilections. That he had no affinity with the pernicious philosophies of the Axis powers whose help he sought during World War II is beyond a shadow of doubt. He stood up to them courageously to maintain India's honor, but, regrettably, not on behalf of the victims of their brutality. The suffering human beings about whose fate he was concerned were the colonially oppressed people for whom World War II presented an opportunity to break the shackles of Western imperialism. He did, on at least three separate occasions, speak of the need for a period of authoritarian rule after independence, to effect the dramatic social and economic transformation he envisioned for India. The empowerment of women, peasants, workers, and the subordinate castes had always figured prominently on his political agenda. The inertia that accompanied the approach of the formally democratic Indian state to the gigantic problems of poverty, illiteracy, and disease might well have exasperated him. Under those circumstances, he may have been tempted to deploy the instruments of a strong party and state to bring about the revolutionary change he sought. Yet it is doubtful that he would have been personally enamored of the trappings of state power. His entire life was characterized by a series of renunciations of wealth and weal, worldly comfort and joy. The streak of self-abnegation was stronger in his character than that of self-assertion.

Nehru and Bose had much in common when it came to their views about the social and economic reconstruction of India. Both believed in variants of socialism, with Bose being a little more attentive to Indian notions of justice and equality. He was also far less impatient than Nehru when faced with expressions of religious or linguistic differences. He did not subscribe to the dogma of secular uniformity, but rather strove for unity by respecting and transcending cultural distinctiveness. This approach toward negotiating the problem of internal differences was closer to that of Gandhi, except that Bose believed in the possibility of forging cultural links between different communities.

Many socialists—such as the scientist Meghnad Saha, whom Bose had appointed to the national planning committee chaired by Nehru—became critics of India's first prime minister, once he embraced the colonial bureaucracy at the helm of a centralized state and obstructed the Congress's longstanding promise to bring about a linguistic reorganization of states.[44] A firm believer in Indian unity, Netaji nevertheless understood the salience of multiple identities, including those based on ties of religion or language.

Prem Kumar Sahgal has recalled that during the height of the Imphal campaign in April 1944, Bose was visiting the Burmese hill town of Maymyo, and there he analyzed Jawaharlal Nehru's "greatness and his weaknesses." The young military secretary sat with his leader many a night after the day's work had been done, "listening to him, enthralled," as he held forth on a variety of subjects. In addition to Nehru, the topics included the philosophy of nonviolence, Mahatma Gandhi's role in Indian politics, the causes of the Germans' defeat in World War I, their current mistakes in Europe, the reasons for Mussolini's failure, and the "inevitability of the partition of India if the British were not driven out of India before the Allies finally won the war." Sahgal marveled at his leader's "great intellect and the clarity of his vision"—the achievement of a man who, sadly, had been born in a "slave country." Sahgal believed that Netaji, in a land of the free, would have found his place as "the greatest teacher of his times."[45]

In free India, Bose was always regarded as a great popular hero; but official recognition of his stature was somewhat muted during the prime ministership of his rival, Jawaharlal Nehru, until 1964. Nehru's daughter, Indira Gandhi, admired Netaji for his courage and his vision. Yet the Indian National Congress, to which he had been twice elected president, truly acknowledged him as one of its own only during the 1990s, when under Narasimha Rao it ceased to be under dynastic control. Having become an icon among icons of the freedom struggle, Netaji has been subject to political appropriation, especially on the eve of elections. The Hindu right lauds his military heroism, ignoring his deep commitment to Hindu-Muslim unity and the rights of religious minorities. The communists, who were his harshest Indian critics and derided him as Tojo's stooge during World War II, have changed their mind since the late 1970s. Every January 23, they now garland his statues and express remorse for the blunder they made in their assessment of this great patriot.[46]

"When he is seen, in statue or portrait," an acute contemporary observer has noted, "a thirst is slaked but not satiated; a promise is seen, but not saturated; a hope is seen, but not with the regret that shadows most hopes." Netaji serves in a sense as "an alter-ego to the nation's power structure."[47] Whenever justice is threatened, wherever freedom is menaced, he continues to be invoked. His life's adventures followed itineraries far beyond the nation's frontiers. He played a dramatic role—a heroic one, against tremendous odds—on a global stage. It is by the magnitude of his conception of a world free from imperialist domination and from the corrosive degradation of colonial rule that his place in history must be assigned.

"In this mortal world, everything perishes and will perish," Subhas Chandra Bose had written in 1940, "but ideas, ideals and dreams do not." As he prepared for a fast unto death, he was confident that the idea for which one individual was prepared to die would incarnate itself in a thousand lives. That, he believed, was how the wheels of evolution turned and how the ideas, ideals, and dreams of one generation were "bequeathed to the next." "No idea has ever fulfilled itself in this world," he asserted, "except through an ordeal of suffering and sacrifice."[48] It is his immense *sacrifice*—in the sense of *tyag* as taught by Ramakrishna and Vivekananda, and *kurbani* as enshrined on the INA memorial—that has made him the heir to a life immortal.

Notes

GFO   German Foreign Office
IOR, BL   India Office Records, British Library
NAI   National Archives of India
NMML   Nehru Memorial Museum and Library
NRB   Netaji Research Bureau
TNA   The National Archives of the United Kingdom, Kew

1. A Flaming Sword Forever Unsheathed

1. *New York Times,* February 8, 1946.

2. D. G. Tendulkar, *Mahatma: Life of Mohandas Karamchand Gandhi,* vol. 7, *1945–1947* (New Delhi: Publications Division, Government of India, 1962), p. 113.

3. Ibid., p. 68.

4. Louis Fischer, *A Week with Gandhi* (London: George Allen and Unwin, 1943), pp. 7, 58–59, 63; *Harijan,* June 14, 1942.

5. Sugata Bose and Ayesha Jalal, *Modern South Asia: History, Culture, Political Economy* (London: Routledge, 2004), pp. 128–132.

6. Fischer, *A Week with Gandhi,* pp. 7, 28–29, 57.

7. "Jab hum phir Lal Kile Delhi pe jakar wahan hamare victory parade karenge . . . ," Video and audio recordings of Bose's July 4, 1943, speech (NRB). Subhas Chandra Bose, "Hunger, Thirst, Privation, Forced Marches and Death," in Bose, *Chalo Delhi: Netaji Subhas Chandra Bose, Collected Works,* vol. 12, ed. Sisir K. Bose and Sugata Bose (Calcutta: Netaji Research Bureau; and Delhi: Permanent Black, 2007), pp. 39–44.

8. "To Delhi, to Delhi," in Bose, *Chalo Delhi,* pp. 45–48.

9. "Why I Left Home and Homeland," ibid., pp. 51–54.

10. "At Bahadur Shah's Tomb" and "The Great Patriot and Leader," ibid., pp. 97–99, 249–253.

11. "Proclamation of the Provisional Government of Free India," ibid., pp. 117–120.

12. "The Roads to Delhi Are Many" and "India Shall Be Free," ibid., pp. 407–410.

13. Jawaharlal Nehru, "Foreword," in Moti Ram, *Two Historic Trials in Red Fort* (New Delhi: Roxy Printing Press, 1946), p. iii.

14. W. McK Wright, New Delhi, to Major Courtenay Young, Intelligence Division, C.I.C.B., H.Q. SACSEA, Singapore, February 19, 1946, no. C-5, Intelligence Bureau, Home Department, New Delhi, File 273, INA (NAI).

15. Sri Aurobindo, *The Doctrine of Passive Resistance* (Calcutta: Arya Publishing House, 1948; composed in 1907), pp. 87–88.

16. Bhulabhai Desai, "Address of Counsel for Defense, Red Fort Trial, 1 December 1945," *The Oracle*, 15, no. 4 (October 1993), 31–55.

17. Moti Ram, *Two Historic Trials in Red Fort*, pp. 109–110.

18. Tendulkar, *Mahatma*, vol. 7, pp. 77–78.

19. K. K. Ghosh, *The Indian National Army: Second Front of the Indian Independence Movement* (Meerut: Meenakshi Prakashan, 1969), pp. 215–216.

20. Ibid., pp. 229, 232. Sisir K. Bose, *Bosubari* (Calcutta: Ananda, 1985), pp. 200–201.

21. Tendulkar, *Mahatma*, vol. 7, pp. 107–108.

22. Christopher Bayly and Tim Harper, *Forgotten Armies* (Cambridge, Mass.: Harvard University Press, 2004), p. 29.

23. The leaders of the secular Jammu and Kashmir Liberation Front, such as Amanullah Khan and Yasin Malik, have often spoken of their admiration for Bose, as have Naga leaders like Phizo and Muivah, along with some of the Tamil rebels in Sri Lanka.

24. Audio recording of Sheikh Mujibur Rahman, January, 1972 (NRB).

25. Audio and video recording of Nelson Mandela's speech at the Eden Gardens cricket stadium, Calcutta, 1990 (NRB).

26. Presidential address by Padmaja Naidu, Governor of West Bengal, at the sword ceremony on March 19, 1967, *Bulletin of the Netaji Research Bureau*, 9–10 (1968–1969), 6.

27. Address by Indira Gandhi, Prime Minister of India, at the Red Fort, Delhi, December 17, 1967, ibid., p. 18.

28. Subhas Chandra Bose, *An Indian Pilgrim: Netaji Subhas Chandra Bose, Collected Works*, vol. 1, ed. Sisir K. Bose and Sugata Bose (Calcutta: Netaji Research Bureau; and Delhi: Oxford University Press, 1997), p. 122.

29. Audio and video recording of interview with Mehboob Ahmed, May 1991 (NRB).

30. Carl Sandburg, "Lincoln Day Address to a Joint Session of Congress," February 12, 1959 (Abraham Lincoln's 150th birthday), in Robert C. Torricelli and An-

drew Carroll, eds., *In Our Own Words: Extraordinary Speeches of the American Century* (New York: Kodansha, 1999), p. 214.

31. S. A. Ayer, *Unto Him a Witness: The Story of Netaji Subhas Chandra Bose in Southeast Asia* (Bombay: Thacker, 1951), p. 12.

32. D. G. Tendulkar, *Mahatma: Life of Mohandas Karamchand Gandhi,* vol. 8, *1947–1948* (Delhi: Publications Division, Government of India, 1963), p. 277.

2. God's Beloved Land

1. Janakinath Bose, Diary, January 23, 1897 (NRB).

2. "The Famine in India," *The Times,* January 23, 1897.

3. Romesh Chunder Dutt, *The Economic History of India in the Victorian Age: From the Accession of Queen Victoria in 1837 to the Commencement of the Twentieth Century,* vol. 2 (New York: Augustus M. Kelley, 1969; first pub. 1904), p. v.

4. Mike Davis, *Late Victorian Holocausts: El Niño Famines and the Making of the Third World* (New York: Verso, 2001).

5. M. G. Ranade, *Miscellaneous Writings of the Late Hon'ble Mr. Justice M. G. Ranade,* ed. Ramabai Ranade (Delhi: Sahitya Akademi, 1992), p. 180.

6. William Digby, *"Prosperous" British India: A Revelation from Official Records* (London: T. F. Unwin, 1901).

7. Davis, *Late Victorian Holocausts,* p. 158.

8. Subhas Chandra Bose, *An Indian Pilgrim: An Unfinished Autobiography and Letters to 1921, Netaji Subhas Chandra Bose, Collected Works,* vol. 1, ed. Sisir K. Bose and Sugata Bose (Calcutta: Netaji Research Bureau; and Delhi: Oxford University Press, 1997), p. 3. The original manuscript is preserved in the archives of the Netaji Research Bureau.

9. Ibid., p. 15.

10. Ibid., p. 19.

11. Ibid., p. 5. Sisir Kumar Bose, "My Mother's Face," *The Oracle,* 18, nos. 3–4 (July–October 1996), 2.

12. Bose, *An Indian Pilgrim,* pp. 22–23.

13. Ibid., pp. 25–27.

14. Ranajit Guha, "Nationalism and the Trials of Becoming," *The Oracle,* 24, no. 2 (August 2002), p. 11.

15. Bose, *An Indian Pilgrim,* pp. 34–35.

16. Ibid., pp. 35–36; Guha, "Nationalism."

17. Bose, *An Indian Pilgrim,* pp. 36–38, 48; Guha, "Nationalism," pp. 15–17.

18. Bose, *An Indian Pilgrim,* pp. 39–40, 49–50.

19. Ibid., p. 45.

20. Ibid., p. 38.

21. Guha, "Nationalism," p. 16.

22. Subhas Chandra Bose to Prabhabati Bose, 1912, in Bose, *An Indian Pilgrim,* p. 143. The original letters from Subhas to his mother are preserved in the archives of the Netaji Research Bureau.

23. Subhas Chandra Bose to Prabhabati Bose, 1912, ibid., pp. 128, 136–138, 144.

24. Subhas Chandra Bose to Sarat Chandra Bose, August 22, 1912; idem, September 17, 1912; idem, October 11/16, 1912; and idem, January 8, 1913; all ibid., pp. 148–156. The original letters from Subhas to his brother Sarat are preserved in the archives of the Netaji Research Bureau. The lines he quoted from Washington Irving appear in Irving, *The Sketchbook of Geoffrey Crayon: The Voyage,* first published in 1819–1820. It is a striking illustration of the wide range of the fifteen-year-old Subhas's reading.

25. Bose, *An Indian Pilgrim,* pp. 49–50.

26. Ibid., p. 51.

27. Subhas Chandra Bose to Prabhabati Bose, March 1913, ibid., p. 148.

28. Bose, *An Indian Pilgrim,* pp. 51, 53.

29. Ibid., p. 54.

30. Ibid., pp. 63–64.

31. Ibid., p. 67.

32. Ibid., pp. 68–69, 71.

33. Ibid., p. 74.

34. Dilip Kumar Roy, *Netaji, the Man: Reminiscences* (Bombay: Bharatiya Vidya Bhavan, 1966), p. 10.

35. Bose, *An Indian Pilgrim,* pp. 76–77; "Discipline in Presidency College: Government Statement and Report of the Enquiry Committee," in Sisir Kumar Bose, ed., *Netaji and India's Freedom* (Calcutta: Netaji Research Bureau, 1975), pp. 39–53; Government of India, Department of Education, June 1916, nos. 122–127; see also Government of India, L/P&J/1861/1916 (IOR, BL).

36. Edward Farley Oaten, "The Bengal Student as I Knew Him," in Bose, *Netaji and India's Freedom,* p. 33.

37. Bose, *An Indian Pilgrim,* pp. 77–78.

38. Ibid., pp. 77, 233; Krishna Bose, "Basanti Devir kaachhe shona Kahini," in *Prasanga Subhaschandra* (Calcutta: Ananda Publishers, 1993), p. 57; author's conversations with Sisir Kumar Bose.

39. "Discipline in Presidency College," in Bose, *Netaji and India's Freedom,* p. 48.

40. Rabindranath Tagore, "Indian Students and Western Teachers," *Modern Review* (April 1916); Tagore's Bengali essay on similar lines appeared in the monthly magazine *Sabuj Patra.*

41. "Discipline in Presidency College," in Bose, *Netaji and India's Freedom,* p. 50. The Enquiry Committee had three British and two Indian members. One of the Indian members, Heramba Chandra Moitra, dissented from this view. See also

Government of India, Department of Education, June 1916, nos. 122–127; Government of India, L/P&J/1861/1916 (IOR, BL).

42. Bose, *An Indian Pilgrim,* pp. 79–80.

43. See Krishna Bose, "The Professor Who Made a Verb," *The Statesman,* October 31, 1971.

44. Bose, *An Indian Pilgrim,* pp. 82–85.

45. Ibid., pp. 88–89.

46. *Scottish Churches College Magazine,* 8, no. 5 (March 1918), 218–219; ibid., 9, no. 2 (September 1918), 59–60.

47. Bose, *An Indian Pilgrim,* pp. 91–92.

48. Ibid., pp. 97–98.

49. Ibid., pp. 99–101, 105. For a discussion of the books read by Subhas at Cambridge, see Leonard A. Gordon, *Brothers against the Raj: A Biography of Indian Nationalists Sarat and Subhas Chandra Bose* (New York: Columbia University Press, 1990), pp. 56, 63.

50. Bose, *An Indian Pilgrim,* pp. 101–104.

51. Subhas Chandra Bose to Mrs. Dharmavir, May 7, 1921.

52. Roy, *Netaji,* pp. 161–162.

53. Subhas Chandra Bose to Charu Chandra Ganguly, March 23, 1920, in Bose, *An Indian Pilgrim,* pp. 205–206.

54. Bose, *An Indian Pilgrim,* pp. 105–106.

55. File L/P&J/6238/20 (IOR, BL).

56. Guha, "Nationalism," p. 19.

57. Subhas Chandra Bose to Sarat Chandra Bose, September 22, 1920, in Bose, *An Indian Pilgrim,* pp. 206–209. All of the original letters from Subhas to Sarat concerning the Indian Civil Service are preserved in the archives of the Netaji Research Bureau.

58. Subhas Chandra Bose to Sarat Chandra Bose, January 26, 1921, ibid., pp. 109–110.

59. Subhas Chandra Bose to Sarat Chandra Bose, February 16, 1921, ibid., pp. 217–219.

60. Subhas Chandra Bose to Deshbandhu Chittaranjan Das, February 16, 1921, ibid., pp. 210–214.

61. Subhas Chandra Bose to Deshbandhu Chittaranjan Das, March 2, 1921, ibid., pp. 214–217.

62. Subhas Chandra Bose to Sarat Chandra Bose, February 23, 1921, ibid., pp. 219–222.

63. Subhas Chandra Bose to Sarat Chandra Bose, April 6, 1921, ibid., pp. 222–225.

64. Ibid., pp. 225–227.

65. Subhas Chandra Bose to Sarat Chandra Bose, April 20, 1921, ibid., pp. 227–229.

66. Subhas Chandra Bose to E. S. Montagu, Secretary of State for India, April 22, 1921, ibid., p. 229. The original of this letter can be found in L/P&J/6238/20 (IOR, BL).

67. Subhas Chandra Bose to Sarat Chandra Bose, April 23, 1921, ibid., pp. 230–236.

68. Bose, *An Indian Pilgrim,* pp. 115–117.

69. Subhas Chandra Bose to Sarat Chandra Bose, May 18, 1921, ibid., pp. 236–237.

70. Subhas Chandra Bose to E. S. Montagu, Secretary of State for India, April 22, 1921, ibid., p. 229.

71. Subhas Chandra Bose to Charu Chandra Ganguly, April 22, 1921, ibid., p. 230.

3. Dreams of Youth

1. Subhas Chandra Bose, *The Indian Struggle, 1920–1942: Netaji Subhas Chandra Bose, Collected Works,* vol. 2, ed. Sisir K. Bose and Sugata Bose (Calcutta: Netaji Research Bureau; and Delhi: Oxford University Press, 1997), pp. 58–59.

2. Ibid., pp. 64–65.

3. Ibid., p. 60.

4. Krishna Bose, "Basanti Devir kaachhe shona Kahini," in *Prasanga Subhaschandra* (Calcutta: Ananda Publishers, 1993), pp. 58–59.

5. Janakinath Bose to Sarat Chandra Bose, December 12, 1921 (NRB).

6. Bose, *The Indian Struggle,* pp. 73–75.

7. Ibid., p. 82.

8. Mohandas Karamchand Gandhi, "Tampering with Loyalty," first published in *Young India,* September 29, 1921, reprinted in *The Collected Works of Mahatma Gandhi,* vol. 21 (Delhi: Government of India, Publications Division, 1958), pp. 221–223.

9. Gandhi, "A Puzzle and Its Solution" and "Shaking the Manes," first published in *Young India,* December 15, 1921, and February 23, 1922 (respectively), and reprinted in *The Collected Works of Mahatma Gandhi,* vol. 22, pp. 28–29, 457–458.

10. Ibid., pp. 90–91; Hemendranath Dasgupta, *Subhas Chandra* (Calcutta: Jyoti Prakashalaya, 1946), p. 55.

11. *Amrita Bazar Patrika,* July 17, 1924.

12. Mohandas Karamchand Gandhi, *The Collected Works of Mahatma Gandhi,* vol. 24 (Delhi: Government of India, Publications Division, 1958), p. 479.

13. Krishna Bose, "Basanti Devir kaachhe shona Kahini," p. 63.

14. Bose, *The Indian Struggle,* p. 141.

15. Government of Bengal, Political Department, File 257/25.

16. Idem, File 840/32.

17. Sarat Chandra Bose to Subhas Chandra Bose, November 24, 1924; idem,

December 12, 1924; Subhas Chandra Bose to Sarat Chandra Bose, December 8, 1924; Sarat Chandra Bose to Subhas Chandra Bose, July 10, 1926, enclosing Ray Knight to J. A. Jones, December 18, 1924; all in Subhas Chandra Bose, *In Burmese Prisons: Netaji Subhas Chandra Bose, Collected Works,* vol. 3, ed. Sisir K. Bose (Calcutta: Netaji Research Bureau; and Delhi: Permanent Black, 2009), pp. 21–26, 315–322. The three newspapers were the *Catholic Herald,* the *Englishman,* and the *Statesman.* Subhas Chandra won the suits against the first two, while the third was let off by the British judge on the grounds that it had not asserted facts but merely commented on a speech by the governor.

18. C. R. Das's speech of October 29, 1924, in *Calcutta Municipal Gazette,* 1, no. 7 (1924–1925).

19. Sri Aurobindo, *The Doctrine of Passive Resistance* (Calcutta: Arya Publishing House, 1948), pp. 27–30.

20. *Indian Annual Register,* 1 (1924), 671.

21. Dasgupta, *Subhas Chandra,* pp. 66–67.

22. Subhas Chandra Bose to Sarat Chandra Bose, December 16, 1924, in Bose, *In Burmese Prisons,* pp. 26–29.

23. Bose, *The Indian Struggle,* pp. 142–143.

24. Subhas Chandra Bose to Sarat Chandra Bose, February 12, 1925; idem, March 14, 1925; idem, March 28, 1925; all in Bose, *In Burmese Prisons,* pp. 39–41, 46–49, 51.

25. Subhas Chandra Bose to N. C. Kelkar, August 20, 1925, ibid., pp. 112–115.

26. Subhas Chandra Bose to Dilip Kumar Roy, May 2, 1925, ibid., pp. 55–59.

27. Subhas Chandra Bose to Dilip Kumar Roy, June 25, 1925, ibid., pp. 82–84.

28. Subhas Chandra Bose to Sarat Chandra Bose, June 19, 1925, ibid., pp. 71–72.

29. "Deshbandhu Chittaranjan Das," Subhas Chandra Bose to Hemendranath Dasgupta, February 20, 1926, in Subhas Chandra Bose, *The Essential Writings of Netaji Subhas Chandra Bose,* ed. Sisir K. Bose and Sugata Bose (Calcutta: Netaji Research Bureau; and Delhi: Oxford University Press, 1997), pp. 61–76.

30. Patrick Pearse, excerpt from "The Rebel," quoted in Bose, "Analysis of Books Read," in Subhas Chandra Bose, *Netaji Subhas Chandra Bose, Collected Works,* vol. 5, ed. Sisir K. Bose (Calcutta: Netaji Research Bureau, 1985), pp. 33–70.

31. Subhas Chandra Bose to Dilip Kumar Roy, September 11, 1925; Subhas Chandra Bose to Sarat Chandra Bose, May 17, 1926; idem, May 14, 1926; all in Bose, *In Burmese Prisons,* pp. 85–87, 287–296.

32. Subhas Chandra Bose to Sarat Chandra Bose, March 14, 1925, ibid., pp. 47–49.

33. Subhas Chandra Bose to Dilip Kumar Roy, June 25, 1925, ibid., pp. 82–84.

34. Dilip Kumar Roy to Subhas Chandra Bose, September 27, 1925; November 21, 1925; idem, November 28, 1925; Subhas Chandra Bose to Dilip Kumar Roy, October 9, 1925; Rabindranath Tagore to Dilip Kumar Roy, November 1925; all ibid., pp. 88–91, 129–138, 345–347.

35. Subhas Chandra Bose to Sarat Chandra Chattopadhyay, August 12, 1925, ibid., pp. 107–111.

36. "Tomari lagiya kalanker bojha / Bahite amaar sukh." Subhas Chandra Bose to Anath Bandhu Dutta, December 1925, in Bose, *Netaji, Collected Works,* vol. 4, pp. 130–133.

37. Subhas Chandra Bose to Bivabati Bose, September 11, 1925; idem, December 16, 1925; idem, February 12, 1926; idem, July 28, 1926; all in Bose, *In Burmese Prisons,* pp. 118–123, 168–174, 216–219, 343–344. Subhas Chandra Bose to Bivabati Bose, February 7, 1927, in Bose, *Netaji, Collected Works,* vol. 4, pp. 163–164.

38. Subhas Chandra Bose and other state prisoners to the Superintendent, Mandalay jail, August 7, 1925; idem to the Chief Secretary, Government of Burma, August 10, 1925; Subhas Chandra Bose to the Governor of Burma, 1925; Subhas Chandra Bose and other state prisoners to the Chief Secretary, Government of Burma, February 16, 1926; all in Bose, *In Burmese Prisons,* pp. 101–104, 185–187, 221–226.

39. Subhas Chandra Bose to Sarat Chandra Bose, March 26, 1926, ibid., 269–271.

40. Subhas Chandra Bose to Sarat Chandra Bose, March 17, 1926, ibid., pp. 258–261.

41. Sarat Chandra Bose to Subhas Chandra Bose, March 20, 1926, ibid., pp. 255–257.

42. Subhas Chandra Bose to Sarat Chandra Bose, August 13, 1926; idem, September 1, 1926; idem, September 3, 1926; idem, October 9, 1926; idem, November 6, 1926; idem, November 13, 1926; Sarat Chandra Bose to Subhas Chandra Bose, August 6, 1926; idem, August 21, 1926; idem, August 27, 1926; idem, September 2, 1926; idem, September 8, 1926; idem, September 15, 1926; idem, October 2, 1926; idem, October 11, 1926; idem, October 18, 1926; idem, November 1, 1926; all in Bose, *Netaji, Collected Works,* vol. 4, pp. 23–33, 39–40, 52–58, 62–64, 77–84, 87–91.

43. Sisir K. Bose, *Bosubari* (Calcutta: Ananda Publishers, 1985), p. 33.

44. Subhas Chandra Bose to Basanti Devi, December 20, 1926; idem, December 30, 1926; both in Bose, *Netaji, Collected Works,* vol. 4, pp. 118–121.

45. Kabe pran khuli balite paribo
    Peyechhi amaar shesh.
    Tomra sakale esho mor pichhe
    Guru tomader sabare dakichhe,
    Amaar jibane labhiya jiban
        Jagore sakal desh.
Subhas Chandra Bose to Bhupendranath Bandyopadhyay, 1926, ibid., pp. 133–138. Translation by Sisir Kumar Bose.

46. "Tomar pataka jare dao / Tare bahibare dao shakti." Subhas Chandra Bose to Gopal Lal Sanyal, April 5, 1927, ibid., pp. 204–205. Translation by Sisir Kumar Bose.

47. Subhas Chandra Bose to the Governor of Burma, March 19, 1927; idem, March 21, 1927; Subhas Chandra Bose to the Inspector General of Prisons, March 21, 1927; all ibid., pp. 174–181.

48. Subhas Chandra Bose to Jatindra Nath Chakrabarty, April 2, 1927, ibid., pp. 193–195.

49. Subhas Chandra Bose to Sarat Chandra Bose, April 4, 1927, ibid., pp. 196–203.

50. Sarat Chandra Bose to Subhas Chandra Bose, April 16, 1927; A. N. Moberly to Sarat Chandra Bose, April 15, 1927; O. M. Martin to Sarat Chandra Bose, April 16, 1927; all ibid., pp. 209–212, 325–327.

51. Subhas Chandra Bose to the superintendent, Insein jail, April 11, 1927, in Ibid., pp. 213–215.

52. Subhas Chandra Bose to Sarat Chandra Bose, May 6, 1927, ibid., pp. 224–226.

53. Bose, *The Indian Struggle*, p. 155.

54. Subhas Chandra Bose to Basanti Devi, July 17, 1927; idem, July 30, 1927; idem, October 15, 1927; all in Bose, *Netaji, Collected Works*, vol. 4, pp. 231–234, 238–240, 262–265.

55. Sisir K. Bose, *Bosubari*, pp. 33–34.

56. Subhas Chandra Bose to Bivabati Bose, 1927, in Bose, *Netaji, Collected Works*, vol. 4, pp. 253–255.

57. Bose, *Netaji, Collected Works*, vol. 5, pp. 242–254.

58. Subhas Chandra Bose to Motilal Nehru, July 18, 1928, in Bose, *Netaji, Collected Works*, vol. 4, p. 268–269.

59. Professor Ranajit Guha's reminiscence, *The Oracle*, 15, no. 1 (January 2003), 13.

60. Bose, *Netaji, Collected Works*, vol. 5, pp. 275–278.

61. Subhas Chandra Bose, *Netaji Subhas Chandra Bose, Collected Works*, vol. 6 (Calcutta: Netaji Research Bureau, 1987), pp. 10–13.

62. A. G. Noorani, *The Trial of Bhagat Singh: Politics of Justice* (Delhi: Oxford University Press, 2008), pp. 84–89; Neeti Nair, "Bhagat Singh as *Satyagrahi*: The Limits to Non-Violence in Late Colonial India," *Modern Asian Studies*, 43, no. 3 (2009), 649–681.

63. Sarba kharbatare dahe taba krodha daha—
he Bhairav, shakti dao, bhakta-pane chaha.
Door karo Maharudra jaha mugdha jaha khudra—
mrityure karibe tuchha pranera uthsaha.
Dukhero manthanabege uthibe amrita,

shanka hote raksha pabe jara mrityubheeta.

Taba deepta roudrateje nirjharia galibe je

prastarashrinkhalonmukta tyagera prabaha.

(English translation by Sugata Bose.)

64. Sisir K. Bose, *Bosubari,* p. 40.

65. Bose, *Netaji, Collected Works,* vol. 6, pp. 42–53.

66. Subhas Chandra Bose to Kalyani Devi, October 26, 1929, in Bose, *Netaji, Collected Works,* vol. 4, pp. 272–273.

67. Subhas Chandra Bose to Basanti Devi, November 5, 1929, ibid., pp. 273–274.

68. Subhas Chandra Bose to Basanti Devi, January 23, 1930, ibid., p. 276.

69. Bose, *The Indian Struggle,* p. 190.

70. Ibid., pp. 205–206.

71. Jawaharlal Nehru, *An Autobiography* (Delhi: Oxford University Press, 1982; first pub. 1936), pp. 174–176.

72. Bose, *The Indian Struggle,* pp. 227–229.

73. Bose, *Netaji, Collected Works,* vol. 6, pp. 149–162.

74. Ibid., pp. 190–196.

75. Ibid., p. vii; Bose, *The Indian Struggle,* pp. 236–237.

76. Subhas Chandra Bose to a friend, February 27, 1932; idem, April 22, 1932; idem, April 29, 1932; idem, May 14, 1932; all in Bose, *Netaji, Collected Works,* vol. 4, pp. 277–285.

77. Home Department File 44/8/1/1933-Poll. (NAI).

78. Sisir K. Bose, *Bosubari,* pp. 49, 54.

79. Ibid., pp. 49–51.

80. Bose, *Netaji, Collected Works,* vol. 6, pp. 262–263.

4. Exile in Europe

1. Robert Musil, *The Man without Qualities* (London: Picador, 1971); Carl Schorske, *Fin-de-Siècle Vienna: Politics and Culture* (New York: Vintage Books, 1981).

2. Subhas Chandra Bose to Kantilal Parekh, March 15, 1933, in Subhas Chandra Bose, *Netaji Subhas Chandra Bose, Collected Works, 1933–1937,* vol. 8, ed. Sisir Kumar Bose and Sugata Bose (Calcutta: Netaji Research Bureau; Delhi: Oxford University Press, 1994), pp. 6–7.

3. Home Department File 22/37/1933-Poll. (NAI).

4. Subhas Chandra Bose to Satyendra Nath Majumdar, April 28, 1933, in Bose, *Netaji Collected Works,* vol. 8, pp. 8–10. The reference is to a famous Tagore song: "Jadi tor dak shune keu na ashe, tabe ekla chalo re."

5. Subhas Chandra Bose to J. T. Sunderland, May 18, 1933, ibid., p. 12.

6. "Patel-Bose Manifesto, May 1933" (NRB).

7. L/P&J/174/Part 1/1935 (IOR, BL); Krishna Bose, *Itihaser Sandhane* (Calcutta: Ananda, 1972), pp. 25–26.

8. "The Anti-Imperialist Struggle and *Samyavada*," June 10, 1933; and Subhas Chandra Bose to Kitty Kurti, February 23, 1934; in Bose, *Netaji Collected Works*, vol. 8, pp. 241–263, 56–57.

9. Home Department File 35/11/1933-Poll. (NAI).

10. Subhas Chandra Bose to Santosh Kumar Basu, mayor of Calcutta, May 11, 1933; May 23, 1933; June 18, 1933; Subhas Chandra Bose to Naomi Vetter, May 31, 1933; all in Bose, *Netaji Collected Works*, vol. 8, pp. 10–14, 16–17.

11. Subhas Chandra Bose to Naomi Vetter, June 29, 1933; July 10, 1933; Subhas Chandra Bose to Santosh Kumar Basu, mayor of Calcutta, July 9, 1933; Subhas Chandra Bose to V. Lesny, November 10, 1933; ibid., pp. 18–21, 38. Krishna Bose, *Itihaser Sandhane*, pp. 5–7.

12. L/P&J/174/Part 1/1935 (IOR, BL); Krishna Bose, *Itihaser Sandhane*, p. 26.

13. Subhas Chandra Bose to Naomi Vetter, July 15, 1933; Subhas Chandra Bose to Santosh Kumar Basu, mayor of Calcutta, March 14, 1934; "A Friend of India in Poland"; all in Bose, *Netaji Collected Works*, vol. 8, pp. 22, 57–60, 340–342.

14. Sisir Kumar Bose, Alexander Werth, and S. A. Ayer, *A Beacon across Asia* (Hyderabad: Orient Longman, 1973), p. 42.

15. Adolf Hitler, *Mein Kampf* (Boston: Houghton Mifflin, 1943), p. 657.

16. For an analysis of Hitler's rational decisions, see Adam Tooze, *The Wages of Destruction: The Making and Breaking of the Nazi Economy* (Harmondsworth: Penguin, 2006).

17. Subhas Chandra Bose to Naomi Vetter, July 22, 1933; idem, August 4, 1933; idem, August 10, 1933; idem, August 25, 1933; all in Bose, *Netaji Collected Works*, vol. 8, pp. 23–26.

18. Kitty Kurti, *Subhas Chandra Bose as I Knew Him* (Calcutta: Firma K. L. Mukhopadhyay, 1966), pp. 2–5, 8, 38–43.

19. Subhas Chandra Bose to Naomi Vetter, August 31, 1933; September 21, 1933; Subhas Chandra Bose to Kantilal Parekh, October 3, 1933; Subhas Chandra Bose to Satyendra Nath Majumdar, October 19, 1933; all in Bose, *Netaji Collected Works*, vol. 8, pp. 26–28, 30–31, 35–36.

20. "Vithalbhai Patel's Will," August 1934, in Bose, *Netaji Collected Works*, vol. 8, pp. 283–284.

21. Subhas Chandra Bose to E. Woods, October 12, 1933; idem, December 7, 1933; both in Bose, *Netaji Collected Works*, vol. 8, pp. 33–34, 40–41.

22. Subhas Chandra Bose to Sunil Mohan Ghosh Moulik, December 7, 1933; Subhas Chandra Bose to Naomi Vetter, December 21, 1933; idem, January 12, 1934; all in Bose, *Netaji Collected Works*, vol. 8, pp. 42, 44–47.

23. Krishna Dutta and Andrew Robinson, eds., *Selected Letters of Rabindranath Tagore* (Cambridge: Cambridge University Press, 1997), pp. 332–337, 393–394.

24. Mahatma Gandhi, *Collected Works*, vol. 58, pp. 429–430.

25. Subhas Chandra Bose to Sunil Mohan Ghosh Moulik, February 15, 1934, in Bose, *Netaji Collected Works*, vol. 8, pp. 50–51.

26. Subhas Chandra Bose to C. R. Prufer, April 5, 1934, ibid., pp. 61–64.

27. Subhas Chandra Bose to A. C. N. Nambiar, July 10, 1934; Subhas Chandra Bose to V. Lesny, July 25, 1934; all ibid., pp. 72–75. On British views in 1939 looking back at Bose's formation of Indian students associations in Germany and Austria, see "Indian Societies and Associations in Germany," L/P&J/12/410 (IOR, BL).

28. Subhas Chandra Bose to Naomi Vetter, May 11, 1934; idem, May 18, 1934; idem, May 21, 1934; idem, June 3, 1934; all in Bose, *Netaji Collected Works*, vol. 8, pp. 67–70.

29. Subhas Chandra Bose to Emilie Schenkl, March 1936, in Subhas Chandra Bose, *The Essential Writings of Netaji Subhas Chandra Bose*, ed. Sisir K. Bose and Sugata Bose (Calcutta: Netaji Research Bureau; Delhi: Oxford University Press, 1997), pp. 160–161.

30. Krishna Bose, "Basanti Debir kaachhe shona Kahini," in *Prasanga Subhaschandra* (Calcutta: Ananda, 1993), pp. 57–64.

31. Krishna Bose, "Important Women in Netaji's Life," in *The Illustrated Weekly of India* (August 13 and 20, 1972); Krishna Bose, *Itihaser Sandhane*, pp. 16–17; my conversations with Emilie Schenkl, 1993.

32. Subhas Chandra Bose to Naomi Vetter, August 14, 1934, in Bose, *Netaji Collected Works*, vol. 8, pp. 77–78.

33. Subhas Chandra Bose to Naomi Vetter, September 24, 1934; "Karlsbad and Other Watering Places of Czechoslovakia" (first pub. *Calcutta Municipal Gazette*, December 31, 1937); both in Bose, *Netaji Collected Works*, vol. 8, pp. 81–82, 436–441. Krishna Bose, *Itihaser Sandhane*, p. 12.

34. Subhas Chandra Bose, *The Indian Struggle, 1920–1942: Netaji Subhas Chandra Bose, Collected Works*, vol. 2 (Calcutta: Netaji Research Bureau; Delhi: Oxford University Press, 1997), pp. 327–333.

35. Bose, *The Indian Struggle*, pp. 350–353.

36. Subhas Chandra Bose to Emilie Schenkl, November 30, 1934; idem, December 1, 1934; idem, December 2, 1934; idem, December 20, 1934; all in Subhas Chandra Bose, *Letters to Emilie Schenkl, 1934–1942: Netaji Subhas Chandra Bose, Collected Works*, vol. 7, ed. Sisir K. Bose and Sugata Bose (Calcutta: Netaji Research Bureau; Delhi: Permanent Black, 1994, 2004), pp. 1–3, 5–8.

37. Sisir Kumar Bose, *Bosubari* (Calcutta: Ananda, 1985), pp. 57–58.

38. Ibid., pp. 59–60; Subhas Chandra Bose to Emilie Schenkl, December 7, 1934, in Bose, *Letters to Emilie*, pp. 4–5.

39. Subhas Chandra Bose, "Italy" (letter to *Amrita Bazaar Patrika*, March 9, 1935), in Bose, *Netaji Collected Works*, vol. 8, p. 291; Asoke Nath Bose, *My Uncle Netaji* (Bombay: Bharatiya Vidya Bhavan, 1989), p. 109.

40. Subhas Chandra Bose to Emilie Schenkl, December 31, 1934; idem, Janu-

ary 8, 1935; idem, January 20, 1935; idem, January 22, 1935; idem, January 25, 1935; all in Bose, *Letters to Emilie,* pp. 8–13.

41. Bose, *Letters to Emilie,* p. xv.

42. Bose, *The Indian Struggle,* pp. ix–x; the various reviews were compiled in Home Department File 22/29/1935-Poll. (NAI).

43. Home Department File 39/15/35-Poll. (NAI).

44. Bose, *The Indian Struggle,* p. xi.

45. Interview of A. C. N. Nambiar with Sisir Kumar Bose and Krishna Bose, September 1971; Krishna Bose, *Itihaser Sandhane,* pp. 81–82; Krishna Bose, "Important Women in Netaji's Life."

46. Subhas Chandra Bose to Naomi Vetter, March 25, 1935, in Bose, *Netaji Collected Works,* vol. 8, p. 94.

47. "What Romain Rolland Thinks," in Bose, *Netaji Collected Works,* vol. 8, pp. 302–309.

48. Sisir Kumar Bose, *Bosubari,* p. 63.

49. Subhas Chandra Bose to Naomi Vetter, May 15, 1935; idem, June 16, 1935; idem, September 6, 1935; Subhas Chandra Bose to Amiya Chakravarty, July 23, 1935; Subhas Chandra Bose to J. T. Sunderland, August 6, 1935; all in Bose, *Netaji Collected Works,* vol. 8, pp. 97–98, 100–101, 103–106; Asoke Nath Bose, *My Uncle Netaji,* pp. 115, 119–122.

50. Subhas Chandra Bose to Jawaharlal Nehru, October 4, 1935, in Bose, *Netaji Collected Works,* vol. 8, pp. 109–110.

51. Krishna Bose, *Itihaser Sandhane,* pp. 11–12; Asoke Nath Bose, *My Uncle Netaji,* p. 121; author's conversations with Emilie Schenkl, 1993.

52. Subhas Chandra Bose to Naomi Vetter, October 12, 1935; October 25, 1935; November 29, 1935; in Bose, *Netaji Collected Works,* vol. 8, pp. 110–111; 121–122.

53. Subhas Chandra Bose to E. Woods, December 21, 1935, in Bose, *Netaji Collected Works,* vol. 8, pp. 124–125.

54. Subhas Chandra Bose to Emilie Schenkl, January 13, 1936; idem, January 15, 1936; idem, January 17, 1936; idem, January 19, 1936; idem, January 20, 1936; idem, January 22, 1936; idem, January 24, 1936; idem, January 25, 1936; idem, January 30, 1936; all in Bose, *Letters to Emilie,* pp. 14–18; Subhas Chandra Bose to Naomi Vetter, January 30, 1936, in Bose, *Netaji Collected Works,* vol. 8, pp. 138–141.

55. Subhas Chandra Bose to Emilie Schenkl, January 30, 1936; idem, February 7, 1936; idem, February 11, 1936; all in Bose, *Letters to Emilie,* pp. 19–23; Subhas Chandra Bose to Santosh Kumar Sen, January 23, 1936, in Bose, *Netaji Collected Works,* vol. 8, pp. 134–135; *Irish Independent,* February 4, 1936; Amiya Chakravarty, "Subhaschandra," in Biswanath De, ed., *Subhas Smriti* (Calcutta: Sahityam, 1970), p. 265.

56. "The Visit to Dublin" and "Impressions of Ireland," in Bose, *Netaji Collected Works,* vol. 8, pp. 343–345, 350–352; Krishna Bose, "Irish *Swadhinata Andolan:*

de Valera *o* Netaji," in *Prasanga Subhaschandra,* pp. 105–110; Kate O'Malley, *Ireland, India and Empire: Indo-Irish Radical Connections, 1919–1964* (Manchester: Manchester University Press, 2008), pp. 100–113.

57. Subhas Chandra Bose to E. Woods, March 5, 1936; idem, March 30, 1936; both in Bose, *Netaji Collected Works,* vol. 8, pp. 148–149, 168–170.

58. Subhas Chandra Bose to Naomi Vetter, March 17, 1936, ibid., pp. 158–160.

59. "The Indian Situation and World Opinion," ibid., pp. 347–350.

60. Subhas Chandra Bose to Naomi Vetter, February 26, 1936; idem, March 5, 1936; Subhas Chandra Bose to E. Woods, March 5, 1936; all ibid., pp. 142, 147–149.

61. Subhas Chandra Bose to Santosh Kumar Sen, March 3, 1936, ibid., p. 143.

62. Subhas Chandra Bose to Jawaharlal Nehru, March 4, 1936, ibid., pp. 144–145.

63. "The Secret of Abyssinia and Its Lesson," November 1935, ibid., pp. 309–326.

64. Subhas Chandra Bose to Amiya Chakravarty, March 11, 1936, ibid., pp. 151–153.

65. Subhas Chandra Bose to Franz Thierfelder, March 25, 1936, ibid., pp. 165–168.

66. "Meeting the Press: Situation in India, India and Germany, League of Nations," Geneva, March 2, 1936, ibid., pp. 345–347.

67. Subhas Chandra Bose to Kitty Kurti, December 22, 1935, ibid., p. 126.

68. Kurti, *Subhas Chandra Bose as I Knew Him,* pp. 48–49.

69. J. W. Taylor to Subhas Chandra Bose, March 12, 1936, in Bose, *Netaji Collected Works,* vol. 8, p. 154.

70. Subhas Chandra Bose to Amiya Chakravarty, March 17, 1936, ibid., pp. 154–155.

71. Subhas Chandra Bose to Jawaharlal Nehru, March 13, 1936, ibid., pp. 155–157.

72. Jawaharlal Nehru to Subhas Chandra Bose, March 26, 1936, in Jawaharlal Nehru, *Selected Works,* vol. 7 (New Delhi: Orient Longman, 1972), p. 407; Home Department File 4/6/1936-Poll. (NAI).

73. Romain Rolland to Subhas Chandra Bose, March 20, 1936; Subhas Chandra Bose to Romain Rolland, March 25, 1936; both in Bose, *Netaji Collected Works,* vol. 8, pp. 161, 163.

74. Subhas Chandra Bose to Emilie Schenkl, March 1936, in Bose, *The Essential Writings of Netaji Subhas Chandra Bose,* pp. 160–161. Emilie Schenkl made this letter available on June 24, 1994, after a family celebration in Augsburg on the sixtieth anniversary of her first meeting with Subhas. "This is a love letter," Emilie said as she handed over the letter to her niece-in-law Krishna Bose. The letter itself is undated, but the envelope in which it came bears the postmark of March 5,

1936. On March 4 Subhas had written, "Today or tomorrow I shall write another letter to you. Please call for it. It is beautiful here and quiet. Plenty of snow. How are you?" (Bose, *Letters to Emilie*, p. 28). Subhas added at the bottom of the letter, "Please destroy after perusal." This historian is glad that Emilie disobeyed this instruction.

75. Subhas Chandra Bose to Emilie Schenkl, March 15, 1936, in Bose, *Letters to Emilie*, pp. 40–41.

76. My conversations with Emilie Schenkl, June 1993 and June 1994. In June 2008, during a visit to Badgastein with Krishna Bose, Anita Pfaff (daughter of Subhas and Emilie), Martin Pfaff, and Sumantra Bose, we were able to locate Kurhaus Hochland and Grüner Baum.

77. Subhas Chandra Bose to Sunil Mohan Ghosh Moulik, March 17, 1936, in Bose, *Netaji Collected Works*, vol. 8, pp. 160–161.

78. Subhas Chandra Bose to Naomi Vetter, March 26, 1936, ibid., p. 168.

79. Subhas Chandra Bose to Emilie Schenkl, March 26, 1935; March 28, 1935; in Bose, *Letters to Emilie*, pp. 44–49. The first letter included a corrected version of an article on the Balkans which Subhas wanted Emilie to send to the paper *Hindu* in India.

80. Subhas Chandra Bose to Emilie Schenkl, March 29, 1936, ibid., pp. 49–53.

81. Subhas Chandra Bose to Emilie Schenkl, March 31, 1936, ibid., pp. 56–57. For details of Bose's conversation with Nahas Pasha in January 1935, see "Passing through Cairo," in Bose, *Netaji Collected Works*, vol. 8, pp. 291–297.

82. Subhas Chandra Bose to Emilie Schenkl, March 30, 1936, in Bose, *Letters to Emilie*, pp. 53–56.

83. Subhas Chandra Bose to Emilie Schenkl, April 8, 1936; idem, May 11, 1936; both ibid., pp. 57–59.

84. Home Department File 4/6/1936-Poll. (NAI); Nehru, *Selected Works*, vol. 7, pp. 414–415.

85. Subhas Chandra Bose to Emilie Schenkl, May 11, 1936; idem, May 22, 1936; both in Bose, *Letters to Emilie*, pp. 58–61.

86. Subhas Chandra Bose to Santosh Kumar Basu, January 3, 1936, in Bose, *Netaji Collected Works*, vol. 8, pp. 129–130.

87. Subhas Chandra Bose, "Through Congress Eyes," ibid., pp. 355–357.

88. Subhas Chandra Bose to Emilie Schenkl, June 11, 1936; idem, June 22, 1936; both in Bose, *Letters to Emilie*, pp. 61–66; Sisir Kumar Bose, *Bosubari*, p. 66.

89. Home Department File 44/26/1936-Poll. (NAI).

90. Home Department File 22/92/1936-Poll. (NAI).

91. Home Department File 27/40/1936-Poll. (NAI).

92. Subhas Chandra Bose to Emilie Schenkl, July 15, 1936; Emilie Schenkl to Subhas Chandra Bose, August 17, 1936; both in Bose, *Letters to Emilie*, pp. 66–69, 77–80.

93. Subhas Chandra Bose to Jawaharlal Nehru, June 30, 1936, in Bose, *Netaji Collected Works,* vol. 8, pp. 175–176.

94. Subhas Chandra Bose to Kitty Kurti, July 25, 1936, ibid., pp. 179–181.

95. Subhas Chandra Bose to Emilie Schenkl, July 30, 1936; idem, August 12, 1936; idem, August 29, 1936; idem, September 12, 1936; idem, September 26, 1936; idem, November 9, 1936; idem, December 15, 1936; Emilie Schenkl to Subhas Chandra Bose, August 3, 1936; idem, August 17, 1936; idem, August 18, 1936; idem, September 8, 1936; idem, December 4, 1936; all in Bose, *Letters to Emilie,* pp. 69–97.

96. Subhas Chandra Bose to Emilie Schenkl, January 10, 1937, ibid., pp. 100–102.

97. Subhas Chandra Bose to Rabindranath Tagore, January 30, 1937, in Bose, *Netaji Collected Works,* vol. 8, p. 190.

98. Emilie Schenkl to Subhas Chandra Bose, January 1, 1937, in Bose, *Letters to Emilie,* pp. 97–100.

99. Subhas Chandra Bose to Naomi Vetter, February 3, 1937, in Bose, *Netaji Collected Works,* vol. 8, pp. 190–192.

100. Subhas Chandra Bose to Emilie Schenkl, March 15, 1937, in Bose, *Letters to Emilie,* pp. 114–115. For detailed medical reports on Bose, see Home Department File 22/113/1936-Poll. (NAI).

101. Government of India, Home Political File 44/26/36 (NAI).

102. Subhas Chandra Bose to Emilie Schenkl, March 18, 1937; idem, March 25, 1937; idem, April 5, 1937; all in Bose, *Letters to Emilie,* pp. 117–119, 121–122.

103. Subhas Chandra Bose, "Calcutta" (speech at public reception, April 6, 1937), in Bose, *Netaji Collected Works,* vol. 8, pp. 389–393; *Calcutta Municipal Gazette,* April 10, 1937.

104. Dilip Kumar Roy, *Netaji, the Man: Reminiscences* (Bombay: Bharatiya Vidya Bhavan, 1966), p. 133.

105. Subhas Chandra Bose to Emilie Schenkl, April 22, 1937; idem, May 1, 1937; idem, May 6, 1937; idem, May 11, 1937; Emilie Schenkl to Subhas Chandra Bose, May 20, 1937; all in Bose, *Letters to Emilie,* pp. 126–128, 130–133.

106. Subhas Chandra Bose to Sita Dharmavir, May 9, 1937; idem, May 22, 1937; idem, July 7, 1937; all in Bose, *Netaji Collected Works,* vol. 8, pp. 196, 199–200.

107. Subhas Chandra Bose to Emilie Schenkl, May 27, 1937; undated (May 1937); June 3, 1937; June 10, 1937; in Bose, *Letters to Emilie,* pp. 135–138, 141–143.

108. Subhas Chandra Bose to Anil Chandra Ganguly, August 8, 1937, in Bose, *Netaji Collected Works,* vol. 8, pp. 215–217.

109. Subhas Chandra Bose to Naomi Vetter, May 27, 1937, ibid., pp. 200–203.

110. Subhas Chandra Bose, "Europe—Today and Tomorrow," ibid., pp. 397–410.

111. Subhas Chandra Bose to Kitty Kurti, February 23, 1934, ibid., pp. 56–57.

112. Subhas Chandra Bose, "Japan's Role in the Far East," ibid., pp. 411–429.

113. Subhas Chandra Bose to E. Woods, September 9, 1937, ibid., pp. 225–226.

114. Subhas Chandra Bose to Emilie Schenkl, August 12, 1937; idem, August 19, 1937; idem, August 27, 1937; in Bose, *Letters to Emilie,* pp. 156–159.

115. Subhas Chandra Bose to Emilie Schenkl, October 13, 1937, ibid., pp. 173–174.

116. Sisir Kumar Bose, *Bosubari,* p. 72.

117. Subhas Chandra Bose to Jawaharlal Nehru, October 17, 1937, in Bose, *Netaji Collected Works,* vol. 8, pp. 226–227; Jawaharlal Nehru to Subhas Chandra Bose, October 20, 1937 (NMML).

118. Rabindranath Tagore to Subhas Chandra Bose, October 19, 1937; and Tagore's press statement on "Bande Mataram," October 30, 1937; both cited in Nepal Majumdar, *Rabindranath o Subhaschandra* (Calcutta: Saraswati, 1987), pp. 56–57, 59–60.

119. Majumdar, *Rabindranath o Subhaschandra,* pp. 60–66; Subhas Chandra Bose's letter to the editor, *Hindusthan Standard,* November 23, 1937, in Bose, *Netaji Collected Works,* vol. 8, pp. 435–436.

120. Sisir Kumar Bose, *Bosubari,* pp. 72–77.

121. Ibid., pp. 77–78; Subhas Chandra Bose, "On the Bengal Situation" (press statement, November 18, 1937), in Bose, *Netaji Collected Works,* vol. 8, pp. 434–435.

122. Subhas Chandra Bose to Mrs. J. Dharmavir, December 6, 1937, in Bose, *Netaji Collected Works,* vol. 8, pp. 234–235.

123. Subhas Chandra Bose to Emilie Schenkl, November 4, 1937; idem, November 16, 1937; in Bose, *Letters to Emilie,* pp. 174–176.

124. Subhas Chandra Bose to Maggiore Rapicavoli, November 25, 1937; idem, December 31, 1937; both in Bose, *Netaji Collected Works,* vol. 8, pp. 232–233, 238–239.

125. Subhas Chandra Bose to Mrs. J. Dharmavir, December 6, 1937, ibid., pp. 234–235.

126. Subhas Chandra Bose, *An Indian Pilgrim: Netaji Subhas Chandra Bose, Collected Works,* vol. 1, ed. Sisir K. Bose and Sugata Bose (Calcutta: Netaji Research Bureau; Delhi: Oxford University Press, 1997).

127. Ibid., pp. xii–xiii. The original manuscript is available in the archives of the Netaji Research Bureau.

128. Ibid., p. 56.

129. Ibid., pp. 118–124.

130. A. K. Chettiar, "I Meet Subhas-babu," *The Oracle,* 28, no. 1 (January 2008).

131. My conversations with Emilie Schenkl, June 1993. The secrecy resorted to by Subhas Chandra Bose and Emilie Schenkl caused some confusion about the date of their marriage, even within the family. Emilie Schenkl clearly told two other historians about the December 1937 marriage: first, B. R. Nanda, who interviewed

her for the Nehru Museum's oral history project on November 11, 1971; and second, Leonard A. Gordon, who interviewed her on October 14, 1978. She had asked Nanda not to include her answer in his typescript, but did not impose any such restriction on Gordon. See Leonard A. Gordon, *Brothers against the Raj: A Biography of Indian Nationalists Sarat and Subhas Chandra Bose* (New York: Columbia University Press, 1990), p. 701.

132. Subhas Chandra Bose to Emilie Schenkl, March 1936, in Bose, *The Essential Writings of Netaji Subhas Chandra Bose*, pp. 160–161. I have borrowed words and insights from Sisir K. Bose and P. Lal on the Subhas-Emilie relationship. See their speeches on the occasion of the "Release Ceremony of *Netaji Collected Works*, vol. 7: *Letters to Emilie Schenkl, 1934–1942*," *The Oracle*, 16, no. 3 (July 1994), 4–13.

133. Subhas Chandra Bose to Emilie Schenkl, January 8, 1938; idem, January 10, 1938; idem, January 11, 1938; all in Bose, *Letters to Emilie*, pp. 176–177.

134. Subhas Chandra Bose to the Marquis of Zetland, November 25, 1937, in Bose, *Netaji Collected Works*, vol. 8, pp. 233–234.

135. *Calcutta Municipal Gazette*, January 15, 1938.

136. Subhas Chandra Bose to Emilie Schenkl, January 16, 1938, in Bose, *Letters to Emilie*, pp. 177–178.

137. *Calcutta Municipal Gazette*, January 15, 1938.

138. Subhas Chandra Bose, "On Congress and the Constitution, Fascism and Communism" (report of an interview with Rajani Palme Dutt, published in the *Daily Worker*, January 24, 1938), in Subhas Chandra Bose, *Congress President: Netaji Subhas Chandra Bose, Collected Works*, vol. 9, ed. Sisir K. Bose and Sugata Bose (Calcutta: Netaji Research Bureau; Delhi: Permanent Black, 2004), pp. 1–3.

139. Lord Zetland's report on his meeting with Subhas Chandra Bose, Government of India, L/PO/57 (IOR, BL).

140. Government of India, L/PO/57 (IOR, BL) and *Calcutta Municipal Gazette*, January 22, 1938.

141. *News Chronicle*, January 11, 1938, in L/PO/57 (IOR, BL).

142. Subhas Chandra Bose to E. Woods, December 18, 1937; idem, December 30, 1937; both in Bose, *Netaji Collected Works*, vol. 8, pp. 236–238.

143. Subhas Chandra Bose to E. Woods, January 16, 1938, in Bose, *Congress President*, p. 252.

144. Subhas Chandra Bose to Naomi Vetter, January 21, 1938, ibid., p. 253.

145. *Manchester Guardian*, January 1938, cited in Bose, Werth, and Ayer, *A Beacon across Asia*, p. 71.

146. Subhas Chandra Bose to Emilie Schenkl, January 16, 1938; idem, January 19, 1938; idem, January 20, 1938; idem, January 21, 1938; all in Bose, *Letters to Emilie*, pp. 177–179.

147. Hemendranath Dasgupta, *Subhas Chandra* (Calcutta: Jyoti Prakashalaya, 1946), p. 155.

148. Subhas Chandra Bose to Emilie Schenkl, January 24, 1938; idem, January 25, 1938; idem, February 8, 1938; all in Bose, *Letters to Emilie*, pp. 179–182.

5. The Warrior and the Saint

1. Aurobindo Ghose [Sri Aurobindo], "The Morality of Boycott," in idem, *The Doctrine of Passive Resistance* (Calcutta: Arya Publishing House, 1948), pp. 87–88.

2. Subhas Chandra Bose to Emilie Schenkl, February 8, 1938, in Subhas Chandra Bose, *Letters to Emilie Schenkl: Netaji Subhas Chandra Bose, Collected Works*, vol. 7, ed. Sisir K. Bose and Sugata Bose (Calcutta: Netaji Research Bureau; Delhi: Permanent Black, 2004), pp. 181–182.

3. Sisir Kumar Bose, *Bosubari* (Calcutta: Ananda, 1985), pp. 79–81.

4. Subhas Chandra Bose to Basanti Devi, February 6, 1938, in Subhas Chandra Bose, *Congress President: Netaji Subhas Chandra Bose, Collected Works*, vol. 9, ed. Sisir K. Bose and Sugata Bose (Calcutta: Netaji Research Bureau; Delhi: Permanent Black, 2004), p. 257.

5. Nandalal Bose, *Vision and Creation* (Calcutta: Visva Bharati, 1999), p. 235.

6. Video and audio recording (NRB).

7. "The Haripura Address," in Bose, *Congress President*, pp. 3–6.

8. Ibid., pp. 6–15.

9. Ibid., pp. 15–16.

10. Subhas Chandra Bose to Sita Dharmavir, July 7, 1937, in Subhas Chandra Bose, *Netaji Subhas Chandra Bose, Collected Works*, vol. 8, ed. Sisir K. Bose and Sugata Bose (Calcutta: Netaji Research Bureau; Delhi: Oxford University Press, 1994), pp. 209–210.

11. "The Haripura Address," in Bose, *Congress President*, pp. 15–16.

12. Ibid., p. 16.

13. Ibid., p. 13.

14. Ibid., pp. 24–25.

15. Ibid., pp. 27–30.

16. Photographs, audio recordings, and video recordings (NRB). A. K. Chettiar, "I Meet Subhas-babu," *The Oracle*, 30, no. 1 (January 2008), 58.

17. Subhas Chandra Bose to Emilie Schenkl, March 6, 1938, in Bose, *Letters to Emilie*, pp. 182–183.

18. *Time*, March 7, 1938.

19. "Municipal Socialism," in Bose, *Congress President*, pp. 31–35.

20. "Science and Politics," ibid., pp. 43–48.

21. "The Industrial Problems of India," ibid., pp. 48–53.

22. Subhas Chandra Bose to Jawaharlal Nehru, October 19, 1938, ibid., p. 183.

23. Jawaharlal Nehru to Subhas Chandra Bose, June 21, 1939, in Jawaharlal Nehru, *Selected Works*, vol. 9 (New Delhi: Orient Longman, 1972–1982), p. 397.

24. Subhas Chandra Bose to Emilie Schenkl, May 9, 1938, in Bose, *Letters to Emilie*, pp. 186–188.

25. Jawaharlal Nehru to M. A. Jinnah, March 17, 1938, in Jawaharlal Nehru, *A Bunch of Old Letters* (Delhi: Oxford University Press, 1989), p. 278.

26. Ayesha Jalal, *The Sole Spokesman: Jinnah, the Muslim League and the Demand for Pakistan* (Cambridge: Cambridge University Press, 1985).

27. Subhas Chandra Bose to M. A. Jinnah, May 15, 1938; idem, June 21, 1938; idem, June 27, 1938; idem, July 25, 1938; idem, August 16, 1938; idem, October 2, 1938; idem, December 16, 1938; M. A. Jinnah to Subhas Chandra Bose, May 16, 1938; idem, June 6, 1938; idem, August 2, 1938; idem, October 9, 1938; all in Bose, *Congress President*, pp. 112–122.

28. M. K. Gandhi, "That Unfortunate Walkout," *Harijan*, 6 (October 15, 1938).

29. N. B. Khare, *My Political Memoirs* (Nagpur: J. R. Joshi, 1959), pp. 48–49.

30. "On the Federal Scheme," in Bose, *Congress President*, pp. 39–43.

31. Sugata Bose, *Agrarian Bengal: Economy, Social Structure and Politics, 1919–1947* (Cambridge: Cambridge University Press, 1986), p. 206.

32. Sarat Chandra Bose to Jawaharlal Nehru, August 14, 1937, AICC Papers, File P-5, 1937 (NMML).

33. Bose, *Agrarian Bengal*, pp. 206–210.

34. Mahatma Gandhi to Subhas Chandra Bose, December 18, 1938, in Mahatma Gandhi, *Collected Works*, vol. 68 (Delhi: Government of India, 1958–1983), p. 218; Subhas Chandra Bose to Mahatma Gandhi, December 21, 1938, in Bose, *Congress President*, pp. 122–126.

35. Subhas Chandra Bose to Mahatma Gandhi, December 21, 1938, in Bose, *Congress President*, p. 125.

36. "Congress Medical Mission to China"; Subhas Chandra Bose to Amala Nundy (Shankar), November 11, 1938; S. C. Bose, "The European Crisis: Analysis of the Debacle"; idem, "On Kemal Atatürk"; all in Bose, *Congress President*, pp. 36–39, 58–61, 279.

37. Mahatma Gandhi to Amrit Kaur, June 25, 1938, in Gandhi, *Collected Works*, vol. 67, p. 137.

38. Subhas Chandra Bose to Mrs. J. Dharmavir, March 22, 1938, in Bose, *Congress President*, pp. 260–261.

39. Subhas Chandra Bose to Emilie Schenkl, March 28, 1938; idem, April 5, 1938; idem, April 9, 1938; idem, May 9, 1938; idem, May 20, 1938; idem, May 24, 1938; idem, May 26, 1938; idem, June 8, 1938; idem, June 26, 1938; idem, June 27, 1938; idem, July 8, 1938; idem, July 14, 1938; idem, July 27, 1938; idem, September 3, 1938; idem, October 13, 1938; idem, October 17, 1938; idem, October 19, 1938; idem, December 6, 1938; idem, December 10, 1938; idem, December 26, 1938; all in Bose, *Letters to Emilie*, pp. 183–206.

40. Subhas Chandra Bose to Emilie Schenkl, December 6, 1938, ibid., pp. 203–204.

41. Nepal Majumdar, *Rabindranath o Subhaschandra* (Calcutta: Saraswat Library, 1968), pp. 93–107; Gandhi, *Collected Works,* vol. 68, pp. 144, 161.

42. Milan Hauner, *India in Axis Strategy: Germany, Japan and Indian Nationalists in the Second World War* (Stuttgart: Klett-Cotta, 1981), pp. 644–653.

43. Subhas Chandra Bose to Emilie Schenkl, January 4, 1939, in Bose, *Letters to Emilie,* pp. 206–207.

44. Rabindranath Tagore to Subhas Chandra Bose, November 20, 1938; idem, December 12, 1938; idem, January 14, 1938; idem, January 19, 1938; Subhas Chandra Bose to Rabindranath Tagore, December 14, 1938; all in Bose, *Congress President,* pp. 236–239.

45. "Tagore's Call to Bose" and "Bose's Response to Tagore," ibid., pp. 240–246.

46. "The Tripuri Presidential Election Debate," ibid., pp. 67–87.

47. Sisir Kumar Bose, *Bosubari,* pp. 86–87.

48. Nripendra Nath Mitra, *The Indian Annual Register January to June 1939* (Calcutta: Annual Register Office, 1939), pp. 45–46.

49. These telegrams are available in the archives of the Netaji Research Bureau. One cable from Gujarat lamented the inability of that province to join the radical tide.

50. "Statement of Mahatma Gandhi," January 31, 1939; "Statement of Subhas Chandra Bose, February 4, 1939"; both in Bose, *Congress President,* pp. 87–90.

51. M. N. Roy to Subhas Chandra Bose, February 1, 1939, ibid., pp. 280–283.

52. Subhas Chandra Bose to Emilie Schenkl, February 11, 1939, in Bose, *Letters to Emilie,* pp. 208–209.

53. "My Strange Illness," in Bose, *Congress President,* pp. 95–101.

54. "The Tripuri Address," ibid., pp. 90–94.

55. "My Strange Illness," ibid., p. 103.

56. Rabindranath Tagore to Mahatma Gandhi, March 29, 1939; Mahatma Gandhi to Rabindranath Tagore, April 2, 1939; both quoted in Majumdar, *Rabindranath o Subhaschandra,* p. 133.

57. Mahatma Gandhi to Subhas Chandra Bose, March 24, 1939; idem, March 25, 1939; idem, March 26, 1939; idem, March 30, 1939; idem, March 31, 1939; idem, April 1, 1939; idem, April 2, 1939; idem, April 4, 1939; idem, April 5, 1939; Subhas Chandra Bose to Mahatma Gandhi, March 24, 1939; idem, March 25, 1939; idem, March 26, 1939; idem, March 29, 1939; idem, March 31, 1939; idem, April 1, 1939; idem, April 3, 1939; idem, April 5, 1939; all in Bose, *Congress President,* pp. 126–149.

58. Subhas Chandra Bose to Mahatma Gandhi, April 6, 1939, ibid., pp. 149–155.

59. Subhas Chandra Bose to Mahatma Gandhi, April 7, 1939; idem, April 10,

1939; idem, April 13, 1939; Mahatma Gandhi to Subhas Chandra Bose, April 7, 1939; idem, April 10, 1939; all ibid., pp. 156–172.

60. Subhas Chandra Bose to Jawaharlal Nehru, March 28, 1939, ibid., pp. 193–216.

61. Taya Zinkin, *Reporting India* (London: Chatto and Windus, 1962), p. 217.

62. Jawaharlal Nehru to Subhas Chandra Bose, April 3, 1939, in Bose, *Congress President,* pp. 217–232.

63. Jawaharlal Nehru to Mahatma Gandhi, April 17, 1939, in Nehru, *Selected Works,* vol. 9, pp. 553–554.

64. Rabindranath Tagore to Subhas Chandra Bose, April 3, 1939, in Bose, *Congress President,* p. 250.

65. Subhas Chandra Bose to Jawaharlal Nehru, April 15, 1939; idem, April 20, 1939; Jawaharlal Nehru to Subhas Chandra Bose, April 17, 1939; Subhas Chandra Bose to Mahatma Gandhi, April 15, 1939; idem, April 20, 1939; all ibid., pp. 173–176, 178–180, 233–236.

66. Subhas Chandra Bose to Mahatma Gandhi, April 22, 1939; Mahatma Gandhi to Subhas Chandra Bose, April 29, 1939; both ibid., pp. 180–181.

67. "Statement on Resignation from Congress Presidentship," ibid., pp. 107–109.

68. Rabindranath Tagore to Subhas Chandra Bose, April 30, 1939, ibid., p. 109.

69. Rabindranath Tagore, "Deshnayak," ibid., pp. 247–249.

70. "My Strange Illness," ibid., pp. 101–106.

71. Subhas Chandra Bose to Emilie Schenkl, May, 14, 1939; idem, June 16, 1939; idem, June 21, 1939; idem, July 4, 1939; in Bose, *Letters to Emilie,* pp. 211–215.

72. "Glimpses of My Tour"; Dr. Satyapal to Subhas Chandra Bose, January 23, 1940; Mian Akbar Shah to Subhas Chandra Bose, February 19, 1940; idem, February 29, 1940; N. G. Ranga to Subhas Chandra Bose, February 20, 1940; Indulal Yagnik to Subhas Chandra Bose, February 20, 1940; idem, March 2, 1940; Swami Sahajanand Saraswati to Subhas Chandra Bose, February 28, 1940; all in Subhas Chandra Bose, *The Alternative Leadership: Netaji Subhas Chandra Bose, Collected Works,* vol. 10, ed. Sisir K. Bose and Sugata Bose (Calcutta: Netaji Research Bureau; Delhi: Permanent Black, 2004), pp. 20–31, 206–209, 211–214.

73. "Glimpses of My Tour," in Bose, *Alternative Leadership,* pp. 30–31.

74. Bengal Provincial Congress Committee, *Working Committee and Bengal Congress* (Calcutta: BPCC, 1940), pp. 1–20; Mitra, *Indian Annual Register, July–December 1939,* pp. 224–225, 271–275; AICC Papers, File P-5, 1939–1940 (NMML).

75. "Statement on Disciplinary Action," in Bose, *Alternative Leadership,* pp. 7–8.

76. "The House of the Nation: Mahajati Sadan," ibid., pp. 8–10.

77. Audio and video recording of Tagore's speech (NRB). My translation.

78. "The Need of the Hour," August 26, 1939, in Bose, *Alternative Leadership,* pp. 13–15.

79. Subhas Chandra Bose to Emilie Schenkl, April 19, 1939; idem, June 21, 1939; idem, July 6, 1939; all in Bose, *Letters to Emilie,* pp. 209–211, 213–216.

80. Subhas Chandra Bose, *The Indian Struggle: Netaji Subhas Chandra Bose, Collected Works,* vol. 2, ed. Sisir K. Bose and Sugata Bose (Calcutta: Netaji Research Bureau; Delhi: Oxford University Press, 1997), p. 379.

81. "Heart Searching," in Bose, *Alternative Leadership,* pp. 18–20.

82. Bose, *Indian Struggle,* p. 381.

83. Mitra, *Indian Annual Register, June–December 1939,* pp. 40–45.

84. Phanu Bhusan Chakravarti (Acting Governor of West Bengal), "Presidential Address" after Hari Vidhnu Kamath's Netaji Oration, January 23, 1963, in *Bulletin of the Netaji Research Bureau,* January 1964.

85. Rabindranath Tagore to Mahatma Gandhi, December 1939; Mahatma Gandhi to C. F. Andrews, January 15, 1940; Gandhi, "The Charkha," in *Harijan,* January 13, 1940; all in Gandhi, *Collected Works,* vol. 71, pp. 50, 94, 113–114.

86. "The Correct Line," in Bose, *Alternative Leadership,* pp. 50–53.

87. "An Address to Students of India," ibid., pp. 58–64.

88. *Proceedings of the Bengal Legislative Assembly,* 55, no. 3 (December 13, 1939), 71–80. Sarat is quoting Roger Casement.

89. "Danger Ahead," in Bose, *Alternative Leadership,* pp. 64–68.

90. "Stem the Rot," ibid., pp. 72–75.

91. "The Ramgarh Address," ibid., pp. 83–88.

92. "The New Parade," ibid., pp. 96–98.

93. Ayesha Jalal, *Self and Sovereignty: Individual and Community in South Asian Islam since 1850* (New York: Routledge, 2000), pp. 396–399.

94. Abul Mansur Ahmed, *Amaar Dekha Rajnitir Panchash Bachhar* [Fifty Years of Politics as I Saw It] (Dhaka: Khishroj, 1984), pp. 147–150.

95. "Congress and Communal Organizations," in Bose, *Alternative Leadership,* pp. 98–100.

96. Ibid. See also Subhas Chandra Bose to M. A. H. Ispahani, October 14, 1940, ibid., p. 221.

97. Abul Mansur Ahmed, *Amaar Dekha Rajnitir Panchash Bachhar,* pp. 150–154.

98. "Act Quickly," in Bose, *Alternative Leadership,* pp. 103–104.

99. "A Provisional National Government," ibid., pp. 109–111.

100. "Long Live Deshbandhu," ibid., pp. 111–112.

101. "The Nagpur Address," June 18, 1940, ibid., pp. 115–126.

102. "Task before the Country," June 29, 1940, ibid., pp. 126–128.

103. "Holwell Monument," ibid., pp. 128–129.

104. Krishna Bose, *Prasanga Subhaschandra* (Calcutta: Ananda, 1993), pp. 167–171.

105. Subhas Chandra Bose to Sarat Chandra Bose, October 24, 1940; idem, October 31, 1940; both in Bose, *Alternative Leadership,* pp. 158–161.

106. "On the Bengal Congress Tangle," ibid., pp. 144–152.

107. "My Conscience Is My Own," ibid., pp. 143–144.

6. One Man and a World at War

1. The legend was based on Jonathan Holwell's exaggerated "eyewitness" account propagated by Macaulay and Curzon. See Nicholas Dirks, *The Scandal of Empire* (Cambridge, Mass.: Harvard University Press, 2006), pp. 1–5; Brijen K. Gupta, *Sirajuddaullah and the East India Company, 1756–1757: Background to the Foundation of British Power in India* (Leiden: E. J. Brill, 1966), pp. 70–80.

2. Subhas Chandra Bose to H.E. The Governor of Bengal, The Hon. Chief Minister and the Council of Ministers, November 26, 1940, in Subhas Chandra Bose, *The Alternative Leadership: Netaji Subhas Chandra Bose, Collected Works,* vol. 10, ed. Sisir K. Bose and Sugata Bose (Calcutta: Netaji Research Bureau; Delhi: Permanent Black, 1998, 2004), p. 197.

3. Subhas Chandra Bose to The Hon. Chief Minister and the Council of Ministers, December 2, 1940, ibid., p. 199.

4. Governor John Herbert to Viceroy Linlithgow, August 22, 1940, L/P&J/S/147 (IOR, BL).

5. Viceroy Linlithgow to Secretary of State for India, December 6, 1940, L/P&J 5562 (IOR, BL).

6. Governor John Herbert to Viceroy Linlithgow, December 11, 1940, L/P&J/S/147 and R/3/2/16 (IOR, BL).

7. The man who took the photographs in Badgastein in December 1937 saw them displayed in Bose's bedroom when he visited in 1940. See A. K. Chettiar, "I Meet Subhas-babu," *The Oracle,* 28, no. 1 (January 2008).

8. Herbert to Linlithgow, December 11, 1940, L/P&J/S/147 and R/3/2/16 (IOR, BL).

9. Report by agent C207 in "Secret" file labeled "Activities of Subhas Chandra Bose since his release from Jail on 5.12.40," R/3/2/16-17-18 (IOR, BL), p. 2. There were at least fourteen secret police agents keeping watch on Bose; they were numbered AS95, AS249, C107, C112, C115, C116, C195, C207, CB18, CB21, JP97, JP312, TL31, and TP52, and their reports were compiled in this dossier.

10. Sisir Kumar Bose, *The Great Escape* (Calcutta: Netaji Research Bureau, 2000), p. 4.

11. Ibid., p. 7.

12. Report by agent C207 in "Secret" file labeled "Activities of Subhas Chandra Bose," p. 2.

13. Sisir Kumar Bose, *Great Escape,* pp. 14–18; Mian Akbar Shah, "Netaji's Escape: An Untold Chapter," in Bose, *Great Escape,* Appendix 1, p. 75.

14. Bose, *Alternative Leadership,* p. 155.

15. "Secret" file labeled "Activities of Subhas Chandra Bose," p. 5. On the same day, agent CB21 reported that Bose was planning to start an agitation against the sales tax on Independence Day, January 26, 1941.

16. Sisir Kumar Bose, *Great Escape,* pp. 24–28.

17. Ibid., pp. 28–31.

18. Sisir Kumar Bose, *Bosubari* (Calcutta: Ananda, 1985), p. 111.

19. Sisir Kumar Bose, *Great Escape,* pp. 31–39.

20. Ibid., pp. 39–40.

21. Mian Akbar Shah, "Netaji's Great Escape," pp. 78–81; Krishna Bose, "Netajir Shange Mian Akbar Shah," in Krishna Bose, *Prasanga Subhaschandra* (Calcutta: Ananda, 1993), pp. 117–125.

22. Mian Akbar Shah, "Netaji's Great Escape," pp. 78–81; "Bhagat Ram's Story," Interrogation Report on Bhagat Ram Talwar following his arrest in November 1942, WO 208/773 (TNA), pp. 1–2; Bhagat Ram Talwar, "My Fifty-five Days with Netaji Subhas Chandra Bose," in Sisir Kumar Bose, ed., *Netaji and India's Freedom* (Calcutta: Netaji Research Bureau, 1975), pp. 159–161. Bhagat Ram Talwar's accounts are slightly inaccurate with respect to the exact dates, which I have cross-checked with other sources. See Sisir Kumar Bose, *Great Escape,* p. 60.

23. Mian Akbar Shah, "Netaji's Great Escape," p. 85; "Bhagat Ram's Story," WO 208/773 (TNA), p. 2; Bhagat Ram Talwar, "My Fifty-five Days," pp. 161–177; Sisir Kumar Bose, *Great Escape,* p. 60. I have corrected the inaccuracies in reporting exact dates in Bhagat Ram Talwar's accounts.

24. Sisir Kumar Bose, *Great Escape,* pp. 40–43.

25. Viceroy Linlithgow to Secretary of State, January 30, 1941, L/P&J/400 (BL, IOR).

26. Government of India, Home Department, Political Confidential File 135/41 (NAI).

27. Sisir Kumar Bose, *Remembering My Father* (Calcutta: Netaji Research Bureau, 1988), pp. 108–109.

28. Home Political 135/41 (NAI); J. V. B. Janvrin, Secret report "Subhas Bose" dated January 27, 1941; J. V. B. Janvrin, Special Branch, Calcutta, to G. H. Puckle, Intelligence Bureau, New Delhi, January 29, 1941, R/3/2/20–21–22 (IOR, BL).

29. J. G. Laithwaite, Viceroy's House, New Delhi, to M. O. Carter, Governor's House, Calcutta, February 4, 1941, R/3/2/20 (IOR, BL).

30. Home Political 135/41 (NAI).

31. Sisir Kumar Bose, *Great Escape,* p. 40.

32. "Bhagat Ram's Story," WO 208/773 (TNA), p. 2; Bhagat Ram Talwar, "My Fifty-five Days," pp. 180–185.

33. Telegram from Pilger, Kabul, to Reich Foreign Minister, Berlin, February 5, 1941, Political Department (GFO archives).

34. Woermann to State Secretary, February 8, 1941, Political Department (GFO archives).

35. "Bhagat Ram's Story," WO 208/773 (TNA), p. 3; Bhagat Ram Talwar, "My Fifty-five Days," pp. 192–210.

36. Quaroni, Kabul, to Italian Foreign Office, Rome, "Plan of Indian Revolution: Report of an Interview, Kabul, April 2, 1941, Sub: Subhas Chandra Bose— His Proposals about India, in continuation of telegram no. 124," in Subhas Chandra Bose, *Azad Hind: Writings and Speeches 1941–1943, Netaji Subhas Chandra Bose, Collected Works,* vol. 11, ed. Sisir K. Bose and Sugata Bose (Calcutta: Netaji Research Bureau; Delhi: Permanent Black, 1998, 2002), p. 36.

37. Bhagat Ram Talwar, "My Fifty-five Days," p. 215.

38. Special Operations Executive (SOE) war diary, March 7, 1941, HS7/217 (TNA).

39. Count Friedrich Werner von der Schulenburg, Moscow, to German Foreign Minister, Berlin, March 3, 1941, Political Department (GFO archives).

40. Subhas Chandra Bose, "Forward Bloc: Its Justification," Kabul thesis, March 1941, in Bose, *Azad Hind,* pp. 13–14, 27–29, 31. The original handwritten manuscript is in the archives of the Netaji Research Bureau.

41. Count Friedrich Werner von der Schulenburg, Moscow, to German Foreign Minister, Berlin, March 31, 1941 (GFO, microfilm in NRB).

42. Subhas Chandra Bose, *Letters to Emilie Schenkl, 1934–1942, Netaji Subhas Chandra Bose, Collected Works,* vol. 7, ed. Sisir K. Bose and Sugata Bose (Calcutta: Netaji Research Bureau; Delhi: Permanent Black, 1994, 2004), p. 216.

43. Subhas Chandra Bose to Emilie Schenkl, June 15/21, 1939, and July 4/6, 1939, ibid., pp. 214–215.

44. Subhas Chandra Bose to Emilie Schenkl, April 3, 1941, ibid., p. 217.

45. See Kris Manjapra, "The Mirrored World" (Ph.D. diss., Harvard University, 2007).

46. On Sarat Chandra Bose's visit to Rabindranath Tagore, see Sisir Kumar Bose, *Bosubari,* p. 142. The title of Tagore's short story is "Badnaam."

7. The Terrible Price of Freedom

1. Subhas Chandra Bose, "After Paris," in Subhas Chandra Bose, *The Alternative Leadership: Netaji Subhas Chandra Bose, Collected Works,* vol. 10, ed. Sisir K. Bose and Sugata Bose (Calcutta: Netaji Research Bureau; Delhi: Permanent Black, 2004), pp. 112–114.

2. A. C. N. Nambiar, "Foreword," in N. G. Ganpuley, *Netaji in Germany: A Little-Known Chapter* (Bombay: Bharatiya Vidya Bhavan, 1959), p. viii. See also the discussion in M. R. Vyas, *Passage through a Turbulent Era: Historical Reminiscences of the Fateful Years, 1937–47* (Bombay: Indo-Foreign Publications, 1982), pp. 266–272.

3. Quaroni, Kabul, to Italian Foreign Office, Rome, "Plan of Indian Revolution: Report of an Interview, Kabul, April 2, 1941, Sub: Subhas Chandra Bose—His Proposals about India, in continuation of telegram no. 124," in Subhas Chandra Bose, *Azad Hind: Writings and Speeches, 1941–1943, Netaji Subhas Chandra Bose, Collected Works,* vol. 11, ed. Sisir K. Bose and Sugata Bose (Calcutta: Netaji Research Bureau; Delhi: Permanent Black, 1998, 2002), pp. 34–37.

4. "Secret Memorandum to the German Government," Berlin, April 9, 1941, ibid., pp. 38–49.

5. "Record of Conversations between Ribbentrop and Bose, 1941–1942" (GFO).

6. "Supplementary Memorandum to the German Government," Berlin, May 3, 1941, in Bose, *Azad Hind,* pp. 50–52.

7. "Draft of the Free India Declaration by Mazzotta," May 1941, AA-A/Kult.R., vol. 8, England (GFO), reproduced ibid., pp. 57–58.

8. O. Mazzotta to Dr. Woermann, July 5, 1941, ibid., p. 59.

9. "Report of a Conversation with the German Foreign Office," by Woermann, July 17, 1941, ibid., pp. 60–62.

10. Gieselher Wirsing, *Indien-Asiens Gefährliche Jahre* (Düsseldorf: Diederichs, 1968), pp. 8–9.

11. Subhas Chandra Bose to Joachim von Ribbentrop, August 15, 1941, in Bose, *Azad Hind,* pp. 63–65.

12. Interview of A. C. N. Nambiar by Sisir K. Bose and Krishna Bose, 1971 (NRB); Krishna Bose, *Itihaser Sandhane* (Calcutta: Ananda, 1972), pp. 99–102; "Statement of A. C. N. Nambiar," September 17, 1945 (TNA), pp. 9–20; A. C. N. Nambiar, "A Memorable Meeting in Paris with Netaji Subhas Chandra Bose," *The Oracle,* 4, no. 1 (January 1982), 61–62.

13. "Swami: Notes Taken in Singapore, Sept./Oct. 1945, When Swami Came to Tea" (TNA); interview of Abid Hasan by Sisir K. Bose, Krishna Bose, Sugata Bose, and Rabindra Kumar Ghosh, transcribed by Sarmila Bose, published as Abid Hasan, "A Soldier Remembers," *The Oracle,* 6, no. 1 (January 1984), 24–28.

14. Girija Mookerjee, *This Europe* (Calcutta: Saraswaty Library, 1950), p. 131; Vyas, *Passage through a Turbulent Era,* pp. 271, 310–311.

15. Alexander Werth, "An Eye-Witness Account of Indian Freedom Struggle in Europe during World War II," in Alexander Werth and Walter Harbich, *Netaji in Germany* (Calcutta: Netaji Research Bureau, 1970), pp. 14–16.

16. Viceroy of India to Secretary of State for India, May 26, 1941, L/PS/12/487 (IOR, BL).

17. SOE (Special Operations Executive) war diary, 16/17 June 1941, HS7/220. Italian minister, Kabul, to Rome, March 26, 1941, HW12/263 (TNA).

18. SOE war diary, June 18, 1941, HS7/220 (TNA).

19. Vyas, *Passage through a Turbulent Era,* p. 324.

20. Walter Harbich, "A Report on the Organization and Training of the Free

India Army in Europe, 1941–42," in Werth and Harbich, *Netaji in Germany,* p. 53.

21. Hugh Toye, *The Springing Tiger: A Study of Subhas Chandra Bose* (London: Cassell, 1959), p. 70.

22. Hasan, "A Soldier Remembers," pp. 29–32.

23. Ganpuley, *Netaji in Germany,* p. 95.

24. Hasan, "A Soldier Remembers," pp. 42–44.

25. Sisir K. Bose, *The Great Escape* (Calcutta: Netaji Research Bureau, 2000), pp. 47–48, 58–59; "Bhagat Ram's Story" (TNA).

26. Most Secret File C/7488, for Prime Minister enclosing B. J. Report no. 095161, September 5, 1941, initialed "C" by Churchill, HW 1/48 (TNA).

27. Sisir K. Bose, *Remembering My Father* (Calcutta: Netaji Research Bureau, 1988), pp. 109–114; Home Political File 94/26/41 (NAI); Governor of Bengal to Viceroy of India, December 7, 1941; idem, December 8, 1941; idem, December 9, 1941; idem, December 10, 1941; A. K. Fazlul Huq to John Herbert, Governor of Bengal, December 10, 1941; J. G. Laithwaite, Viceroy's Camp, Patna, to M. O. Carter, Governor's House, Calcutta (enclosing Secretary of State L. S. Amery's telegram to Viceroy Linlithgow dated December 10, 1941), December 11, 1941; all in R/3/2/30 (IOR, BL).

28. Sisir K. Bose, S. A. Ayer, and Alexander Werth, *A Beacon across Asia* (Bombay: Orient Longman, 1973), pp. 133–134.

29. "The Fall of Singapore," Bose's broadcast on Azad Hind Radio, February 19, 1941, in Bose, *Azad Hind,* pp. 67–68.

30. Krishna Bose, *Itihaser Sandhane,* p. 31.

31. "India Has No Enemy outside Her Own Frontiers," March 19, 1942, in Bose, *Azad Hind,* pp. 75–79.

32. Mohandas Gandhi, *The Collected Works of Mahatma Gandhi,* vol. 76 (New Delhi: Government of India Publications Division, 1958–1978), pp. 87, 105, 114, 120, 242, 381.

33. Linlithgow, Viceroy of India, to L. S. Amery, Secretary of State for India, January 21, 1942, in Nicholas Mansergh, ed., *The Transfer of Power,* vol. 1 (London: HMG, 1970–1983), doc. 23.

34. "Draft Declaration on India," February 22, 1942, reproduced in facsimile from the GFO archives in Sisir Kumar Bose, ed., *Netaji and India's Freedom* (Calcutta: Netaji Research Bureau, 1975), pp. 306–309.

35. German naval staff memoranda of February 12 and 20, 1942, and Raeder-Hitler naval conferences on February 13, March 12, and April 13, 1942, cited in Milan Hauner, "India and the Axis Powers," in Sisir Kumar Bose, ed., *Netaji and India's Freedom,* p. 292.

36. Milan Hauner, *India in Axis Strategy: Germany, Japan and Indian Nationalists in the Second World War* (Stuttgart: Klett-Cotta, 1981), pp. 402, 429–435.

37. "My Death Is Perhaps an Instance of Wishful Thinking," in Bose, *Azad*

Hind, pp. 80–83; Vyas, *Passage through a Turbulent Era,* pp. 365–367; Sisir Kumar Bose, *Bosubari* (Calcutta: Ananda, 1985), p. 147.

38. Abul Kalam Azad, *India Wins Freedom* (Hyderabad: Orient Longman, 1988), p. 40.

39. Hauner, *India in Axis Strategy,* pp. 446–448.

40. Martin Bormann's record of Hitler's ruminations in February 1945, in *The Testament of Adolf Hitler* (Boring, Oregon: CPA Book Publisher, 1990), p. 21.

41. Luigi Barzini, "With Chandra Bose in His Home," *Popolo d'Italia,* April 19, 1942.

42. Galeazzo Ciano, *Ciano's Diary, 1939–1943,* ed. Malcolm Muggeridge (London: William Heinemann, 1947), p. 465.

43. "My Allegiance," in Bose, *Azad Hind,* pp. 94–99.

44. Subhas Chandra Bose to Joachim von Ribbentrop, May 22, 1942, ibid., pp. 100–101.

45. "Bose-Hitler Interview," English translation of Paul Schmidt's account in the GFO archives, in Sisir Kumar Bose, ed., *Netaji and India's Freedom,* pp. 310–315.

46. Ibid.

47. Werth and Harbich, *Netaji in Germany,* p. 36; Mookerjee, *This Europe,* p. 134; Krishna Bose, "Hitler o Netaji," in *Prasanga Subhaschandra* (Calcutta: Ananda, 1993), p. 87.

48. Rajmohan Gandhi, *Mohandas: The Man, His People and the Empire* (Delhi: Penguin, 2007), p. 421.

49. "Differentiate between Internal and External Policy," June 17, 1942, in Bose, *Azad Hind,* pp. 117–121.

50. Gandhi, *Collected Works,* vol. 76, pp. 87, 105, 114, 120, 242, 381.

51. Cited in Hauner, *India in Axis Strategy,* p. 493.

52. "The Quit India Movement," August 17, 1942, in Bose, *Azad Hind,* pp. 132–139.

53. "The USA, Britain and India," October 15, 1942, ibid., pp. 162–169.

54. "The Quit India Movement," August 17, 1942, ibid., pp. 132–139.

55. Ganpuley, *Netaji in Germany,* p. 89.

56. Mookerjee, *This Europe,* pp. 139, 153.

57. Vyas, *Passage through a Turbulent Era,* p. 326.

58. Hasan, "A Soldier Remembers," 40–41.

59. Toye, *The Springing Tiger,* pp. 68–69; Hauner, "India and the Axis Powers," in Bose, *Netaji and India's Freedom,* p. 301.

60. Toye, *The Springing Tiger,* p. 74.

61. "Free India and Her Problems," in Bose, *Azad Hind,* pp. 148–156.

62. "India and Germany," ibid., pp. 157–161.

63. Krishna Bose, *Itihaser Sandhane,* p. 102.

64. My conversations with Emilie Schenkl, 1993.

65. "Statement of A. C. N. Nambiar," September 17, 1945 (TNA), paragraphs 160–179; Bureau of Secretary of State, India, Serial no. 195, vol. 3, 13955–140026 (GFO, microfilm in NRB).

66. Subhas Chandra Bose to Emilie Schenkl, September 15, 1942; idem, September 26, 1942; idem, October 1, 1942; October 6, 1942; all in Subhas Chandra Bose, *Letters to Emilie Schenkl, 1934–1942, Netaji Subhas Chandra Bose, Collected Works,* vol. 7, ed. Sisir K. Bose and Sugata Bose (Calcutta: Netaji Research Bureau; Delhi: Permanent Black, 1994, 2004), pp. 218–220.

67. Subhas Chandra Bose to Emilie Schenkl, November 5, 1942; idem, November 7, 1942; idem, November 16, 1942; idem, November 18, 1942; all ibid., pp. 223–224; "Statement of A. C. N. Nambiar," September 17, 1945 (TNA), paragraph 171.

68. Krishna Bose, *Itihaser Sandhane,* p. 104.

69. Subhas Chandra Bose to Emilie Schenkl, n.d. [December 1942]; idem, December 19, 1942; both in Bose, *Letters to Emilie,* pp. 225–227.

70. "Statement of A. C. N. Nambiar," September 17, 1945 (TNA), paragraph 172.

71. Subhas Chandra Bose to Ribbentrop, December 5, 1942, in Bose, *Azad Hind,* pp. 170–172.

72. "The Bluff and Bluster Corporation of British Imperialists" and "The 24th Anniversary of the Bloodbath of Amritsar," ibid., pp. 193–204.

73. "Independence Day," ibid., pp. 182–192.

74. Subhas Chandra Bose to Sarat Chandra Bose, February 8, 1943, ibid., p. 205. After this letter reached Sarat, he visited Vienna in 1948 with his wife, Bivabati, and three of his children—Sisir, Roma, and Chitra—and warmly welcomed Emilie and Anita into the Bose family.

75. "Statement of A. C. N. Nambiar," September 17, 1945 (TNA), para. 177; "Swami: Notes Taken in Singapore, Sept./Oct. 1945, When Swami Came to Tea" (TNA).

76. Hasan, "A Soldier Remembers," p. 52.

77. Christopher Bayly and Tim Harper, *Forgotten Armies: The Fall of British Asia, 1941–1945* (Cambridge, Mass.: Harvard University Press, 2004), p. 278.

78. Mansergh, ed., *Transfer of Power,* vol. 3, February 8, 1943, p. 632.

79. Ibid., p. 690.

80. Ibid., February 26, 1943, p. 737.

81. Hasan, "A Soldier Remembers," p. 53; Bose, Werth, and Ayer, *A Beacon across Asia,* p. 160.

82. Hasan, "A Soldier Remembers," pp. 53–56.

83. Ibid., pp. 57–61.

84. Hasan, "A Soldier Remembers" (second installment), *The Oracle,* 7, no. 1 (January 1985), 19–20, 23.

85. Ibid., p. 21; Bose, Werth, and Ayer, *A Beacon across Asia,* pp. 161–162.

86. Hasan, "A Soldier Remembers," p. 22; Bose, Werth, and Ayer, *A Beacon across Asia,* p. 163.

87. Hasan, "A Soldier Remembers," p. 22; Bose, Werth, and Ayer, *A Beacon across Asia,* pp. 163–164.

88. Hasan, "A Soldier Remembers," pp. 22–25; Bose, Werth, and Ayer, *A Beacon across Asia,* pp. 164–166; audio recording of Bose's June 1943 broadcast from Tokyo (NRB).

8. Roads to Delhi

1. Fujiwara Iwaichi, *F. Kikan: Japanese Army Intelligence Operations in Southeast Asia during World War II,* trans. Akashi Yoji (Hong Kong: Heinemann Asia, 1983), p. 89.

2. "Link Up Indian Nationalists All Over the World," message to the Bangkok conference, June 15, 1942, Subhas Chandra Bose, *Azad Hind: Writings and Speeches, 1941–1943, Netaji Subhas Chandra Bose, Collected Works,* vol. 11, ed. Sisir K. Bose and Sugata Bose (Calcutta: Netaji Research Bureau; Delhi: Permanent Black, 2002), pp. 115–116.

3. See Sugata Bose, *A Hundred Horizons: The Indian Ocean in the Age of Global Empire* (Cambridge, Mass.: Harvard University Press, 2006).

4. Original document in NRB archives.

5. Joyce Lebra, *Jungle Alliance: Japan and the Indian National Army* (Singapore: Asia Pacific Press, 1971), pp. 114–116; Abid Hasan, "A Soldier Remembers" (transcript of interview), *The Oracle,* 6, no. 1 (January 1984), 61–65; Seizo Arisue, "My Memories of Subhas Chandra Bose," *The Oracle,* 1, no. 1 (January 1979), 19–24.

6. Fujiwara Iwaichi, *F. Kikan,* pp. 71–91.

7. Ibid., pp. 180–187; Lebra, *Jungle Alliance,* pp. 37–38; Peter Ward Fay, *The Forgotten Army: India's Armed Struggle for Independence, 1942–1945* (Ann Arbor: University of Michigan Press, 1993), pp. 73–86.

8. Monograph no. 3, "The Incidence of Volunteers and Non-Volunteers," compiled by Lieutenant Colonel G. D. Anderson and his staff in May 1946, L/WS/2/45 (IOR, BL).

9. Fujiwara Iwaichi, *F. Kikan,* pp. 201–212; Lebra, *Jungle Alliance,* pp. 67–71.

10. Nakajima Takeshi, *Bose of Nakamuraya: An Indian Revolutionary in Japan,* trans. Prem Motwani (New Delhi: Promilla, 2009).

11. Lebra, *Jungle Alliance,* pp. 98–101; Fay, *Forgotten Army,* pp. 137–152.

12. "The magic of Bose enchanted Tojo immediately," writes Joyce Lebra, an American scholar of Japanese history. Lebra, *Jungle Alliance,* p. 116.

13. Ibid.; "Subhas Chandra Bose and Japan," 4th Section, Asian Bureau, Ministry of Foreign Affairs, Government of Japan, August 1956, English translation in Sisir K. Bose, ed., *Netaji and India's Freedom* (Calcutta: Netaji Research Bureau, 1975), pp. 336–337.

14. "Bose and Japan," Japan Foreign Ministry, in Sisir K. Bose, *Netaji and India's Freedom*, pp. 337–339; "What British Imperialism Means for India," in Subhas Chandra Bose, *Chalo Delhi: Writings and Speeches, 1943–1945*, Netaji Subhas Chandra Bose, *Collected Works*, vol. 12, ed. Sisir K. Bose and Sugata Bose (Calcutta: Netaji Research Bureau; Delhi: Permanent Black, 2007), pp. 17–19.

15. "Our National Honor" (broadcast from Tokyo, June 21, 1943); "The Blood of Freedom-Loving Indians" (broadcast from Tokyo, June 1943); "The War and Its Significance" (broadcast from Tokyo, June 24, 1943); all in Bose, *Chalo Delhi*, pp. 20–33.

16. Audio and video recordings (NRB).

17. "Hunger, Thirst, Privation, Forced Marches and Death" (Presidential Address to the East Asia Delegates Conference at Singapore, July 4, 1943), in Bose, *Chalo Delhi*, pp. 39–44.

18. "To Delhi, to Delhi!" (speech delivered by Bose as the supreme commander of the INA at a Military Review of the INA in Singapore on July 5, 1943, translated from the original Hindustani), ibid., pp. 45–48.

19. "Why I Left Home and Homeland" (speech at a mass meeting in Singapore, July 9, 1943), ibid., pp. 51–54.

20. Leonard A. Gordon, *Brothers against the Raj: A Biography of Indian Nationalists Sarat and Subhas Chandra Bose* (New York: Columbia University Press, 1990), p. 498; Fay, *The Forgotten Army*, pp. 214, 525–526.

21. Abid Hasan Safrani, "A Soldier Remembers," transcript of a taped interview in the archives of the Netaji Research Bureau, 1976, part 5, printed in *The Oracle*, 7, no. 1 (January 1985), 21.

22. "Empire that Rose in a Day Will Vanish in a Night" (speech delivered at a meeting of Indian women held under the auspices of the Woman's Section of the Indian Independence League, Singapore Branch, on July 12, 1943), in Bose, *Chalo Delhi*, pp. 55–59.

23. Lakshmi Sahgal, "The Rani of Jhansi Regiment," *The Oracle*, 1, no. 2 (April 1979), 15–19; and conversations with Lakshmi Sahgal (*née* Swaminathan), 2001.

24. Puan Sri Datin Janaki Athinahappan, "The Rani of Jhansi Regiment," *The Oracle*, 2, no. 1 (January 1980), 29–32; and conversations with Janaki Athinahappan (*née* Thevar), 2006; Manawati Arya, "The Rani of Jhansi Regiment in Burma," and Maya Banerjee, "My Life with the Rani of Jhansi Regiment," both in *The Oracle*, 2, no. 2 (April 1980), 16–24; Shanti Majumdar, "Netaji's Rani of Jhansi Regiment," *The Oracle*, 2, no. 3 (July 1980), 21–26. See also Fay, *The Forgotten Army*, pp. 219–221.

25. Ba Maw, *Breakthrough in Burma: Memoirs of a Revolution, 1939–1946* (New Haven: Yale University Press, 1968), p. 348.

26. "Independent Burma" (press statement on the achievement of Burma's independence, August 1, 1943), in Bose, *Chalo Delhi*, pp. 70–76.

27. Ba Maw, *Breakthrough in Burma*, p. 352.

28. Amartya Sen, *Poverty and Famines: An Essay on Entitlement and Deprivation* (Oxford: Clarendon Press, 1981), pp. 52–85; Sugata Bose, *Agrarian Bengal: Economy, Social Structure and Politics* (Cambridge: Cambridge University Press, 1986), pp. 87–97; Sugata Bose, "Starvation amidst Plenty: The Making of Famine in Bengal, Honan and Tonkin, 1942–1945," *Modern Asian Studies*, 24, no. 4 (1990), 699–727; M. S. Venkataramani, *The Bengal Famine of 1943: The American Response* (Delhi: Vikas, 1973), p. 16.

29. Bose, *Chalo Delhi*, p. 79; WO 208/809, August 20 and 24, 1943, and WO 208/818 (TNA); File 114/43-Poll. (I), September 1, 1943 (IOR, BL); Krishna Bose, *Charanarekha Taba* (Calcutta: Ananda, 1982), pp. 66–67.

30. "At Bahadur Shah's Tomb" (speech given on September 26, 1943), in Bose, *Chalo Delhi*, pp. 97–99.

31. "Bose and Japan," Japan Foreign Ministry, in Sisir K. Bose, *Netaji and India's Freedom*, p. 347.

32. S. A. Ayer, *Unto Him a Witness: The Story of Netaji Subhas Chandra Bose in East Asia* (Bombay: Thacker, 1951), p. 248.

33. Shah Nawaz Khan, *My Memories of I.N.A. and Its Netaji* (Delhi: Rajkamal, 1946), p. 100.

34. Ibid., pp. 100–101; Mohammad Zaman Kiani, *India's Freedom Struggle and the Great INA* (New Delhi: Reliance, 1994), pp. 72–86.

35. Khan, *My Memories*, p. 11; Ayer, *Unto Him a Witness*, pp. 174–176; INA music recordings (NRB); "National Songs," File 151/INA; "New Songs for Rally," File 155/INA; "National Songs," File 156/INA (NAI).

36. Abid Hasan, "A Soldier Remembers," pp. 56–57; Ayer, *Unto Him a Witness*, pp. 168–183, 269.

37. "Proclamation of the Provisional Government of Azad Hind," October 21, 1943, in Bose, *Chalo Delhi*, pp. 108–120; and S. A. Ayer, *Unto Him a Witness*, pp. 163–164.

38. Bose, *Chalo Delhi*, p. 117.

39. "Where Is Your Bank Book?" (speech at the All Malai Chettiars and Other Indian Merchants Conference, October 25, 1943), ibid., pp. 139–145.

40. Fay, *The Forgotten Army*, p. 215. For detailed reports of contributions collected at local branches in Malaya see, for instance, *Young India*, Sunday, September 19, 1943, archives of the Netaji Research Bureau, pp. 12–13.

41. Abid Hasan Safrani, *The Men from Imphal* (Calcutta: Netaji Research Bureau, 1971, 1995), pp. 11–12.

42. "Unification of the Indian Nation" (resolutions of the meeting of the Council of Ministers of the Provisional Government of Azad Hind, December 9, 1943), in Bose, *Chalo Delhi*, pp. 166–168.

43. "Unity of India, Past and Present" (INA platoon lecture), archives of the Netaji Research Bureau; "Gandhiji's Part in India's Fight" (broadcast from Bangkok, October 2, 1943), in Bose, *Chalo Delhi*, pp. 100–105.

44. Ayer, *Unto Him a Witness,* pp. 219–220.

45. Bose, *Chalo Delhi,* p. 131.

46. Bhulabhai Desai, "Address of Counsel for Defence, Red Fort Trial, Delhi, December 1, 1945," *The Oracle,* 15, no. 4 (October 1993), 34.

47. "Bose and Japan," Japan Foreign Ministry, in Sisir K. Bose, *Netaji and India's Freedom,* pp. 358, 364. See also Mamoru Shigemitsu, *Japan and Her Destiny* (London: Hutchinson, 1958), pp. 293–294.

48. "Bose and Japan," Japan Foreign Ministry, in Sisir K. Bose, *Netaji and India's Freedom,* p. 359; Krishna Bose, *Charanarekha Taba,* pp. 55–56.

49. "Bose and Japan," Japan Foreign Ministry, in Sisir K. Bose, *Netaji and India's Freedom,* pp. 361–362.

50. Ibid., pp. 363–366; Krishna Bose, *Charanarekha Taba,* pp. 57, 58.

51. Bose, *Chalo Delhi,* pp. 79, 161–162; Abid Hasan, "A Soldier Remembers" (taped interview, NRB); Krishna Bose, *Prasanga Subhaschandra* (Calcutta: Ananda, 1993), p. 47.

52. "Bose and Japan," Japan Foreign Ministry, in Sisir K. Bose, *Netaji and India's Freedom,* pp. 373–374.

53. "Netaji in Andaman, December 29–31, 1943: A Report," *The Oracle,* 16, no. 1 (January 1994), 11–13.

54. Hugh Toye, *The Springing Tiger: A Study of Subhas Chandra Bose* (London: Cassell, 1959), p. 100.

55. "Statement of Kartar Singh," File 276/INA (NAI); Toye, *The Springing Tiger,* pp. 87–88; K. K. Ghosh, *The Indian National Army: Second Front of the Indian Independence Movement* (Meerut: Meenakshi, 1969), pp. 160–161.

56. Sisir Kumar Bose, *The Great Escape* (Calcutta: Netaji Research Bureau, 2000), pp. 48–49; Santimoy Ganguli, Sudhir Ranjan Baksi, Dhiren Saha Roy, Ratul Roy Chowdhury, and Sisir Kumar Bose, "Netaji's Underground in India during World War II: An Account by Participants in a Daring and Historic Undertaking," *The Oracle,* 1, no. 2 (April 1979), 7–14; Sisir Kumar Bose, *Bosubari* (Calcutta: Ananda, 1985), pp. 159–163; "The Landing of the Following Eight Japanese Agents from a Submarine on the Kathiawar Coast on the Night of 22/23 December 1943"; Criminaire, New Delhi to McDonough, War Emergency Department, Colombo, January 13, 1944; "Statement of Kartar Singh"; J. C. Wilson, "Landing of Japanese Agents"; A. W. Macdonald, "The JIF Landing in Kathiawar, December 1943"; D. Stephens, "The 1939–1945 War and the Indian Police"; all in Mss. E, File 276/INA (NAI), Wilson onward, in Mss. Eur F161/6/3 (IOR, BL); E. W. Wace, "Indian National Army" ("Indian Police Collection," Mss. Eur. F161/6/3) (IOR, BL); Richard Tottenham, "Extract from Home Department War Histories" ("Indian Police Collection," Mss. Eur. F161/4/4) (IOR, BL).

57. Sisir Kumar Bose, *Bosubari,* p. 159.

58. *Young India* (Singapore), 46 (January 16, 1944), cited in Ghosh, *Indian National Army,* p. 171.

59. Khan, *My Memories,* pp. 99–100, 110.

60. Ibid., pp. 101–104.

61. Ibid., pp. 114–120; Ghosh, *Indian National Army,* pp. 174–175.

62. "Homage to the Mother of the Indian People" (statement on the death of Shrimati Kasturba Gandhi, February 22, 1944), in Bose, *Chalo Delhi,* pp. 190–191.

63. Gordon, *Brothers against the Raj,* p. 511.

64. "Indian National Army in Action" (addresses to the INA and statements issued by Netaji during the months January to March 1944), in Bose, *Chalo Delhi,* pp. 173–189.

65. Ghosh, *Indian National Army,* p. 178; "Bose and Japan," Japan Foreign Ministry, in Sisir K. Bose, *Netaji and India's Freedom,* pp. 388–390; A. C. Chatterji, *India's Struggle for Freedom* (Calcutta: Chuckervertty, 1947), pp. 163–173.

66. Gordon, *Brothers against the Raj,* p. 510.

67. Bhulabhai Desai, "Address of Counsel for Defence," p. 42.

68. Bose, *Chalo Delhi,* p. 197; Toye, *The Springing Tiger,* p. 109.

69. S. Woodburn Kirby, *The War against Japan: The Decisive Battles* (London: U.K. Military Series III, 1961), p. 446; Toye, *The Springing Tiger,* p. 109.

70. Alfred Tyrnauer, "India's Would-Be Führer," *Saturday Evening Post,* March 11, 1944, p. 22.

71. John W. Gerber, "India's Would-Be Quisling," *The Nation,* April 22, 1944.

72. "Renegade's Revenge," *Time,* April 17, 1944.

73. Subhas Chandra Bose to Brahmachari Kailasam, April 16, 1944, in Bose, *Chalo Delhi,* p. 417.

74. Toye, *The Springing Tiger,* pp. 109–110; Khan, *My Memories,* pp. 113–114.

75. Ghosh, *Indian National Army,* pp. 181–184.

76. Khan, *My Memories,* pp. 155–156; M. Z. Kiani, *India's Freedom Struggle,* pp. 107–117.

77. Khan, *My Memories,* pp. 148–149.

78. Toye, *The Springing Tiger,* pp. 110–111.

79. Ibid., p. 114; "Swami: Notes Taken in Singapore, Sept./Oct. 1945, When Swami Came to Tea" (TNA).

80. Toye, *The Springing Tiger,* p. 114.

81. "Father of Our Nation" (message to Mahatma Gandhi, broadcast on July 6, 1944), in Bose, *Chalo Delhi,* pp. 212–222; Toye, *The Springing Tiger,* p. 117; Ayer, *Unto Him a Witness,* p. 256.

82. "The Great Patriot and Leader" (speech at Bahadur Shah's tomb, July 11, 1944), in Bose, *Chalo Delhi,* pp. 249–243.

83. Krishna Bose, *Prasanga Subhaschandra,* pp. 72–81; and author's conversations with Naga Sundaram, 1997.

84. Abid Hasan, *The Men from Imphal* (Calcutta: Netaji Research Bureau, 1971), pp. 1–6; Khan, *My Memories,* pp. 151–157.

85. William Slim, *Defeat into Victory* (London: Cassell, 1956), pp. 150–151.

86. Hasan, *Men from Imphal*, pp. 1–12; Khan, *My Memories*, pp. 158–159.

87. "Our Baptism of Fire" (press statement, August 21, 1944), in Bose, *Chalo Delhi*, pp. 264–265; Khan, *My Memories*, pp. 162–163.

88. Hasan, *Men from Imphal*, pp. 7–9.

89. Ibid. See also Raja Muhammad Arshad, "The Retreat" (written at the Red Fort, October 1945), *The Oracle*, 16, no. 4 (October 1994), 1–56.

90. Hasan, *Men from Imphal*, p. 11; Toye, *The Springing Tiger*, p. 121; Krishna Bose, *Prasanga Subhaschandra*, p. 51.

91. "Survey of Foreign Intelligence Activities Directed against Indian Security, dated October 2, 1944," WO 208/829 (TNA).

92. Fay, *The Forgotten Army*, p. 296.

93. Khan, *My Memories*, p. 161; "Weekly Intelligence Summary no. 150, September 15, 1944," cited in Fay, *The Forgotten Army*, p. 298.

94. "The Landing of the Following Eight Japanese Agents from a Submarine on the Kathiawar Coast on the Night of 22/23 December 1943"; Criminaire, New Delhi, to McDonough, War Emergency Department, Colombo, January 13, 1944; "Statement of Kartar Singh," File 276/INA (NAI); J. C. Wilson, "Landing of Japanese Agents"; A. W. Macdonald, "The JIF Landing in Kathiawar, December 1943"; all in Mss. Eur. F161, Box 6, File 3 (IOR, BL), from Wilson onward.

95. Sisir Kumar Bose, *The Great Escape*, pp. 49–51, 64–72; Pilger, German Minister, Kabul, to Berlin, May 4, 1944 (GFO); E. H. Le Brocq, "Bengal Police at War" ("Indian Police Collection," Mss. Eur. F161/5/3) (IOR, BL).

96. "Suspected Enemy Activities: Extract from Home Department War Histories, Dated January 23, 1945, by Sir Richard Tottenham, Additional Home Secretary," Mss. Eur. F161, Box 9, File 3 (IOR, BL).

97. Ayer, *Unto Him a Witness*, pp. 265–266.

98. "The Human Spirit Is More Powerful Than Steel and Armour" (broadcast on "Army Day," October 18, 1944), in Bose, *Chalo Delhi*, pp. 269–275.

99. M. Z. Kiani, *India's Freedom Struggle*, pp. 137–144; A. C. Chatterji, *India's Struggle for Freedom*, p. 251; Ayer, *Unto Him a Witness*, p. 16; Krishna Bose, *Charanarekha Taba*, p. 79.

100. "The Fundamental Problems of India" (address to faculty and students of Tokyo University, November 1944), in Bose, *Chalo Delhi*, pp. 285–301.

101. M. Z. Kiani, *India's Freedom Struggle*, p. 141. A Russian translation of Bose's message exists in the KGB archives.

102. Quoted in Toye, *The Springing Tiger*, p. 129; Subhas Chandra Bose to Sri Rama Murti, December 14, 1944, in Bose, *Chalo Delhi*, pp. 443–444.

103. Subhas Chandra Bose to the INA cadets, November 29, 1944, in Bose, *Chalo Delhi*, p. 437.

104. Subhas Chandra Bose to the INA cadets, December 14, 1944, ibid., p. 442.

105. Subhas Chandra Bose to M. Satiavati Thevar, May 14, 1944; idem, June 18, 1944; idem, June 21, 1944; idem, August 4, 1944; idem, August 19, 1944; idem,

May 21, 1945; idem, May 22, 1945; all ibid., pp. 418–420, 422–423, 428–432, 447–449.

106. Fay, *The Forgotten Army,* p. 556.

107. "India and Thailand: Speech by Prime Minister of Thailand at Dinner in Honor of Netaji," January 16, 1945, File 322/INA (NAI).

108. Fay, *The Forgotten Army,* pp. 314–329; "Swami: Notes Taken in Singapore, Sept./Oct. 1945, When Swami Came to Tea" (TNA).

109. Ayer, *Unto Him a Witness,* pp. 203–209.

110. Khan, *My Memories,* pp. 176–178; Gurbaksh Singh Dhillon, "The Nehru Holds the Irrawady," *The Oracle,* 5, no. 4 (October 1993), 1–30.

111. Khan, *My Memories,* pp. 178–181. See also the discussion in Fay, *The Forgotten Army,* pp. 333–334.

112. Khan, *My Memories,* pp. 181–183.

113. Ibid., pp. 183–184; Fay, *The Forgotten Army,* pp. 336–341.

114. Khan, *My Memories,* p. 184.

115. Gurbaksh Singh Dhillon, "The Indo-Burman Relations during World War II," *The Oracle,* 7, no. 3 (July 1985), 15–22. "Aung San's Reply to the Address of Sarat Chandra Bose, 1946," in Sisir K. Bose, ed., *Netaji and India's Freedom* (Calcutta: Netaji Research Bureau, 1974), pp. 69–75.

116. "Bravery and Cowardice" (statement, March 13, 1945), in Bose, *Chalo Delhi,* pp. 314–316.

117. Fay, *The Forgotten Army,* pp. 354–358, 399; Khan, *My Memories,* pp. 218–220.

118. Hasan, *The Men from Imphal.* See also Dhillon, "The Nehru Holds the Irrawady," *The Oracle,* 5, no. 4 (October 1993), 1–30.

119. Fay, *The Forgotten Army,* pp. 359–360; Khan, *My Memories,* pp. 229–232.

120. "End of a Dream" (message on the eve of Netaji's departure from Rangoon for Bangkok on April 24, 1945), in Bose, *Chalo Delhi,* pp. 317–318.

121. "The Future Generations of Indians Will Bless Your Names" (Special Order of the Day, April 24, 1945), ibid., pp. 319–320.

122. Ayer, *Unto Him a Witness,* pp. 14–16; R. M. Arshad, "Netaji Oration 1996," *The Oracle,* 28, no. 2 (April 1996), 7–15; Toye, *The Springing Tiger,* pp. 146–147.

123. Ayer, *Unto Him a Witness,* pp. 17–18.

124. Ibid., p. 23.

125. Janaki Thevar's diary, quoted in Khan, *My Memories,* pp. 239–244.

126. Ayer, *Unto Him a Witness,* p. 25.

127. Kiani, *India's Freedom Struggle,* pp. 154–156.

128. Janaki Thevar's diary, quoted in Khan, *My Memories,* pp. 245–246.

129. "We Fight On" (speech delivered in Bangkok on May 21, 1945), in Bose, *Chalo Delhi,* pp. 321–322.

130. William Slim, *Defeat into Victory* (London: Cassell, 1956).

131. "We Fight On," in Bose, *Chalo Delhi,* p. 324.

132. Ibid., pp. 324–325.

133. Subhas Chandra Bose to Brahmachari Kailasam, June 10, 1945, in Bose, *Chalo Delhi*, p. 450.

134. "We Fight On," ibid., p. 326.

135. Ayer, *Unto Him a Witness*, pp. 42–46; Kiani, *India's Freedom Struggle*, pp. 157–159; Toye, *The Springing Tiger*, p. 155.

136. "Cooperation with Japan," in Bose, *Chalo Delhi*, pp. 385–389.

137. "Liberty or Death" (speech at Singapore on July 4, 1945), ibid., pp. 403–405; Ayer, *Unto Him a Witness*, p. 41.

138. Ayer, *Unto Him a Witness*, pp. 48–55.

139. Ibid., pp. 55–57.

140. Ibid., pp. 58–59; F. Mudie to E. Jenkins, August 23, 1945, Wavell Papers, in Nicholas Mansergh, ed., *The Transfer of Power*, vol. 6 (London: HMG, 1970–1983), document no. 57, pp. 137–140.

141. Ayer, *Unto Him a Witness*, p. 59.

142. Ibid., pp. 59–61; Cyril John Stracey, "How I Came to Join the INA," *The Oracle*, 4, no. 1 (January 1982), 53–56.

143. "The Roads to Delhi Are Many," in Bose, *Chalo Delhi*, pp. 407–408.

144. "India Shall Be Free" (Special Message to Indians in Malaya, Thailand, Indo-China, Java, Sumatra, Borneo, Philippines, Japan, and other parts of East Asia, August 15, 1945), in Bose, *Chalo Delhi*, pp. 409–410.

145. Ayer, *Unto Him a Witness*, pp. 61–62; Kiani, *India's Freedom Struggle*, pp. 162–163.

146. Kiani, *India's Freedom Struggle*, pp. 163–164.

147. Ayer, *Unto Him a Witness*, pp. 63–64.

148. Ibid., pp. 64–65; Krishna Bose, *Charanarekha Taba*, pp. 171–173.

149. Ayer, *Unto Him a Witness*, pp. 66–71; Abid Hasan, "A Soldier Remembers" (taped interview, NRB); Isoda Saburo, "Netaji As I Knew Him," *The Oracle*, 8, no. 1 (January 1986), 11–15; "Bose and Japan," Japan Foreign Ministry, in Sisir K. Bose, *Netaji and India's Freedom*, pp. 414–416; Krishna Bose, *Prasanga Subhaschandra*, pp. 52–56; Krishna Bose, *Charanarekha Taba*, pp. 181–186.

150. Ayer, *Unto Him a Witness*, pp. 71–72.

9. A Life Immortal

1. Krishna Bose, *Itihaser Sandhane* (Calcutta: Ananda, 1972), p. 36.

2. Sisir Kumar Bose to Bivabati Bose, August 27, 1945 (NRB), reproduced in Sisir Kumar Bose, *Bosubari* (Calcutta: Ananda, 1985), p. 196.

3. Sarat Chandra Bose's Prison Diary, August 25, 1945 (NRB), reproduced in Sisir Kumar Bose, *Bosubari*, p. 194.

4. *The Hindu*, August 29, 1945.

5. S. A. Ayer, *Unto Him a Witness: The Story of Netaji Subhas Chandra Bose in East Asia* (Bombay: Thacker, 1951), pp. 78–79, 83.

6. Ibid., pp. 83–86.

7. Ibid., pp. 100, 103–105, 107–108.

8. Ibid., pp. 110–113.

9. Ibid., pp. 113–114.

10. Ibid., pp. 114–115.

11. Ibid., pp. 116–117. According to the Murti family, as an extra precaution, Rama Murti divided up the cremated remains and hid a portion in his home. This is stated by his nephew Anand J. Murti in a signed affidavit attested by the Embassy of India in Tokyo, dated August 18, 2008 (copy in my possession).

12. Ayer, *Unto Him a Witness,* pp. xiv, 117, 120–121, 125–130.

13. Shah Nawaz Khan and S. N. Maitra, *Netaji Inquiry Committee Report* (New Delhi: Government of India, 1956), pp. 32–33. See also Appendix A to CSDIC (I) 2, Section Report 1089, on B1189: "The Last Movements of S. C. Bose (April–August 1945)," WO 208/3812 (TNA).

14. "Subhas Chandra Bose (a) Notes," File 273/INA (NAI).

15. *Harijan,* April 7, 1946, written on March 30, 1946, from Uruli, and quoted in D. G. Tendulkar, *Mahatma: Life of Mohandas Karamchand Gandhi,* vol. 7, *1945–1947* (New Delhi: Government of India, 1953), pp. 84–85.

16. Emilie Schenkl to Mrs. Woods, January 18, 1946 (NAI and NRB).

17. Mss. Eur. C785 (IOR, BL).

18. Ayer, *Unto Him a Witness,* p. 62.

19. Harin Shah, *Verdict from Formosa: The Gallant End of Netaji, Subhas Chandra Bose* (Delhi: Atma Ram and Sons, 1956), pp. 51–72.

20. "Statement of Yoshimi Taneyoshi, Captain (Medical) of the Imperial Japanese Army, with Regard to the Death of One Chandra Bose, Who Died at Taihoku, Formosa, on 18th Day of August 1945," Stanley Gaol, Hong Kong, October 19, 1946, WO 208/3812 (TNA). Dr. Yoshimi repeated this testimony to the Netaji Inquiry Committee in 1956 and spoke on camera in Charles Bruce's film *Enemy of Empire,* broadcast on the BBC in August 1995. See also Leonard A. Gordon, *Brothers against the Raj: A Biography of Indian Nationalists Sarat and Subhas Chandra Bose* (New York: Columbia University Press, 1990), pp. 541–543, 605.

21. See the images and commentary in Sumathi Ramaswamy, *The Goddess and the Nation* (Durham, N.C.: Duke University Press, 2010), pp. 177–236; and in Maria Antonella Pelizzari, ed., *Traces of India* (New Haven: Yale University Press, 2003), pp. 54–55, 276, 288–289.

22. Annexure 21, Appendix 7, *Parliamentary Debates,* Fifth Session, 1952, p. 103.

23. Khan and Maitra, *Netaji Inquiry Committee Report,* pp. 1–4.

24. Ibid., pp. 9–10, 14.

25. Ibid., pp. 15–26. Kono, Sakai, and Nonogaki were interviewed again by the Khosla Commission in the early 1970s and by Leonard A. Gordon in 1979 in the presence of Netaji's daughter Anita. See Gordon, *Brothers against the Raj,* pp. 539–543, 740–741.

26. Khan and Maitra, *Netaji Inquiry Committee Report,* pp. 29–30. Full text of Juichi Nakamura's testimony (NRB).

27. Khan and Maitra, *Netaji Inquiry Committee Report,* pp. 40–42; and Nakamura's testimony (NRB).

28. Khan and Maitra, *Netaji Inquiry Committee Report,* pp. 67–68; Suresh Chandra Bose, *Dissentient Report* (Calcutta: Subarna Prakasani, 1956). For a criticism of the dissenting report, see Gordon, *Brothers against the Raj,* p. 606.

29. Khan and Maitra, *Netaji Inquiry Committee Report,* pp. 24, 35, 50.

30. Ibid., p. 61, quoting 1 Corinthians 15:55.

31. G. D. Khosla, *Report of the One-Man Commission of Inquiry into the Disappearance of Netaji Subhas Chandra Bose* (New Delhi: Government of India, 1977), pp. 123–125.

32. Manoj Mukherjee, interview with *Star Ananda News* (February 2010); Mukherjee commission to Sugata Bose, October 4, 2002 (in my possession).

33. Manoj Mukherjee, *Report of the Commission;* Parliamentary Proceedings, 2006. The portion of Netaji's mortal remains kept in the Murti home was brought back to India in March 2006, in consultation with Netaji's daughter Anita, and the prime minister of India was informed of this development. The urn preserved in Tokyo's Renko-ji temple has not yet (as of 2010) been brought back to India.

34. My conversations with Netaji's associates and numerous speeches and media interviews given by them. For Sisir Kumar Bose's criticism of the proponents of the "so-called mystery" surrounding Netaji's disappearance and the votaries of a "strange and spurious new Bose cult," see S. K. Bose, "Editor's Note," in Sisir Kumar Bose, ed., *Netaji and India's Freedom* (Calcutta: Netaji Research Bureau, 1975), p. vii.

35. Khan and Maitra, *Netaji Inquiry Committee Report,* pp. 35, 63.

36. "My Political Testament," Subhas Chandra Bose to the Governor of Bengal, November 26, 1940, in Subhas Chandra Bose, *The Alternative Leadership: Netaji Subhas Chandra Bose, Collected Works,* vol. 10, ed. Sisir K. Bose and Sugata Bose (Calcutta: Netaji Research Bureau; Delhi: Permanent Black, 2004), p. 197.

37. Tendulkar, *Mahatma,* pp. 313–314.

38. Dilip Kumar Roy, *Netaji, the Man: Reminiscences* (Bombay: Bharatiya Vidya Bhavan, 1966), p. 147.

39. Tendulkar, *Mahatma,* p. 92.

40. K. T. John to S. R. Nathan, August 30, 2000. I am most grateful to President S. R. Nathan of Singapore for sending me a copy of this letter. S. R. Nathan to Sugata Bose, February 21, 2007 (in my possession).

41. A. C. N. Nambiar, who headed the Free India Center in Berlin after Bose's

departure for Asia in February 1943, became free India's first ambassador to the Federal Republic of Germany. In later years, Abid Hasan served as ambassador to Denmark; Mehboob Ahmed, to Canada; Cyril John Stracey, to the Netherlands; and N. Raghavan, to Switzerland. On the role of INA officers in Pakistan's army, see Mohammad Zaman Kiani, *India's Freedom Struggle and the Great INA* (New Delhi: Reliance Publishing House, 1994), pp. xiv–xvi, 209–213. Kiani himself served as political agent in Gilgit in the late 1950s.

42. Habibur Rahman Khan, "Short Note on Mr. Subhas Chandra Bose, Specially on His Last Days" (sent to Tatsuo Hayashida, 1966), full text at NRB; excerpts quoted in Sisir Kumar Bose, Alexander Werth, and S. A. Ayer, *A Beacon across Asia* (Bombay: Orient Longman, 1973), p. 230.

43. Raja Mohammad Arshad, "Netaji Oration, 1996," *The Oracle*, 28, no. 2 (April 1996), 7–15.

44. Sugata Bose, "Instruments and Idioms of Colonial and National Development: India's Experience in Comparative Perspective," in Frederick Cooper and Randall Packard, eds., *International Development and the Social Sciences* (Berkeley: University of California Press, 1998), pp. 45–60.

45. Prem Kumar Sahgal, "The Indian National Army" (Netaji Oration, 1966), *The Oracle*, 15, no. 1 (January 1993), 18.

46. Jyoti Basu, "Looking Back: Netaji and Indian Communists," *The Oracle*, 1, no. 1 (January 1979), 47–51. "He was among the one or two leaders of the first rank," Basu wrote. "I am not saying this as a Bengali, because when he organized the INA, how many Bengalis were there?" On January 23, 2010, the current communist chief minister of West Bengal once more acknowledged the communists' "mistake"; and the general secretary of the Communist party of India (Marxist) led the demand of leftist parties to observe Bose's birthday as Patriots' Day.

47. Gopal Krishna Gandhi, "An Icon of Icons," *The Oracle*, 31, no. 1 (January 2009), 11–15.

48. "My Political Testament," Subhas Chandra Bose to the Governor of Bengal, November 26, 1940, in Bose, *The Alternative Leadership*, p. 197.

Index

9 780674 065963